*WRITE 2: Paragraphs and Essays*
Dave Kemper, Verne Meyer, John Van Rys,
and Patrick Sebranek

Publisher: Lyn Uhl

Director, Developmental English and College Success:
Annie Todd

Development Editors: Leslie Taggart, Karen Mauk

Assistant Editor: Melanie Opacki

Editorial Assistant: Matthew Conte

Media Editor: Amy Gibbons

Marketing Manager: Kirsten Stoller

Marketing Coordinator: Ryan Ahern

Marketing Communications Manager: Stacey Purviance
Taylor

Content Project Manager: Rosemary Winfield

Art Director: Jill Ort

Print Buyer: Susan Spencer

Rights Acquisition Specialist, Image: Jennifer Meyer Dare

Rights Acquisition Specialist, Text: Katie Huha

Production Service: Sebranek, Inc.

Text Designer: Sebranek, Inc.

Cover Designer: Hannah Wellman

Cover Image: Gettyimages.com

Compositor: Sebranek, Inc.

Sebranek, Inc.: Steven J. Augustyn, April Lindau,
Colleen Belmont, Chris Erickson, Mariellen Hanrahan,
Dave Kemper, Tim Kemper, Rob King, Chris Krenzke,
Lois Krenzke, Mark Lalumondier, Jason C. Reynolds,
Janae Sebranek, Lester Smith, Jean Varley

For product information and technology assistance, contact us at
**Cengage Learning Customer & Sales Support, 1-800-354-9706.**
For permission to use material from this text or product,
submit all requests online at **www. cengage.com/permissions.**
Further permissions questions can be emailed to
**permissionrequest@cengage.com.**

Library of Congress Control Number: 2010935708

Student Edition:
ISBN-13: 978-0-618-64286-1
ISBN-10: 0-618-64286-2

Annotated Instructor Edition:
ISBN-13: 978-0-618-64287-8
ISBN-10: 0-618-64287-0

Wadsworth
20 Channel Center Street
Boston, MA 02210
USA

Cengage Learning is a leading provider of customized learning solutions with office
locations around the globe, including Singapore, the United Kingdom, Australia,
Mexico, Brazil, and Japan. Locate your local office at:
**international.cengage.com/region.**

Cengage Learning products are represented in Canada by Nelson Education, Ltd.

For your course and learning solutions, visit **www.cengage.com.**

Purchase any of our products at your local college store or at our preferred online
store **www.cengagebrain.com.**

Printed in the United States of America
1 2 3 4 5 6 7 14 13 12 11 10

# WRITE 2:
## Paragraphs and Essays

## CONTENTS

Blend Images/ColorBlind Images/Collection Mix: Subjects/Getty Images

David Henley/Dorling Kindersley/ Getty Images

Dougal Waters/Digital Vision/Getty Images

S.Borisov,2010 / Used under license from Shutterstock.com

## Part 5: Sentence Workshops   230

raresirimie,2010 / Used under license from Shutterstock.com

# Preface

Our objective with *WRITE 2: Paragraphs and Essays* and its companion *WRITE 1: Sentences and Paragraphs* is to help you function, and even flourish, in college and in the workplace. Now more than ever, you need effective communication skills in order to take your place in our information-driven world. There really is no alternative. Writing, speaking, collaborating, thinking critically—these are the survival skills for the twenty-first century. We have kept this crucial directive clearly in mind during the development of *WRITE 1* and *WRITE 2*.

## Overview of *WRITE 2*

*WRITE 2* covers all of the essential communication skills needed to succeed in the college classroom:

**Part 1** features **writing to learn**, **reading to learn**, and making the **writing-reading** connection.

Fuse/Getty Images

**Part 2** helps you learn about using the **writing process** and the **traits of effective writing.**

**Parts 3 and 4** cover **the forms of paragraph and essay writing** that you will be expected to develop in the college classroom: description, illustration, definition, narration, classification, process, comparison, cause-effect, and argumentation.

**Part 5** provides in-depth **sentence workshops** to help you master sentence basics and overcome sentence challenges.

Demetrio Carrasco/Dorling Kindersley/
Getty Images

**Part 6** offers many **word workshops** to help you understand and master using the parts of speech in your writing.

**Part 7** includes **punctuation and mechanics workshops** that cover commas, apostrophes, quotation marks, italics, and capitalization.

**Part 8** is **a reader with short, medium, and long professional essays** for the major forms of writing covered in parts 3 and 4.

iofoto,2010 / Used under license from Shutterstock.com

Sean Prior 2010/used under license from www.shutterstock.com

# Research-Based Approach

■ **The Writing Process** *WRITE 2* presents writing as a process rather than an end product. Too often, writers try to do everything all at once and end up frustrated, thinking that they can't write.

*WRITE 2* shows you that writing must go through a series of steps before it is ready to submit. As you work on the various writing tasks, you will internalize strategies that you can employ in all of your future writing, whether analytical essays in college or quarterly reports in the workplace.

Prewrite → Write → Revise → Edit → Publish

■ **The Traits of Writing** *WRITE 2* not only explains the steps you should take during a writing project but also tells you what to include—the traits. These traits comprise *ideas, organization, voice, word choice, sentence fluency, conventions,* and *design.*

Working with the traits helps you in two important ways: It (1) identifies the key elements of successful paragraphs and essays and (2) provides a vocabulary for discussing writing with others. This information will give you the background knowledge you need to engage thoughtfully with writing.

■ **Connecting the Process and the Traits** *WRITE 2* helps students address the appropriate traits at different points during the writing process. For example, during your prewriting, or planning, you should focus on the ideas, organization, and intended voice in your writing.

The traits are especially useful when revising an initial draft because they help you know what to look for. All of the revising checklists in *WRITE 2* are traits based.

> **Revise** Improve your writing, using your partner's comments on the response sheet and the following checklist. Continue working until you can answer yes to each question.
>
> **Ideas:**
> 1. Do I compare two subjects—myself and another person? _____
> 2. Do I use three points of comparison? _____
> 3. Do I include details that show instead of tell? _____
>
> **Organization:**
> 4. Do I have a topic sentence, middle, and a closing sentence? _____
> 5. Have I used a point-by-point organizational plan? _____
> 6. Have I used transitions to connect my sentences? _____
>
> **Voice:**
> 7. Do I sound knowledgeable and interested? _____

■ **The Writing-Reading Connection** *WRITE 2* provides you with accessible and exemplary models of sentences, paragraphs, and essays. Before you begin to write, you read and respond both verbally and on the page. And as you write, you will read and respond to other students' works. Numerous activities throughout *WRITE 2* support the reading-writing and speaking-listening connections.

■ **Grammar in Context** *WRITE 2* is designed to provide grammar instruction, as much as possible, within the context of your own writing—to merge skills with craft. Study after study has shown this to be the most effective approach to teaching grammar.

In a typical writing chapter, you are introduced to two or three new grammar skills or concepts. After practicing each skill, you apply what you have learned as you edit your own writing. Additional practice activities are provided in the workshop section of the text.

# Developmental Design

*WRITE 2* employs the following proven strategies:

■ **Helpful Visuals** Research shows that visuals help writers learn new concepts and processes. As a result, charts, graphs, and illustrations are used throughout each chapter; and you are encouraged to use graphic organizers as you develop your own writing.

■ **Structured Instruction** Each chapter in *WRITE 2* is carefully structured and easy to follow, guiding you through the writing process and helping you produce writing that reflects your best efforts. This approach is essential to help you stay with a piece of writing until it is truly ready to submit.

After completing the work in *WRITE 2,* you will have internalized key strategies for producing effective writing.

■ **Clear Format** Objectives, explanations, and directions in *WRITE 2* are clearly marked so you know what you are expected to do and why. In addition, each two-page spread offers definite starting and ending points for your work, eliminating the necessity to page back and forth within a chapter.

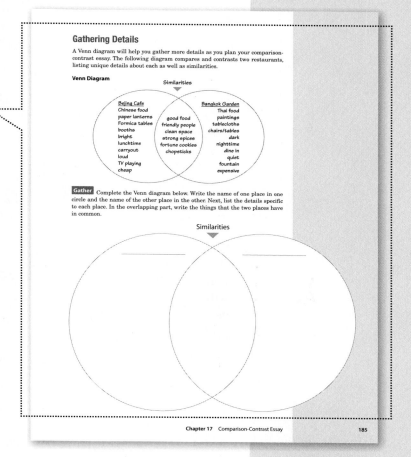

**Gathering Details**

A Venn diagram will help you gather more details as you plan your comparison-contrast essay. The following diagram compares and contrasts two restaurants, listing unique details about each as well as similarities.

**Venn Diagram**

Similarities

**Bejing Cafe**
Chinese food
paper lanterns
Formica tables
booths
bright
lunchtime
carryout
loud
TV playing
cheap

*good food
friendly people
clean space
strong spices
fortune cookies
chopsticks*

**Bangkok Garden**
Thai food
paintings
tablecloths
chairs/tables
dark
nighttime
dine in
quiet
fountain
expensive

**Gather** Complete the Venn diagram below. Write the name of one place in one circle and the name of the other place in the other. Next, list the details specific to each place. In the overlapping part, write the things that the two places have in common.

Similarities

Because *WRITE 2* is so easy to follow, it lends itself to small-group work and independent study.

### ■ Reflection and Reinforcement

*WRITE 2* asks you to reflect on your writing after completing the various paragraph and essay assignments. This self-assessment or reflection is a critical activity, helping you to internalize the different forms and strategies.

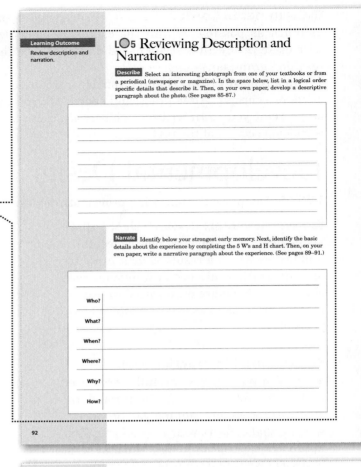

### ■ Familiar Connections

*WRITE 2* compares new, perhaps difficult concepts with old familiar ones, establishing a comfortable context.

### ■ Vocabulary Key terms related to instruction are defined.

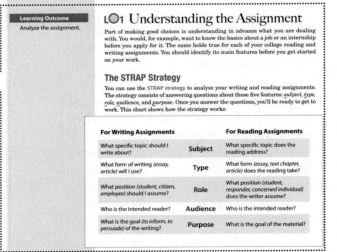

# Additional Special Features

The following features appear as side notes or special call-outs to help you develop your communication skills and to connect your work with other learning situations—both in school and in the workplace.

**Traits**

The traits are used for writing and reading.

**Test Taking**

When appropriate, tips for taking exams are provided.

**Speaking & Listening**

Optional oral activities complement the writing instruction.

**WAC**

Special notes connect your work to writing in different classes.

**Workplace**

Special notes connect your work to writing in the workplace.

# ESL Support

These features will help those who speak English as a second language to improve their understanding as they complete the activities in *WRITE 2*.

**Insight**

The insights explain or reinforce concepts for students who are just learning English.

**Vocabulary**

Challenging words and idioms throughout the book are defined to help ESL students—and any other student.

**Insight**

As the introduction indicates, native English speakers use this order unconsciously because it sounds right to them. If you put adjectives in a different order, a native English speaker might say, "That's not how anybody says it." One way to avoid this issue is to avoid stacking multiple adjectives before nouns.

"I write to discover what I think."
—Joan Didion

# 1 Writing and Learning

In college, the new concepts flooding your way can seem overwhelming. To succeed you must be able retain new knowledge, connect it to other ideas and subjects, and communicate conclusions with your peers and instructors. Writing can help.

You may not think of writing as a learning tool, but writing can make you a better, more efficient learner. Think about it: writing allows you to sort through your thoughts, form new and thoughtful opinions, and communicate what you've learned with others. And these skills translate directly to the workplace. It is no surprise that today's employers place a premium on effective writers.

This chapter is set up in two parts. The first half introduces you to writing as a learning tool, while the second half introduces writing as a means of sharing knowledge. Becoming an effective writer and learner isn't magic, but the result of focus and practice.

## What do you think?

What does the quotation on the previous page say about writing? How does it match up with your opinion of writing?

Answers will vary.

Fuse/Getty Images

## Learning Outcomes

**LO1** Write to learn for yourself.

**LO2** Write to share learning.

**LO3** Consider the range of writing.

**LO4** Review writing and learning.

# LO1 Writing to Learn

Gertrude Stein made one of the more famous and unusual statements about writing when she said, "To write is to write is to write is to write. . . ." The lofty place that writing held in her life echoes in the line. As far as she was concerned, nothing else needed to be said on the subject.

What would cause a writer to become so committed to the process of writing? Was it for fame and recognition? Not really. The real fascination that experienced writers have with writing is the frame of mind it puts them in. The act of filling up a page stimulates their thinking and leads to exciting and meaningful learning.

## Changing Your Attitude

If you think of writing in just one way—as an assignment to be completed—you will never discover its true value. Writing works best when you think of it as an important learning tool. It doesn't always have to lead to an end product submitted to an instructor.

A series of questions, a list, or a quick note in a notebook can be a meaningful form of writing if it helps you think and understand. If you make writing an important art of your learning routine, two things will happen: (1) You'll change your feelings about the importance of writing, and (2) you'll become a better thinker and learner.

**Speaking & Listening**

As a class, discuss this writing experience: Did it help you focus your thinking on the topic? Did you surprise yourself in any way? Could you have written more? If so, about what?

**Reflect** Write nonstop for 5 minutes about one of the three topics below. Don't stop or hesitate, and don't worry about making mistakes. You are writing for yourself. Afterward, checkmark something that surprises you or you learned about yourself.

| What are my talents? | Where do I want to go? | Have I seized opportunities? |
|---|---|---|
| Answers will vary. | | |

# Keeping a Class Notebook

Keeping a class notebook or journal is essential if you are going to make writing to learn an important part of your learning routine. Certainly, you can take notes in this notebook, but it is also helpful to reflect on what is going on in the class. Try these activities:

- **Write freely about anything from class discussions to challenging assignments to important exams.**
- **Discuss new ideas and concepts.**
- **Argue for and against any points of view that came up in class.**
- **Question what you are learning.**
- **Record your thoughts and feelings during an extended lab or research assignment.**
- **Evaluate your progress in the class.**

**WAC**

Note taking is a common form of writing to learn in most classes. Always try to explore your thoughts and feelings alongside the basic notes. This makes note taking more meaningful. (See page 12.)

## Special Strategies

Writing or listing freely is the most common way to explore your thoughts and feelings about your course work. There are, however, specific writing-to-learn strategies that you may want to try:

| | |
|---|---|
| **Sent or Unsent Messages** | Draft messages to anyone about something you are studying or reading. |
| **First Thoughts** | Record your first impressions about something you are studying or reading. |
| **Role-Play** | Write as if you are someone directly involved in a topic you are studying. |
| **Nutshelling** | Write down in one sentence the importance of something you are studying or reading. |
| **Pointed Question** | Keep asking yourself *why?* in your writing to sort out your thoughts about something. |
| **Debate** | Split your mind in two. Have one side defend one point of view, and the other side, a differing point of view. |

"If you can't explain it simply, you don't understand it well enough."
—Albert Einstein

**Practice** For one month, make a commitment to writing to learn. In a notebook or on a laptop, take five minutes after or in between classes to write freely about what you just learned. Also, try a few of the strategies on this page as study tools. Afterward, evaluate how writing to learn worked for you. Did you retain more knowledge? Did you come to new conclusions or understandings?

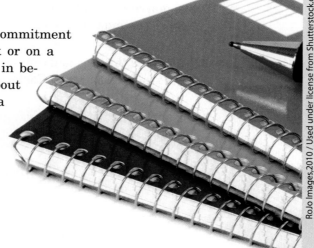

RoJo Images, 2010 / Used under license from Shutterstock.com

# LO2 Writing to Share Learning

The other important function of writing is to share what you have learned. When you write to learn, you have an audience of one, yourself; but when you write to share learning, you have an audience of many, including your instructors and classmates.

All writing projects (paragraphs, essays, blog entries) actually begin with writing to learn, as you collect your thoughts about a topic. But with a first draft in hand, you turn your attention to making the writing clear, complete, and ready to share with others.

**Note:**
Writing is called a process because it must go through a series of steps before it is ready to share. (See pages 26-81.)

## A Learning Connection

As the graphic below shows, improved thinking is the link between the two functions of writing. Writing to learn involves exploring and forming your thoughts; writing to share learning involves clarifying and fine-tuning them.

**Writing to Learn** — **Improved Thinking** — **Writing to Share Learning**

**Speaking & Listening**

As a class, explore the following question: Why is writing often called "thinking on paper"?

**Identify** Label each scenario below as an example of writing to learn (WL) or writing to share learning (WSL).

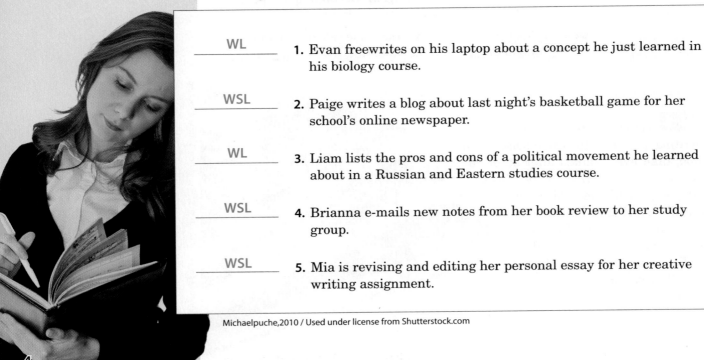

_____WL_____ **1.** Evan freewrites on his laptop about a concept he just learned in his biology course.

_____WSL_____ **2.** Paige writes a blog about last night's basketball game for her school's online newspaper.

_____WL_____ **3.** Liam lists the pros and cons of a political movement he learned about in a Russian and Eastern studies course.

_____WSL_____ **4.** Brianna e-mails new notes from her book review to her study group.

_____WSL_____ **5.** Mia is revising and editing her personal essay for her creative writing assignment.

# LO3 Considering the Range of Writing

The forms of writing to share cover a lot of territory as you can see in the chart below. Some of the forms are quick and casual; others are more thoughtful and formal. As a college student, your writing may cover this entire spectrum, but the instruction you receive will likely focus on the more formal types.

**Learning Outcome**

Consider the range of writing.

## The Writing Spectrum

**Formal and Thoughtful**

Multimedia Reports

Research Papers

Stories/Plays/Poems

Responses to Literature

Persuasive Paragraphs and Essays

Expository Paragraphs and Essays

Business Letters

Personal Narratives

Blogs

E-Mails

Microblogs

**Casual and Quick**  Text Messages

**Insight**

Completeness and correctness are not critical in quick and casual writing, but they are important for all of the other forms on the chart.

**React**  After studying the chart, answer the following questions. Then discuss your responses as a class.

Answers will vary.

1. What form of writing do you most often engage in?

_____

_____

2. How might your writing approach change at different points on the writing spectrum?

_____

_____

3. What characteristics do you associate with casual and quick writing? How about formal and thoughtful?

_____

_____

# LO4 Reviewing Writing and Learning

**Writing to Learn** Answer the following questions about writing as a learning tool. (See pages 2-3.) Answers will vary.

1. How is writing to learn different from traditional writing assignments?

   _____

   _____

2. What are some ways you can write to learn using your classroom notebook or personal laptop?

   _____

   _____

3. How can pointed questions be used as a writing-to-learn strategy? What about debate?

   _____

   _____

   _____

**Writing to Share Learning** Answer the following questions about writing to share learning. (See page 4.) Answers will vary.

1. How is writing to share learning different from writing to learn?

   _____

   _____

2. Why is improved thinking considered the link between writing to learn and writing to share?

   _____

   _____

**The Range of Writing** Rank the following forms of writing in order of casual and quick to formal and thoughtful, with 1 being the most casual.

____2____ On your personal blog, you write a review of a new restaurant.

____4____ You complete a research report on sports in Ancient Greece.

____1____ You send your friend a text message about your plans for the evening.

____3____ You argue for a campus-wide smoking ban in a letter to the editor in your college's newspaper.

> "Reading furnishes the mind only with materials of knowledge;
> it is thinking that makes what we read ours."
> —John Locke

John Giustina/Stone/Getty Images

# 2 Reading and Learning

Reading, as you well know, is a gateway to learning. Textbooks, literature, newspaper articles, and Web sites have fueled much of your formal education. It should come as no surprise then to discover that reading is an essential learning tool in college.

But where much of elementary and secondary school reading material is geared toward gaining a basic understanding of new ideas and concepts, college reading assignments demand a more active reader. Your instructors will expect you not only to retain new information, but also to compare it to what you already know and reflect on what makes the information important. This chapter is set up to help you become a successful college reader.

## Learning Outcomes

**LO1** Read to learn.
**LO2** Use reading strategies.
**LO3** Read graphics.
**LO4** Review reading and learning.

### What do you think?

What message is John Locke trying to get across in his quotation at the top of the page? Do you agree with him?

Answers will vary.

"Some books are to be tasted, others to be swallowed, and some few are to be chewed and digested."

—Francis Bacon

**Traits**

Effective writing has strong ideas, clear organization, appropriate voice, precise words, smooth sentences, correct conventions, and a strong design. Use these traits to understand what you read.

**Vocabulary**

**context cues**
using the words surrounding an unfamiliar term to help unlock its meaning

# LO1 Reading to Learn

Thoughtful, active reading encompasses a number of related tasks: previewing the text, reading it through, taking notes as you go along, and summarizing what you have learned. Active reading gives you control of reading assignments and makes new information part of your own thinking.

## Effective Academic Reading

Follow the guidelines listed below for all of your academic reading assignments. A few of these points are discussed in more detail later in the chapter.

1. **Know the assignment:** Identify its purpose, its due date, its level of difficulty, and so on.
2. **Set aside the proper time:** Don't try to read long assignments all at once. Instead, try to read in 30-minute allotments.
3. **Find a quiet place:** The setting should provide space to read and to write.
4. **Gather additional resources:** Keep on hand a notebook, related handouts, Web access, and so on.
5. **Study the "layout" of the reading:** Review the study-guide questions. Then skim the pages, noting titles, headings, graphics, and boldfaced terms.
6. **Use proven reading strategies:** See pages 10–15.
7. **Look up challenging words:** Also use context cues to determine the meaning of unfamiliar terms.
8. **Review difficult parts:** Reread them, write about them, and discuss them with your classmates.
9. **Summarize what you learned:** Note any concepts or explanations that you will need to study further.

**Reflect** Which of the tips above do you follow? Which do you not follow? Reflect on one tip that could help you improve.

Answers will vary.

# Using a Class Notebook

To thoughtfully interact with a text, you need to write about it, so reserve part of your class notebook for responses to your readings. Certainly, you can take straight notes on the material (see page 12), but you should also personally respond to it. Such writing requires you to think about the reading—to agree with it, to question it, to make connections. The following guidelines will help you get started:

**Insight**

If you are a visual person, you may understand a text best by mapping or clustering its important points. (See page 39 for a sample cluster.)

- **Write whenever you feel** a need to explore your thoughts and feelings. Discipline yourself to write multiple times, perhaps once before you read, two or three times during the reading, and one time afterward.

- **Write freely and honestly** to make genuine connections with the text.

- **Respond to points of view** that you like or agree with, information that confuses you, connections that you can make with other material, and ideas that seem significant.

- **Clearly label and date your responses.** These entries will help you prepare for exams and other assignments.

- **Share your discoveries.** Think of your entries as conversation starters in discussions with classmates.

## Special Strategies

Here are some specific ways to respond to a text:

**Discuss** Carry on a conversation with the author or a character until you come to know him or her and yourself a little better.

**Illustrate** Use graphics or pictures to help you think about a text.

**Imitate** Continue the article or story line by trying to write like the author.

**Express** Share your feelings about a text in a poem.

**Practice** For one of your next reading assignment, carry out at least two of the reading-response strategies described on this page. When you have finished, reflect on the value of responding to the reading.

# Note:

Annotate reading material only if you own the text or if you are reading a photocopy.

**Vocabulary**

**annotating**
the process of underlining, highlighting, or making notes in a text

# LO2 Using Reading Strategies

To make sure that you gain the most from each reading assignment, employ the additional strategies on the next four pages.

## Annotating a Text

**Annotating** a text allows you to interact with the writer's thoughts and ideas. Here are some suggestions:

- Write questions in the margins.
- Underline or highlight important points.
- Summarize key passages.
- Define new terms.
- Make connections to other parts.

### Annotating in Action

### You've Got Hate Mail
#### by Lydie Raschka

***First I expected it; now I'm scared.***

Hate mail confirms a vague, nagging feeling that you've done something wrong. It's a firm tap on the shoulder that says, "The jig is up." So when the first letter came, it was expected. The second, however, was a shock. By the third I was a wreck. How did he know it would take exactly and only three?

*So the hate mail is all coming from one person —a man.*

I started writing a few years ago, after I had a baby. I haven't completely figured out what led me to writing, but it was probably tied up with my son's birth and the attendant emotions that needed sorting.

*Def: related; associated*

I like the solitary work life. I write at a table in the bedroom. I send my ideas out into the void. The bedroom seems a safe enough place. I have been told that I am an introvert. What on earth makes me want to communicate with strangers in this perilous way—standing naked in a field?

*I can relate to this. Also, it exhibits her fear of people judging her.*

"You have to expect these things when you are a writer," my father says about the hate mail. "When you're in the public eye, anyone can read what you write."

The letters are effective and unsettling, to say the least. I have an unusual name, so he thinks I'm foreign. He calls me "Eurotrash." It's a relief because it means he doesn't really know me—although he makes some pretty accurate guesses. He doesn't know that my parents simply like unusual names.

*A shortsighted conclusion*

Carefully read the excerpt below from an essay by John Taylor Gatto. Then annotate the text, according to the following directions:

- Circle the main point of the passage.
- Underline or highlight one idea in the first paragraph that you either agree with, question, or are confused by. Then make a comment about this idea in the margin. AWV
- Do the same for one idea in the second paragraph and one idea in the final paragraph. AWV
- Circle one or two words that you are unsure of. Then define or explain these words in the margin. AWV

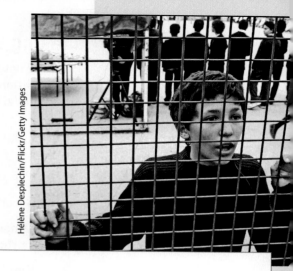

Hélène Desplechin/Flickr/Getty Images

## Why Schools Don't Educate
### by John Taylor Gatto

I accept this award on behalf of all the fine teachers I've known over the years who've struggled to make their transactions with children honorable ones: men and women who are never complacent, always questioning, always wrestling to define and redefine endlessly what the word education should mean. A "Teacher of the Year" is not the best teacher around—those people are too quiet to be easily uncovered—but a standard-bearer, symbolic of these private people who spend their lives gladly in the service of children. This is their award as well as mine. 1 5

We live in a time of great social crisis. Our children rank at the bottom of nineteen industrial nations in reading, writing, and arithmetic. The world's narcotic economy is based upon our own consumption of this commodity. If we didn't buy so many powdered dreams, the business would collapse—and schools are an important sales outlet. Our teenage-suicide rate is the highest in the world—and suicidal kids are rich kids for the most part, not poor. In Manhattan, 70 percent of all new marriages last less than five years. 10 15

Our school crisis is a reflection of this greater social crisis. We seem to have lost our identity. Children and old people are penned up and locked away from the business of the world to an unprecedented degree; nobody talks to them anymore. Without children and old people mixing in daily life, a community has no future and no past, only a continuous present. In fact, the term "community" hardly applies to the way we interact with each other. We live in networks, not communities, and everyone I know is lonely because of that. In some strange way, school is a major actor in this tragedy, just as it is a major actor in the widening gulfs among social classes. Using school as a sorting mechanism, we appear to be on the way to creating a caste system, complete with untouchables who wander through subway trains begging and sleep on the streets. 20 25

# Taking Effective Notes

Taking notes helps you focus on the text and understand it more fully. It changes information you have read about to information that you are working with. Personalizing information in this way makes it much easier to remember and use.

**Insight**

Note taking should be more than writing down what you read. It should also be connecting with and questioning new information.

## Note-Taking Tips

- Use your own words as much as possible.

- Record only key points and details rather than complicated sentences.

- Consider boldfaced or italicized words, graphics, and captions as well as the main text.

- Employ as many abbreviations and symbols as you can (vs., #, &, etc.).

- Decide on a system for organizing or arranging your notes so they are easy to review.

## An Active Note-Taking System

To make your note taking more active, use a two-column system, in which one column (two-thirds of the page) is for your main notes and another column (one-third of the page) is for comments, reactions, and questions.

### Two-Column Notes

You've Got Hate Mail                              March 3
by Lydie Raschka

**Comments, reactions, questions**

At what point would police take action? ⟶

How *do* other authors and musicians react to hate mail? ⟶

This last bullet is interesting. It reminds me of Stockholm Syndrome—when hostages begin having positive feelings toward their captors. ⟶

**Main notes**

- The author has received multiple hate letters from the same person; the first included feces.

- She has contacted the post office and the police, who say there is not much they can do.

- The author admits she is vulnerable to people's opinions of her, so much so she takes what the hate mail says seriously.

- Eventually, she admits she feels a connection to the accuser.

**Practice** Use the two-column note system for one of your next reading assignments. Use the left-hand column to react with questions, comments, and reflections about the information that you record.

# Summarizing a Text

Summarizing a reading assignment is an effective way to test how well you understand the information. Summarizing means to present the main points in a clear, concise form using your own words (except for those few words from the original text that can't be changed). Generally speaking, a summary should be no more than one-third as long as the original.

## Summarizing Tips

- Start with a clear statement of the main point of the text.
- Share only the essential supporting facts and details (names, dates, times, and places) in the next sentences.
- Present your ideas in a logical order.
- Tie all of your points together in a closing sentence.

**WAC**

In many classes, you'll find summarizing skills useful to help you understand and retain content.

## Example Summary

The example below summarizes a three-page essay by Lydie Raschka concerning hate mail that she received.

| | |
|---|---|
| Main points (underlined) | <u>Three occurrences of hate mail from the same sender have</u> 1 <u>left author Lydie Raschka consumed with fear and doubt.</u> Even before the hate mail, Raschka, who admits to being an introvert, struggled with the vulnerability of sharing her writing. She expected hate mail, but, when new letters from the same man 5 |
| Essential supporting facts | kept coming, Raschka contacted the post office and police. Neither helped much. As the unsettling feeling increased, Raschka was unable to continue writing. At some point, she became so consumed by the letters that she began relating to her enemy, even feeling some sympathy for him. For example, he talks in his letters about 10 |
| Closing sentence (underlined) | his aunt and disabled sister; Raschka has a sister and a disabled aunt. <u>In the end, Raschka wishes the sender could realize how much he has in common with her.</u> |

**Practice** Summarize the information in one of the essays on pages 424–w499 or in an essay provided by your instructor. Use the tips and sample above as a guide.

**Vocabulary**

**summarizing**
presenting the main points of a text in a clear, concise form using, for the most part, your own words

# L○3 Reading Graphics

In many of your college texts, a significant portion of the information will be communicated via charts, graphs, diagrams, and drawings. Knowing how to read these types of graphics will help you become a more effective and informed college student. Follow the guidelines listed below when you read a **graphic**.

- **Scan the graphic.** Consider it as a whole to get an overall idea about its message. Note its type (bar graph, pie graph, diagram, table, and so forth), its topic, its level of complexity, and so on.

- **Study the specific parts.** Start with the main heading or title. Next, note any additional labels or guides (such as the horizontal and vertical guides on a bar graph). Then focus on the actual information displayed in the graphic.

- **Question the graphic.** Does it address an important topic? What is its purpose (to make a comparison, to show a change, and so on)? What is the source of the information? Is the graphic dated or biased in any way?

- **Reflect on its effectiveness.** Explain in your own words the main message communicated by the graphic. Then consider its effectiveness, how it relates to the surrounding text, and how it matches up to your previous knowledge of the topic.

**Vocabulary**

**graphic**
a visual representation of information that reveals trends, makes comparisons, shows how something changes over time, and so on

**horizontal**
parallel to ground level, at right angles to the vertical

**vertical**
straight up and down, at right angles to the horizontal

## Analysis of a Graphic

Review the vertical bar graph below. Then read the discussion to learn how all of the parts work together.

Figure 17.3 Percentage of Labor Force by Age Group

*Discussion:* This bar graph compares the labor force in 2001 to the labor force in 2011 for five specific age groups. The heading clearly identifies the subject or topic of the graphic. The **horizontal** line identifies the different age groups, and the **vertical** line identifies the percentage of the labor force for each group. The key in the upper right-hand corner of the graphic identifies the purpose of the color coding used in the columns or bars. With all of that information, the graphic reads quite clearly—and many interesting comparisons can be made.

**React**  Read and analyze the following graphics, answering the questions about each one. Use the information on the previous page as a guide.

## Graphic 1

1. This graphic is called a pictograph rather than a bar graph. What makes it a "pictograph"?

   It is built of pictures of cars.

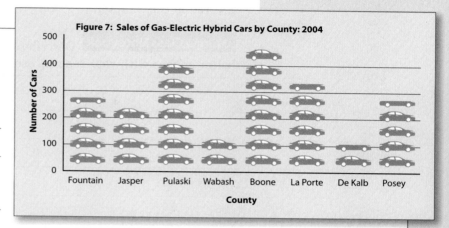

Figure 7: Sales of Gas-Electric Hybrid Cars by County: 2004

2. What is the topic of this graphic?

   Sales of gas-electric hybrid cars in

   eight counties

3. What information is provided on the horizontal line? On the vertical line?

   The eight counties appear on the horizontal line. The number of cars sold appears on the

   vertical line.

4. What comparisons can a reader make from this graphic?

   Numbers of cars sold (in increments of one hundred)

## Graphic 2

1. This graphic is called a line diagram, mapping a structure. What structure does this diagram map?

   A complex Web site

Figure 36.2 Complex Web Site Map

2. What two working parts are used in this diagram: *words* *lines,* and *symbols?* Circle the appropriate choices.

3. How are the different navigational choices on a complex Web site shown on this graphic?

   Straight lines show the hierarchy of pages. Curved lines with arrows show links between

   individual pages.

# L○4 Reviewing Reading and Learning

Complete these activities as needed to help you better understand the concepts covered in this chapter.

**Using a Class Notebook** Describe some activities you can do in your notebook to better engage with your reading assignments. (See page 9.)

Answers will vary.

**Annotating a Text** What is the purpose of annotating a text? (See pages 10–11.)

It allows you to interact with the author's thoughts and ideas.

**Taking Effective Notes** Identify three helpful note-taking tips. (See page 12.)

1. Use your own words. Record only key points and details.

2. Consider boldfaced or italicized words, graphics, and captions as well as the main text.

3. Use abbreviations and symbols. Use an organizing system.

**Reading Graphics** Describe the steps you should take to evaluate the graphics you see in your reading assignments. (See page 14-15.)

1. Scan the graphic.

2. Study the specific parts.

3. Question the graphic.

4. Reflect on its effectiveness.

"It's good to rub and polish our brain against that of others."

—Michel de Montaigne

Blend Images/ColorBlind Images/Collection Mix: Subjects/Getty Images

# 3

# Making the Writing-Reading Connection

Professional writers are well aware of the special connection between writing and reading. Stephen King says, "Reading is the creative center of a writer's life." Joan Aiken says, "Read as much as you possibly can." William Faulkner said, "Read, read, read. Read everything. . . ." These individuals know that reading stimulates writing, while their writing stimulates them to read more.

As a student, you need to make your own special connections between writing and reading. This chapter will get you started because it provides three important strategies that enrich college-level writing and reading.

## Learning Outcomes

**LO1** Analyze the assignment.

**LO2** Use the traits of writing.

**LO3** Use graphic organizers.

**LO4** Review the writing-reading connection.

## What do you think?

How can you connect the de Montaigne quotation to the writing process, the reading process, or both?

Answers will vary.

_____

_____

_____

_____

# LO1 Understanding the Assignment

Part of making good choices is understanding in advance what you are dealing with. You would, for example, want to know the basics about a job or an internship before you apply for it. The same holds true for each of your college reading and writing assignments. You should identify its main features before you get started on your work.

## The STRAP Strategy

You can use the **STRAP strategy** to analyze your writing and reading assignments. The strategy consists of answering questions about these five features: _subject, type, role, audience,_ and _purpose._ Once you answer the questions, you'll be ready to get to work. This chart shows how the strategy works:

| For Writing Assignments | | For Reading Assignments |
|---|---|---|
| What specific topic should I write about? | **Subject** | What specific topic does the reading address? |
| What form of writing (essay, article) will I use? | **Type** | What form (essay, text chapter, article) does the reading take? |
| What position (student, citizen, employee) should I assume? | **Role** | What position (student, responder, concerned individual) does the writer assume? |
| Who is the intended reader? | **Audience** | Who is the intended reader? |
| What is the goal (to inform, to persuade) of the writing? | **Purpose** | What is the goal of the material? |

## The STRAP Strategy in Action

**Test Taking**

The STRAP questions help you quickly understand a writing prompt or a reading selection on a test.

Suppose you were given the following reading assignment in an environmental studies class.

Read the essay "To Drill or Not to Drill" in the online readings. Then write a blog entry, comparing the reading with what you've learned about oil drilling in class discussions.

Here are the answers to the STRAP questions for this assignment:

| | |
|---|---|
| **Subject:** | Drilling for oil in the Arctic National Wildlife Refuge |
| **Type:** | Persuasive essay |
| **Role:** | Advocate of less drilling, more conservation |
| **Audience:** | General consumers |
| **Purpose:** | To persuade readers to accept a new line of thinking |

**Respond** Use the STRAP strategy to analyze the assignment that follows for a reading in *WRITE 2*. Then in the box below, analyze another reading assignment as directed.

**Assignment 1:** Read "Religious Faith Versus Spirituality" starting of page 458 in *WRITE 2*. Then in your class notebook, respond to the reading, noting its key features and your reactions to them.

**Subject:** What specific topic does the reading address?
Religion and spirituality

**Type:** What form *(essay, text chapter)* does the reading take?
Essay

**Role:** What position does the writer assume?
Concerned individual

**Audience:** Who is the intended audience?
Everyone

**Purpose:** What is the goal of the material?
To persuade that religion is not required for spirituality

Before you begin any reading assignment, you should also consider these issues:

- The importance of the assignment
- The time you have to complete it
- The way the assignment fits into the course as a whole

**Assignment 2:** Answer the STRAP questions that follow for a reading assignment in *WRITE 2* or elsewhere that informs or entertains.  Answers will vary.

**Subject:** What specific topic does the reading address?

**Type:** What form *(essay, text chapter)* does the reading take?

**Role:** What position does the writer assume?

**Audience:** Who is the intended audience?

**Purpose:** What is the goal of the material?

**Speaking & Listening**

Work on the second assignment with a partner or a small group if your instructor allows it.

# LO2 Using the Traits

Chapter 4 in *WRITE 2* goes into great detail about using the **traits** to help you with your writing. (See pages 24–34.) You can use these same traits to help you analyze and discuss your reading assignments.

## Previewing the Traits

The traits of writing are highlighted below. Each one addresses an important feature in a reading selection, whether an essay, a chapter, an article, or a piece of fiction. (The questions will help you analyze a reading selection for the traits.)

**Traits**

Throughout *WRITE 2*, the traits are used to help you read and write. Watch for this advice in annotations like this one.

- **Ideas** The information contained in reading material
  *What is the topic of the reading?*
  *What main point is made?*
  *What supporting details are provided?*

- **Organization** The overall structure of the material
  *How does the reading selection begin?*
  *How is the middle part arranged?*
  *How does the selection end?*

- **Voice** The personality of the writing—how the writer speaks to the reader
  *To what degree does the writer seem interested in and knowledgeable about the topic?*
  *To what degree does the writer engage the reader?*

- **Word Choice** The writer's use of words and phrases
  *What can be said about the nouns, verbs, and modifiers in the reading?*
  *Are the words too general, or are they specific and effective?*
  *Does the writer use figurative language?*

- **Sentence Fluency** The flow of the sentences
  *What stands out about the sentences?*
  *Are they varied in length, do they flow smoothly, do they seem stylish, and so on?*

- **Conventions** The correctness or accuracy of the language
  *To what degree does the writing follow the conventions of the language?*

- **Design** The appearance of the writing
  *What, if anything, stands out about the design?*
  *Does it enhance or take away from the reading experience?*

Nikada/iStockphoto.com

**Vocabulary**

**traits**
the key elements found in effective writing

**figurative language**
metaphors, personification, or other creative comparisons used to describe something or to make a point

# A Sample Analysis for a Reading Selection

Here is a traits analysis of "A Modest Proposal: Guys Shouldn't Drive Till 25," an argumentative essay on pages 491–493 in *WRITE 2*.

- ## Ideas

  The essay focuses on a bold proposal (rather than a modest one): raising the driving age for males to 25. The writer presents reliable statistics showing the dangers that young male drivers present. She also addresses main objections to her idea as well as many benefits to it.

- ## Organization

  The beginning paragraph uses dramatic statistics to lead up to her proposal.

  The middle paragraphs cover main objections, benefits, and exceptions to her idea.

  The closing paragraph identifies rules and actions that haven't worked in the past as a dramatic contrast to her bold claim, which she restates here.

- ## Voice

  The writer speaks in a friendly, knowing manner. The use of the pronoun "We" in a few paragraphs helps connect the reader with the writer. At times, she speaks in a tongue in cheek style. For example, she claims a more fit male population in our "paunchy" society would be a side benefit.

- ## Word Choice

  The word choice reflects an essay intended for a general audience—not too challenging nor too basic. The most challenging terms such as *salient* and *carnage* are defined for the reader.

- ## Sentence Fluency

  The sentences are, for the most part, long, and some of them may require a few readings. The varied sentence beginnings help with the flow of the writer's ideas.

- ## Conventions

  The writer clearly follows the conventions.

- ## Design

  The essay is traditional in design except for one long bulleted list.

**Vocabulary**

**tongue in cheek**
an expression or idiom meaning "somewhat humorously" or "not to be taken seriously"

**Respond** Analyze "Spanglish Spoken Here" (page 473–474) in *WRITE 2* for the traits. To develop your analysis, ask and answer each of the specific questions on page 19, or use the questions as a basic response guide, as is done above. (Use your own paper.)

**Speaking & Listening**

Work on this activity with a partner or a small group of classmates if your instructor allows it.

**WAC**

See page 42 for eight common graphic organizers that you can use to organize ideas in any class.

# LO3 Using Graphic Organizers

Graphic organizers help you map out your thinking for writing and reading assignments. You can, for example, use a Venn diagram or a T-graph to arrange your thinking for a comparison essay that you are about to write or for one that you have just read. Other common graphics help you organize your thinking for problem-solution, cause-effect, and narrative writing and reading.

## Graphing a Reading Assignment

Provided below is a time line charting the main actions in a narrative essay starting on page 432 in *WRITE 2*. (A time line identifies the key actions and events, without the related details and explanations.)

**A Doctor's Dilemma**

- The writer, a young doctor, witnesses an accident.
- He finds one injured driver, unconscious and turning blue.
- He moves the driver and tries mouth-to-mouth without success.
- Then he pierces the windpipe with needle shots to initiate breathing.
- An ambulance takes the injured driver to a hospital.
- Three weeks later, the driver leaves the hospital after throat surgery.
- Days later, the writer has a revealing talk with a professor.

**Respond** In the space provided, use a time line to chart the main actions from the narrative essay "Shark Bait," starting on page 427. (Remember to focus on key actions, without all of the related details.)

**Shark Bait**

- Ten males took a motorboat excursion off the Miami coast.
- They ate fried chicken and potato chips.
- The four boys were punching one another.
- The group motored to open sea and dropped anchor.
- They spent some time diving for lobsters.
- Afterward, Larry began fishing and hooked a barracuda.
- Before he could reel it in, a hammerhead shark ate most of it.
- Impressed, the boys were finally quiet.

# LO4 Reviewing the Writing-Reading Connection

Complete these activities as needed to help you better understand the writing-reading connection.

**Analyze the Assignment** Use the STRAP strategy to analyze the following reading assignment. (See pages 18–19.)

Read "Why I Changed My Mind on the Death Penalty" starting on page 489 in your text.

**Subject:** Death penalty

**Type:** Essay

**Role:** Concerned individual

**Audience:** Everyone

**Purpose:** To convince that the death penalty should be abolished

**Use the Traits** Analyze the contents of "Why I Changed My Mind on the Death Penalty" for the following traits. (See pages 20–21.)

**Ideas:** Answers will vary.

**Organization:**

**Word Choice:**

"If you start in the right place and follow all the steps,
you will get to the right end."
—Elizabeth Moon

# 4 Using the Writing Process and the Traits

Have you ever climbed to the top of a lighthouse? You can't get there in one step. You can't get there in a straight line, either. But if you've ever climbed to the top of a lighthouse and looked out for miles over the ocean, you know it's worth the trip.

Writing is the same way. You can't arrive at a final draft in one step or in a straight line. It's going to take some work and a bit of sweat. You may even feel dizzy sometimes. But if you take the steps in the writing process, you'll reach your destination and see things you've never imagined. This chapter will show you the way.

## What do you think?

How can a series of small steps in writing equal a giant leap in thinking?

Answers will vary.

## Learning Outcomes

**LO1** Think about writing as a process.

**LO2** Learn about the steps in the writing process.

**LO3** Learn about the traits of effective writing.

**LO4** Connect the process and the traits.

# LO1 Understanding the Writing Process

When receiving a writing assignment, most writers ask the same question: How will I *ever* get this done? If you struggle to answer this question, you are not alone. Even professional writers labor for the right answer. But have no fear. As the quotation on the previous page explains, a writing project is much less imposing when you approach it as a process rather than as an end product.

This chapter will introduce you to the manageable steps of the **writing process**. Taking those steps one at a time will help you become a better writer and make your next writing assignment a lot less intimidating.

## The Process in Action

The writing process is often considered a process of discovery because while you follow it, you will find out what you want to say.

**Read/React** Read the following quotations from writers who describe the writing process as a means of discovery. Discuss the quotations with a partner or a small group of classmates. Then explain below what one or two of the statements mean to you.

"Writing became such a process of discovery that I couldn't wait to get to work in the morning: I wanted to know what I was going to say."

—Sharon O'Brien

"For most writers, the act of putting words on paper is not the recording of a discovery but the very act of exploration itself."

—Donald Murray

"If you don't allow yourself the possibility of writing something very, very bad, it would be hard to write something very good."

—Steven Galloway

**Reactions:** Answers will vary.

# Thinking About Your Own Writing

**Respond** Answer the following questions about your writing experiences. Be sure to explain each of your answers.

1. Rate your experience as a writer by circling the appropriate star:

   negative ★ ★ ★ ★ ★ positive    Answers will vary.

   Explain. _____

   _____

   _____

   _____

2. What is the easiest part of writing for you? _____

   _____

   _____

   _____

3. What is the hardest part of writing for you? _____

   _____

   _____

   _____

4. What types of writing assignments challenge you the most? _____

   _____

   _____

   _____

5. What is the best thing you have ever written? _____

   _____

   _____

   _____

6. What is the most important thing you have learned about writing?

   _____

   _____

   _____

   _____

   _____

   _____

Kristian Dowling/Getty Images

**Spotlight on** Writing

"Sometimes something discouraging can be encouraging. It's all in how you take it."

The writing career of playwright Suzan-Lori Parks nearly fizzled, thanks in part to resistance from her high school English teacher, who recommended she not pursue an English degree because she was a poor speller. "Still am actually," says Parks.

Following that advice, Parks went to college to pursue a chemistry degree, but rediscovered her passion for writing in a fiction workshop. "What you love comes back to you," she says.

Since that time, Parks has become a renowned playwright. In 2002, her play *Topdog/Underdog* was awarded the Pulitzer Prize for Drama, making her the first African American woman to win the award.

"The first draft is a skeleton—just bare bones."

—Phyllis Reynolds Naylor

# LO2 The Steps in the Process

You cannot change a flat tire in one fell swoop—it takes a number of steps to get the job done right. The same goes for writing. If you expect to finish a paper in one broad attempt, you are going to be disappointed. On the other hand, if you follow the steps of the writing process and pace yourself, you'll get the job done right.

| Process | Activities |
|---|---|
| **Prewriting** | Start the process by (1) selecting a topic to write about, (2) collecting details about it, and (3) finding your focus, the main idea or thesis. |
| **Writing** | Then write your first draft, using your prewriting plan as a general guide. Writing a first draft allows you to connect your thoughts about a topic. |
| **Revising** | Carefully review your first draft and have a classmate read it as well. Change any parts that need to be clearer, and add missing information. |
| **Editing** | Edit your revised writing by checking for style, grammar, punctuation, and spelling errors. |
| **Publishing** | During the final step, prepare your writing to share with your instructor, your peers, or another audience. |

**Explain** On the lines below, tell how the writing process explained above compares with your own way of completing writing assignments. Consider what you usually do first, second, third, and so on.

Answers will vary.

# The Process in Action

As the chart indicates, you will likely move back and forth between the steps in the writing process. For example, after writing a first draft, you may decide to collect more details about your topic, which is actually a prewriting activity.

## Process Chart

**Create** In the space provided below, create a chart that shows your own process—the one you described on page 28. Discuss your chart with a partner or small group of classmates.

## Reasons to Write

The four main reasons to write are given below. Always use the writing process when **writing to show learning** and when **writing to share**.

| Reason | Forms | Purpose |
|---|---|---|
| **Writing to show learning** | Summaries, informational essays | To show your understanding of subjects you are studying |
| **Writing to share** | Personal essays, blog postings, short stories, plays | To share your personal thoughts, feelings, and creativity with others |
| **Writing to explore** | Personal journals, diaries, unsent letters, dialogues | To learn about yourself and your world |
| **Writing to learn** | Learning logs, reading logs, notes | To help you understand what you are learning |

**Explain** Why is using the writing process unnecessary for **writing to explore** and **writing to learn**?

Answers will vary.

**Speaking & Listening**

If you are having trouble explaining your process, talk about it with a partner.

**Test Taking**

When you respond to a prompt on a test, use an abbreviated form of this process. Spend a few minutes gathering and organizing ideas, then write your response. Afterward, read what you have done and quickly revise and edit it.

# LO3 Understanding the Traits of Writing

Think about your favorite song. What makes it great? It's a combination of elements, right? The beat is fresh; the lyrics, inventive; the chorus, catchy.

A combination of elements results in good writing, too. The elements, or **traits**, that you find in the best articles and essays are described below.

■ **Strong Ideas** Good writing contains plenty of good information (ideas and details). And all of the information holds the reader's interest.

> In the world of cloud enthusiasts, 1951 was a special year. It marked the last time a new cloud category was recognized by the International Cloud Atlas. But that may soon change. A photograph of wavy, violent-looking clouds over Cedar Rapids, Iowa, is at the heart of a 2009 cloud debate. Many say the picture reveals a new cloud category known as *undulatus asperatus*. Others say it is just another example of an *undulatus* cloud. A review is underway to determine the answer. Will 2009 become the new 1951?
>
> — Johanna Ruiz

1. Rate the passage for ideas by circling the appropriate star:

   weak ★ ★ ★ ★ ★ strong

   Explain. __Answers will vary.__

   _____

2. What is the main point? __A new cloud category, *undulatus asperatus*, is being debated.__

■ **Logical Organization** Effective writing has a clear overall structure—with a beginning, a middle, and an ending.

> I've experienced all sorts of road trips. Some have been great; others have been lousy. But along the way, I've picked up tips for maximizing the experience. The first is preparation. Before you leave, gather snacks, caffeinated drinks, and a minimum of three of your favorite CDs. Next, carry a notebook to record all the stupid things your friends say. And lastly, drive whatever car is least likely to break down. Now go enjoy the open road!
>
> — T. J. Brown

1. Rate the passage for organization by circling the appropriate star:

   weak ★ ★ ★ ★ ★ strong

   Explain. __Answers will vary.__

   _____

2. How is this passage arranged—by time, by order of importance, by logic?

   __By order of importance__

   _____

3. What transitional phrases does the writer use? _____

   __"But along the way," "before you leave," "next," "and lastly"__

**■ Fitting Voice** In the best writing, you can hear the writer's voice—her or his special way of saying things. It shows that the writer cares about the subject.

**Speaking & Listening**

Read this model aloud to a partner. Then have the partner read the model. How do your different voices and expression affect the overall impact of the model?

> Natural disasters are as ruthless as they are powerful. Too often they leave families, communities, and entire countries broken and helpless. But that's when we must step up and help. You may think one person can't make a world of a difference to people affected by a natural disaster, but you can. Besides donating money, you can give blood, volunteer for relief agencies, and use social media to influence others to help. Will you join the cause?
>
> — Melanie Roberts

1. Rate the passage for voice by circling the appropriate star:

   weak ★ ★ ★ ★ ★ strong

   Explain. Answers will vary.

2. Does the writer seem to care about the topic? Explain.

   Answers will vary.

3. How would you identify the voice in this passage—sincere, silly, bored?

   sincere

**■ Well-Chosen Words** In strong writing, nouns and verbs are specific and clear, and the modifiers add important information.

> The swimmer hunched over the starting line, anticipating the start of the race. "Bang!" The sound thrust her into motion. She dived into the pool, darting through the water like a torpedo. As she approached the other end of the pool, she swiftly spun around, kicked her feet off the concrete side, and swam back to the original end of the pool.
>
> — Joel Gutierrez

1. Rate the passage for word choice by circling the appropriate star:

   weak ★ ★ ★ ★ ★ strong

   Explain. Answers will vary.

2. Which, if any, specific verbs stand out for you?

   hunched   thrust   darting   spun   kicked

3. What other words do you find interesting? (Name two.)

   Answers will vary.

Chanyut Sribua-rawd/iStockphoto.com

**Traits**

The traits help you in two important ways: (1) They name the key elements that you must consider when writing. (2) They provide a vocabulary to discuss writing with your peers.

■ **Smooth Sentences** The sentences in good writing flow smoothly from one to the next. They carry the meaning of the essay or article.

> Have you ever sent so many text messages that your thumbs started to ache? If so, you may be suffering from a condition dubbed "Blackberry thumb." It's true. Repetitive stress on your thumbs from texting can cause tendonitis and nerve damage. Doctors say the chance for injury is greater as you age. Naturally, the remedy is to rest your fingers.
>
> — James Jackson

1. Rate the sentences in the passage by circling the appropriate star:

   weak ★ ★ ★ ★ ★ strong

   Explain. Answers will vary.

   _____

2. In what ways does the writer vary the sentences he uses? _____

   _____ Answers will vary. _____

3. Which sentence do you like best? Why? _____

   _____ Answers will vary. _____

■ **Correct Copy** Strong writing is easy to read because it follows the conventions, or rules, of the language.

> Ella Fitzgerald is one of the most famous jazz vocalists in music history. Known as "the First Lady of Song," Fitzgerald made her singing debut at 17 at the renowned Apollo Theater in Harlem, New York. From there, her career went through three progressions—big band, bebop, and mainstream. In all, her recording career lasted 59 years and produced 13 Grammy Awards.
>
> — Chloe Evans

1. Rate the conventions in the passage by circling the appropriate star:

   weak ★ ★ ★ ★ ★ strong

   Explain. Answers will vary.

   _____

2. What punctuation marks, other than periods, are used in this passage?

   _____ commas    quotation marks    dash _____

3. What do the quotation marks show? (See page 408 for help.)

   _____ Answers will vary. _____

   _____

# ■ Appropriate Design

In the best academic writing, the design follows the guidelines established by the instructor or school.

LaShawna Wilson
Ms. Davis
Forces in Science
February 11, 2011

### Physics of Rainbows

"Why are there so many songs about rainbows?" asks the old tune. Perhaps it's because rainbows are beautiful, multicolored, and huge, arching over cities and mountains. But rainbows have captured human imagination as much because of their mystery as their beauty. In his work with prisms, Sir Isaac Newton demonstrated that something as beautiful and mysterious as a rainbow could be created through the simple property of refraction.

**Basics of Refraction**

The key to understanding rainbows is refraction. When light passes from one medium to another, it bends. Simply look at a straw in a glass, and the apparent break in the straw when it enters the water demonstrates refraction. Light is bending as it passes through the water, showing the straw in a different place.

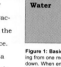

**Figure 1: Basic refraction.** Light moving from one medium to another slows down. When entering at an angle, the light is more sharply refracted.

When light enters a new medium at a sharp angle, the refraction is stronger. That's because one side of the light beam is entering the medium first, thereby slowing down, as the other side of the light beam continues longer at its previous speed. The result is a turn in the angle of the light ("Prism" 13). This effect is demonstrated in Figure 1.

Wilson 2

**Frequencies and Refraction**

Different frequencies of light bend at different angles. The relatively long wavelengths of red light do not bend as much as the relatively short wavelengths of purple light, which is why a prism splits white light into its colors.

A raindrop can do the same thing. Figure 2, derived from the Web site "How Stuff Works," shows how white light is bent when passing through a raindrop.

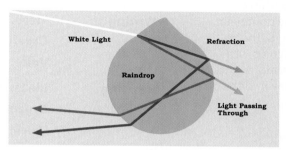

Figure 2: **Refraction of light through a raindrop.** Note that the purple light exits at a higher angle than the red. Drops lower in the air will reflect violet light to viewers' eyes, while higher drops reflect red light. (Source http://science.howstuffworks.com/rainbow2.htm.)

**Bands of Color**

The reason that a rainbow looks like bands of color is that the observer sees only one color coming from each droplet. As Figure 2 shows, a droplet that is higher in the sky will refract red into the eyes of the viewer. A droplet that is lower in the sky will refract violet into the viewer's eyes. This same pattern holds for all of the colors in between—orange, yellow, green, blue, and indigo. This effect creates the bands of color that the person sees when looking at the rainbow.

---

**1.** Rate the design of these pages by circling the appropriate star:

weak ★ ★ ★ ★ ★ strong

Explain. Answers will vary. _____

_____

_____

**2.** What one design feature stands out for you? Answers will vary. _____

_____

_____

**3.** Why is format and design important for a finished piece of writing?

Answers will vary.

_____

_____

APA
MLA

Traits

The first three traits—ideas, organization, and voice—deal with big issues, so they dominate the beginning of the writing process. Words, sentences, conventions, and design become important later.

# LO4 Connecting the Process and the Traits

The writing process guides you as you form a piece of writing. The writing traits identify the key elements to consider in the writing. This chart connects the two. For example, it shows that during prewriting, you should focus on ideas, organization, and voice.

| Process | Traits: Activities |
|---------|--------------------|
| **Prewriting** | **Ideas:** selecting a topic, collecting details about it, forming a thesis |
| | **Organization:** arranging the details |
| | **Voice:** establishing your stance (objective, personal) |
| **Writing** | **Ideas:** connecting your thoughts and information |
| | **Organization:** following your prewriting plan |
| | **Voice:** sounding serious, sincere, interested . . . |
| **Revising** | **Ideas:** reviewing for clarity and completeness |
| | **Organization:** reviewing for structure/arrangement of ideas |
| | **Voice:** reviewing for appropriate tone |
| **Editing** | **Word choice:** checking for specific nouns, verbs, and modifiers |
| | **Sentences:** checking for smoothness and variety |
| | **Conventions:** checking for correctness |
| **Publishing** | **Design:** evaluating the format |

**Think Critically** Team up with a classmate to discuss the following questions. Record your answers on the lines below.

1. Which writing trait interests you the most? Why?

   Answers will vary.

2. Which step in the writing process should probably take the most time? Explain. 

   Answers will vary.

3. How could you use the chart above during a writing project? 

   Answers will vary.

Monkey Business Images, 2010/used under license from www.shutterstock.com

"Bring ideas in and entertain them royally, for one of them may be king."

—Mark Van Doren

David Henley/Dorling Kindersley/ Getty Images

# Prewriting

A process, by definition, is "a series of actions bringing about a result." **Prewriting** is the first action or step in the writing process, and, in many ways, the most important one, because it involves all of the decisions you should make before the actual writing. If you do the necessary prewriting and planning, you will be well prepared to work through the rest of the process. If, on the other hand, you jump right into your first draft, you will find it extremely difficult to develop an effective piece of writing.

In this chapter, you will learn about the following prewriting strategies: selecting a specific topic, gathering details about it, forming a focus or thesis, and organizing your support. Completing each one of these activities puts you in control of your writing. And for extended writing assignments, like research papers, thorough prewriting becomes even more important.

## Learning Outcomes

**LO1** Analyze the assignment.

**LO2** Select a topic.

**LO3** Gather details about a topic.

**LO4** Use graphic organizers.

**LO5** Establish a focus.

**LO6** Understand patterns of organization.

**LO7** Organize your information.

**LO8** Review prewriting.

## What do you think?

In the quotation above, what does Van Doren mean by "bring ideas in and entertain them royally"? How does this thought relate to prewriting?

### Vocabulary

**prewriting**
the first step in the writing process, preparation for the actual writing

Answers will vary.

# LO1 Analyzing the Assignment

Suppose a student writes an essay explaining the main features of a weight-training program, but the instructor really wanted an evaluation of its effectiveness. The student will have missed the purpose of the assignment (*to evaluate*). To make sure that this doesn't happen to you, always analyze your writing assignments.

## Using the STRAP Strategy

In *WRITE 1*, you were introduced to the STRAP strategy for analyzing assignments. This strategy asks you to answer key questions about an assignment.

| | |
|---|---|
| **Subject:** | What specific topic should I write about? |
| **Type:** | What form of writing (*essay, article, report*) should I use? |
| **Role:** | What position (*student, citizen, employee, family member*) should I assume? |
| **Audience:** | Who (*classmates, instructor, government official, parent*) is the intended reader? |
| **Purpose:** | What is the goal (*to inform, to analyze, to persuade, to share*) of the writing? |

**Respond** Analyze the following assignment using the STRAP strategy.

**Assignment:** In a class blog posting, reflect on the significance of a social custom from another culture. In your writing, consider the history of the custom, its relationship to similar customs in other cultures, and your reasons for choosing this particular custom.

**Subject:** What topic should I write about?

A social custom from another culture, its history, its relationship to other customs, and my reasons for choosing it

**Type:** What form of writing should I use?

Blog post

**Role:** What position should I assume?

Student

**Audience:** Who is the intended reader?

Classmates

**Purpose:** What is the goal of the writing?

To analyze and to share

**Test Taking**

For some assignments, you may not find a direct answer to every STRAP question. Use your best judgment when this happens.

**Vocabulary**

**STRAP strategy**
a strategy helping a writer identify the key features of an assignment—the subject, type of writing, writer's role, audience, and purpose

# Understanding Key Words in Assignments

A key word in a writing assignment identifies your purpose; more specifically, it tells you what you should do in your writing. For example, in the assignment on the previous page, the key word is *reflect*. Other common key words include *explain, persuade, describe,* and so on. But what exactly does it mean to reflect or explain? The following chart shares the meanings and implications of key terms in your writing assignments.

**Tip**

*Reflecting* may include other writing and thinking moves, such as *explaining, describing,* and *comparing.*

## Common Key Words

Here are key words that you will find in many of your assignments.

| | |
|---|---|
| Analyze | Break down a topic into its parts. |
| Argue or persuade | Defend a position with logical arguments and support. |
| Compare | Show the similarities and differences. |
| Describe | Show in detail what something or someone is like. |
| Evaluate | Consider the truth, usefulness, or value of something. |
| Explain or inform | Give reasons, list steps, or discuss something. |
| Reflect | Share your well-considered thoughts and feelings about a topic. |
| Summarize | Restate someone else's ideas briefly in your own words. |

*Think about it...*

Once you find out the due date for the assignment, set up a schedule to complete your work. Be sure to give yourself enough time for each step in the writing process— prewriting, writing, revising, and editing.

**Identify** Circle the key word in each of the following assignments. Then explain how this key word will direct your writing. (The first one is done for you.)

1. In a movie review suitable for a school publication, (evaluate) one of Quentin Tarantino's latest films.

   To evaluate a movie means to identify its main features, its strengths and weaknesses, and

   its value (whether or not it is worth seeing).

2. In a personal essay, (describe) a time when the "better angels of your nature" took control.

   Answers will vary.

3. Write a letter to your representative in Congress, (arguing) for or against a piece of immigration legislation.

   Answers will vary.

4. (Explain) in an informational essay the causes of a serious health condition affecting a large number of people.

   Answers will vary.

> "There are few experiences quite so satisfactory as getting a good idea. . . .
> You're pleased with it, and feel good."
> —Lancelot Law Whyte

# LO2 Selecting a Topic

Personal essayist Andy Rooney of *60 Minutes* fame stated, "I don't pick subjects so much as they pick me." He is lucky in that he can write about anything that interests him, and he comes across so many interesting subjects that they seem to "pick" him. You are not so lucky in most of your writing assignments because your choices are usually limited. Even so, always try to select a topic that you have strong feelings about. Otherwise, you will find it very difficult to do your best work.

## Narrowing Your Choices

Some assignments will tell you specifically what you should write about, but in most cases, they will identify a general subject area that serves as a starting point for a topic search. This graphic shows how the selecting process should work, moving from the general subject area to a specific topic.

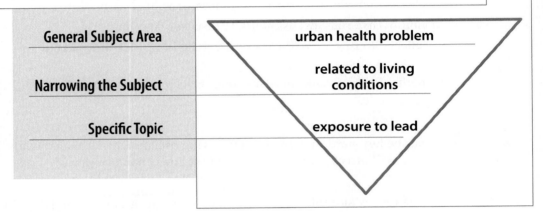

**Assignment:** Analyze the cause and effects of an urban health problem.

| General Subject Area | urban health problem |
| Narrowing the Subject | related to living conditions |
| Specific Topic | exposure to lead |

Traits

A topic for an extended assignment such as a research paper must be broad enough to offer plenty of information. For a more limited assignment (a one- or two-page essay), the topic should be more specific.

**Choose** Identify a specific topic for the following assignment. (Use the example above as a guide.)

**Assignment:** In a persuasive essay, argue for or against a new or proposed mode of transportation.

A new or proposed mode of transportation

Answers will vary.

Answers will vary.

1. What is the general subject area?

2. How can you narrow this subject?

3. What is one specific topic that you could write about?

# Selecting Strategies

If you can't think of a suitable topic for an assignment, be sure to review your class notes, your text, and relevant Web sites for ideas. You may also want to use a selecting strategy to help you identify possible topics.

**Clustering** Begin a cluster with the general subject area or a narrowed subject. Circle it and then cluster related words around it.

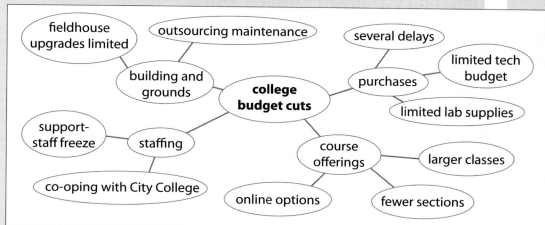

**Extend**

If one of the clustering ideas interests you, write about it for 5 minutes to see what you can discover.

**Freewriting** Write nonstop for 5–10 minutes about your assignment to discover possible topics. Begin by writing down a particular thought about the assignment. Then record whatever comes to mind without stopping to judge, edit, or correct your writing.

**Developing a Dialogue** Create a dialogue between yourself and another person to identify possible topics for a writing assignment.

**Practice** Use the format below to create a dialogue for the following writing assignment. Afterward, circle any possible writing ideas. (Use your own paper to continue the conversation.)

**Vocabulary**

dialogue
a composition in the form of a written conversation

**Assignment:** Write a brief personal essay in which you reflect on something that really bugs you about school life or the workplace.

You: _So what is one thing that really bugs you about this school?_

Other person: _Answers will vary._
_____

You: _Answers will vary._
_____

Other person: _Answers will vary._
_____

> "Writing comes more easily if you have something to say."
> —Sholem Asch

# LO3 Gathering Details

After selecting a writing topic, you'll need to learn as much as you can about it. Writing your first draft will go smoothly if you have collected plenty of information about your topic, so use strategies like those below and on the next page to gather facts and details.

## Deciding What You Already Know

To review what you already know about a topic, try one of these strategies:

**Five W's of Writing** Answer the five W's (who? what? when? where? and why?) to identify basic information about your subject. Add *how?* to the list for more thorough coverage.

**Listing** List your first thoughts about your topic as well as questions about it. Work rapidly, recording ideas nonstop for as long as you can.

**Clustering** Create a cluster with your specific topic as the starting point. (See page 39.)

**Focused Freewriting** Write freely about your topic for at least 5 minutes to see what thoughts and feelings you can uncover. Keep writing for as long as you can.

**Dialoguing** Discuss your topic in a creative dialogue between you and another person of your choice. (See page 39.)

**Explore** Using one of the strategies above, collect your first thoughts about a topic you identified on the previous page, or one of the topics listed here. (Use your own paper if you need more room.)

- the benefits (or drawbacks) of taking online college courses
- a promising career choice
- a particular trend in fashion or music

Answers will vary.

# Collecting Additional Information

For most writing assignments, gathering your own thoughts will just be a starting point, unless, of course, you're writing about a personal experience. Conducting primary and secondary research is the main way to learn more about a topic. Here is the main difference between the two types of research:

**Primary research** consists of information you gather by observing the topic in action, participating in it, and so on.

**Secondary research** consists of learning what others have already written about the topic.

# Questioning

Your questions will naturally guide your search for additional information about a topic. Whether your topic is a **problem** (school budget cuts), a **policy** (graduation requirements), or a **concept** (a weight-training program), the questions in the following chart will lead you to pertinent facts and details.

|  | Description | Function | History | Value |
|---|---|---|---|---|
| **Problems** | What is the problem? | Who or what is affected by it? | What or who caused it? | What is its significance? |
| **Policies** | What are the most important features? | What is the policy designed to do? | What brought this policy about? | What are its advantages and disadvantages? |
| **Concepts** | What type of concept is it? | Why is it important? | When did it originate? | What value does it hold? |

**Collect** Fill in the first blank below with a specific topic. (See the previous activities in this chapter for ideas.) Then indicate the topic's category—either a problem, policy, or concept. Finally, choose two appropriate questions from the chart above and answer them. (You may have to do some quick research to answer your questions.) Answers will vary.

Topic: _____  Category: _____

Question 1: _____  Question 2: _____

_____  _____

Answer: _____  Answer: _____

_____  _____

**Vocabulary**

**primary research** information gained through firsthand experience such as participating, observing, or interviewing

**secondary research** information gained through reading what others have learned about a topic

**Traits**

A graphic organizer helps you to put the information you are collecting in good order.

# LO4 Using Graphic Organizers

Researching a topic is one thing; keeping track of all of the new information is quite another. To remember key points, take notes, write summaries (see pages 12–13), or use a graphic organizer.

## Sample Graphic Organizers

**Time Line** Use for personal narratives to list actions or events in the order they occurred.

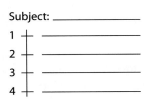

**Process Diagram** Use to collect details for science-related writing, such as the steps in a process.

**Line Diagram** Use to collect and organize details for informational essays.

**Venn Diagram** Use to collect details to compare and contrast two topics.

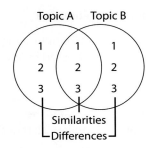

**Cause-Effect Organizer** Use to collect and organize details for cause-effect essays.

**Problem-Solution Web** Use to map out problem-solution essays.

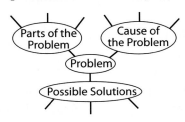

**Evaluation Chart** Use to collect supporting details for essays of evaluation.

Subject:

| Points to Evaluate | Supporting Details |
| --- | --- |
| 1 | |
| 2 | |
| 3 | |
| 4 | |

**Cluster** Use to collect details for informational essays.

**Choose** Identify the best graphic organizer for collecting information about each of the following topics.

1. A personal experience that changed your thinking

   Graphic organizer: _____time line_____

2. The features of a new recycling system

   Graphic organizer: _____line diagram, process diagram, or cluster_____

3. Vandalism in the dormitories

   Graphic organizer: _____cause-effect organizer or problem-solution web_____

4. Effects of a specific oil spill

   Graphic organizer: _____cause-effect organizer_____

5. Examining two similar movies

   Graphic organizer: _____Venn diagram_____

**Complete** Use the appropriate graphic organizer to record information about the topic you worked with on page 41, or for the first topic above. (You may have to do more research to help you fill in the graphic organizer.)

Answers will vary.

# LO5 Establishing a Focus

There are really two parts to prewriting. Part one involves selecting an appropriate topic and collecting information about it. Part two deals with planning how to use this information in the actual writing. To **initiate** this plan, you must establish a writing focus.

## Choosing the Special Part of a Topic

A skilled photographer decides how to **focus** or center the subject before taking a photograph. You should do the same before you begin writing. A thoughtful focus dictates what information to include in your writing, and what information to leave out.

Suppose you were writing an essay on the effects of the 2010 Gulf oil leak on a local shrimping community. To focus your writing and enhance its interest, you could cover how the spill has affected one particular shrimping family or business.

**Topic:** Effects of 2010 Gulf oil spill on (name of local shrimping community)

**Focus:** The spill's effect on a particular family or business

**Review** Rate the effectiveness of each focus below by circling the appropriate star. Consider whether the focus is clear, reasonable, and worth developing.

1. **Topic:** My personal ambitions
   **Focus:** A direct result of my mother's influence

   weak ★ ★ ★ ★ ★ strong

   strong

2. **Topic:** Barbie dolls
   **Focus:** Have been around a long time

   weak ★ ★ ★ ★ ★ strong

   weak

3. **Topic:** American art museums
   **Focus:** Why government funding is questionable

   weak ★ ★ ★ ★ ★ strong

   strong

4. **Topic:** Dog food
   **Focus:** What does it really taste like?

   weak ★ ★ ★ ★ ★ strong

   weak

# Forming a Thesis Statement

You will state your focus in a **thesis statement** for an essay and in a **topic sentence** for a paragraph. An effective thesis statement identifies a special part of a topic or shares a particular feeling about it. The following formula can be used to write a thesis statement or a topic sentence.

| A specific topic | **+** | A particular feeling, feature, or part | **=** | An effective thesis statement or topic sentence |
|---|---|---|---|---|
| Wearing *hijab*—Islamic covering | | Mixed feelings about it | | To wear *hijab*—Islamic covering—invites mixed feelings in me. |

**Tip**

You may have to write two, three, or even four versions of a thesis statement until it says exactly what you want it to say.

**Create** Identify a focus and then write a topic sentence or thesis statement for each of the following assignments. The first one is done for you.

1. **Writing assignment:** Paragraph describing a specific type of exercise

   **Specific topic:** Pilates

   **Focus:** a thoughtful approach to fitness

   **Topic sentence:** Pilates provides a thoughtful approach to physical fitness.

   _____

2. **Writing assignment:** Paragraph explaining a type of ethnic food

   **Specific topic:** Tex-Mex cuisine

   **Focus:** Answers will vary.

   **Topic sentence:** _____

   _____

3. **Writing assignment:** Essay reflecting on a modern social problem

   **Specific topic:** Affordable living spaces

   **Focus:** Answers will vary.

   **Thesis statement:** _____

   _____

4. **Writing assignment:** Essay analyzing a favorite or important movie

   **Specific topic:** (Your choice)

   **Focus:** Answers will vary.

   **Thesis statement:** _____

   _____

**Vocabulary**

**thesis statement**
the controlling idea in an essay, highlighting a special part or feature of a topic or expressing a particular feeling about it

**topic sentence**
the controlling idea in a paragraph

# LO6 Understanding Patterns of Organization

After identifying your thesis, you'll need to decide how to organize the information that supports it. You have many patterns of organization to choose from. Here's how to proceed:

1. **Study your thesis statement.** It will usually indicate how to organize your ideas. For example, consider the following thesis statement:

   > Viewers love *The Simpsons* because it **parodies** daily live in the United States.

   As a point to be proved, this thesis suggests arranging the information by order of importance. As an idea to be shared and explained, it suggests a deductive organization of supporting information.

2. Then **review the information you have gathered.** Decide which ideas support your thesis and arrange them according to the appropriate method of organization. For example, if you are trying to prove a point about *The Simpsons,* you would arrange your reasons either from most important to least important or vice versa.

## Patterns of Organization

Listed below are some of the common patterns that you will use in your writing.

- Use **chronological order** (time) when you are sharing a personal experience, telling how something happened, or explaining how to do something.

- Use **spatial order** (location) for descriptions, arranging information from left to right, top to bottom, from the edge to the center, and so on.

- Use **order of importance** when you are taking a stand or arguing for or against something. Arrange your reasons either from most important to least important or the other way around.

- Use **deductive organization** if you want to follow your thesis statement with basic information—supporting reasons, examples, and facts.

- Use **inductive organization** when you want to present specific details first and conclude with your thesis statement.

- Use **compare-contrast organization** when you want to show how one topic is different from and similar to another one.

### Traits

For some writing assignments, you will use one main pattern of organization, and **complement** it with one or more additional patterns. For example, in an essay organized by order of importance, you may also need to make a comparison or describe someone or something.

**Choose** Study each of the following thesis statements. Then choose the method of organization that the thesis suggests. Explain each of your choices. The first one is done for you.

Work on this activity with a partner if your instructor allows it.

1. **Thesis statement:** The boardwalk makes Coney Island different from any other New York neighborhood.

   **Appropriate method of organization:** spatial order

   **Explain:** The thesis suggests that the writer will describe the boardwalk, so spatial organization makes sense.

2. **Thesis statement:** I am a Korean, but I am an American, too.

   **Appropriate method of organization:** compare-contrast organization

   **Explain:** Answers will vary.

3. **Thesis statement:** Multicultural education is vital to a society made up of many different peoples.

   **Appropriate method of organization:** deductive organization

   **Explain:** Answers will vary.

4. **Thesis statement:** I did something totally out of character for me; I jumped off a bridge with nothing more than a giant rubber band attached to my ankles.

   **Appropriate method of organization:** chronological order

   **Explain:** Answers will vary.

5. **Thesis statement:** (Choose one that you wrote on page 45.)

   **Appropriate method of organization:** Answers will vary.

   **Explain:**

"The essay is a literary device for saying almost everything about almost anything."

—Aldous Huxley

# LO7 Organizing Your Information

Here are three basic strategies for arranging your supporting information after identifying an appropriate pattern of organization.

**Make a quick list** of main points.

**Create an outline**—an organized arrangement of main points and subpoints.

**Fill in a graphic organizer,** arranging main points and details in a chart or diagram. (See pages 42.)

> "Complicated outlines tempt you to think too much about the fine points of organization, at a time when you should be blocking out the overall structure."
>
> —Donald Murray

## Using a Quick List

A quick list works well when you are writing a short piece, such as a paragraph, or when your planning time is limited. Here is a quick list for an informational essay about comets. (The main pattern of organization is chronological.)

**Sample Quick List**

**Topic sentence:** The appearance of comets in the night skies has puzzled people for thousands of years.

- very early on, thought to be planets
- Aristotle, the result of air escaping from atmosphere
- by 15th & 16th centuries, thought to be heavenly bodies
- all along, considered a sign of impending disaster
- really a gaseous body around a core of ice and dust
- head, hundreds of miles in diameter; tail millions of miles in length

**Create** Write a thesis statement and a quick list for an essay explaining why a certain book is one of your favorites. Answers will vary.

**Thesis statement:** _____

_____

_____

**Quick list:**

_____

_____

_____

_____

_____

# Using an Outline

An effective outline shows how ideas fit together and serves as a blueprint for your writing. Topic and sentence outlines follow specific guidelines: If you have a "I," you must have at least a "II." If you have an "A," you must have at least a "B," and so on. You can also **customize** an outline to meet your own needs.

## Sample Customized Outline

What follows is the first part of a customized outline that includes main points stated in compete sentences and supporting details stated as phrases.

**Thesis statement:** Activist Charlotte Perkins Gilman rejected commonly held notions of male superiority.

1. Gilman's beliefs did little to prepare her for domestic life.
   – in 1884, married Charles W. Stetson
   – gave birth to a daughter
   – visited CA shortly after to mentally and emotionally recuperate
   – while there, wrote a book about a pregnant woman locked in a room

2. During the next stage in her life, Gilman became a leading feminist.
   – delivered speeches on women's rights
   – following a divorce in 1894, edited *Impress* for Women's Press Associate
   – from 1895-1900, continued lecturing on women's rights
   – in 1896, a delegate to the National Socialist and Labor Congress in London

**Create** Develop the first part of a customized outline for an essay about television viewing. A thesis statement and two main points are provided. Put the main points in a logical order and make up two or three details to support each one.

**Thesis statement:** **Unregulated** television viewing has harmful effects on young viewers.

**Main points:** Television is reactive, requiring no skill or thinking. Television viewing takes away from study and reading time.

1. _Answers will vary._
   – _____
   – _____
   – _____

2. _____
   – _____
   – _____
   – _____

**Vocabulary**

**customize**
to change or alter

**unregulated**
not controlled

# LO8 Reviewing Prewriting

Complete these activities as needed to help you better understand the key prewriting strategies.

**Selecting a Topic** Select a specific topic for the following general subject area (or for one of your own choosing): *a helpful Web site*. (See page 38.) Answers will vary.

1. General subject area: _____

2. Narrowing the subject: _____

3. Specific topic: _____

**Forming a Thesis Statement** Fill in the top spaces with the formula for writing thesis statements. Then write a thesis statement for the topic you identified above. (See page 45.)

| A specific topic | **+** | A particular feeling, feature, or part | **=** | An effective thesis statement or topic sentence. |
|---|---|---|---|---|
| Answers will vary. | | Answers will vary. | | Answers will vary. |

**Choosing a Pattern of Organization** Identify the best pattern of organization for developing each of the following thesis statements. (See pages 46–49.)

1. **Thesis statement:** Believe it or not, the environment can take care of itself.

   **Pattern of organization:** Deductive organization

2. **Thesis statement:** The animated movie *Fantasia* may be more than 60 years old, but it is still a timeless work of art.

   **Pattern of organization:** Order of importance

> "You have to write a lot; let the words flow. . . ."
>
> —Benjamin Percy

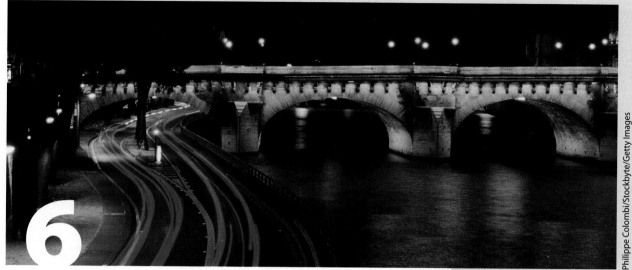

Philippe Colombi/Stockbyte/Getty Images

# 6 Drafting

When developing a piece of writing, you don't have to get it right the first time, the second time, or even the third time. Knowing this should help you feel less anxious about writing first drafts. You have a **singular** task at this point in the process—connecting your thoughts and feelings about your topic. These thoughts and feelings don't have to be perfectly worded or in the best order; they just have to be put on paper so you have something to work with.

Of course, drafting goes most smoothly when you have done the necessary prewriting, including information gathering, focusing, and organizing. Prewriting provides a road map for the writing that follows.

If you remember to approach a first draft as your *first look* at an emerging writing idea, you'll do fine. This chapter provides many additional tips and guidelines about the drafting process.

## Learning Outcomes

**LO1** Follow a drafting plan.
**LO2** Form a meaningful whole.
**LO3** Create an effective opening.
**LO4** Develop the middle part.
**LO5** Write a strong closing.
**LO6** Review drafting.

## Vocabulary

**singular**
one of a kind, unique

## What do you think?

How can Benjamin Percy's advice about writing a lot and letting the words flow be applied to writing a first draft?

Answers will vary.

51

**Traits**

In order to do your best work, you must have strong feelings about your topic.

# LO1 Following a Drafting Plan

When writing a first draft, you're writing to see how well you match up with the topic and if your initial planning still makes sense.

Writing a first draft helps you decide how to proceed with your writing idea. If you're lucky, everything will turn out just as you had planned, and you'll continue to develop your writing. On the other hand, you may discover that you need to learn more about the topic, adjust your focus, or start over.

## A Writing Plan

Use the following points as your drafting guide.

- Focus on developing your thoughts and feelings, not on trying to produce a final copy.

- Follow your prewriting and planning notes, but also feel free to include new ideas that come to mind as you write.

- Continue writing until you cover all of your main points or until you come to a logical stopping point.

- Express yourself honestly and sincerely, using other sources of information to support what you have to say.

- If you get stuck, employ one of these strategies:

  Write as if you are in a conversation with the reader.

  Write in short, fluid bursts of 3-5 minutes.

  Start in the middle by simply identifying your topic and going from there.

**Write** Answer the following questions related to the drafting process.

1. Why is a first draft commonly called a rough draft?

   Answers will vary.

2. In what way does writing a first draft set in motion the rest of the writing process?

   Answers will vary.

3. Some instructors suggest turning down the **resolution** on your computer if you have trouble writing a first draft. How do you think this action would help?

   Answers will vary.

# LO2 Forming a Meaningful Whole

Writer Lillian Hellman said, "There are a thousand ways to write, and each is as good as the other if it fits you." That is certainly true when writing a first draft, once you understand that it doesn't have to be perfect. You must also understand that when developing a first draft, your goal is to form a meaningful whole or a complete initial writing.

Forming a meaningful whole for a paragraph means including a topic sentence, body sentences, and a closing sentence. For an essay, it means including an opening paragraph (with a thesis statement), multiple supporting paragraphs, and a closing paragraph.

> "Just get it on paper, and then we'll see what to do with it."
> —Maxwell Perkins

## Graphically Speaking

The graphics below show the structure of both basic forms of writing.

### Paragraph Structure

**Topic Sentence**
A **topic sentence** names the topic.

**Detail Sentences**
**Detail sentences** support the topic.

**Closing Sentence**
A **closing sentence** wraps up the paragraph.

### Essay Structure

**Opening Paragraph**
The **opening paragraph** draws the reader into the essay and provides information that leads to a thesis statement. The thesis statement tells what the essay is about.

**Middle Paragraphs**
The **middle paragraphs** support the thesis statement. Each middle paragraph needs a topic sentence, a variety of detail sentences, and a closing sentence.

**Closing Paragraph**
The **closing paragraph** finishes the essay by revisiting the thesis statement, emphasizing an important detail, providing the reader with an interesting final thought, and/or looking toward the future.

> "The best advice on writing I've ever received is 'Knock 'em dead with the lead sentence.'"
>
> —Whitney Balliett

# LO3 Creating an Effective Opening

In many situations, first impressions are important—say, for instance, when you're interviewing for a job or introducing yourself to a roommate or a coworker. First impressions are important in writing, too, because the first few ideas help set the **tone** for the rest of the piece. The information that follows will help you make a positive impression in the opening part of your essays.

## The Basic Parts

The opening paragraph (or part) of an essay usually does these three things: (1) identifies the topic, (2) **engages** the reader, (3) and states the thesis. Before stating your thesis, you may also need to include a sentence or two of background information.

### Starting Strategies

Listed below are a few strategies to help you introduce the topic and engage the reader.

- Begin with a surprising or little-known fact about the topic.

    Thousands of babies are born each year with alcohol-related defects, making fetal alcohol syndrome one of the leading causes of mental retardation.

- Ask an interesting or challenging question about the topic.

    What exactly do the signs held up by homeless people tell us?

- Start with a telling quotation.

    "We live here and they live there," Bigger Thomas says in *Native Son*. "We black and they white. They got things and we ain't. They do things and we can't."

- Share a brief, dramatic story.

    It was May 1945. World War II had just ended and Yugoslavia had been overtaken. The town of Vrhnika, Yugoslavia, was no longer safe. Russian and communist troops would break into houses, take what they wanted, and even kill.

- Open with a bold statement.

    Barbie's boobs and spacious mansion helped cause the decay of to-day's youth, or so say some experts.

jon le-bon/2010. Used under license from Shutterstock.com

54

## Sample Opening Paragraph

**Analyze**  Carefully read the following opening paragraph from an essay about a **degenerative** bone disease called Legg-Calve-Perthes (pronounced leg-cal-VAY-PER-theez). Then answer the questions below.

**Traits**

Once the beginning part is set, you'll find it much easier to develop the rest of your writing.

Allie Mason acted like a typical high school freshman. She was bubbly, 1
energetic, and extremely friendly. She was also a **conscientious** student,
belonged to the Honors Art Club, and enjoyed golfing. What set Allie apart was
a **debilitating** physical condition that caused one of her legs to be noticeably
shorter than the other one and forced her to limp. As a result, she had to endure 5
endless medical procedures and missed out on typical school activities such as
gym and dances. She also had to endure more than her share of insensitive
remarks. She remembered, "My classmates would tease me and call me names."
Their comments obviously hurt, especially those made by her friends. The reason
for Allie's suffering was Legg-Calve-Perthes, a painful bone disease that truly 10
challenges the sufferer.

**Vocabulary**

**degenerative**
gradual loss of use or function

**conscientious**
caring, hard-working

**debilitating**
weakening, draining the strength or health

1. What strategy does the writer use to introduce the topic and engage the reader? (See the previous page.)

    She gives a brief dramatic story.

2. What, if any, background information is provided about the topic?

    The effects are shaped before the condition is named.

3. What special part of or feeling about the topic is identified in the thesis statement?

    The pain and challenge of Legg-Calve-Perthes disease.

**Create**  Write a sample opening paragraph for an essay about one of the topics that you worked with in "Prewriting" (pages 35–50). Use your own paper if you need more room.

Answers will vary.

# LO4 Developing Your Ideas

In the middle paragraphs, you should develop all of the main points that support your thesis statement. Use your planning (quick list, outline, graphic organizer) as a general guide when you develop this part of an essay. Here are a few tips for getting started:

- **Keep your thesis statement in mind as you write.** All of your main points should support or advance this statement.
- **Develop each main point in a separate paragraph (or two).** State the main point in the form of a topic sentence and follow with detail sentences that support it.
- **Use plenty of details** to fully explain your points.
- **Use your own words,** except on those few occasions when you employ a quotation to add authority to your writing.
- **Be open to new ideas that occur to you,** especially if they will improve your essay.
- **Try any of the following writing moves** that are appropriate to your topic.

> "When your writing is filled with details, it has a lot more impact."
>
> —Ivan Levison

## Basic Writing Moves

The paragraphs in the middle part of an essay should, among other things, *explain, describe, define, classify,* and so on. What follows is a list and definitions of these basic writing moves.

**WAC**

Most writing assignments use one of these basic writing words to identify the key focus of your work—to *describe,* to *explain,* and so on.

| | |
|---|---|
| **Narrating** | — sharing an experience or a story |
| **Describing** | — telling how someone or something appears, acts, or operates |
| **Explaining** | — providing important facts, details, and examples |
| **Analyzing** | — carefully examining a subject or breaking it down |
| **Comparing** | — showing how two subjects are similar and different |
| **Defining** | — identifying or clarifying the meaning of a term |
| **Reflecting** | — connecting with or wondering about |
| **Evaluating** | — rating the value of something |
| **Arguing** | — using logic and evidence to prove something is true |

**Special Challenge** Read two different essays on pages 424–499 in *WRITE 2*. On your own paper, list the different moves that the writer uses in the middle paragraphs of her or his writing. For example, the writer may *explain* in one or more paragraphs, *reflect* in another, and so on.

## Sample Middle Paragraph

**Analyze** Carefully read the following middle paragraph from an essay on Legg-Calve-Perthes. Then answer the questions below.

**Tip**

Keep your reader in mind as you write. Try to anticipate and answer any questions your audience may have about your topic.

Legg-Calve-Perthes is both rare and mysterious. The disease affects only *1* 5 of every 100,000 children, usually when they are between the ages of five and twelve. While boys suffer from the disease far more frequently than girls do by a ratio of 4 to 1, when girls do develop Legg-Calve-Perthes, they tend to suffer more severely from it. At this point, researchers are not really sure of *5* the cause of the disease. They are, however, fairly certain that it is not genetic. They also know that a reduction of blood flow at the hip joint contributes to the disease and causes the bone tissue to collapse or react in other strange ways. Usually, the rounded part of the femur bone that fits into the hip joint becomes deformed. In Allie's case, the top of her femur bone grew to double its normal *10* size, a condition that produced extreme pain when she tried to walk. It's hard to imagine how Allie or anyone else is able to deal with this condition during the active childhood years.

1. What specific part or special feature of the topic is identified in the topic sentence?

   The rarity and mysteriousness of Legg-Calve-Perthes disease

2. What basic writing move (or moves) does the writer use in this paragraph? (See the previous page.)

   describing, explaining, analyzing, defining

**Create** Write a middle paragraph to go along with the opening paragraph that you wrote on page 55. You may either carry out some quick research or simply make up details to complete your paragraph. Use your own paper if you need more room.

Answers will vary.

## Traits

You may need to write two or three versions of your closing before it says exactly what you want it to say.

# LO5 Writing a Strong Closing

While the opening part of your writing offers important *first* impressions, the closing part should offer important *final* impressions. More specifically, it should help the reader better understand and appreciate the importance of your topic or thesis.

## The Working Parts

Consider the strategies below when writing your closing. In most cases, you will want to use more than one of them; but whatever you choose to do, your closing must flow smoothly from your last middle paragraph.

- Remind the reader of the thesis.

  Legg-Calve-Parthes is like a cancer in how it affects an individual and her or his family.

- Summarize the main points or highlight one or two of them.

  Ultimately, both Alan and Bigger (two literary characters) fail to gain real control over the outside forces in their lives. Alan **forfeits** his interest in life, and Bigger forfeits life itself.

- Reflect on the explanation or argument you've presented in the main part.

  It would be a shame to lose these amazing creatures (humpback whales). We don't want their mysterious song to be a thing of the past. And we can't turn to zoos when the numbers shrink to a precious few.

- Offer a final idea to keep the reader thinking about the topic.

  If the country waits until an **agroterrorist** attack happens, people may become ill, the overall economy could be damaged, and the agricultural economy may never recover.

Noam Armonn/2010. Used under license from Shutterstock.com

## Sample Closing Paragraph

**Analyze** Carefully read the following closing paragraph for an essay on Legg-Calve-Perthes. Then answer the questions below.

Legg-Calve-Perthes is like a cancer in how it affects an individual and her *1* family. In Allie's case, the debilitating effects started with her painful efforts to walk and has continued with attempts to address the condition with operations, therapy, and braces. Through all of this, she and her family have missed out on so much. Her mother had to quit her job, and her sister felt ignored. As Allie *5* recalled, "My sister has always felt jealous of all of the attention I get from my parents." But knowing that the condition should, in time, resolve itself certainly must help sufferers like Allie meet each new challenge. It must also help them to know that young people suffering from Legg-Calve-Perthes usually do quite well in the long term. Unfortunately, the chance of permanent hip damage exists *10* as well.

1. In what way does the first sentence remind the reader of the thesis statement?

   It focuses on the way the disease affects the sufferer.

2. What other strategy or strategies does the writer use?

   The author shares more anecdotes about Allie's suffering.

**Create** Write a closing paragraph to go along with the opening and middle paragraphs that you have written in this chapter. Use the sample above and the information on page 58 as a guide.

Answers will vary.

**Traits**

Feel free to include new information in your closing, especially if you feel it will help you emphasize the importance of your topic.

# LO6 Reviewing Drafting

Complete these activities as needed to help you better understand key strategies in this chapter.

**Follow a Drafting Plan** What are two things that you can do if you get stuck when drafting? (See page 52.)

1. See the list under the final bullet point on page 52.
2. See the list under the final bullet point on page 52.

**Create an Effective Opening** What are the three main things that you should accomplish in the opening part of an essay? (See page 54.)

1. Identify the topic.
2. Engage the reader.
3. State the thesis.

**Develop the Middle Part** Answer these questions about the basic writing moves a writer may use. (See page 56.)

1. What does it mean to narrate in a paragraph? 
   Sharing an experience or a story

2. When explaining, what types of information will a writer include? 
   Important facts, details, and examples

3. When a writer evaluates, what is she or he actually doing? 
   Rating the value of something

**Write a Strong Closing** What are two strategies that you can use to develop a closing? (See page 58.)

1. See the bulleted list on page 58.
2. See the bulleted list on page 58.

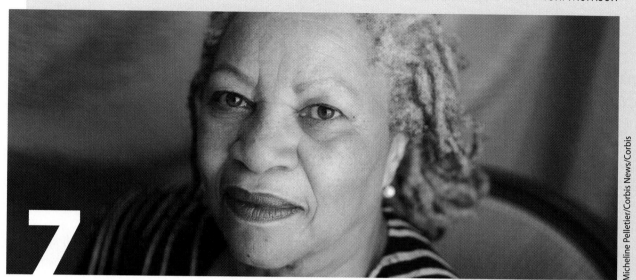

"If [you] write a lot, that's good.
If [you] revise a lot, that's even better."
—Toni Morrison

# 7 Revising

You would never expect a musician to perform or record a song after putting lyrics and music together for the first time. In fact, the real work would have just begun. There would be questions to answer: Does the song have potential? If so, what needs to be done to get it performance-ready? Then would come the work of arranging and practicing the song, again and again, until everything—lyrics, rhythm, timing, beat—was just right.

In the same way, you should never expect to share a first draft of your writing as if it were a finished piece. You still have a lot of work ahead of you—reviewing your writing, and then revising any confusing, incomplete, or out-of-order parts. Each revision you make brings you closer to an effective piece of writing.

This chapter provides guidelines and strategies for revising a first draft, with the traits of strong writing, and a fine finished draft, in clear view.

## Learning Outcomes

LO1 Understand the revising process.

LO2 Recognize the traits of strong writing.

LO3 Check for completeness.

LO4 Check for coherence.

LO5 Learn the basics of peer reviewing.

LO6 Review revising.

## What do you think?

In the quotation, why does Morrison state that revising a lot is even better than writing a lot?

Answers will vary.

"If you haven't revised, you're not finished."

—Patricia T. O'Conner

**Traits**

Don't pay undue attention to surface issues—usage, spelling, punctuation—at this point in the process. Instead, focus on the **content** of your writing.

# LO1 Understanding Revising

Revising is the process of improving the message in your writing. To make the best revising decisions, follow these guidelines:

- **Take some time away from your writing.** This will help you see your first draft more clearly, and with a fresh outlook.
- **Read your first draft a number of times,** silently and out loud, to get an overall impression of your work.
- **Have a trusted peer or two react to your writing.** Their questions and comments will help you decide what changes to make.
- **Check your overall focus or thesis.** Decide if it still works and if you have provided enough support for it.
- **Then review your work, part by part.** Pay special attention to the opening, since it sets the tone of your writing, and the closing, since it serves as your final word on the topic.
- **Plan a revising strategy** by deciding what you need to do first, second, and third.

**Evaluate** Rate each sample below in terms of its potential as an effective starting point for a piece of writing. Explain your choices.

> I've met a lot of people. Some were interesting and some were enemies. Some I hardly knew. Whenever I see kids building a snow fort, I ask myself, "Whatever happened to Keyton Kaul, the most feared girl in my old neighborhood?" Keyton was a bully, and she had done a lot to earn that label. I also remember Mary Osmond. . . .

weak ★ ★ ★ ★ ★ strong

Weak. Explanations will vary.

> Though Howard Hughes died more than 20 years ago, his legend lives on. He represented the American Dream turned on itself because he was a victim of the multibillion-dollar empire he single-handedly created. We all are fascinated by celebrities, heroes, the wealthy, and the sick. Hughes was all of these things and more. . . .

weak ★ ★ ★ ★ ★ strong

Strong. Explanations will vary.

# Additional Considerations

What follows are two additional aspects of the revising process to consider.

## Revisit Your Purpose and Audience

Before you revise a first draft, be sure to have the purpose of your writing clearly in mind: *Are you writing to explain, to persuade, to describe, or to share?* With a clear understanding of the purpose, you will find it much easier to know what changes to make. Also consider your readers: *Have you anticipated and answered the questions they may have about the topic?*

## Understand the Basic Revising Moves

You have four basic ways to make changes in your writing—adding, cutting, rewriting, or reordering information. Each change or improvement that you make will bring you closer to a strong finished piece.

---

**Add information to . . .**
- make a main supporting point more convincing.
- complete a specific explanation.
- improve the flow of your writing.

**Cut information if it . . .**
- doesn't support the thesis.
- seems repetitious.

**Rewrite information if it . . .**
- seems confusing or unclear.
- appears too complicated.
- lacks the proper **voice**.

**Reorder information if it . . .**
- seems out of order.
- would be more significant in another spot.

---

**Vocabulary**

**voice**
a writer's manner of expression, the "sound" of his or her words (A strong voice signals an interested, knowledgeable writer.)

**React**  Carefully read this first draft. As you will see, it has a number of problems. Then follow the directions below the writing.

---

Winning the lottery must be everyone's number one dream! If I won the lottery, my life would be wonderful. First, I'd travel to other countries. I've always wanted to go to Italy and eat spaghetti in a gondola. ~~Yeah I'm definitely going to keep buying those lottery tickets.~~ Then I'd buy a retooled Mustang with a stardust paint job. My dad says that old Fords have mechanical problems. But he's just an old dude who doesn't know cars. Everyone knows Mustangs are totally hot-looking cars. I'd buy my mom a car, too. She'd probably want a dull, dependable car like a Volvo or something dull like that, but a Jeep is something I'd talk her out of undoubtedly for sure. Some 4x4 action would spice up her life.

1. **Underline** one sentence or idea that could be improved if information were added.

2. **Put** a line through one idea that should be cut because it is unnecessary or unneeded.

3. **Draw** a wavy line under one idea that should be rewritten because it is unclear.

4. **Circle** one idea that should be moved; draw an arrow to show where you would move it.
   Answers will vary.

---

**Special Challenge**  Rewrite this paragraph, making the changes that you marked on the original. Feel free to make other changes as well. Afterward, share your revised writing with your classmates.

# LO2 Recognizing Strong Writing

Understanding the traits of writing will help you revise your first drafts. Think of the traits (*ideas, organization,* and so on) as the key ingredients in writing, each one contributing to the development of a piece of writing. The traits-based checklist below can serve as an effective guide when you revise. If your writing doesn't "pass" certain descriptors, then you should make the necessary changes.

> "There is no such thing as good writing, only good rewriting."
>
> —Louis Brandeis

## Revising Checklist

**Ideas**

☐ 1. Does an interesting and relevant topic serve as a starting point for the writing?

☐ 2. Is the writing focused, addressing a specific feeling about or a specific part of the topic? (The focus is usually expressed in the thesis statement.)

☐ 3. Are there enough specific ideas, details, and examples to support the thesis?

☐ 4. Overall, is the writing engaging and informative?

**Organization**

☐ 5. Does the writing form a meaningful whole—with opening, middle, and closing parts?

☐ 6. Does the writing follow a logical pattern of organization?

☐ 7. Do transitions connect ideas and help the writing flow?

**Voice**

☐ 8. Does the writer sound informed about and interested in the topic?

☐ 9. In addition, does the writer sound sincere and genuine?

**Word Choice**

☐ 10. Does the word choice clearly fit the purpose and the audience?

☐ 11. Does the writing include specific words as much as possible?

**Sentence Fluency**

☐ 12. Are the sentences clear and do they flow smoothly?

☐ 13. Are the sentences varied in terms of their beginnings and length?

**Traits**

Word choice and sentence fluency are not as important as the other traits at this point. But they become very important during the editing step.

**React** Carefully read the following paragraphs from a persuasive essay. Then answer the questions below that address the first three traits: *ideas, organization,* and *voice.* (Use your own paper for your answers.)

# Learn to Earn

   Lack of student motivation is a main topic of discussion when it comes to today's underachieving schools. The experts ask, how can we motivate our students to learn? And how can we keep them in school long enough to prepare for the twenty-first century workplace? These questions are especially important in urban areas, where the drop-out rate is alarming, especially among nonnative English students. One answer appears quite logical: Give them money. In other words, if we want our students to succeed in school, we should pay them.

   Students, in one way, are already bribed to attend school. The whole point of academic scholarships is based on receiving a monetary reward for being a good student. Calling a cash award a "scholarship" doesn't alter the fact that what's being offered is money. Presently, only the best students or the best athletes pick up all the cash. That does not seem fair. What about the student that doesn't want to go to college? Why not pay everyone for going to school the same way they would get paid for doing any other job?

   Many students drop out of school because they are forced to work to help support their families. When it comes to choosing between going to school or going to work, the latter usually wins out for practical reasons. If these same students were paid a minimum wage for attending school, they wouldn't have to worry about choosing between education and keeping their jobs. In the long run, it would probably be less expensive to keep these students in school by paying them than to have them drop out of school with no skills.

*(line numbers: 1, 5, 10, 15, 20)*

**Ideas**  Answers will vary.

   **1.** Is the topic relevant and interesting? Explain.

   **2.** Is the focus or thesis of the essay clear? Explain.

   **3.** Does the essay contain a variety of specific details? Explain.

**Organization**

   **1.** Does the first paragraph include the key elements
   of an effective opening? (See pages 54–55.)
   Explain. Answers will vary.

   **2.** Do these paragraphs follow a logical pattern
   of organization? If so, which one?
   (See pages 46–49.) Deductive organization
   or order of importance.

**Voice** Answers will vary.

   **1.** Does the writer sound informed and
   interested in the topic? Explain.

   **2.** Does the writer sound sincere and
   honest? Explain.

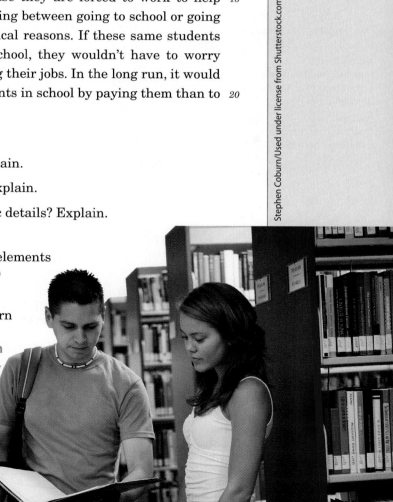

"The first great gift we can bestow on others is a good example."
—Thomas Morell

# LO3 Checking for Completeness

Your college instructors expect you to support the main points in your essays with plenty of details. Details help you develop complete explanations and arguments.

## Types of Details

The following list identifies the common types of details.

**Facts and statistics** give specific information that can be checked.

> Legg-Calve-Perthes affects only 5 of every 100,000, usually when they are between the ages of five and twelve.

**Examples** demonstrate or show something.

> Donald, two years younger than me, has always been more daring. (main point)
>
> When we were younger, he was the first to jump off the cliffs at the quarry. (example)

**Definitions** explain new terms.

> The *American Heritage College Dictionary* defines sexual harassment as "unwanted and offensive sexual advances or sexually **derogatory** remarks."

**Reasons** answer "why" after a main point.

> Watching television is a **reactive** activity. (main point)
>
> It takes absolutely no skill or thinking. (reason)

**Quotations** provide the thoughts of people knowledgeable about the topic.

> Tuyen stated, "In the Chinese tradition, the superior person assumes loving responsibility for the inferior, and the inferior person shows respect and obedience to the superior."

**Reflections** offer the writer's thoughts.

> For most young people, growing up means being told to act like an adult while being treated like a child. It means receiving an abundance of advice but having little patience. It means wanting to be independent but realizing just how dependent you are.

**Identify** In the essay on page 65, record one example for each type of detail listed below. (Use your own paper if you need more room.) Answers will vary.

Facts: _____

Examples: _____

Reasons: _____

Quotations: _____

# Levels of Detail

Effective essays are thorough, meaning that they contain different levels of information to fully explain or develop each main point. Here are three basic levels of detail in writing.

> **Level 1:** A **controlling sentence** names a topic (usually a topic sentence) or makes a main point.
>
> **Level 2:** A **clarifying sentence** explains a level 1 sentence.
>
> **Level 3:** A **completing sentence** adds details to complete the point.

**Traits**

To "complete" some main points, a writer may add another level of detail (level 4).

## Details in Action

The passage that follows uses three different levels of detail. Notice that the level 1 sentence (a topic sentence) is supported by three level 2 sentences. Two level 3 sentences complete the last level 2 sentence.

> **(Level 1)** Legg-Calve-Perthes is both rare and mysterious. **(Level 2)** The disease affects only 5 of every 100,000 children, usually when they are between the ages of five and twelve. **(Level 2)** Boys suffer from the disease far more frequently than girls do, by a ratio of 4 to 1, which makes Allie's experience all the more unusual. **(Level 2)** At this point, researchers are not really sure of the cause of the disease. **(Level 3)** They are, however, fairly certain that it is not genetic. **(Level 3)** They also know that a reduction of blood flow . . .

**Identify** Carefully read the following passage; then label its levels of detail. (Work on this activity with a partner if your instructor allows it.)

> ( __controlling__ ) Plato, an ancient Greek philosopher and educator, was the first to write about the lost continent of Atlantis in his book *Critias*. ( __clarifying__ ) Most scholars agree that Plato's book includes only legendary events, not real history. ( __completing__ ) When Plato described Atlantis, he painted a picture of a people of fabulous wealth who ruled over a great and wonderful empire. ( __completing__ ) He also claimed that the continent of Atlantis sank beneath the sea in one day's time.

**Special Challenge** Write a paragraph of at least five or six sentences about one of the following topics: *types of sports fans, your favorite type of music, the best piece of technology ever invented, the one time you really "roughed it."* Afterward, label your sentences with the numbers 1, 2, or 3, depending on the level of detail they include.

"I tell [students] to use transitions, to start each paragraph with an interlocking nut, a thread, so that the story is seamless."

—Steve Lovelady

# LO4 Checking for Coherence

When a paragraph or essay is coherent, all of its ideas work together and flow smoothly from one point to the next. Transitions, or linking words and phrases like *such as, on the other hand,* and *in addition,* help create coherence because they connect ideas. Transitions can show location or time, compare and contrast things, and so on.

## Words used to show location:

| | | | |
|---|---|---|---|
| above | behind | down | on top of |
| across | below | in back of | onto |
| against | beneath | in front of | outside |
| along | beside | inside | over |
| among | between | into | throughout |
| around | beyond | near | to the right |
| away from | by | off | under |

## Words used to show time:

| | | | |
|---|---|---|---|
| about | during | next | today |
| after | finally | next week | tomorrow |
| afterward | first | second | until |
| as soon as | immediately | soon | when |
| at | later | then | yesterday |
| before | meanwhile | third | |

## Words used to compare things (show similarities):

| | | |
|---|---|---|
| also | in the same way | likewise |
| as | like | similarly |

## Words used to contrast things (show differences):

| | | | |
|---|---|---|---|
| although | even though | on the other hand | still |
| but | however | otherwise | yet |

## Words used to emphasize a point:

| | | | |
|---|---|---|---|
| again | for this reason | particularly | to repeat |
| even | in fact | to emphasize | truly |

## Words used to conclude or summarize:

| | | | |
|---|---|---|---|
| all in all | finally | in summary | therefore |
| as a result | in conclusion | last | to sum up |

## Words used to add information:

| | | | |
|---|---|---|---|
| additionally | and | equally important | in addition |
| again | another | finally | likewise |
| along with | as well | for example | next |
| also | besides | for instance | second |

## Words used to clarify:

| | | | |
|---|---|---|---|
| for instance | in other words | put another way | that is |

# Linking Words and Phrases in Action

Note the use of transitions in the following passages. Each one adds to the coherence and readability of the ideas.

- Jazz ballet provides me with all of the exercise that I need. *To begin with,* it combines gymnastics with dance. All of the gymnastic-like splits, leaps, kicks, and high jumps provide the ultimate cardiovascular workout. *(The transition is used to add information.)*

- Alan experiences the pressure of working as a clerk at Bryson's Appliance Store. The customers are demanding, and the many products and brand names are confusing. *Later,* under hypnosis, he admits that his "foes" are the myriad brand names he is challenged to locate. *(The transition is used to show time.)*

- In response to Motz's idea that Barbies make girls dependent on males, I say, "Phooey." I played with the dolls for years, and I have often been free from any type of romantic attachment. *In fact,* I am now a happy single girl. *(The transition emphasizes a point.)*

**Traits**

Use transitions as needed in your writing, but be careful not to overuse them. Too many transitions can actually get in the way and draw undue attention to themselves.

**Identify** Circle the transition or transitions used in each of the following passages. In the space below each passage, identify the purpose of the transition—*to show location, to show time,* and so on.

- Humpbacks, like other whales, must migrate. Some humpbacks begin their journey in October. Mature females accompanied by their yearling calves set off (first. Next) the immature males and females begin the journey. . . .

  to show time

- American art museums represent a confusing mix of public and private interests. Without question, (however,) the primary function of the museum is to serve the public.

  to contrast things (show differences)

- What set Allie apart was a debilitating physical condition that caused one of her legs to be noticeably shorter than the other one. (As a result,) she had to endure endless medical procedures, . . .

  to conclude or summarize

- This crude tent-like structure was to be my home. (Around the base,) four strong poles stick straight up. On the top, a crisscrossing of long branches and thatch serves as a roof. . . .

  to show location

**Special Challenge** Review the paragraph you may have written on page 67, looking for transitions. Did you use any? If not, could the paragraph benefit from a transition or two? Which ones?

Learn the basics of peer reviewing.

"Keep away from people who try to **belittle** your ambitions." —Mark Twain

Responding to each other's writing builds a community spirit among classmates. It will help you appreciate writing as a process of learning rather than just another assignment.

**belittle**
lessen, make smaller, criticize

**constructively**
in a helpful manner

# LO5 Reviewing with Peers

Having your peers react to your writing helps you decide what changes need to be made. They can tell you if your writing keeps their interest, answers their main questions about the topic, and makes sense from start to finish.

## The Role of the Writer

1. **Have a complete piece of writing to share.** Make a copy for each group member.

2. **Set the scene** by making a few introductory comments about your work. But don't say too much.

3. **Read your work out loud.** Don't stop for explanations; just read the text as clearly as you can.

4. **Afterward, listen carefully to the reactions,** and answer any questions. Don't try to defend yourself or your writing. Just listen and take notes on important points.

5. **Ask for help** if you have concerns about certain parts.

## The Role of the Listeners/Responders

1. **Pay careful attention during the reading.** Take brief notes if you think it would help. Then read the text silently.

2. **React positively and constructively.** Instead of saying "Nice start," for example, say something more exact, such as "Sharing that dramatic story in the beginning really made me take notice."

3. **Comment on specific things you noticed.** Saying "It would be good to add more style to your writing" isn't very helpful. But saying "Many of the sentences start in the same way" gives the writer a specific idea for improving the writing.

4. **Question the writer** if you are unsure of something. "What is the purpose of . . . ?" or "Why did you start the . . .?"

5. **Show that you are really interested in helping.** Have at least one positive comment and one suggestion to offer. Also listen to others' comments and add to them.

**Write** Develop a first draft in which you reflect and/or comment upon a current event in any area of life—political affairs, the environment, sports, entertainment, and so on. (Use your own paper if you need more room.)

Answers will vary.

_____

_____

_____

_____

_____

_____

_____

_____

_____

_____

_____

_____

_____

_____

_____

_____

_____

_____

_____

_____

_____

_____

**Share** Review your first draft in a peer-responding session, following the guidelines on the previous page. (Work with one partner or a small group of your peers.) Then list two helpful suggestions that were made. Answers will vary.

1. _____

_____

2. _____

_____

# LO6 Reviewing Revising

Complete these activities as needed to help you better understand the revising process.

**Understand the Revising Process** List below the four basic revising moves. (See page 63.)

1. Add information.

2. Cut information.

3. Rewrite information.

4. Reorder information.

**Recognize Strong Writing** What questions should you ask about your writing to check it for effective organization? Identify two of them. (See page 64.)

1. See checklist points 5, 6, and 7 on page 64.

2. See checklist points 5, 6, and 7 on page 64.

**Check for Completeness** Identify the type of detail used in each of the following examples. (See page 66.)

1. _____Facts and statistics_____ According to *Modern Style Magazine,* a face-lift costs $5,000-$15,000; nose jobs are $4,000-$8,000; and hair transplants are $6,000–$10,000.

2. _____Examples_____ Charlotte Perkins Gilman contributed to the women's movement. *(main point)* She developed the idea of collective child care and attacked misconceived notions of womanhood and motherhood.

**Check for Coherence** Circle the transitions used in each passage and tell the purpose of each one: to show time, to emphasize a point, and so on. (See pages 68–69.)

1. The assortment of food whisking by me is astonishing. (Below me,) a father and his two sons are just completing their third trip to the food court. _to show location_

2. I made French toast this morning for my family. It was an American treat, and they praised its taste. (Afterward,) we all watched an old movie. _to show time_

3. A tactful person not only expresses herself sensitively, but truthfully as well. Doctors, (for example,) must be truthful when dealing with their patients and the patients' families. _to add information_

A Carmichael/Stone/Getty Images

"I love the taste of words. They have a taste and a weight and a colour as well as a sound and a shape." —Philip Pullman

# 8

# Editing

There's a time during the writing process when **editing** for style and correctness makes the most sense. And that time comes after you have done everything possible to make your main message logical and complete. Always think content before anything else.

Editing writing is like buffing out the smudges and scratches on a car after it's been painted. The buffing is certainly important, but only after the main work—the actual painting—is complete.

The first part of this chapter provides tips for checking the word choice and sentence fluency in your writing. The second part provides, among other things, strategies for editing for correctness and an explanation of Standard English.

## What do you think?

How can Pullman's quotation serve as a guide for selecting words for your writing?

Answers will vary.

## Learning Outcomes

**LO1** Edit for style.

**LO2** Learn how to check for correctness.

**LO3** Understand Standard English.

**LO4** Use a common errors list.

**LO5** Review editing.

### Vocabulary

**editing**
the step in the writing process when you check the style (word choice and sentence fluency) and accuracy of your revised writing

73

# LO1 Editing for Style

When editing your writing for style, you are checking the quality of its words and sentences. You want to make sure that they are clear, interesting, and honest (sounding like they come from you). Trying to force style into your writing by using **flowery language**, for example, will diminish its overall quality.

## Checking for Word Choice

Suppose some five-alarm buffalo wings actually bring you to tears. Then you write about the experience: "I ate some hot food." Did you capture the moment, or the pain? Or course not. General words like "hot" and "food" do not compare favorably to specific words like "five-alarm" and "buffalo wings."

### Using Specific Nouns and Verbs

It's especially important to use specific nouns and verbs because they carry most of the meaning in your writing. Note that the subjects and verbs in the following sentences are specific.

> **noun**  **verb**
> The five-alarm buffalo wings scorched my mouth.
> **noun**  **verb**
> Charlotte Perkins Gilman rejected the belief in male superiority.

**Traits**

Watch for the overuse of the "be" verbs (*is, are, was, were*) in your writing. Often, a more vivid verb can be made from another word in the sentence.

**Analyze** Study the photograph to the right. Then list examples of specific nouns and verbs that could be associated with it. Afterward, compare lists with your classmates.

Answers will vary.

Paul Cowan/2010. Used under license from Shutterstock.com

| Specific Nouns | Specific Verbs |
| --- | --- |
| | |

**Create** On your own paper, write a brief descriptive paragraph about the photograph using some or all of the words that you listed above.

# Checking for Sentence Fluency

To check the fluency of your sentences, read your writing out loud, or have someone read it out loud to you.

## Sentence Trouble Spots

Pay special attention to the following two problems.

### Slow-Moving Sentences

If too many of your sentences contain passive verbs, your writing will plod along. To fix this problem, edit the sentences so that they contain active, forward-moving verbs. (See page 352 for more information.)

**Sentence with Passive Verb:**

> The 16-ounce porterhouse was dragged along the kitchen counter by the Chihuahua. *(The subject "porterhouse" is being acted upon.)*

**Sentence with Active Verb:**

> The Chihuahua dragged a 16-ounce porterhouse along the kitchen counter. *(The subject "Chihuahua" is performing the action.)*

### Sentences with Qualifiers

If you use too many qualifiers in your sentences (*maybe, it seems to me, I think*), you will sound unsure of yourself. To sound confident, simply omit these words.

**Sentence with Qualifiers:**

> Although McDonald's is a leading fast-food chain, *it seems to me* that they have *maybe* introduced some healthy alternatives to fried food. *(The qualifiers create uncertainty.)*

**Sentence without Qualifiers:**

> Although McDonald's is a leading fast-food chain, they have introduced some healthy alternatives to fried food. *(Removing the qualifiers creates assurance.)*

**Traits**

Also check your writing for series of short, choppy sentences. These sentences can often be combined.

**Vocabulary**

**monarch**
a ruler, such as a king or queen, who usually has limited authority

**Edit** Rewrite these sentences to fix the trouble spots discussed above.

Answers will vary.

1. Ryan Braun was being held at first base by Albert Pulois. The pitcher was signaled by the catcher Yavier Molina to throw a pitch out.

2. I think that Queen Elizabeth II is the **monarch** of the United Kingdom, but, if I'm not mistaken, the prime minister actually governs the country.

"While I grumble about the imperfections of spellcheckers, mine does find those embarrassing word repetitions (*the the*) I can't see myself."
—Patricia T. O'Conner

# LO2 Checking for Correctness

Correctness should be the last element that you address in a piece of writing. When editing for correctness, you check your writing for punctuation, capitalization, spelling, and grammar errors.

## Strategies for Editing

When checking for errors, examine your writing word for word and sentence by sentence. The following strategies will help you edit thoroughly and effectively.

- Work with a clean copy of your writing, one that incorporates your revisions and stylistic changes.
- Check one element at a time—spelling, punctuation, and so on.
- For spelling, start at the bottom of the page to force yourself to look at each word. (Remember that your spell-checker will not catch all errors.)
- For punctuation, circle all the marks to force yourself to look at each one.
- Read your work aloud at least once, noting any errors as you go along.
- Refer to a list of common errors. (See page 80.)
- Have an editing guide (see pages 230–422 in this text) and a dictionary handy.
- Ask a trusted classmate to check your work as well.

**Preview** When you have questions about punctuation, grammar, or any other convention, turn to pages 230-422 in *WRITE 2*. This part of the book is divided into three major workshops. Answer the following questions about this section.

1. What are the names of the three workshops in this section?

   Sentence Workshops, Word Workshops, and Punctuation and Mechanics Workshops

2. How will these workshops prove helpful when you are editing your writing?

   Answers will vary.

3. Which one or two of these workshops will you probably turn to more than the others? Why?

   Answers will vary.

# Using Editing Strategies

You can use editing symbols to mark errors in your writing. Listed below are some of the most common symbols.

| | | | |
|---|---|---|---|
| <u>C</u><br>c̲h̲icago | Capitalize a letter. | first<br>my ∧ speech | Insert here. |
| Ƒall | Make lowercase. | ∧ ∧ ∧ | Insert a comma, a colon, or a semicolon. |
| Mr⊙Ford | Insert (add) a period. | ⌄ ⌄ ⌄ | Insert an apostrophe or quotation marks. |
| Sp. or ⟨recieve⟩ | Correct spelling. | ? !<br>∧ ∧ | Insert a question mark or an exclamation point. |
| Mr. Lott he | Delete (take out) or replace. | ⟨possible⟩worst | Switch words or letters. |

**Edit** Use the editing symbols above to mark errors in this writing sample and show how they should be corrected. The first error has been marked for you.

During the last few decades ∧ this Nation has become obsessed with dieting and    *1*

**caloric intake**. While many of us are counting calories, not everyone understands

what it is were are counting. <u>b</u>y definition, a calorie is a measure of the heat

~~similar to that~~ required to raise the temperature of one gram of water by one

degree Celsius. Our bodies can be thought of as ⟨biocemical⟩ machines that burn    *5*

the food we eat for fuel⊙ The amount of burning that takes place is measured

in calories. <u>h</u>ow much energy is produced by burning calories is determined

by how active we are. By just sitting and resting ∧ we **expend** about a calorie

each
∧ minute. That means that just to stay alive our body ~~it~~ must burn 1440 calories

per day. The more active we are, the more calories we will ⟨up⟩burn. How many    *10*

calories do we burn up when we engage hard exercise ?∧

Evangelos2010. Used under license from Shutterstock.com

> "My attitude toward punctuation is that it ought to be as **conventional** as possible."
> —Ernest Hemingway

## Vocabulary

**conventional**
usual or accepted

**caloric intake**
the total number of calories taken in

**expend**
use up, burn

**Insight**

A grammatical form that is not used in SE may be acceptable in another dialect. So this chart is identifying variations, not errors.

"Standard English is not a language—but a variety of English among many."
—Peter Trudgill

# LO3 Understanding Standard English

Standard English (SE) is the **dialect** of English that is considered appropriate in business, government, and education. You have been learning to use SE throughout your years in school, and just about every career choice you make requires that you know and effectively use SE.

Surprisingly, there are not many grammatical differences between SE and other common dialects, and you may already be aware of most of them. As one linguist put it, "The difference boils down to the details." The chart below shows some of the common differences between non-Standard variations of American English (NS) and SE.

| Differences in . . . | NS | SE |
|---|---|---|
| 1. Expressing plurals after numbers | 10 mile | 10 miles |
| 2. Expressing **habitual** action | He always be early. | He always is early. |
| 3. Expressing ownership | My friend car . . . | My friend's car . . . |
| 4. Expressing the third-person singular verb | The customer ask . . . | The customer asks . . . |
| 5. Expressing negatives | She doesn't never . . . | She doesn't ever . . . |
| 6. Using reflexive pronouns | He sees hisself . . . | He sees himself . . . |
| 7. Using demonstrative pronouns | Them reports are . . . | Those reports are . . . |
| 8. Using forms of *do* | He done it. | He did it. |
| 9. Avoiding double subjects | My manager he . . . | My manager . . . |
| 10. Using *a* or *an* | I need new laptop. She had angry caller. | I need a new laptop. She had an angry caller. |
| 11. Using the past tense of verbs | Carl finish his . . . | Carl finished his . . . |
| 12. Using *isn't* or *aren't* versus using *ain't* | The company ain't . . . | The company isn't . . . |

Underline any Standard English error that you find in the following descriptive essay. Then write the number that describes each error, based on the chart on the previous page. (The first one has been done for you.)

**Speaking & Listening**

Work on this activity with a partner or in small groups if your instructor allows it.

---

                          9

My <u>grandparents they</u> used to baby-sit for me when my mom had to work   *1*

weekends. They were never too busy to have me. Whenever I <u>be bored</u> with

playing outside, I would head into the two-car garage and "help" Grandpa.

His garage was really just a collection place for all of his old machines. He <u>be</u>

always <u>putzing</u> around with something in there. I think <u>Grandpa saw hisself</u> as   *5*

a master repairman.

    Upon entering this ancient structure, the burnt smell of oil was the first

thing that I would notice. Once my eyes adjusted to the gloom, I could begin to

make out different parts of the collection. On the right wall, he had picture of

everyone in the Smith family. On certain days I had to stand <u>four inch</u> from the   *10*

picture to see the grinning faces. Glaring sunbeams would shoot through <u>them</u>

<u>dusty, yellowish curtains</u> covering the one window.

    In one corner, there was a dirty old refrigerator <u>fill</u> with cans of soda and

new canisters of snuff, just in case he ran out while working on a project. You

see, <u>Grandpa he</u> always had a pinch of snuff in his mouth. Because of this nasty   *15*

habit, he would occasionally spit into an old coffee can, <u>object</u> I avoided at all

costs. Other than that, he was a great person to be around because he <u>be so</u>

<u>patient and interested</u> in working with me.

    Occupying the entire left side of the garage was <u>Grandpa pride and joy,</u>

his tractor. He could spend hours working on it. And then, of course, there was   *20*

my <u>grandfather dog</u>, Max, who sometimes chased me and once tried to pull my

pants down. When I was eight or nine, I <u>didn't never</u> want to be anyplace else.

---

**Vocabulary**

**putzing**
keeping busy; cleaning, fixing, and so on

**Discuss** Afterward, discuss your work as a class. How easy or difficult was it to find the errors?

# LO4 Using a Common Errors List

You can find top-ten lists covering just about any topic: top business schools, top crime novels, even top angry comedians. Here is a list of 10 common writing errors to watch for. (The corrections are shown in blue.) Turn to this list whenever you edit your writing.

1. **Missing Comma After Long Introductory Phrase(s)**

   Because of the fitness craze in this country, many people are suffering from sore muscles and pulled tendons.

2. **Confusing Pronoun Reference**

   While Serena met with Ms. Randall, her cell phone rang two different times. *Ms. Randall's*

3. **Missing Comma in a Compound Sentence**

   For job-searching advice, consulting a school's placement service is a good first step, but there are many other options to consider as well.

4. **Missing Comma(s) with a Nonrestrictive Phrase or Clause**

   Traveling, which is usually tiring, is absolutely brutal when you experience flight delays or cancellations.

5. **Comma Splices**

   People are affected differently by the sun; each person's system produces different amounts of skin pigment or melanin.

6. **Subject-Verb Agreement Errors**

   Every one of the senators *wants* want the president to call a special meeting.

7. **Missing Comma in a Series**

   Stephen Hawkings became a renowned physics professor, author, and theorist despite suffering from **ALS**.

8. **Pronoun-Antecedent Agreement Errors**

   Neither Carlos nor Manny has completed *his* their first-aid requirements for the job.

9. **Missing Apostrophe to Show Ownership**

   The left front tire on Martha's car needs to be replaced.

10. **Misusing *Its* and *It's***

    *It's* Its a fact that a hummingbird beats *its* it's wings more than 75 times a second.

# LO5 Reviewing Editing

Complete these activities as needed to help you better understand the editing process.

**Checking for Sentence Fluency** In the space provided below, explain what is meant by the two sentence problems.

**Slow-moving sentences:** Sentences that plod because of passive verbs (See page 75.)

**Sentences with qualifiers:** Sentences that seem uncertain due to phrases like "maybe" and "I think" (See page 75.)

**Editing for Correctness** Edit the following sentences using the symbols on page 77 to mark the errors.

London is a fascinating city, its filled with historical buildings such as the british museum and st pauls cathedral

**Understanding Standard English** Answer the following questions about Standard English (SE). (See pages 78–79.)

1. How should you express habitual action when you are using SE versus a typical non-Standard (NS) usage? Conjugate the "be" verb (I am, you are, she is, and so on).

2. How should you express the past tense in SE versus how it is often expressed in a NS dialect? Use the past tense form of the verb (e.g., "ran," "finished," "ate") instead of the infinitive ("run," "finish," "eat").

**Using a Common Errors List** Answer the following questions about the common errors list on page 80.

1. What punctuation mark is often missing in compound sentences? comma between the clauses

2. What is an antecedent, and what word in the sentence must it agree with? An antecedent is the noun a pronoun refers to. The two must agree.

"To write about people you have to know people, to write about bloodhounds you have to know bloodhounds, to write about the Loch Ness monster you have to find out

# 9 Description and Narration

What sets human beings apart from other animals is, among other things, our curiosity. We have a deep-seated need to know what is happening around us, what things look like, and what our world means. It is not an exaggeration to say that the world as we know it would not exist if people weren't obsessed with a need to know.

Whenever you describe a particular topic or explore some aspect of your life, you are satisfying, in one small way, your **innate** curiosity. In the first part of this chapter, you will analyze a descriptive paragraph and then write a paragraph of your own. In the second part, you will analyze a narrative paragraph before recalling and writing about one of your own memorable experiences.

As you develop each of your paragraphs in this section, you will learn valuable strategies that you can apply to all of your writing, including establishing a focus, using specific details, and following a clear pattern of organization.

## What do you think?

What does Thurber's quotation say about the importance of research in the writing process, especially as it applies to descriptive writing?

Answers will vary.

Jeremy Woodhouse/Photodisc/Getty Images

## Learning Outcomes

**LO1** Analyze a descriptive paragraph.

**LO2** Write a descriptive paragraph.

**LO3** Analyze a narrative paragraph.

**LO4** Write a narrative paragraph.

**LO5** Review description and narration.

## Vocabulary

**innate**
inborn or automatic

# LO1 Analyzing a Descriptive Paragraph

When writing a description, you are using words to represent a topic. An effective description creates a clear, interesting image in the reader's mind.

**Read/React** Read the following descriptive paragraph; then answer the questions at the bottom of the page.

## Matchmaker, Matchmaker

**The topic sentence** identifies the topic and focus of the paragraph.

**Body sentences** share descriptive details plus interesting background information about the topic.

**The closing sentence** reestablishes the importance of the topic.

One particular Capewell photo is proudly displayed in our house. It is a portrait-style black-and-white photograph of two people neatly attired in their best military uniforms, and it was taken during World War II in a small studio in Leicester, England. One of the individuals is wearing the uniform of the British Royal Air Force; the other, the uniform of the United States Army Air Force. Both people are clearly very happy. The person positioned to the left has huge dimples, an infectious smile, and bright, dark eyes. The one to the right has a more understated smile and lighter, happy eyes. The first has thick, wavy black hair worn in a fashionable turned-under military style; the second has neatly trimmed fairer hair. What makes this photograph so special to our family is the occasion that prompted it. It is my great-grandparents' wedding picture. My great-grandmother was born in England and my great-grandfather was born in the States, and they were both on leave to get married. Their honeymoon had to wait until after the war. This photograph is one of the few keepsakes that we have left from their military experience and wedding day, and we take very special care of it.

1. What does the paragraph describe?

   A wedding photograph from the World War II era with a bride and groom

   from different nations.

2. What physical features of the two people are highlighted?

| Specific Features | Woman | Man |
|---|---|---|
| uniform | British Royal Air Force | U.S. Air Force |
| face | dimples, big smile, dark eyes | subtler smile, lighter eyes fair, neatly trimmed |
| hair | black, wavy | |

# L○2 Writing a Descriptive Paragraph

The next three pages provide guidelines for writing a descriptive paragraph, starting with prewriting below.

**Learning Outcome**

Write a descriptive paragraph.

**Vocabulary**

**keepsakes**
small items reminding people of specific events or times

**indispensable**
essential, absolutely necessary

## Prewriting

**List/Select**  Under each category below, list potential topics. Then circle the one topic that you will describe in your paragraph. On the lines provided at the bottom of the chart, explain the reason for your choice. Answers will vary.

| Favorite **Keepsakes** | Special Photographs | **Indispensable** Tools or Gadgets |
|---|---|---|
| _____ | _____ | _____ |
| _____ | _____ | _____ |
| _____ | _____ | _____ |

_____

_____

_____

**Collect**  Study your topic; then list specific details that describe it. Try to list them in a logical order: from top to bottom, bottom to top, side to side, and so on.

Answers will vary.

_____

_____

_____

_____

_____

**Create**  Write a topic sentence for your paragraph following this formula:

| A specific topic | **+** | a particular feeling, feature, or part | **=** | an effective topic sentence. |
|---|---|---|---|---|
| a Capewell photograph | | proudly displayed in our house | | One particular Capewell photo is proudly displayed in our house. |

Answers will vary.

_____

_____

# Writing

**Write** Create a first draft of your descriptive paragraph, using the following paragraph outline as a guide.

### Paragraph Outline

**Topic Sentence:** Begin with your topic sentence from the previous page.

**Body Sentences:** Follow with sentences that describe and explain your topic. Organize your details according to the order that you determined during prewriting.

**Closing Sentence:** Write a sentence that sums up the topic's essential meaning.

Answers will vary.

# Revising

**Revise** Read your paragraph and, if possible, have someone else read it as well. Then use the following checklist to guide your revision. Keep revising until you can check off each item in the list.

**Ideas**

- [ ] **1.** Does my paragraph describe a special keepsake, photo, or tool?
- [ ] **2.** Do I include plenty of specific details?
- [ ] **3.** Do I include background information to tie the details together?

**Organization**

- [ ] **4.** Does my topic sentence name the topic and focus of the paragraph?
- [ ] **5.** Do the body sentences present details in a logical order (top to bottom, left to right, most important to least important)?
- [ ] **6.** Does my closing sentence tell what the object means to me?

**Voice**

- [ ] **7.** Does my writing voice reflect my feelings about the topic?
- [ ] **8.** Does my voice sound knowledgeable?

# Editing

**Edit** Create a clean copy of your revised paragraph and use the following checklist to check it for style and conventions.

**Words**

- [ ] **1.** Have I used specific nouns and verbs? (See page 74.)
- [ ] **2.** Have I used specific modifiers? (See page 143.)

**Sentences**

- [ ] **3.** Have I varied the beginnings and lengths of sentences? (See pages 264, 266.)
- [ ] **4.** Have I combined short, choppy sentences? (See page 262.)
- [ ] **5.** Have I avoided fragments and run-ons? (See pages 297–302, 306–307.)

**Conventions**

- [ ] **6.** Do I use correct verb forms (*he saw,* not *he seen*)? (See page 356.)
- [ ] **7.** Do my subjects and verbs agree (*she speaks,* not *she speak*)? (See pages 282–291.)
- [ ] **8.** Have I used the right words (*their, there, they're*)?
- [ ] **9.** Have I capitalized first words and proper nouns and adjectives? (See page 414.)
- [ ] **10.** Have I used commas after long introductory word groups? (See page 396.)
- [ ] **11.** Have I carefully checked my spelling?

# LO3 Analyzing a Narrative Paragraph

The starting point for all writers is their own story. Everything they create stems, in some way, from their own experiences. Keeping this point in mind gives you a new perspective whenever you read another's writing.

**Read/React** Read the following narrative paragraph; then answer the questions at the bottom of the page.

---

### Attention!

**The topic sentence** identifies the topic and focus of the paragraph.

     Mr. Brown, my middle school gym teacher, did not allow any goofing around in his class. Unfortunately two of my friends learned this the hard way. At the end of the first day of flag football, Mr. Brown blew his whistle to signal that time was up. Most of us knew enough to stop and **fall in line**. He had made it very clear on the first day of class that when he blew his whistle, we had to stop whatever we were doing. Immediately! Randy Steger and Joe Johnson, being brave or stupid, decided to test Mr. Brown, so they continued throwing a football to each other. With fire in his eyes, "the drill sergeant" quickly sent us in and went after the two **transgressors**. We all watched from the locker-room doorway while Mr. Brown gave them an earful and then made them **duckwalk** across the field. After 10 yards or so, we could tell that duckwalking was not easy because they were already struggling. He sent them in after another 10 yards when their duckwalk had turned into more of a crawl. We couldn't help giving a few duck calls when Randy and Joe got into the locker room, but we didn't "quack" too loudly. We didn't want Mr. Brown to make us walk like a duck, or any other animal.

**Body sentences** shares details about the memory.

**The closing sentence** brings the experience to a satisfying ending.

*(line numbers in margin: 1, 5, 10, 15)*

---

**1.** This paragraph (1) shares a specific experience and (2) introduces you to a memorable individual. What details stand out about either one? Name two.

    Answers will vary.

**2.** What questions, if any, do you have about the experience?

    Answers will vary.

**3.** What is the **tone** of this paragraph (serious, sarcastic, interesting/entertaining)? Explain.

    Answers will vary.

---

**Vocabulary**

**fall in line**
an idiom meaning, in this case, to line up as a group

**transgressors**
people who act in violation of (against) the rules or laws

**duckwalk**
to walk in a crouching or squatting position

**tone**
the writer's attitude toward the topic

# LO4 Writing a Narrative Paragraph

The next three pages provide guidelines for writing a narrative paragraph, starting with prewriting below.

## Prewriting

**Select** List below four or more experiences that you have had with memorable individuals. Consider school-related, work-related, sports-related, and family-related experiences. Circle the one experience that you would like to share in a narrative paragraph. On the lines that follow, explain the reason for your choice.

Answers will vary.

_____    _____    _____

_____    _____    _____

_____

_____

_____

_____

_____

_____

**Collect** Gather details for your paragraph by answering the 5 W's and H about the experience. Answers will vary.

Who? _____

_____

What? _____

_____

When? _____

_____

Where? _____

_____

Why? _____

_____

How? _____

# Writing

**Write** Create the first draft of your narrative paragraph, using the following paragraph outline as a guide.

**Paragraph Outline**

**Topic Sentence:** Begin with a topic sentence that identifies the topic and focus of your paragraph. (See page 85 for a formula to follow.)

**Body Sentences:** Write sentences that cover the 5 W's and H of the experience. Be sure to include plenty of specific details.

**Closing Sentence:** Write a sentence that brings the experience to a satisfying or natural stopping point.

Answers will vary.

# Revising

**Revise** Read your paragraph, and, if possible, have someone else read it as well. Then use the following checklist to guide your revision. Continue making improvements until you can check off each item in the list.

**Ideas**

- [ ] **1.** Does my paragraph share a specific experience related to a memorable person?
- [ ] **2.** Have I answered the 5 W's and H about the experience?
- [ ] **3.** Do I include plenty of specific details?

**Organization**

- [ ] **4.** Does my topic sentence name the topic and focus of the paragraph?
- [ ] **5.** Do the body sentences present details in chronological (time) order?
- [ ] **6.** Does my closing sentence bring the experience to a satisfying end?

**Voice**

- [ ] **7.** Does my voice reflect my feelings about the topic?
- [ ] **8.** Does my voice create interest in the reader?

# Editing

**Edit** Create a clean copy of your revised paragraph and use the following checklist to check it for style and conventions.

**Words**

- [ ] **1.** Have I used specific nouns and verbs? (See page 74.)
- [ ] **2.** Have I used specific modifiers? (See page 143.)

**Sentences**

- [ ] **3.** Have I varied the beginnings and lengths of sentences? (See pages 264, 266.)
- [ ] **4.** Have I combined short, choppy sentences? (See page 262.)
- [ ] **5.** Have I avoided fragments and run-ons? (See pages 297–302, 306–307.)

**Conventions**

- [ ] **6.** Do I use correct verb forms (*he saw,* not *he seen*)? (See page 356.)
- [ ] **7.** Do my subjects and verbs agree (*she speaks,* not *she speak*)? (See pages 282–291.)
- [ ] **8.** Have I used the right words (*their, there, they're*)?
- [ ] **9.** Have I capitalized first words and proper nouns and adjectives? (See page 414.)
- [ ] **10.** Have I used commas after long introductory word groups? (See page 396.)
- [ ] **11.** Have I carefully checked my spelling?

# LO5 Reviewing Description and Narration

**Describe** Select an interesting photograph from one of your textbooks or from a periodical (newspaper or magazine). In the space below, list in a logical order specific details that describe it. Then, on your own paper, develop a descriptive paragraph about the photo. (See pages 85–87.)

Answers will vary.

**Narrate** Identify below your strongest early memory. Next, identify the basic details about the experience by completing the 5 W's and H chart. Then, on your own paper, write a narrative paragraph about the experience. (See pages 89–91.)

Answers will vary.

| Who? | |
|---|---|
| What? | |
| When? | |
| Where? | |
| Why? | |
| How? | |

"Knowledge is of two kinds: We know the subject ourselves
or we know where we can find information upon it."

—Samuel Johnson

Todd Davidson/Getty Images

# 10

# Illustration and Process

The best informational writing succeeds because it (1) focuses on an interesting topic and (2) provides plenty of supporting facts and examples. This fact holds true for newspaper stories, magazine articles, text chapters, blogs, and academic essays. Readers of informational texts want to be **engaged** and informed.

In this chapter you will read examples of two basic forms of informational writing: illustrating a main point and explaining a process. Each one is intended to be interesting and informative. After each sample, you will write an illustration or process paragraph of your own.

## What do you think?

According to the Johnson quotation, what are the two kinds of knowledge? How does the quotation relate to informational writing?

Answers will vary.

## Learning Outcomes

LO1 Analyze an illustration paragraph.

LO2 Write an illustration paragraph.

LO3 Analyze a process paragraph.

LO4 Write a process paragraph.

LO5 Review illustration and process.

### Vocabulary

**engaged**
fully and actively occupied

# LO1 Analyzing an Illustration Paragraph

Illustrating in writing is the process of clarifying or explaining with examples. Think of the examples in this type of writing as the legs that support the table-top, or main point.

**Read/React** Read the following illustration paragraph; then answer the questions below.

## Super Sleuths

The **topic sentence** states the topic and focus.

The best mystery writers have created **iconoclastic** super *1* **sleuths.** Edgar Allan Poe created the first detective, before the term detective even existed. The name of this character is C. Auguste Dupin, a French gentleman who is able to enter the criminal mind to help him solve murders. Some people say that Arthur Conan *5* Doyle modeled the most famous detective of all after Dupin. Doyle's detective, of course, is Sherlock Holmes, the **eccentric** private investigator who uses his incredible powers of deduction to solve difficult mysteries. Another British writer—Agatha Christie, the **grand dame** of mystery writers—created the well-known Jane *10* Marple, an elderly woman who happens to show up at murder scenes to offer her crime-solving abilities, and Hercule Poirot, an odd, but skilled detective from Belgium. Writer Raymond Chandler became famous in this country with Philip Marlowe, an intelligent, tough, hard-drinking detective. Not to be outdone, writer Robert Parker *15* created Spenser (no first name), a Boston private investigator who is tough, but also philosophical, funny, and afraid of nothing. Lee Child has also created a Spenser-like sleuth named Jack Reacher, who simply wanders around the States solving complicated crimes. It will be interesting to see if future mystery writers will break out *20* of this super-sleuth model, and, if so, in what direction they will go.

**Body sentences** give examples that illustrate or support the topic sentence.

The **closing sentence** keeps the reader thinking.

*Yuri Samsonov/2010. Used under license from Shutterstock.com*

1. What is the main point of the paragraph?

   Popular mystery writers create unique, unusual characters as their

   fictional detectives.

2. List at least four examples that support the main point.

   Answers will vary.

# LO2 Writing an Illustration Paragraph

## Prewriting

**Select**  To select a topic for your paragraph, answer the following question:

What is your favorite type of television show, movie, music, literature, magazine, or Internet feature? (*The writer of the sample paragraph identified his favorite type of literature—mysteries.*)

Answers will vary.

**Focus**  Then decide on a feature of this topic that you could illustrate in your paragraph. Explain your choice below. (*The writer of the sample paragraph decided to illustrate the memorable detectives created by the best mystery writers.*)

Answers will vary.

**Identify**  List at least four examples that illustrate this feature.

Answers will vary.

**Create**  On the lines below, write a topic sentence for your paragraph. Be sure that your sentence identifies the topic and the feature you are going to illustrate. (See page 85 for a formula to follow.)

Answers will vary.

# Writing

**Write** Develop a first draft of your illustration paragraph, using the outline below as a guide. Be sure to refer to the sample on page 94 for additional help.

**Paragraph Outline**

**Topic Sentence:** Begin with the topic sentence that you wrote on page 95.

**Body Sentences:** Present the supporting examples that you listed on page 95. Include explanations or background information as needed to connect the examples.

**Closing Sentence:** Write a sentence that keeps the reader thinking about your topic.

**Traits**

The topic sentence gives the reader a summary of the material in the paragraph.

Answers will vary.

# Revising

**Revise** Read your paragraph, and, if possible, have someone else read it as well. Then use the following checklist to guide your revision. Continue making improvements until you can check off each item in the list.

**Ideas**

☐ **1.** Does my paragraph address an interesting topic?

☐ **2.** Have I included at least four examples that illustrate the topic?

☐ **3.** Do I include additional background details as needed?

**Organization**

☐ **4.** Does my topic sentence name the topic and focus of the paragraph?

☐ **5.** Are the body sentences presented in a logical order?

☐ **6.** Does my closing sentence keep the reader thinking about the topic?

**Voice**

☐ **7.** Does my voice reflect my feelings about the topic?

☐ **8.** Does my voice create interest in the topic?

# Editing

**Edit** Create a clean copy of your revised paragraph and use the following checklist to check it for style and conventions.

**Words**

☐ **1.** Have I used specific nouns and verbs? (See page 74.)

☐ **2.** Have I used specific modifiers? (See page 143.)

**Sentences**

☐ **3.** Have I varied the beginnings and lengths of sentences? (See pages 264, 266.)

☐ **4.** Have I combined short, choppy sentences? (See page 262.)

☐ **5.** Have I avoided fragments and run-ons? (See pages 297–302, 306–307.)

**Conventions**

☐ **6.** Do I use correct verb forms (*he saw*, not *he seen*)? (See page 356.)

☐ **7.** Do my subjects and verbs agree (*she speaks*, not *she speak*)? (See pages 282–291.)

☐ **8.** Have I used the right words (*their, there, they're*)?

☐ **9.** Have I capitalized first words and proper nouns and adjectives? (See page 414.)

☐ **10.** Have I used commas after long introductory word groups? (See page 396.)

☐ **11.** Have I carefully checked my spelling?

# LO3 Analyzing a Process Paragraph

Process paragraphs explain how to do something *(apply for a passport)* or how something works *(photosynthesis)*. The paragraph that follows explains how to do something.

**Read/React** Read the following process paragraph; then answer the questions below.

Maximmal/2010. Used under license from Shutterstock.com

## Two Steps Forward, One Step Back

The **topic sentence** introduces the process.

**Body sentences** explain the materials needed and the steps to follow.

The **closing sentence** provides the reader with a final thought about the topic.

Walking the streets of Rome for the first time requires patience *1* and a sense of adventure. Before you set out, be sure to wear a comfortable pair of shoes. Roman streets, at least the most interesting ones, are **cobbled**. Also dress in light layers, even if you see most of the **natives** dressed in heavy coats. They must have thinner blood *5* than the rest of us. Then plan a route on a street map by circling the sites you want to visit and the streets you need to follow. As you start, enjoy all that the **cityscape** has to offer. Then within the first 10 or 15 minutes, expect to get lost. Roman streets, other than the main thoroughfares, are never straight, seldom marked, and rarely *10* labeled on the street map you have in hand. When this happens, you can try to retrace your steps or continue on. If you are at all adventurous, just keep going and enjoy what that part of the city has to offer. You won't be disappointed, and sooner or later, you'll come across a plaza or church square that will be marked on your *15* map. Once you get your bearings, proceed, but again, expect to get lost in no time at all. You can continue in this way from plaza to plaza, enjoying the sites that you come across as well as stopping for some refreshments or a meal. When you've had enough, find a taxi or tram for the return trip—you'll never find your way by foot.

1. What specific feeling about the topic is expressed in the topic sentence?

   Amused affection.

2. What steps are offered for the walking tourist in Rome?

   Answers will vary.

**Vocabulary**

**cobbled**
uneven, rough

**natives**
those who are born in a place or country

**cityscape**
the part of a city viewed, the sights in part of a city

# L○4 Writing a Process Paragraph

## Prewriting

**Select**  Complete the following sentence starters in at least two ways. (Avoid food-related topics.)  Answers will vary.

> **1.** I learned the hard way how to . . .
>
> _____    _____
>
> **2.** I may be one of the few people who knows how to . . .
>
> _____    _____
>
> **3.** In case of an emergency, I would like to be able to . . .
>
> _____    _____
>
> **4.** Choose a topic and explain your choice.
>
> _____

**Collect**  Identify the materials needed and the steps in your process.

| Materials | Steps |
|---|---|
| Answers will vary. | |

**Create**  Write a topic sentence for your paragraph. This sentence should identify the topic and focus of your writing. (See page 85 for a formula to follow.)

> Answers will vary.
>
> _____
>
> _____

# Writing

**Write** Create a first draft of your process paragraph, using the following paragraph outline as a guide.

**Paragraph Outline**

**Topic Sentence:** Begin with the topic sentence that you wrote on the previous page.

**Body Sentences:** First, discuss any materials that may be needed. Then clearly explain the steps to complete the process. Add other information as needed to connect all of your ideas.

**Closing Sentence:** Write a sentence that sums up the process.

Answers will vary.

# Revising

**Revise** Read your process paragraph and, if possible, have someone else read it as well. Then use the following checklist to guide your revision. Continue to make improvements until you can check off each item in the list.

### Ideas

☐ **1.** Have I selected an interesting process to explain?

☐ **2.** Do I identify the necessary materials and provide all of the steps?

### Organization

☐ **3.** Does my topic sentence identify the topic and focus of my paragraph?

☐ **4.** Have I put the body sentences that explain the steps in good order?

☐ **5.** Does my closing sentence effectively sum up the process?

### Voice

☐ **6.** Does my writing voice sound knowledgeable?

☐ **7.** Does my voice create interest in this process?

# Editing

**Edit** Create a clean copy of your revised paragraph and use the following checklist to check it for style and conventions.

### Words

☐ **1.** Have I used specific nouns and verbs? (See page 74.)

☐ **2.** Have I used more action verbs than "be" verbs? (See page 348.)

### Sentences

☐ **3.** Have I varied the beginnings and lengths of sentences? (See pages 264, 266.)

☐ **4.** Have I combined short, choppy sentences? (See page 262.)

☐ **5.** Have I avoided fragments and run-ons? (See pages 297–302, 306–307.)

### Conventions

☐ **6.** Do I use correct verb forms (*he saw,* not *he seen*)? (See page 356.)

☐ **7.** Do my subjects and verbs agree (*she speaks,* not *she speak*)? (See pages 282–291.)

☐ **8.** Have I used the right words (*their, there, they're*)?

☐ **9.** Have I capitalized first words and proper nouns and adjectives? (See page 414.)

☐ **10.** Have I used commas after long introductory word groups? (See page 396.)

☐ **11.** Have I carefully checked my spelling?

# LO5 Reviewing Illustration and Process

**Illustration** Fill in the top blank with a career that truly interests you. Then write four statements that illustrate or explain your choice. On your own paper, write an illustration paragraph about this career. (See pages 95–97.)

Career: Answers will vary. _____

Example: _____

Example: _____

Example: _____

Example: _____

**Process** On the top blanks, list possible topics for a paragraph explaining how something works. Consider pieces of technology, features on the Internet, a natural phenomenon *(evaporation)*, a governmental process *(how to become a U.S. citizen)*, and so on. Circle the one that you would like to write about.

Next, list any materials needed and the steps taken to complete the process. Then, on your own paper, write a paragraph explaining the process. (See pages 99–101.)

**Topics (how something works)**   Answers will vary.

_____   _____   _____

**Materials**

_____

_____

**Steps**

_____

_____

_____

_____

_____

_____

_____

> "My father told me that words and letters hold the secrets of the universe. That in their shape and sounds I could find everything, could see beyond myself to something special . . . perfect."
>
> —Eliza, in the movie *Bee Season*

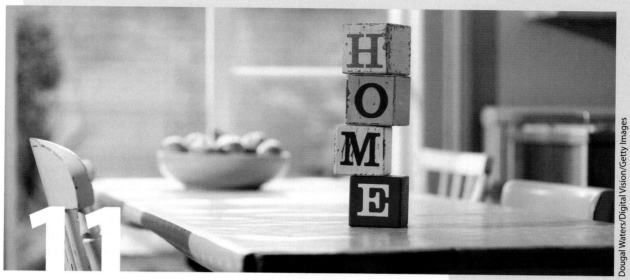

Dougal Waters/Digital Vision/Getty Images

# Definition and Classification

Each new course presents you with a set of words and concepts to learn. (Just think of all of the vocabulary lists you've received over the years.) One of the best ways to understand these new terms and topics is to write about them. Writing **extended** definition and **classification** paragraphs allows you to do just that.

Each type of writing requires you to research a word or concept and then understand and **synthesize** the information you have gathered. As you develop these paragraphs, you may consult several sources—from traditional dictionaries to a variety of online sites. As you hunt down information, your topic will take shape before you

## Learning Outcomes

**LO1** Analyze a definition paragraph.

**LO2** Write a definition paragraph.

**LO3** Analyze a classification paragraph.

**LO4** Write a classification paragraph.

**LO5** Review definition and classification.

### Vocabulary

**extended**
fully explained, added to

**classification**
systematic or organized grouping

**synthesize**
combine multiple ideas to form new understandings

## What do you think?

How can words "hold the secrets of the universe"?

Answers will vary.

# LO1 Analyzing a Definition Paragraph

A definition paragraph explains a new or, perhaps, misunderstood term. This type of paragraph may include a dictionary definition, the history of the term, examples of it, related words, and so on. Providing extended definitions like this is an important part of academic writing.

**Read/React** Read this definition paragraph; then follow the directions at the bottom of the page.

Frontpage/2010. Used under
license from Shutterstock.com

**Vocabulary**

**influenza**
a contagious viral
infection

**infectious**
capable of being
spread from person
to person

**globetrotting**
traveling often
and widely

## A Word of Warning

The **topic sentence** identifies the term and focus of the paragraph.

**Body sentences** explore the term in a number of ways.

The **closing sentences** keep the reader thinking about the term.

One word in medical reports strikes fear into people every- *1* where, and that word is *pandemic*. One report might say, "The threat of a pandemic flu hitting the United State exists"; another one might say, "The World Health Organization has raised the level of the **influenza** pandemic alert." Who wouldn't be scared by threats *5* such as these? So what exactly is a pandemic and where did this word come from? A pandemic is an "**infectious** disease covering a wide geographic area and affecting a large proportion of the population." Being "infectious" is a key feature because a disease cannot become a pandemic unless it can be spread by humans over *10* a very wide area. So influenza can be pandemic, but cancer cannot. Some people use *pandemic* interchangeably with *epidemic*. But an epidemic doesn't become pandemic until it covers an extremely widespread area, such as a series of countries. *Pandemic* comes from the Greek *pandēmos*: The Greek root *pan* means "every" or *15* "all" and *demos* means "common people." Thus, *pandēmos* means "all the people," so the connection with pandemic is clear. Two pandemics that are often cited are the Black Death during the Dark Ages and the flu pandemic in 1918 that killed from 40 to 50 million people. Current pandemics include H1N1, an infectious flu *20* virus, and HIV. Here's a scary final thought: **Globetrotting** provides an easy way for pandemics to occur.

This paragraph defines *pandemic* by providing the following types of details. Identify each detail from the paragraph.

Dictionary definition: <u>Infectious disease covering a wide geographic area and</u>
<u>affecting a large proportion of the population</u>

History of the word: <u>From the Greek word *pandēmos*, *pan* meaning "every" and</u>
<u>*dēmos* meaning "common people"</u>

Examples: <u>Black Death; flu pandemic of 1918; current H1N1 virus and HIV</u>

Related word: <u>epidemic (though an epidemic isn't widespread)</u>

Explanations: <u>Answers will vary.</u>

# LO2 Writing a Definition Paragraph

The next three pages provide guidelines for writing a definition paragraph, starting with prewriting below.

## Prewriting

**Identify** Read a few articles (online or in print) about medical, scientific, or technological topics. On the blanks below, list four to six terms you encountered that sparked your interest. Then circle one term that you would be interested in writing about. On the lines that follow, explain the reason for your choice.

Answers will vary.

**Collect** On the lines below, gather information for your paragraph. Look for the following types of details:

| | | |
|---|---|---|
| Dictionary definitions | History of the word | Related words |
| Examples | Quotations | Explanations |
| Interesting facts | Personal definition | What it means to others |

Answers will vary.

# Writing

As the model on page 104 shows, definition writing is key to science.

**Write** Create a first draft of your paragraph, using the outline that follows as a guide.

**Paragraph Outline**

**Topic Sentence:** Write a topic sentence that names the term and identifies a personal feeling or special feature about it. (See the formula on page 85.)

**Body Sentences:** Write sentences that explore the term in a variety of different ways. Organize the details in a logical way, perhaps starting with the dictionary definition.

**Closing Sentence:** Write a sentence that leaves the reader with a final thought about the term.

Answers will vary.

# Revising

**Revise** Read your paragraph and, if possible, have someone else read it as well. Then use the following checklist to guide your revision. Keep revising until you can check off each item in the list.

**Ideas**

- ☐ **1.** Does my paragraph focus on an interesting term?
- ☐ **2.** Do I explore the term in a number of different ways?

**Organization**

- ☐ **3.** Does my topic sentence name the term and focus of the paragraph?
- ☐ **4.** Are the body sentences arranged in a logical way?
- ☐ **5.** Does my closing sentence leave the reader with an interesting final thought?

**Voice**

- ☐ **6.** Does my writing voice demonstrate a clear understanding of the term?
- ☐ **7.** Does my voice engage the reader?

# Editing

**Edit** Create a clean copy of your revised paragraph and use the following checklist to check it for style and conventions.

**Words**

- ☐ **1.** Have I used specific nouns and verbs? (See page 74.)
- ☐ **2.** Have I used more action verbs than "be" verbs? (See page 348.)

**Sentences**

- ☐ **3.** Have I varied the beginnings and lengths of sentences? (See pages 264, 266.)
- ☐ **4.** Have I combined short, choppy sentences? (See page 262.)
- ☐ **5.** Have I avoided fragments and run-ons? (See pages 297–302, 306–307.)

**Conventions**

- ☐ **6.** Do I use correct verb forms (*he saw,* not *he seen*)? (See page 356.)
- ☐ **7.** Do my subjects and verbs agree (*she speaks,* not *she speak*)? (See pages 282–291.)
- ☐ **8.** Have I used the right words (*their, there, they're*)?
- ☐ **9.** Have I capitalized first words and proper nouns and adjectives? (See page 414.)
- ☐ **10.** Have I used commas after long introductory word groups? (See page 396.)
- ☐ **11.** Have I carefully checked my spelling?

# LO3 Analyzing a Classification Paragraph

A classification paragraph identifies the types or varieties of something. Classifying is a common form of thinking and writing used in the sciences.

**Read/React** Read the following classification paragraph; then answer the questions at the bottom of the page.

## Nighttime Blues

The **topic sentence** identifies the topic and focus.

Most people are familiar with eating disorders and learning disorders, but they may not be quite as familiar with sleeping disorders. Experts in the field identify four basic types of sleep disorders. The first one, insomnia, is linked to the other disorders because it covers the inability to fall asleep or stay asleep at night. Sleep apnea is another sleep disorder, and it is characterized by snoring, snorting, and even gasping. These irritating sound effects are produced when the sufferer tries to force air through a blockage of the airway during sleep. Narcolepsy, a third disorder, is characterized by excessive sleepiness during the day. It is caused by a chemical imbalance in the part of the brain that controls sleeping and staying awake. One narcoleptic stated that the sleepiness can come on suddenly in much the same way as an epileptic attack comes on. The fourth type of sleep disorder is restless leg syndrome. People suffering from this disorder feel a twitching, pulling, or aching in their legs, which forces them to move or kick them. The syndrome most often strikes during the night, but it can also occur during the day. Exploring the basics of sleeplessness makes it clear why we have sleep disorder clinics: There are a lot of people who aren't getting a good night's sleep.

**Body sentences** provide examples that classify the topic.

The **closing sentence** provides a final thought.

*1*

*5*

*10*

*15*

*20*

1. What are the topic and focus of the paragraph?

   Sleep disorders

2. How many types of the topic are identified? What are they?

   Four types: insomnia, apnea, narcolepsy, restless leg syndrome

3. How does the closing connect with the beginning?

   Answers will vary.

# LO4 Writing a Classification Paragraph

## Prewriting

**Select** On the blanks that follow, list possible topics as they come to mind. Try to fill in the entire chart with ideas. Afterward, review your list and circle one topic that you would like to write about in a classification paragraph. (Two ideas are provided for you.) Answers will vary.

| Types of . . . | | |
|---|---|---|
| weight trainers | | |
| instructors | | |
| | | |
| | | |

**Collect** Complete the following chart to gather details for your paragraph. In the first column, list the types of your topic. In the second column, explain or define each one. (You may have to do some quick research to gather information.)

| Types/Varieties | Explanation/Definition |
|---|---|
| Answers will vary. | |

# Writing

**Write** Create a first draft of your classification paragraph, using the following outline as a guide.

**Paragraph Outline**

**Topic Sentence:** Write a sentence that identifies the topic and focus of your paragraph. (See page 85 for a formula.)

**Body Sentences:** Write sentences that name and explain each type. Add information as needed to tie everything together.

**Closing Sentence:** Write a sentence that connects with the beginning or that keeps the reader thinking about the topic.

Answers will vary.

# Revising

**Revise** Read your paragraph and, if possible, have someone else read it as well. Then use the following checklist to guide your revision. Keep making improvements until you can check off each item in the list.

**Ideas**

☐ **1.** Does my paragraph focus on an interesting or important topic?

☐ **2.** Do I fully explain or classify the important types or varieties of the topic?

☐ **3.** Do I include plenty of specific details to explain each type?

**Organization**

☐ **4.** Does the topic sentence name the topic and focus of my writing?

☐ **5.** Are the body sentences arranged in a logical way.

☐ **6.** Does my closing sentence bring the paragraph to a satisfying end?

**Voice**

☐ **7.** Does my writing voice show my interest in the topic?

☐ **8.** Do I sound knowledgeable about the topic?

# Editing

**Edit** Create a clean copy of your revised paragraph and use the following checklist to check it for style and conventions.

**Words**

☐ **1.** Have I used specific nouns and verbs? (See page 74.)

☐ **2.** Have I used specific modifiers? (See page 143.)

**Sentences**

☐ **3.** Have I varied the beginnings and lengths of sentences? (See pages 264, 266.)

☐ **4.** Have I combined short, choppy sentences? (See page 262.)

☐ **5.** Have I avoided fragments and run-ons? (See pages 297–302, 306–307.)

**Conventions**

☐ **6.** Do I use correct verb forms (*he saw,* not *he seen*)? (See page 356.)

☐ **7.** Do my subjects and verbs agree (*she speaks,* not *she speak*)? (See pages 282–291.)

☐ **8.** Have I used the right words (*their, there, they're*)?

☐ **9.** Have I capitalized first words and proper nouns and adjectives? (See page 414.)

☐ **10.** Have I used commas after long introductory word groups? (See page 396.)

☐ **11.** Have I carefully checked my spelling?

# LO5 Reviewing Definition and Classification

**Define** In the chart that follows, identify a term that interests you from one of your classes. Next, collect details that will help you define and explain the term. (Complete at least four of the categories.) Then, on your own paper, develop a definition paragraph about the term. (See pages 105–107.)

**Term:** _Answers will vary._

Dictionary definition: _____

_____

Personal definition: _____

_____

History of the word: _____

_____

Related words: _____

_____

Quotations: _____

_____

**Classify** At the top of the chart below, list two or three style-related topics. Consider topics that can be broken down into types or varieties. Circle the one that you would like to write about. Next, complete the chart by identifying the types of your topic and an explanation of each one. Then, on your own paper, write a classification paragraph about the topic. (See pages 109–111.)

_Answers will vary._

| Types/Varieties | Explanation/Definition |
|---|---|
| | |

Digital Composite/Lifesize/Lifesize/Getty Images

# 12

# Cause-Effect and Comparison-Contrast

We lead cause-effect lives. One person shops for a scooter *(effect)* because he can't afford a car anymore *(cause)*. Another person can still fit into her swimsuit *(effect)* because she's been careful about her diet *(cause)*. Someone else has had it with a neighbor's barking dog *(cause)*, so she's looking for a new apartment *(effect)*.

A lot of academic writing deals with causes and effects as well. Stated in another way, writing often deals with the logical relationship between events and outcomes. Comparing and contrasting related topics is another important form of academic writing. These two-part forms of writing require analytical thinking and planning to complete.

## What do you think?

How would you explain Eleanor Roosevelt's contention that "understanding is a two-way street"?

Answers will vary.

## Learning Outcomes

**LO1** Analyze a cause-effect paragraph.

**LO2** Write a cause-effect paragraph.

**LO3** Analyze a comparison-contrast paragraph.

**LO4** Write a comparison-contrast paragraph.

**LO5** Review cause-effect and comparison-contrast.

# LO1 Analyzing a Cause-Effect Paragraph

These two starter sentences identify the type of thinking involved in cause-effect writing: *Because of . . . , we now . . .* or *Since . . . happened, we have had to . . . .* Keep this thought pattern in mind as you read and analyze cause-effect writing.

**Read/React**  Read the following cause-effect paragraph; then answer the questions at the bottom of the page.

Africa Studio ,2010 / Used under license from Shutterstock.com

### Problems in Print

The **topic sentence** identifies the topic and focus of the paragraph.

**Body sentences** explore the causes and effects.

Students interested in pursuing a career in traditional 1 journalism may want to think carefully about this decision. The reason is simple: Fewer and fewer people are buying newspapers. Most of them, instead, are getting all or most of their news on the Internet. Fewer buyers of newspapers and magazines mean less 5 income from subscriptions and newsstand sales. Fewer readers also mean fewer ad dollars, a main source of income for publishers. As a result, newspapers are going out of business or cutting back, and magazines are folding. This state of affairs has left publishers unsure about how to re-form for survival. News sources do offer 10 electronic alternatives to their print products, but readers get this news for free or pay a limited fee that in no way offsets the huge losses publishers are experiencing. Because of this situation, there simply are not enough jobs for experienced journalists, let alone recent graduates. So **prospective** journalism students must 15 realize that their chances of working in a traditional newsroom are slim to none. However, all is not lost. The Internet may offer exciting new career options for journalists, especially those who are strong researchers and communicators and well versed in the new opportunities that the **information age** has to offer. 20

The **closing sentence** expands on the main point.

1. What are the topic and focus of this paragraph?

   Traditional journalism as a career is declining dramatically.

2. What are the main causes and effects explained in the paragraph?

   **Causes:**  Fewer buyers of traditional newspapers; less income from electronic news; less income from ads

   **Effects:**  Fewer dollars to pay salaries; more competition for existing jobs

# LO2 Writing a Cause-Effect Paragraph

To write a cause-effect paragraph, use the guidelines on the next three pages, starting with prewriting below.

## Prewriting

**Select** In the first column, list careers or jobs that you are interested in or have had some experience with. In the second column, explain the **status** of each one. Afterward, put a check next to the job that you would like to write about in a cause-effect paragraph. On the lines at the bottom of the chart, explain the reason for your choice. (One example is provided.) Answers will vary.

| Careers or Jobs | Status |
|---|---|
| journalist | Career opportunities are shrinking and changing. |

**Consider** To plan your paragraph, consider the causes and effects of the current status of your topic. You may have one main cause and multiple effects, multiple causes and one main effect, or multiple causes and effects. Answers will vary.

| Causes | Effects |
|---|---|
| | |

**Traits**

In the sample paragraph, there is one main cause (fewer readers of print media) and one main effect (fewer traditional opportunities).

**Vocabulary**

**status**
current situation, standing, or state of affairs

# Writing

By practicing cause-effect writing now, you will be better prepared for cause-effect writing prompts on tests.

**Write** Create a first draft of your cause-effect paragraph, using the following outline as a guide.

**Paragraph Outline**

**Topic Sentence:** Begin with a topic sentence identifying your topic and focus. (See page 85 for a helpful formula.)

**Body Sentences:** Explain the causes and effects of the topic. Arrange these ideas in a logical way, dealing with causes first and then the effects, or vice versa.

**Closing Sentence:** Write a sentence that revisits or expands upon the main point.

Answers will vary.

116

# Revising

**Revise** Read your paragraph and, if possible, have someone else read it as well. Then use the following checklist to guide your revision. Keep making improvements until you can check off each item in the list.

**Ideas**

&#9633; **1.** Does my paragraph address an interesting and **timely** topic?

&#9633; **2.** Do I provide appropriate and clear "cause and effect" information?

**Organization**

&#9633; **3.** Does my topic sentence identify the topic and focus of my paragraph?

&#9633; **4.** Do the body sentences follow a logical order: causes first, then effects; effects first, then causes?

&#9633; **5.** Does my closing sentence revisit or expand upon the main point?

**Voice**

&#9633; **6.** Do I sound knowledgeable about the topic?

&#9633; **7.** Does my voice create interest in the topic?

# Editing

**Edit** Create a clean copy of your revised paragraph and use the following checklist to check it for style and conventions.

**Words**

&#9633; **1.** Have I used specific nouns and verbs? (See page 74.)

&#9633; **2.** Have I used specific modifiers? (See page 143.)

**Sentences**

&#9633; **3.** Have I varied the beginnings and lengths of sentences? (See pages 264, 266.)

&#9633; **4.** Have I combined short, choppy sentences? (See page 262.)

&#9633; **5.** Have I avoided fragments and run-ons? (See pages 297–302, 306–307.)

**Conventions**

&#9633; **6.** Do I use correct verb forms *(he saw,* not *he seen)*? (See page 356.)

&#9633; **7.** Do my subjects and verbs agree *(she speaks,* not *she speak)*? (See pages 282–291.)

&#9633; **8.** Have I used the right words *(their, there, they're)*?

&#9633; **9.** Have I capitalized first words and proper nouns and adjectives? (See page 414.)

&#9633; **10.** Have I used commas after long introductory word groups? (See page 396.)

&#9633; **11.** Have I carefully checked my spelling?

**Vocabulary**

**timely**
well-timed,
important now

matka_Wariatka,2010 / Used under license from Shutterstock.com

**Vocabulary**

**advocacy**
active support, arguing in favor of something

**battery mate**
in terms of baseball, the combination of a pitcher and catcher; in more general terms, partners in an activity or occupation

# LO3 Analyzing a Comparison-Contrast Paragraph

Comparison-contrast writing may emphasize both the similarities and differences between two topics, or it may focus more attention on how the topics are either alike or different.

**Read/React** Read the following comparison-contrast paragraph; then answer the questions at the bottom of the page.

## Order in the Court

The **topic sentence** identifies the topics and focus of the paragraph.

**Body sentences** share details about the two topics.

The **closing sentence** provides a final thought about the topics.

Both solicitors and barristers serve the public in the British    1
legal system, but they do so in different ways. Someone in Great
Britain seeking legal help contacts a solicitor, who will usually
be part of a law firm. A solicitor then serves as a client's legal
representative, providing legal guidance and advice, and even    5
representing a client in some court cases. When a client needs
specialized legal help and **advocacy** before the high court, a solicitor
will contact his legal **battery mate**, a barrister. Unlike a solicitor, a
barrister has no attachment to any firm but instead is a member
of chambers, a group of barristers that share legal aides and such.    10
A barrister's main responsibility is to argue a client's case before a
judge and jury, so his or her independence from any firm provides
an unbiased voice in the law proceedings. When in "uniform" in
front of the judge and jury, barristers have traditionally worn
elaborate horsehair wigs, stiff white collars, and long gowns. This    15
legal division of power has served the British public well for ages,
even though solicitors are now gaining more responsibility before
the courts.

1. What are the topics of this paragraph?

   Solicitors and barristers in the British court system

2. Does the paragraph focus on similarities, differences, or both? Explain.

   Both. Answers will vary.

3. What are two important things that you learned about the topics?

   Answers will vary.

# LO4 Writing a Comparison-Contrast Paragraph

To write a comparison-contrast paragraph, follow the guidelines on the next three pages, starting with prewriting below.

## Prewriting

**Select** Think of jobs or positions that are closely related. For example, within the dental profession, there are dental assistants and dental **hygienists**. In the automotive field, there are automotive technicians and car mechanics. After listing a number of related jobs, circle the pair you would like to write about in a comparison-contrast paragraph.   Answers will vary.

> **Related Jobs or Positions**

**Collect** In the space provided below, gather information about your two topics. Consider training, job description, opportunities, and so on. (Use your own paper if you need more room.)   Answers will vary.

> **Job or Position One:** _____    **Job or Position Two:** _____

**Plan** Decide how you will organize your paragraph: Are you going to share all the information about one topic and then the other? Or are you going to cover the two topics point by point, first showing how they compare or contrast in terms of training, then in terms of job description, and so on?

# Writing

**Write** Create a first draft of your comparison-contrast paragraph, using the following outline as a guide.

**Paragraph Outline**

**Topic Sentence:** Begin with a topic sentence that identifies the related topics and focus of your paragraph. (See page 85 for a formula.)

**Body Sentences:** Develop the body sentences, following your planning at the bottom of the previous page.

**Closing Sentence:** Write a sentence (or two) that provides a final thought about the topics.

Answers will vary.

# Revising

**Revise** Read your paragraph and, if possible, have someone else read it as well. Then use the following checklist to guide your revisions. Keep making improvements until you can check off each item in the list.

**Ideas**

- [ ] **1.** Does my paragraph address two related jobs in an interesting field?
- [ ] **2.** Do I provide an adequate number of important similarities and/or differences?

**Organization**

- [ ] **3.** Does my topic sentence identify the topics and focus of the paragraph?
- [ ] **4.** Do the comparisons and/or contrasts follow a logical order?
- [ ] **5.** Does my closing sentence provide an important final thought about the topics?

**Voice**

- [ ] **6.** Do I sound knowledgeable about the topics?
- [ ] **7.** Does my voice engage the reader?

# Editing

**Edit** Create a clean copy of your revised paragraph and use the following checklist to check it for style and conventions.

**Words**

- [ ] **1.** Have I used specific nouns and verbs? (See page 74.)
- [ ] **2.** Have I used specific modifiers? (See page 143.)

**Sentences**

- [ ] **3.** Have I varied the beginnings and lengths of sentences? (See pages 264, 266.)
- [ ] **4.** Have I combined short, choppy sentences? (See page 262.)
- [ ] **5.** Have I avoided fragments and run-ons? (See pages 297–302, 306–307.)

**Conventions**

- [ ] **6.** Do I use correct verb forms (*he saw,* not *he seen*)? (See page 356.)
- [ ] **7.** Do my subjects and verbs agree (*she speaks,* not *she speak*)? (See pages 282–291.)
- [ ] **8.** Have I used the right words (*their, there, they're*)?
- [ ] **9.** Have I capitalized first words and proper nouns and adjectives? (See page 414.)
- [ ] **10.** Have I used commas after long introductory word groups? (See page 396.)
- [ ] **11.** Have I carefully checked my spelling?

# LO5 Reviewing Cause-Effect and Comparison-Contrast

**Cause-Effect** Fill in the following chart with causes and effects related to this photograph of a shantytown.    Answers will vary.

| Causes | Effects |
|--------|---------|
|        |         |

On the lines below, write a topic sentence for a cause-effect paragraph about the shantytown. Write the paragraph on your own paper. (See pages 115–117.)

**Topic Sentence:** _____

_____

_____

**Comparison-Contrast** List two pairs of related gestures, actions, or feelings. Giggling and snickering, for example, are two types of laughter. Circle the pair that you would like to write about in a comparison-contrast paragraph.

1. Answers will vary. _____    2. _____ _____

Next, use this Venn diagram to collect details about your topic. Write the paragraph on your own paper. (See pages 119–121.)

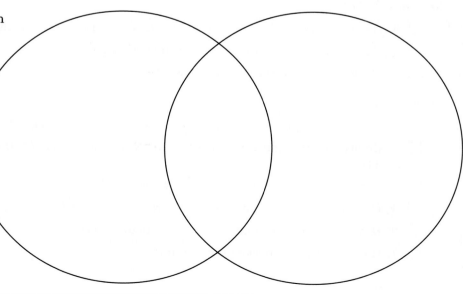

"You're entitled to your own opinion. But you're not entitled to your own facts."

—Daniel Patrick Moynihan

David Madison/Photographer's Choice/Getty Images

# 13
# Argument and Problem-Solution

Writing is really thinking on paper. When you explain or describe, you are demonstrating your ability to understand information. When you compare or classify, you are involved in analyzing, a higher level of thinking. When you persuade, you move even higher up the thinking **food chain**.

Writing persuasively is essentially the process of arguing for or against a particular point of view. In order to form a thoughtful opinion, you first must thoroughly understand and analyze the subject. Developing a problem-solution paragraph is a closely related form because it involves analyzing and recommending.

You'll be expected to writing persuasively in almost all of your college course work, so the strategies that you learn in this chapter will prove very helpful.

## What do you think?

What does Moynihan have to say about the relationship between opinions and facts?

Answers will vary.

## Learning Outcomes

**LO1** Analyze a persuasive paragraph.

**LO2** Write a persuasive paragraph.

**LO3** Analyze a problem-solution paragraph.

**LO4** Write a problem-solution paragraph.

### Vocabulary

**food chain**
the connection from the lowest life forms to the highest; here, a metaphor for different levels of thinking

# LO1 Analyzing an Argument Paragraph

A persuasive paragraph presents a mini-argument by expressing an opinion and supporting it with reliable facts and details. The test of this form of writing is whether or not the reader accepts the **validity** of the argument.

**Read/React** Read the following persuasive paragraph; then answer the questions at the bottom of the page.

## Evening the Odds

The **topic sentence** states the writer's opinion.

Barbed hooks should be banned from lure fishing to protect the fish stocks. Fishing was once a way to put food on the table, so using barbed hooks may have made sense in the past, but in today's word, fishing for almost everyone is a form of recreation. A properly set barbed hook often inflicts serious injury to the fish, especially the smaller ones. Many small fish are kept because the angler knows that releasing them would be inhumane, while others are released with portions of their jaws severely damaged or missing. Using a smooth, barbless hook, on the other hand, is much easier to remove from a fish's mouth, leaving only a small puncture in the jaw area, and giving anglers the opportunity to release undamaged fish. In this way, barbless hooks help to preserve our limited fish stocks. Supporters of barbed hooks say that banning them would decrease the number of fish they are able to catch and that their enjoyment would decrease. They are partially correct because playing a fish is difficult without a barb. However, many anglers using barbless hooks report that they actually find fishing more enjoyable because it adds another challenge. To maintain a healthy fish population for recreational fishing, barbed hooks no longer belong in an angler's tackle box.

**Body sentences** provide support for the writer's position.

The **closing sentence** reinforces the writer's position.

*(Line numbers: 1, 5, 10, 15, 20)*

Sean Gladwell,2010 / Used under license from Shutterstock.com

1. What is the writer arguing for or against?
   Against barbed hooks in lure fishing

2. What part of the paragraph addresses a **counterargument**? (Identify the lines.)
   13-15

3. How would you rate the effectiveness of this argument? Explain your choice.

   | weak | | | | | | | | | strong |
   |---|---|---|---|---|---|---|---|---|---|
   | 1 | 2 | 3 | 4 | 5 | 6 | 7 | 8 | 9 | 10 |

   Answers will vary.

# L○2 Writing an Argument Paragraph

To write an argument paragraph, follow the guidelines on the next three pages, starting with prewriting below.

## Prewriting

**Select** In the space that follows, list activities (hobbies, sports, other pastimes) that you participate in or have strong feelings about. Then circle one that you could write about in a persuasive paragraph.

**Activities:**

Answers will vary.

**Form** After thinking about the topic, write a working opinion statement. (You can always adjust or change it later on.) Use the formula below as a guide.

| Topic | + | position | = | opinion statement |
|---|---|---|---|---|
| Barbed hooks | | should be banned from lure fishing to protect the fish stock | | Barbed hooks should be banned from lure fishing to protect the fish stock. |

Answers will vary.

**Collect** Fill in the chart below with two or three supporting details (facts, statistics, quotations, and so on), and, if possible, one main counterargument. Answers will vary.

**Supporting Details**

1. _____

2. _____

3. _____

**Counterargument**

_____

_____

_____

# Writing

**Write** Create a first draft of your persuasive paragraph, using the following paragraph outline as a guide.

WAC

Problem-solution writing is key to both social sciences and real sciences.

Vocabulary

reaffirm
to restate to emphasize or stress

**Paragraph Outline**

**Topic Sentence:** Begin with your opinion statement from page 125.

**Body Sentences:** Write sentences that develop your supporting details from page 125. Work in a counterargument if you feel it is necessary. (Note how the sentences in the sample paragraph flow from one to another.)

**Closing Sentences:** Write a sentence that **reaffirms** your opinion.

Answers will vary.

# Revising

**Revise** Read your paragraph and, if possible, have someone else read it as well. Then use the following checklist to guide your revision. Keep making improvements until you can check off each item in the list.

**Ideas**

☐ **1.** Does my paragraph address a timely and/or important topic?

☐ **2.** Do I provide a convincing argument (opinion and supporting points)?

☐ **3.** Do I address an important counterargument (optional)?

**Organization**

☐ **4.** Does my opinion statement make a **reasonable** claim?

☐ **5.** Are the body sentences presented in a logical order?

☐ **6.** Does the closing sentence reaffirm my opinion or position?

**Voice**

☐ **7.** Does my writing voice reflect my feelings about the topic?

☐ **8.** Do I sound logical and knowledgeable?

# Editing

**Edit** Create a clean copy of your revised paragraph. Then edit your writing for style and conventions using the following checklist as a guide.

**Vocabulary**

reasonable
practical and intelligent

**Words**

☐ **1.** Have I used specific nouns and verbs? (See page 74.)

☐ **2.** Have I used specific modifiers? (See page 143.)

**Sentences**

☐ **3.** Have I varied the beginnings and lengths of sentences? (See pages 264, 266.)

☐ **4.** Have I combined short, choppy sentences? (See page 262.)

☐ **5.** Have I avoided fragments and run-ons? (See pages 297–302, 306–307.)

**Conventions**

☐ **6.** Do I use correct verb forms (*he saw,* not *he seen*)? (See page 356.)

☐ **7.** Do my subjects and verbs agree (*she speaks,* not *she speak*)? (See pages 282–291.)

☐ **8.** Have I used the right words (*their, there, they're*)?

☐ **9.** Have I capitalized first words and proper nouns and adjectives? (See page 414.)

☐ **10.** Have I used commas after long introductory word groups? (See page 396.)

☐ **11.** Have I carefully checked my spelling?

# LO3 Analyzing a Problem-Solution Paragraph

Problem-solution paragraphs and essays can be expository or persuasive. If the problem and solution happened in the past, the writing is expository. If the essay focuses on a current problem, the writing is persuasive.

**Read/React** Read the following problem-solution paragraph; then answer the questions at the bottom of the page.

© Glenn Bo/iStockphoto.com

## Lead Alert

**The topic sentence** states the topic and focus of the paragraph.

**Body sentences** explain the problem and offer one or more solutions.

**The closing sentence** reminds readers of the importance of the problem.

Young children unprotected from almost any amount of lead may suffer serious health problems. Lead poisoning can lead to everything from headaches and periods of confusion to learning disabilities and behavioral problems. As the Alliance for Healthy Homes reports, the problem is most **acute** in large urban areas where families live in substandard housing. Inner city dwellings built before 1960 likely contain lead-based paints, the major source of the problem. If the lead paint in these dwellings is peeling, very young children will eat the paint chips, but even the dust from the paint is potentially harmful. It can settle on anything, and eventually get in the mouths of the very young. Unfortunately, once someone suffers from lead poisoning, there are no complete cures. The best solution for families is to take **preventative** measures such as daily house cleaning and regular washing of hands. Long-term measures include painting over old lead paint, but without sanding before hand. The Mayo Clinic Web site on lead poisoning reminds renters that they have rights protecting their health and safety. Landlords by law are required to find and address sources of lead. Growing up poor is hard enough. Problems only become magnified if the living conditions expose dwellers to the dangers of lead.

1. What are the topic and focus of the paragraph?

   **Topic:** Children exposed to lead paint    **Focus:** children of urban poor

2. What are two things that you learned about the problem?

   Answers will vary.

3. What two or three solutions did you learn about?

   Answers will vary.

# LO4 Writing a Problem-Solution Paragraph

To write a problem-solution paragraph, use the next three pages as a guide, starting the prewriting below.

## Prewriting

**Select** List two or three problems in your community such as *lack of public transportation* or *loud noises*. Also list two or three problems related to school life such as *crowded classrooms* or *limited access to courses*. Then circle one that you could write about in a problem-solution paragraph.    Answers will vary.

| Community-related problems: | School-related problems: |
|---|---|
| | |

**Collect** Gather information for your paragraph by following the directions below.    Answers will vary.

**Problem**

State the problem: _____

Identify who is affected by it: _____

_____

Identify the causes of the problem: _____

_____

_____

Explain its significance: _____

_____

**Solutions**

State two or three possible solutions: (*Circle the best one.*)

_____

_____

_____

_____

Problem-solution writing is key to both social sciences and natural sciences.

# Writing

**Write** Create a first draft of your problem-solution paragraph, using the following paragraph outline as a guide.

**Paragraph Outline**

**Topic Sentence:** Start your paragraph with a clear statement of the problem. (See the formula on page 125 for help.)

**Body Sentences:** Write sentences that explain the problem and offer the best solutions. You may want to lead up to the best solution. Include additional explanations as necessary to connect your ideas.

**Closing Sentence:** End with a sentence that reminds the reader about the importance of the problem.

Answers will vary.

# Revising

**Revise** Read your paragraph and, if possible, have someone else read it as well. Then use the following checklist to guide your revision. Keep making improvements until you can check off each item in the list.

### Ideas

☐ **1.** Does my paragraph address an important current problem?

☐ **2.** Do I effectively explore the problem and solutions?

☐ **3.** Do I offer additional explanations as needed?

### Organization

☐ **4.** Does my topic sentence clearly identify the problem?

☐ **5.** Are the body sentences arranged in a logical way?

☐ **6.** Does my closing sentence stress the important of the problem?

### Voice

☐ **7.** Do I sound interested in and knowledgeable about the problem?

☐ **8.** Do I speak sincerely to the reader?

# Editing

**Edit** Create a clean copy of your paragraph; then use the following checklist to edit your writing for style and conventions.

### Words

☐ **1.** Have I used specific nouns and verbs? (See page 74.)

☐ **2.** Have I used specific modifiers? (See page 143.)

### Sentences

☐ **3.** Have I varied the beginnings and lengths of sentences? (See pages 264, 266.)

☐ **4.** Have I combined short, choppy sentences? (See page 262.)

☐ **5.** Have I avoided fragments and run-ons? (See pages 297–302, 306–307.)

### Conventions

☐ **6.** Do I use correct verb forms *(he saw,* not *he seen)*? (See page 356.)

☐ **7.** Do my subjects and verbs agree *(she speaks,* not *she speak)*? (See pages 282–291.)

☐ **8.** Have I used the right words *(their, there, they're)*?

☐ **9.** Have I capitalized first words and proper nouns and adjectives? (See page 414.)

☐ **10.** Have I used commas after long introductory word groups? (See page 396.)

☐ **11.** Have I carefully checked my spelling?

"I never travel without my diary. One should
always have something sensational to read on the train."

# 14 Narrative Essay

Memories seemingly alter reality, taking your mind to another time and place. They can flood your brain for hours, make a lengthy car ride go by in a flash, or get you through a particularly mind-numbing classroom lecture. When your mind drifts to that special place and remembers a past experience, you are reflecting on your own unique story.

An essay that shares a memory or story from your own life is called a personal narrative. The goal of such writing is to bring the memory to life with details that will help the reader see, hear, touch, and taste the experience.

This chapter will guide you through the process of writing a narrative essay about an important past experience.

## What do you think?

What sensational stories might be included in the diary of your own life?

Answers will vary.

## Learning Outcomes

**LO1** Understand narrative essays.

**LO2** Plan a narrative essay.

**LO3** Write the first draft.

**LO4** Revise the first draft.

**LO5** Edit the essay.

**LO6** Reflect on the experience.

133

# LO1 Reviewing a Narrative Essay

A narrative essay tells a story. In the following essay, a writer shares a personal story about a memorable experience.

**Read/React** Read the following essay. Then complete the analysis on the next page.

## Tripped Up Road Trip

The **opening paragraph** starts in the middle of the action.

Jammed in our aging royal blue Chevy Astro van with no air conditioning, no radio, and limited legroom, sat my parents, my two sisters, and our beloved golden retriever, Max. It was mid-June and we were traveling along historic Route 66 near the New Mexico-Arizona border, on our way to Grand Canyon National Park. *1* *5*

The first **middle paragraph** uses dialogue to push the story along.

This was not exactly my idea of a fun family vacation. Sweat beads trickled down my brow, and a feeling of dread washed over me as I noticed the low-battery sign blinking on my mp3 player. Couldn't we go to a resort with a swimming pool? "Just six hours left," Mom commented from the front seat. Six hours? You could watch *Avatar* twice in that same amount of time. *10*

The next **paragraph** describes the key moment in the narrative.

What happened next seemed like a scene from a bad comedy movie. Out of nowhere, grayish smoke billowed from under the hood of the van and up the windshield, completely blocking my dad's view of the road. As Dad pulled off to the side, Max started barking, startling my slumbering sisters, who started screaming as smoke spilled into the car through the open windows. When the car was parked, I flung open the door and ran out into the desert sun. This was the worst vacation ever. *15* *20*

The **closing paragraph** describes the action that followed the key moment and provides closure.

Dad discovered the engine had overheated, and we were stuck. "Is this thing going to blow up?" asked my younger sister Michelle. "I have like a bunch of clothes in there." Luckily Mom had brought a cooler stocked with bottled water and snacks, so we survived the hot sun while we waited for a tow truck. It must have been a funny sight for the truck driver when he pulled up. All six of us sat in a circle, sweating and looking miserable. We did eventually make it to the Grand Canyon, but not before Mom admitted, "A pool would feel really nice right now." *25*

# A Closer Look

This essay relied on three basic building blocks of narrative writing: action, dialogue, and description. **Action** uses active verbs to describe what is happening. *Out of nowhere, grayish smoke billowed from under the hood of the van.* **Dialogue** reveals the unique personalities of the people involved in the story. *"I have like a bunch of clothes in there," said Michelle.* And **description** uses vivid details to describe people, places, and things. *Sweat beads trickled down my brow.*

**Analyze** Reread the essay on the facing page. As you do, record any examples of action, dialogue, and description in the following chart.  Answers will vary.

| Action | Dialogue | Description |
|--------|----------|-------------|
|        |          |             |

**Explain** What type of sensory detail are you most interested in hearing about from a writer? Why?  Answers will vary.

_____

_____

_____

_____

_____

# LO2 Prewriting: Planning

In your own essay, you will write about an experience from your past. Think of a time, a place, or an event that sticks out as a particularly memorable moment in your life.

## Selecting a Topic

**Select** In the space below, list four experiences from your own life to consider for a narrative essay. Remember, the experiences don't have to be big or life altering. Small events, even ones that may seem inconsequential, can make interesting topics for narrative essays.  **Answers will vary.**

1. _____    2. _____

3. _____    4. _____

## Using Chronological Order

Once you have selected a topic, think carefully about the order of events in your memory. In almost all cases, narrative essays are arranged **chronologically**, or according to time.

**Identify** Use the time line below to list the main details of your topic in chronological (time) order.  **Answers will vary.**

1. _____

2. _____

3. _____

4. _____

5. _____

6. _____

7. _____

8. _____

# Gathering Details

The most vivid narrative essays use plenty of sensory details. Such details allow the reader to picture, hear, and touch what you describe. The following chart describes the sensory details in a narrative essay about a special memory.

| Sights | Sounds | Smells | Tastes | Textures |
|---|---|---|---|---|
| ceiling fan | buzz of the phone | eggs frying | burn of the bourbon drink | lump in the throat |
| egg in the frying pan | conversation with Mom | | | watery eyes |
| sparkle of brown eyes | Grandpa's deep laugh | | | |
| arthritic hands | | | | |

**Gather** Complete the sensory chart below. Collect any sights, sounds, smells, tastes, or textures about your subject in the appropriate column. Answers will vary.

| Sights | Sounds | Smells | Tastes | Textures |
|---|---|---|---|---|
| | | | | |

The best dialogue captures a person's unique voice, so write the way a speaker actually speaks.

**WAC**

Though some academic forms of writing restrict use of first-person pronouns, *I, you,* and *we,* are acceptable in narrative essays.

# L○3 Writing: Creating a First Draft

In a first draft you follow your plan and organize your details to create a narrative story. Provided below is a sample narrative essay about a memorable moment in the writer's life.

**Read/React** Read the essay, noting how the writer created an effective opening and closing for his personal narrative.

## Remembering Gramps

**Opening paragraph**

It was sometime after eight o'clock on a Saturday morning when I received the call about my grandfather's death. I was already awake, cracking eggs into a skillet, when my cell phone buzzed on the countertop. A little early for a phone call, I thought. It was my mom. "Are you awake?" she asked, her voice cracking. Sensing her distress, I asked what was wrong. She told me my grandfather had suffered a stroke during the night and didn't make it. *1*

*5*

**Middle paragraph 1**

After talking through the funeral plans, I wobbled over to my cushy, leather couch and stared blankly at the circulating blades on the ceiling fan. Memories of my grandfather spun around in my head, like the time he taught me how to throw a curveball, and the fishing trip we took together on the Gulf Coast, and the day he poured me a Coke, but instead mistakenly handed me his glass of bourbon and ice. *10*

**Middle paragraph 2**

Of course, those were old memories. By the time I reached college, Grandpa wasn't as active anymore. Tired and overworked from his years of hard labor at the steel yard, his back eventually gave out and his joints swelled up with arthritis. He lived alone in the modest two-bedroom home he built for my grandmother after they married. But even after she was gone, he never lost the sparkle in his brown eyes. Nor did he lose his sense of humor, punctuated by a deep baritone laugh. *15*

*20*

**Closing paragraph**

And so I sat there, staring at the ceiling and reminiscing about Grandpa. Sure, I had a lump in my throat and tears filled my eyes; but I felt thankful for the memories of times we had together, and hopeful that one day I could be as good a grandfather as he had been to me. *25*

Laura Doss/Fancy/Corbis

# Creating an O

The opening paragr                                    r into the story.
Here are some strat

- **Set the st**
  Show whe                                    se details
  that appe
  > It was                                    when I
  > receiv

- **Jump int**
  Quickly es                                    ic, and have
  them do
  > Jamm                                    ir
  > condit                              s, my two
  > sisters, and our beloved golden retriever, Max.

- **Focus on an interesting detail.**
  Offer a powerful sensory or **thought detail** to introduce an amazing or
  surprising part of the story.
  > I should have listened to my brother. I never should have
  > walked in that room.

**Vocabulary**

**thought details**
a writer's impressions,
emotions, or reflections about
an experience

**Write** Create your opening paragraph. Start with a sentence that uses one of the
strategies above. Then write sentences that continue to introduce the story.

Answers will vary.

# Creating Middle Paragraphs

**Write** As you write your middle paragraphs, include action, description, and dialogue. (See page 135.) Use these narrative elements to build suspense until the story reaches its most exciting moment. Finally, use transition words to move the story along in time order. (Refer to "Traits" at the left.) Answers will vary.

# Creating a Closing Paragraph

The closing paragraph should explain the outcome of the narrative. Consider the following strategies:

- **Use a final piece of dialogue.**
  Close with an appropriate quotation from someone involved in the narrative.
- **Explain the event's impact.**
  In a sentence, describe how you or the world around you changed after the experience.
- **Reveal a new understanding.**
  Explain what you learned from the experience.

**Write** Create the closing paragraph for your narrative essay.   Answers will vary.

Speaking & Listening

Have your partner read your essay aloud. Then complete the response sheet.

# LO4 Revising: Improving the Writing

Revising your first draft involves adding, deleting, rearranging, and reworking parts of your writing. Revision begins with a peer review.

## Peer Review

Sharing your writing at various stages is important, especially when you review and revise a first draft. The feedback that you receive will help you change and improve your essay.

**Respond** Complete this response sheet after reading the first draft of a classmate's essay. Then share the sheet with the writer. (Keep your comments helpful and positive.)  Answers will vary.

Essay title: _____

Writer: _____ Reviewer: _____

1. Which part of the essay seems to work best—opening, middle, or closing? Why?

   _____
   _____
   _____

2. Which part of the essay needs work—opening, middle, or closing? Why? _____

   _____
   _____
   _____

3. Which details in the story caught your attention? Name three.

   a. _____

   b. _____

   c. _____

4. Does the writer include appropriate dialogue? Explain.

   _____
   _____
   _____

5. Identify a phrase or two that show the writer's level of interest.

   _____
   _____

# Adding Specific Verbs and Modifiers

You can strengthen your essay by adding specific verbs and modifiers. Such improvements in word choice make your writing more interesting.

| Verbs | | | Modifiers | |
|---|---|---|---|---|
| **General** | **Specific** | | **General** | **Specific** |
| grew | swelled | | baseball hat | flat-billed New York Yankees hat |
| came | advanced | | curly hair | wavy auburn hair |
| run | sprint | | sweet sauce | tangy barbeque sauce |
| lives | roams | | | |
| wear | adorn | | | |

**Revising in Action**

Read aloud the unrevised and then the revised version of the following excerpt. Note how specific verbs and adjectives make the writing come alive.

> wobbled     cushy, leather     circulating     ceiling
> I ~~walked~~ over to my couch and stared blankly at the blades on the fan.

**Revise** Improve your writing, using the following checklist and your partner's comments on the response sheet. Continue working until you can check off each item in the list.

**Ideas**

☐ **1.** Do I focus on one specific experience or memory?

☐ **2.** Do I include sensory details and dialogue?

☐ **3.** Do I use specific verbs and modifiers?

**Organization**

☐ **4.** Does the essay have an opening, a middle, and a closing?

☐ **5.** Is the story organized chronologically?

☐ **6.** Have I used transitions to connect my sentences?

**Voice**

☐ **7.** Is my interest in the story obvious to the reader?

☐ **8.** Does my writing voice fit my personality?

# LO5 Editing: Correcting Your Writing

The main work of editing is correcting your revised first draft.

## Quotation Marks and Dialogue

**Dialogue** enlivens a story and reveals the personalities of its characters. When you recall or create conversations between people using the speaker's exact words, you must use quotation marks before and after the **direct quotation.** However, when you use an **indirect quotation**—one that does not use the speaker's exact words—quotation marks are not needed. See the examples that follow.

> **Direct Quotation**
>
> Before we left class, our teacher said, **"Next week's final will be comprehensive."**
>
> **Indirect Quotation**
>
> I recall the teacher saying **that the final will be comprehensive.**
>
> *Note:* The word *that* often indicates dialogue that is being reported rather than quoted.

**Punctuation Practice** Read the sentences below. Place quotation marks ("") before and after the speaker's exact words in direct quotations. If the sentence contains no direct quotations, write "C" for correct on the blank following the sentence.

1. "Who is your favorite actress?" asked Veronica. _____

2. The salesman suggested that I should take the truck for a test-drive. __C__

3. Frank said that if we want to make it in time, we should leave by noon. __C__

4. "On my way out today," Jessie said, "I forgot my cell phone." _____

5. "Pull over to the side of the road," said the police officer. _____

6. After glancing at her test score, Jillian said, "Spring break can't come soon enough." _____

7. "And with this new cell phone model," said the saleswoman, "you can play music, get driving directions, and check your e-mail." _____

8. Jana said that she is in love with her new summer dress. __C__

**Apply** Read your narrative essay. If you included any direct quotations, make sure they are properly marked with quotation marks. If you did not use any direct quotations, you may consider adding one or two to reveal the uniqueness of the people in your story.

# Punctuation of Dialogue

As you edit your narrative essay, check for the correct punctuation of dialogue. In general, there are three rules you should follow.

- **When a period or comma follows the quotation, place the period or comma *before* the quotation mark.**
    "You should check your voice messages**,**" advised Mr. Lee.
    "As you will soon discover**,**" advised Reggie, "the wrap station in the cafeteria is the best choice for lunch**.**"

- **When a question mark or an exclamation point follows the quotation, place it *before* the quotation mark if it belongs with the quotation. Otherwise, place it after.**
    I asked Sheryl, "Where can I get some good soul food**?**"
    Did you hear Veronica say, "I quit"**?**

- **When a semicolon or colon follows the quotation, place it after the quotation mark.**
    Trey only said, "I have other plans"**;** he didn't mention his fear of heights.

**Punctuation Practice**   In each sentence that follows, correct the punctuation and capitalization of the quotations.

1. "Let's focus on solutions, not problems"，offered Haley.

2. Jack promised he would, "Try his best to make it;" however, I know he's not coming.

3. "It's not the size of the dog in the fight", suggested Mark Twain "，it's the size of the fight in the dog."

4. "It's about time you showed up"! exclaimed Karen.

5. "Should I apply for the job"? asked my roommate.

6. What did you mean when you said, "There is more to the story than you think"?"

7. "We are doing everything in our power to regain your trust"，said the company spokesperson.

**Apply**   Read your narrative essay. Closely check the punctuation of your dialogue.

# Marking an Essay

Before you finish editing your revised essay, you can practice by editing the following model.

**Editing Practice**  Read the following narrative essay, looking for problems listed in the checklist on the facing page. Also refer to the list of common errors on page 80. Correct the model using the marks listed to the left. One correction has been done for you.

## Correction Marks

| | |
|---|---|
| ✄ | delete |
| d̲ | capitalize |
| ɒ̸ | lowercase |
| ∧ | insert |
| ⌃ | add comma |
| ? ∧ | add question mark |
| word ∧ | add word |
| ⊙ | add period |
| ⬭ | spelling |
| ᶰᶸ | switch |

## Whale Watchers

On a sunny afternoon off the coast of San Diego, my friend Natalie     1
and I set off on our great whale-watching adventure. In the winter months,
some 20,000 gray whales migrate through the Pacific waters along the coast
of c̲alifornia, and we wanted to see the majestic creatures in (there) natural
habitat.                                                                         5

As we stepped aboard the 100-foot tour boat nicknamed "Night and
Day", Natalie reminded me to take some medication to prevent seasickness.
                                            six
Good thing she did, because the captain announced we would hit 6̸-foot swells
on our journey. (Their) were about 40 other passengers onboard with us.

About 15 minutes off the shoreline, a passenger shouted, "There she     10
                                    saw
blows"! Indeed, about 20 yards ahead of us, I s̶e̶e̶n̶ a spray of white water
rocket vertically from the ocean surface ⊙ w̲e had spotted our first whale! As
the boat crept closer, we could see the bumpy gray backs of two more whales
rising above the undulating waves. I was so excited that ∧high-fived Natalie so
hard it made my hand sting.                                                     15

We ended up seeing five (diffrant) gray whales, two packs of dolphins, and
too many pelicans to count. s̲eeing this beautiful sea life in the wild was an
experience I'll never forget. Learning that the whales are endangered goes to
show that we must boost our efforts to protect them from extinction.

146

# Correcting Your Essay

Now it's time to correct your own essay.

**Edit** Prepare a clean copy of your essay and use the following checklist to look for errors. Continue working until you can check off each item in the list.

**Words**

☐ **1.** Have I used specific nouns and verbs)? (See page 74.)

☐ **2.** Have I used more action verbs than "be" verbs? (See page 348.)

**Sentences**

☐ **3.** Have I used sentences with varying beginnings and lengths? (See pages 264, 266.)

☐ **4.** Have I avoided improper shifts in sentences? (See pages 314–315.)

☐ **5.** Have I avoided fragments and run-ons? (See pages 297–302, 306–307.)

**Conventions**

☐ **6.** Do I use correct verb forms (*he saw*, not *he seen*)? (See page 356.)

☐ **7.** Do my subjects and verbs agree (*she speaks*, not *she speak*)? (See pages 282–291.)

☐ **8.** Have I used the right words (*their, there, they're*)?

☐ **9.** Have I capitalized first words and proper nouns and adjectives? (See page 414.)

☐ **10.** Have I used commas after long introductory word groups and to separate items in a series? (See page 396.)

☐ **11.** Have I correctly punctuated any dialogue? (See pages 144–145.)

☐ **12.** Have I carefully checked my spelling?

# Adding a Title

Make sure to add an attention-getting title. Here are three simple strategies for writing narrative-essay titles.

- **Use a phrase from the paragraph:** Remembering Gramps
- **Use alliteration, the repetition of a consonant sound:** Whale Watchers
- **Use a play on words:** Tripped Up Road Trip

# LO6 Reviewing Narrative Writing

Complete these activities as needed to help you better understand how to write narrative essays.

**Fill In** Description, especially relating to the five senses, makes up a key component of narrative writing. Imagine you are at the carnival in the picture on this page. What sensory details—sights, smells, sounds, and so on—might you experience? Fill in as many as you can in this sensory chart. (See page 137.)

| Sights | Sounds | Smells | Tastes | Textures |
|--------|--------|--------|--------|----------|
|        |        | Answers will vary. |        |          |

Kenneth Sponsler,2010 / Used under license from Shutterstock.com

**Explain** What are the three key elements of narrative writing? What purpose does each element serve?   Answers will vary.

_____

_____

_____

_____

_____

_____

**Sort** Circle the transitions that *show time*. (See page 140.)

(after)     below     (before)     near     (next)     (then)

S.Borisov,2010 / Used under license from Shutterstock.com

# 15

# Classification Essay

Say you're starting a flower garden, but you don't know what type of flowers you want to plant. You've got hundreds of options, and you feel overwhelmed. What should you do? Your best plan might be to break down the wide variety of available flowers into categories, or subgroups, that fit your preferences. Think about the color, shape, style, and growing patterns that will work best in your garden. And, eventually, narrow down your choices to a more manageable list.

A classification essay works in the same way: It breaks down a multifaceted topic into manageable subgroups, so that you can look at the individual components and consider the relationships between them.

## Learning Outcomes

**LO1** Understand classification essays.

**LO2** Plan a classification essay.

**LO3** Write the first draft.

**LO4** Revise the essay.

**LO5** Edit the essay.

**LO6** Reflect on the experience.

## What do you think?

Reread the quotation at the top of the page. How might there be unity in variety? Explain.

Answers will vary.

# LO1 Reviewing a Classification Essay

A classification essay analyzes a topic by breaking it down into different categories or types.

**Read/React** Read the following essay. Then complete the analysis on the next page.

## Five Branches of the United States Armed Forces

The **opening** gets the reader's attention and establishes criteria for dividing the topic into subgroups.

They serve on land, in the air, and at sea. Their bases reside in at least 135 countries. They are made up of 1.4 million brave men and women, protecting the freedom and ideals of the United States. That's just part of the story behind the United States armed forces, the unified military force of the United States. Look closer and you will find five different branches, each carrying out distinct roles in order to serve one unifying goal. [1–6]

The United States Army is the largest and oldest branch of armed forces. Its role is to serve land-based military operations, a responsibility it has had since its formation on June 14, 1775, as the Continental Army during the American Revolution. [7–11]

Shortly thereafter, another branch of military was founded— the United States Navy (then called the Continental Navy) on October 13, 1775. The U.S. Navy is the primary sea branch of the armed forces and is currently the second biggest branch within the armed forces with 332,000 personnel. [12–16]

The **middle paragraphs** describe the subgroups, explain their distinct traits, and show the relationships between them.

The next oldest branch of the armed forces—the United States Marine Corps—is actually a part of the U.S. Navy. Founded on November 10, 1775, the Marine Corps carries out the role of naval infantry, often engaging in amphibious or hybrid warfare. They work closely with but separately from the U.S. Navy. [17–21]

The United States Coast Guard is a fourth branch of the U.S. armed forces. It was founded in 1790 and is responsible for maritime law enforcement as well as maritime search and rescue. Along with being the smallest branch of the military, the USCG is the only branch under the direction of the Department of Homeland Security. All other branches of the armed forces are under the direction of the Department of Defense. [22–27]

The newest branch is the United States Air Force. Once a part of the U.S. Army, the USAF was established as a separate branch in 1947 and is responsible for aerial, space, and cyber warfare. It is the third largest military branch. [28–32]

The **closing** reunites the subgroups for a final look at the topic.

Together the Army, Navy, Marine Corps, Air Force, and Coast Guard make up the United States armed forces. Throughout the last 200 years, each branch has played a role in shaping not only what the United States has become, but also what the world has become. [33–37]

# A Closer Look

**List** Complete the chart below by writing the names of each branch of military, the role of that branch, and details about it, including the year it was founded. The first one has been done for you.

**Branches of U.S. Armed Forces**

| | Definition/Role | Details |
|---|---|---|
| **Subgroup 1** Army | Responsible for land-based military operations | - Founding date: June 14, 1775<br>- Largest branch |
| **Subgroup 2** Navy | Primary sea branch | Founding date: October 13, 1775<br>Second largest branch |
| **Subgroup 3** Marine Corps | Naval infantry | Founding date: November 10, 1775<br>Amphibious or hybrid warfare |
| **Subgroup 4** Coast Guard | Maritime law<br>Maritime search/rescue | Founding date: 1790<br>Smallest branch<br>Only branch reporting to Department of Homeland Security |
| **Subgroup 5** Air Force | Aerial, space, and cyber warfare | Founding date: 1947<br>Originally part of the Army<br>Third largest branch |

**Explain** The writer chose to distinguish each branch (subgroup) by role, size, and founding date. What other features or points could the writer have used to distinguish the different branches of armed forces? Explain.

Answers will vary.

Olga Lyubkina,2010 / Used under license from Shutterstock.com

# LO2 Prewriting: Planning

In your own classification essay, you will explore the categories, or subgroups, of a topic of your choice. These two pages will help you select a topic and gather details about it.

**Explore** Read through the "Essentials of Life" list below. Select four general subject areas you would like to explore. Then, for each subject, write a possible topic. An example has been done for you.

## Essentials of Life

| | | |
|---|---|---|
| food | intelligence | resources |
| clothing | personality | energy |
| shelter | senses | money |
| education | emotions | government |
| work | goals | laws |
| entertainment | health | rights |
| recreation | environment | science |
| religion | plants | measurement |
| family | animals | machines |
| friends | land | tools |
| community | literature | agriculture |
| communication | arts | business |

Answers will vary.

1. **Subject Area:**

   Clothing _____

   **Topic:**

   Types of  Athletic shorts _____

2. **Subject Area:**

   _____

   **Topic:**

   Types of _____

3. **Subject Area:**

   _____

   **Topic:**

   Types of _____

4. **Subject Area:**

   _____

   **Topic:**

   Types of _____

5. **Subject Area:**

   _____

   **Topic:**

   Types of _____

**Select** Review the topics you've listed above and select one that has three to six types (a number you could comfortably cover in a classification essay).

# Researching Your Topic

Once you have selected a topic, you may need to find out more about it. Search Internet sites, encyclopedias, school texts, and other sources as necessary. As you break down your topic into types or categories, consider the following points:

### Types or categories should be . . .

- **exclusive**, which means that one example doesn't fit into more than one category.
- **consistent**, which means that examples of this category have the same traits.

**Organize** In this chart, write your topic within the parentheses. Then list the subgroups, or types, in the first column, define each in the second column, and provide details about each in the third.   Answers will vary.

| Types of (          )  | Definition | Details |
|------------------------|------------|---------|
| **Subgroup 1** | | |
| **Subgroup 2** | | |
| **Subgroup 3** | | |
| **Subgroup 4** | | |

# LO3 Writing: Creating a First Draft

After you have completed planning and gathering, you are ready to start the drafting stage. Provided below is a sample classification essay.

**Read/React** Read the essay, noting how the writer classified the topic into four distinct subgroups.

## To Work Out or Not to Work Out

**Opening paragraph**

**Thesis statement**

The Greek philosopher Plato once said, "Lack of activity destroys the good condition of every human being." The American comedian Phyllis Diller once joked, "My idea of exercise is a good brisk sit." Clearly, different people pursue different levels of physical activity. $_5$

**Subgroup 1**

Diller's attitude best aligns with someone living a "sedentary lifestyle." A person with a sedentary lifestyle exercises fewer than three times per week. This type of lifestyle is linked to weight gain and an increased risk of developing diseases such as type 2 diabetes. $_{10}$

**Subgroup 2**

A second level of physical activity is known simply as "lifestyle active." This level describes a person who performs everyday lifestyle activities such as walking to and from the grocery store, doing yard work, or playing pick-up basketball. Engaging in regular lifestyle activities can help control cholesterol levels and $_{15}$ reduce body fat.

**Subgroup 3**

Someone who follows a cardio-respiratory exercise program for 20 to 60 minutes, three to five days per week, lives a "moderate physical lifestyle," the third level of physical activity. This type of person might be a regular runner, weight lifter, or power walker. $_{20}$ A moderate physical lifestyle helps a person become physically fit while reducing the risk of chronic diseases.

**Subgroup 4**

Finally, the highest level of physical activity is a "vigorous physical lifestyle." People on this level exercise 20 to 60 minutes most days of the week and follow a routine of aerobic exercises, $_{25}$ strength training, and stretching exercises. A vigorous physical lifestyle achieves the same benefits of moderate physical activities, while also promoting a greater level of fitness.

**Closing paragraph**

Many factors contribute to a person's level of physical activity—work environment, family obligations, and other personal $_{30}$ responsibilities. Depending on the time of year, a person may live a moderate physical lifestyle one week and a sedentary lifestyle the next week. What's most important, though, is to live a healthy lifestyle. And a healthy lifestyle requires some level of exercise.

# Creating an Opening Paragraph

The objective of the opening paragraph is to gain the reader's attention, introduce the topic, and present your thesis statement. Here are some strategies for beginning your essay:

- **Set the mood.**

  > They serve on land, in the air, and at sea. Their bases reside in at least 135 countries. They are made up of 1.4 million brave men and women, protecting the freedom and ideals of the United States.

- **Begin with a question.**

  > What makes a baseball so hard to hit?

- **Use a quotation.**

  > American comedian Phyllis Diller once joked, "My idea of exercise is a good brisk sit."

## Writing a Thesis Statement

To create a thesis statement for your essay, follow this formula.

| A Specific Topic | + | Overview of Subgroups | = | Thesis Statement |
|---|---|---|---|---|
| physical activity | | different people pursue different levels | | Different people pursue different levels of **physical activity**. |

**Write** Create your opening paragraph. Start with a sentence that uses one of the strategies above. Then write sentences that build to your thesis statement.

Answers will vary.

**Transition words that classify:**

one type / a second / a third / the last / the simplest / a more complex / an advanced / the most complex / the most common / a less common / a rare / a very rare / the earliest / a later / a recent / the newest

# Creating Middle Paragraphs

**Write**  Refer to the chart on page 153 to help organize the middle paragraphs of your essay. Use the paragraphs to describe the subgroups of your topic and their respective traits. Include a topic sentence in each paragraph and use transitional words or phrases (like those at the left) to help your writing flow.

Answers will vary.

# Creating a Closing Paragraph

The closing paragraph should bring the subgroups together again for a final look at the topic. Consider showing how the subgroups are related to one another, or leave the reader with some other thought.

**Write** Answer the following questions to help you sum up your essay.

1. What characteristics do the subgroups have in common?

   Answers will vary.

2. What is a key difference between the subgroups?

**Write** Create the closing paragraph for your classification essay.

Answers will vary.

**Speaking & Listening**

Have your partner read your essay aloud. Then complete the response sheet together.

# LO4 Revising: Improving the Writing

Revising your first draft involves adding, deleting, rearranging, and reworking parts of your writing. Revision begins with a peer review.

## Peer Review

Sharing your writing at various stages is important, especially when you review and revise a first draft. The feedback that you receive will help you change and improve your essay.

**Respond** Complete this response sheet after reading the first draft of a classmate's essay. Then share the sheet with the writer. (Keep your comments helpful and positive.)  Answers will vary.

---

Essay title: _____

Writer: _____  Reviewer: _____

1. Which part of the essay seems to work best—opening, middle, or closing? Why?

   _____

   _____

2. Which part of the essay needs work—opening, middle, or closing? Why? _____

   _____

   _____

   _____

3. Do the middle paragraphs explain the distinct traits of the subgroups? Explain.

   _____

   _____

   _____

4. Name two of your favorite details.

   _____

   _____

   _____

5. Identify a phrase or two that shows the writer's level of interest.

   _____

   _____

   _____

---

# Clarifying Special Terms

Depending on the topic, your essay may contain special terms or words that are unfamiliar to your reader. Keep this potential problem in mind and always clarify such terms in the text of your essay. Consider the following strategies:

■ **Provide an actual definition.**

> A person with a sedentary lifestyle exercises fewer than three times per week.

■ **Use an appositive before or after the term.**

> The pitcher threw a slider, a pitch that breaks sideways and downward at a slower speed than a straight fastball. (The appositive is set off with a comma and defines the term *slider* in this example.)

■ **Give word clues.**

> The African vuvuzelas blared throughout the stadium, a collective buzz from thousands of plastic horns. (Words like *African, blared, buzz, plastic,* and *horns* help the reader understand what *vuvuzelas* are.)

**Revising in Action:**

Read aloud the unrevised and then the revised version of the following excerpt. Note how the specific words energize the writing.

> Some baseball pitchers will throw a knuckleball *, an extremely slow pitch with little to no spin*.
>
> Tim Wakefield *, a pitcher for the Boston Red Sox,* is known for throwing mostly knuckleballs. Many batters are fooled by this specialty pitch because of its wacky movement.

**Respond** Improve your writing, using the following checklist and your partner's comments on the response sheet. Continue until you can check off each item.

**Ideas**

☐ **1.** Do I focus on one specific topic?
☐ **2.** Do I name and define the types or categories of the topic?
☐ **3.** Do I provide details about the traits of each type?
☐ **4.** Have I clarified any special terms?

**Organization**

☐ **5.** Does my essay have effective opening, middle, and closing paragraphs?
☐ **6.** Do I use transition words and phrases to show the relationship between types?

**Voice**

☐ **7.** Does my voice sound knowledgeable and interested?

**Vocabulary**

**appositive**
a word or phrase that identifies or renames a preceding noun or pronoun

**Insight**

For more practice with comma use, see pages 392–402.

# LO5 Editing: Correcting Your Writing

The main work of editing is correcting your revised draft.

## Commas Used with Extra Information

When words add information that can be removed from a sentence without changing its basic meaning, those words should be set off with commas. Here are three examples:

> Marc Jacobs, a famous American designer, is the creative director for the Louis Vuitton fashion line.
>
> (The appositive adds information about Marc Jacobs.)

> The road construction barrels, which were orange with white stripes, littered the side of the interstate for miles.
>
> (The clause adds a description of the barrels.)

> A cannoli, found at many Italian-American delis, is a popular Sicilian pastry.
>
> (The phrase adds a tip about where you might find cannolis.)

**Comma Practice** Indicate where commas are needed in the following sentences. If no commas are needed, write "correct" on the blank next to the sentence.

1. Internship coordinators, found at most colleges and universities, help students apply for and gain valuable internship experience.                    _____

2. Shakira, a Colombian recording artist, has enjoyed crossover success in the Latin pop and American pop markets.                    _____

3. The famous American architect Frank Lloyd Wright was born in a small farming community in Wisconsin.                    <u>correct</u>

4. In *Slumdog Millionaire,* which won ten Academy Awards, a young man from the slums wins the Indian version of *Who Wants to Be a Millionaire?*                    _____

**Apply** Read the sentences in your classification essay and watch for extra information that ought to be set off with commas. If you find any errors, correct them. (For more information, see page 400.)

# Commas After Introductory Phrases

Use a comma after a long introductory phrase.

## Introductory Phrase

Despite her craving for ice cream, Candace opted for an apple.

**Note:** The comma is usually omitted if the phrase comes at the end of the sentence.

Candace opted for an apple despite her craving for ice cream.

**Note:** You may omit the comma after a short (four or fewer words) introductory phrase unless it is needed to ensure clarity.

At 6:30 a.m. Rita would brew her favorite coffee.

olly.2010 / Used under license from Shutterstock.com

**Comma Practice** Indicate where commas are needed in the following sentences. If no commas are needed, write "correct" on the blank next to the sentence.

1. Even before turning around to check Vince sensed someone was following him. _____

2. At risk of sounding outlandish the smell of chocolate-covered bacon is making my mouth water. _____

3. At midnight Willis decided to call it a night. _correct_

4. After the concert we stopped at a late-night diner for some grub. _correct_

5. On the left side of the tool shed I found the circular saw. _____

6. Eventually this rain should subside. _correct_

7. Before making any harsh judgments you should know I considered all options prior to deciding. _____

8. Based on her preliminary research Hanna felt she was ready to begin drafting an essay. _____

**Apply** Read the sentences in your classification essay, paying special attention to long introductory phrases that ought to be set off with commas. If you find any errors, correct them. (For more information, see page 396.)

# Marking an Essay

Before you finish editing your revised essay, you can practice by editing the following model.

**Editing Practice** Read the following classification essay, looking for problems listed in the checklist on the facing page. Also refer to the list of common errors on page 80. Correct the model using the marks listed to the left. The first correction has been done for you.

## Correction Marks

| | |
|---|---|
| ✄ | delete |
| d ̳ | capitalize |
| ⌀ | lowercase |
| ∧ | insert |
| ⌄̑ | add comma |
| ?∧ | add question mark |
| word ∧ | add word |
| ⊙ | add period |
| ◯ | spelling |
| ∿ | switch |

## Fast Ballers

What makes a baseball so hard to hit? Well, besides being the size of an orange and traveling at faster velocities than vehicles on an interstate, baseballs do funny things in the air, depending on the way their thrown. There are four main types of pitches thrown by baseball players, Each with different speeds and trajectories.

The most frequently thrown pitch is a fastball. As its name suggests, fastball travel at the highest velocity of any pitch. Generally a fastball's trajectry is straight through the air and into the catcher's glove.

A second type of pitch, a changeup, is used to trick hitters into thinking its a fastball. However, the changeup is thrown at a much slower speed and tails slightly downward as it reaches the plate.

A third pitch is called a curveball. It is hard to hit because it travels with topspin that causes it to curve sharply both laterally and downward. A hitter might think a curveball is coming right at them before it curves over the plate and into the strike zone. Because of a curveball's trajectory, its slower than a fastball but faster than a changeup.

A fourth comman pitch is called a slider. The slider is similar to a curveball in that it break laterally and downward as it reaches the batter. However, a slider's break is shorter than a curveball's. It is also thrown at a faster speed than a curveball.

When a pitcher is able to throw all four of these pitches, hitting becomes a guessing game for the batter. if the batter is expecting a fastball but receives a changeup, he or she might swing to early. No wonder baseballs is so hard to hit.

# Correcting Your Essay

Now it's time to correct your own essay.

**Edit** Prepare a clean copy of your essay and use the following checklist to look for errors. Continue working until you can check off each item in the list.

---

### Editing Checklist

**Words**

- [ ] **1.** Have I used specific nouns and verbs? (See page 74.)
- [ ] **2.** Have I used more action verbs than "be" verbs? (See page 348.)

**Sentences**

- [ ] **3.** Have I used sentences with varying beginnings and lengths? (See pages 264, 266.)
- [ ] **4.** Have I combined short choppy sentences? (See page 262.)
- [ ] **5.** Have I avoided improper shifts in sentences? (See pages 314–315.)
- [ ] **6.** Have I avoided fragments and run-ons? (See pages 297–302, 306–307.)

**Conventions**

- [ ] **7.** Do I use correct verb forms (*he saw,* not *he seen*)? (See page 356.)
- [ ] **8.** Do my subjects and verbs agree (*she speaks,* not *she speak*)? (See pages 282–291.)
- [ ] **9.** Have I used the right words (*their, there, they're*)?
- [ ] **10.** Have I capitalized first words and proper nouns and adjectives? (See page 414.)
- [ ] **11.** Have I used commas after long introductory word groups and to set off extra information? (See page 396.)
- [ ] **12.** Have I carefully checked my spelling?

---

# Adding a Title

Make sure to add an attention-getting title. Here are three simple strategies for creating one.

- **Describe the classification:** Five Branches of the United States Armed Forces
- **Think creatively:** To Work Out or Not to Work Out
- **Use a play on words:** Fast Ballers

**Create** Prepare a clean final copy of your essay and proofread it.

Cheryl Casey, 2010 / Used under license from Shutterstock.com

# LO6 Reviewing Classification Writing

Complete these activities as needed to help you better understand how to write classification essays.

**Classify** Study the photo on this page. In the first column of the chart below, break down the peppers into subgroups, or types. Then define each type in the second column and write at least one detail about each in the third.

Answers will vary.

| Types of Peppers | Definition | Details |
|---|---|---|
| **Subgroup 1** | | |
| **Subgroup 2** | | |
| **Subgroup 3** | | |

Victor Medina-San Andrés/Flickr/ Getty Images

**Match** Draw a line from each sentence starter below to the correct description on the right.

1. The opening of a classification essay should . . .

2. The middle of a classification essay should . . .

3. The closing of a classification essay should . . .

■ reconnect the subject and its subgroups and present the reader with a final thought.

■ introduce the topic and lead up to the thesis statement.

■ describe the subgroups and traits relating to those subgroups.

> "The vision must be followed by the venture. It is not enough to stare up the steps—we must step up the stairs."
>
> —Vance Havner

John Lumb,2010 / Used under license from Shutterstock.com

# 16
# Process Essay

From the beginning of this book, you have approached writing as a process. You know that tackling a writing challenge in one giant step won't get the job done. Instead, it takes a series of steps to create a thoughtful and polished piece of writing. As with good writing, many of the great accomplishments we see around us are born out of a process.

By definition a process is a series of actions or operations that produce a particular result. In this chapter, you will describe or explain a process, lay out its steps, and write about it clearly enough for your least knowledgeable reader to understand it.

## Learning Outcomes

LO1 Understand process essays.

LO2 Plan a process essay.

LO3 Write the first draft.

LO4 Revise the essay.

LO5 Edit the essay.

LO6 Reflect on the experience.

### What do you think?

Reread the definition of a process at the beginning of the second paragraph. Describe the steps you take to get ready for school or work in the morning.

Answers will vary.

# LO1 Reviewing a Process Essay

A process essay explains how something works by laying out the specific steps that will take you to a particular result.

**Read/React**  Read the following essay. Then complete the analysis on the next page.

## Making Cheese

The **opening** introduces the topic and gives an overview of the steps.

Can you imagine a pizza without mozzarella? A cheeseburger   *1*
sans cheddar? A wine and cheese party with no cheese platters?
Simply put, cheese packs some powerful eating enjoyment. And
while it comes in an assortment of flavors, textures, and forms,
every cheese begins as high quality fresh milk. From there,   *5*
the various types are tweaked from a common cheese-making
process.

The first **middle paragraph** describes the first few steps.

Cheese making starts by heating the milk to kill off any unsafe
bacteria. The milk comes from a variety of sources—from cows and
goats to sheep and buffalo. Once the milk is heated, a starter culture   *10*
is added to curdle it. The culture contains different enzymes and
bacteria that give cheese its unique flavor. For example, Swiss-
cheese culture contains the bacterium *Propianibacter shermanii,*
while cheddar-cheese culture includes the enzyme *chymosin.* Next,
the cheese sits for a day, until the milk has curdled into solids. The   *15*
solids are called *curds,* while the leftover liquid is called *whey.*

The second **middle paragraph** describes the last few steps.

After the cheese maker separates the curds from the whey, the
process continues by reheating the curds, letting them settle, and
stirring away as much liquid as possible. This step is repeated until
the cheese maker believes the cheese is sufficiently solid. When   *20*
the cheese solidifies, it is poured into molds of different shapes and
sizes. Finally, the cheese is placed in cooler temperatures so that it
can ripen. The total ripening time depends on the cheese type and
the flavor desired by the cheese maker. Some cheese types take a
month to ripen, while others may take just one week. When the   *25*
cheese is ripened, it's ready to eat.

The **closing** revisits the process as a whole.

Cheese is produced in small batches by hand or mass-
produced by machine, but along the way it follows the same process:
heating milk, adding culture, separating the curds from the whey,
reheating, stirring, pouring, and ripening. The result is a food as   *30*
diverse as it is delicious. Behold the power of cheese, indeed.

# A Closer Look

This essay discusses the process of producing cheese. The writer explains each step in chronological order, using transitions to move logically from one step to the next.

**Identity**   Reread the essay on the facing page paying attention to the steps in the process. Then, in the graphic below, briefly describe each step and the transition word (or words) used to introduce it. The first step has been done for you.

**Topic:** Making cheese

| Transitions | Steps |
|---|---|
| **1.** Starts | Heat the milk to kill any bad bacteria. |
| **2.** Once | Add a starter culture. |
| **3.** Next | Let it sit a day to curdle. |
| **4.** After | Reheat and settle repeatedly, to dry the curds. |
| **5.** When | Pour it into molds. |
| **6.** Finally | Place it in a cooler temperature to ripen. |

**Explain**   The writer of this essay clearly shows an interest in the subject in the opening paragraph. What words, phrases, or sentences demonstrate this interest?

Answers will vary.

# LO2 Prewriting: Planning

In your own process essay, you will explain how something works or is made. The topic information below will help you select a process to write about.

## Selecting a Topic

Use the following ideas to generate possible process-essay topics.

Consider a process that . . .
- relates to your major or academic concentration.
- keeps you healthy or unhealthy.
- relates to your favorite entertainment—sports, music, theater, and so on.
- is in the news.
- impacts the world around you.

**Select** On the lines below, list four potential topics for your process essay. They may be topics you know a lot about or ones you need to research more thoroughly. Circle the one you would like to write about.  **Answers will vary.**

1. _____   2. _____

3. _____   4. _____

## Researching a Process

Once you have selected a topic, review what you know about it and, if necessary, supplement your information with additional research.

**Identify** Complete the research questions below.  **Answers will vary.**

**1.** What is the process?_____

**2.** Why is it important? _____

_____

**3.** What steps are needed to complete it?_____

_____

**4.** What is the outcome? _____

_____

# Gathering Details

You can use a time line to gather details about the steps in you process. The following example lists the steps needed to purify drinking water.

**Topic:** Purifying drinking water

**Steps**

1. Pretreatment
2. Coagulation
3. Filtration
4. Disinfection
5. Outcome: Clean drinking water

**Gather** Complete the time line below. Start by writing down the topic of your process essay. Then fill in the steps that will complete the process and bring you to the desired outcome. (Use your own paper if you are writing about a process with more than six steps.)  Answers will vary.

**Topic:** _____

**Steps**

1. _____

2. _____

3. _____

4. _____

5. _____

6. _____

7. **Outcome:** _____

# LO3 Writing: Creating a First Draft

Creating a first draft puts all your planning and gathering into concrete form. Provided below is a sample process essay about water treatment.

**Read/React**  Read the essay, noting how the writer uses the opening paragraph to describe the significance of the process, and then uses the middle paragraphs to explain its steps in chronological order.

## Making Dirty Water Drinkable

**Opening paragraph**

One of the most overlooked luxuries of living in the United States is access to clean drinking water. Statistics show roughly one-eighth of the world's population lacks access to safe water supplies, while as many as 2.5 billion people live without sanitized water. Untreated water is full of unhealthy chemicals and contaminants that, if consumed, lead to uncomfortable and sometimes fatal disease, including dysentery and diarrhea. Water purification plants remove these harmful impurities through a process of pretreatment, coagulation, filtration, and disinfection, making our water safe to drink. *1* ... *5* ... *10*

**First two steps in the process**

The first step in water purification is pretreatment. During pretreatment, water is pumped in from its source and screened to remove any large twigs, leaves, or other debris before reaching the holding tanks. Next, coagulation begins. Coagulation removes dirt and other particles from the water by adding a chemical that forms sticky particles called "floc." The floc combines with dirt particles as the water moves to a sedimentary basin. Once inside the basin, the combined weight of the dirt and floc causes it to sink to the floor as sedimentation. The sedimentation is then removed from the water, giving water its clear, colorless quality. *15* ... *20*

**Final two steps in the process**

While coagulation removes the sedimentation from the water, the filtration phase pushes the remaining particles and unsettled sedimentation through filters of sand or charcoal. Filtration reduces particles in the water by about 90 to 95 percent. Lastly the water is pumped to a disinfection tank. During disinfection, chlorine is added to kill any lingering viruses or bacteria. Some plants also introduce fluorine into the water to prevent tooth decay. After the process is completed, the water is tested for safety and then released from the treatment plant for safe consumption. *25*

**Closing paragraph**

Make no mistake: the process of water purification in treatment plants is vitally important to the health of its consumers. By removing dirt and sludge through pretreatment and coagulation, then filtering the lingering particles, and finally disinfecting with chlorine and other chemicals, water purification plants make certain that the water our bodies desperately need to survive will do its job. *30* ... *35*

# Creating an Opening Paragraph

The objective of the opening paragraph is to gain the reader's interest, introduce the topic, state its importance, and provide a thesis statement that gives an overview of the steps. Here are some strategies for beginning your essay:

**Building Interest:**

- **Find an eye-popping statistic.**

  Roughly one-eighth of the world's population lacks access to safe water supplies, while as many as 2.5 billion people live without sanitized water.

- **Ask a question.**

  Can you imagine a pizza without mozzarella?

- **Make a bold statement.**

  Simply put, cheese packs some powerful eating enjoyment.

# Writing a Thesis Statement

To create a thesis statement for your essay, follow this formula.

**A Specific Process** + **Outcome** = **Thesis Statement**

process of water purification **+** safe drinking water **=** Water purification plants remove harmful impurities through a process of pretreatment, coagulation, filtration, and disinfection, making our water safe to drink.

**Write**  Create your opening paragraph. Start with a sentence that uses one of the strategies above. Then write sentences that build to your thesis statement.

Answers will vary.

# Creating Middle Paragraphs

**Write**  Clearly describe each step in the process. Cover the first few steps in the first middle paragraph and the last few steps in the second middle paragraph. Present the steps in a way that your least knowledgeable reader will be able to follow and understand. Also remember to include topic sentences in your paragraphs and use transitional words or phrases (see page 167) to make the writing flow.

Answers will vary.

# Creating a Closing Paragraph

The closing paragraph should describe the process as a whole, restate the key steps, and provide a closing thought.

**Write** Create the closing paragraph for your process essay.

Answers will vary.

Speaking & Listening

Have your partner read your essay aloud. Then complete the response sheet together.

# L○4 Revising: Improving the Writing

Revising your first draft involves adding, deleting, rearranging, and reworking parts of your writing. Revision begins with a peer review.

## Peer Review

Sharing your writing at various stages is important, especially when you review and revise a first draft. The feedback that you receive will help you change and improve your essay.

**Respond** Complete this response sheet after reading the first draft of a classmate's essay. Then share the sheet with the writer. (Keep your comments helpful and positive.)   Answers will vary.

Essay title: _____

Writer: _____     Reviewer: _____

1. Which part of the essay seems to work best—opening, middle, or closing? Why?

   _____

   _____

   _____

2. Which part of the essay needs work—opening, middle, or closing? Why? _____

   _____

   _____

   _____

   _____

3. Do the middle paragraphs clearly present each step of the process? Explain.

   _____

   _____

   _____

4. Do you understand the process after reading the essay?

   _____

   _____

5. Identify a phrase or two that shows the writer's level of interest.

   _____

   _____

# Using Transitions That Show Time Order

Transitions or linking words connect ideas by showing the relationships between them. In process writing, time-order transition words provide a link between the steps of the process and add coherence to the writing overall. Refer to the following list of transitional words as you revise your essay.

### Transitions That Show Time Order

before, during, after, next, finally, first, second, third, then, later, when, once, while, at, meanwhile

### Revising in Action

Read aloud the unrevised and then revised version of the following excerpt. Note how transitional words tie the steps of the process together while improving the flow of the writing.

The first step in water purification is pretreatment. *During pretreatment,* Water is pumped in from its source. *Next, c*oagulation begins. Coagulation removes dirt and other particles from the water by adding a chemical that forms sticky particles called "floc." . . . *Once inside the basin,* The combined weight of the dirt and floc causes it to sink to the floor as sedimentation.

**Revise** Improve your writing, using the following checklist and your partner's comments on the response sheet. Continue revising until you can check off each item in the list.

### Revising Checklist

**Ideas:**

☐ 1. Do I explain an interesting process?
☐ 2. Do I include all the steps in the process?

**Organization:**

☐ 3. Does the essay have effective opening, middle, and closing paragraphs?
☐ 4. Are the steps in a logical time order?
☐ 5. Have I used transitions to connect my ideas?

**Voice:**

☐ 6. Do I use an informed, respectful voice?
☐ 7. Does my interest in the topic come through?

**Traits**

Transition words signal organization and improve sentence fluency.

# LO5 Editing: Correcting Your Writing

The main work of editing is correcting your revised draft. The next two activities will help you avoid two common errors that occur with modifiers.

## Dangling Modifiers

Dangling modifiers can confuse the reader. Such modifiers describe a word that is not in the sentence.

**Dangling modifier:**

After handing in his paper, the teacher began the lecture.
(It sounds as if the teacher handed in the paper.)

**Corrected:**

After Landon handed in his paper, the teacher began the lecture.

For more practice with fixing dangling and misplaced modifiers, see page 312.

**Editing Practice** Correct any dangling modifiers below by rewriting the sentence. If a sentence contains no modifying error, write a C on the line. (The first one has been done for you.)

1. After radioing for clearance, the plane was landed.

   After radioing for clearance, the pilot landed the plane.

2. While scrambling eggs, the mailcarrier rang the doorbell.

   While I was scrambling eggs, the mail carrier rang the doorbell.

3. After waiting in the lobby for hours, the doctor arrived with an update.

   After we had waited in the lobby for hours, the doctor arrived
   with an update.

4. After we finished the main course, the server wheeled out the dessert tray.

   C

5. Stretching under the car, my tennis ball was retrieved.

   Stretching under the car, I retrieved my tennis ball.

**Apply** Read through your essay, looking for dangling modifiers. Correct any that you find by rewriting the sentence so that the modifier clearly describes the correct word.

# Misplaced Modifiers

Misplaced modifiers are similar to dangling modifiers in that they create a confusing or illogical idea. They occur when a modifier appears to modify the wrong word in a sentence.

> **Misplaced modifier:**
>
> The tornado siren has **nearly** been **blaring** for an hour. (Nearly been ringing?)
>
> **Corrected:**
>
> The tornado siren has been blaring for nearly an hour.

**Editing Practice** Underline the misplaced modifier in each of the following sentences. Then correct the error by rewriting the sentence. (The first one has been done for you.)

1. That sedan is my favorite car in the showroom <u>with the shiny blue paint</u>.

   *That sedan with the shiny blue paint is my favorite car in the showroom.*

2. The soda is my first choice <u>with the most caffeine</u>.

   The soda with the most caffeine is my first choice.

3. The car's headlights <u>nearly</u> turned on after three miles.

   The car's headlights turned on after nearly three miles.

4. Please review the report on global warming <u>enclosed</u>.

   Please review the enclosed report on global warming.

**Apply** Read through your essay, checking for misplaced modifiers. Correct any that you find by rewriting the sentence so that the modifier is placed next to the appropriate word.

# Marking an Essay

Before you finish editing your revised essay, you can practice by editing the following model.

**Editing Practice**  Read the following process essay, looking for problems listed in the checklist on the facing page. Also refer to the list of common errors on page 80. Correct the model using the marks to the left. The first correction has been done for you.

## Correction Marks

| | |
|---|---|
| ⌒ | delete |
| d | capitalize |
| Ø | lowercase |
| ∧ | insert |
| ⌃ | add comma |
| ? | add question mark |
| word | add word |
| ⊙ | add period |
| ◯ | spelling |
| ⌢ | switch |

## Fighting the Flu

Flu season is a bummer. For some people, ~~its~~ it's downright dangerous. 1
Every year from November through April, some 60 million Americans will
contract the flu bug. Many people opt to receive a yearly flu vaccine, which
reduce there (s) chances of getting the flu. The type of influenza vaccine given out
each year ~~are~~ is created through a multifaceted process. 5

The first step is surveyllance⃝ Throughout the year, scientists survey the
globe to predict which strains of the influenza virus will dominate the next flu
season. A vaccine can protect against three different strains, so this step helps
decide which strains to put in the vaccine. Next, the World Health Organization
confirms the dominant strains and submits ~~their~~ its recommendation to the Food 10
and drug Administration (FDA). The FDA then distributes seeds of the three
strains to manufacturers for production.

After surveillance and strain selection, the manufacturing of vaccines
begins. In this step, each virous⃝ strain is produced separately. Later combined
to make one vaccine. Manufacturing begins by injecting millions of chicken eggs 15
with the virus strains, which develop. The virus fluid is then given a chemical
treatment, so that the virus is disrupted and will stop spreading. What's left
of the strain is combined. With the other two strains. Lastly, the FDA tests the
vaccine concentrate to make sure it is acceptable for immunization.

The result is an influenza vaccine that is distributed in viles⃝ and syringes 20
to clinics throughout the world during flu season. After the vaccine is injected,
it takes about two weeks for a body to develop immunity to the three strains.
When flu season ends, the process of creating next year's vaccine begins
again.

# Correcting Your Essay

Now it's time to correct your own essay.

**Edit**  Create a clean copy of your essay and use the following checklist to look for errors. Continue working until you can check off each item in the list.

---

### Editing Checklist

**Words**

☐ **1.** Have I used specific nouns and verbs? (See page 74.)

☐ **2.** Have I used more action verbs than "be" verbs? (See page 348.)

**Sentences**

☐ **3.** Have I varied the beginnings and lengths of sentences? (See pages 264, 266.)

☐ **4.** Have I combined short choppy sentences? (See page 262.)

☐ **5.** Have I avoided improper shifts in sentences? (See pages 314–315.)

☐ **6.** Have I avoided fragments and run-ons? (See pages 297–302, 306–307.)

**Conventions**

☐ **7.** Do I use correct verb forms (*he saw,* not *he seen*)? (See page 356.)

☐ **8.** Do my subjects and verbs agree (*she speaks,* not *she speak*)? (See pages 282–291.)

☐ **9.** Have I used consistent verb tense in all steps? (See page 314.)

☐ **10.** Have I used the right words (*their, there, they're*)?

☐ **11.** Have I capitalized first words and proper nouns and adjectives? (See page 414.)

☐ **12.** Have I used commas after long introductory word groups? (See page 396.)

☐ **13.** Have I carefully checked my spelling?

---

# Adding a Title

Make sure to add an attention-getting title. Here are two simple strategies for creating one.

- **Use alliteration:** Fighting the Flu
- **Describe the process:** Making Cheese; Making Dirty Water Drinkable

**Create**  Prepare a clean copy of your essay and carefully proofread it.

# LO6 Reviewing Process Writing

Complete these activities as needed to help you better understand how to write process essays.

**Organize** Think about your professional goals. What do you want to do? Where do you want to work? How can you get there? In the graphic below, identify your goal and lay out five steps to achieving it. For each step, write a transition word or phrase that links the first steps to the second and so on. (See page 175.)

**Goal:** _Answers will vary._

| Transitions | Steps |
| --- | --- |
| 1 | |
| 2 | |
| 3 | |
| 4 | |
| 5 | |

**Explain** In your own words, explain the difference between a dangling modifier and a misplaced modifier. Give an example of each error and show how you would correct it. (See pages 176–177.)

Answers will vary.

> "The murals in restaurants are on par with the food in museums."
>
> —Peter De Vries

# 17

# Comparison-Contrast Essay

The photo above is full of contrasts: bare glass versus painted brick, straight lines versus curves and jags, tan walls versus an explosion of color, architecture versus painting. The photo also contains some surprising comparisons. The building and the mural both serve the neighborhood. There are even buildings painted in the mural.

By looking at the similarities and differences between two things, you can come to understand both things better. An essay that examines similarities and differences is called a comparison-contrast essay.

This chapter will guide you through the process of writing an essay that compares and contrasts two places that you know well.

## What do you think?

What similarities and differences are there between artwork and food?

Answers will vary.

## Learning Outcomes

**LO1** Understand comparison-contrast essays.

**LO2** Plan a comparison-contrast essay.

**LO3** Write the first draft.

**LO4** Revise the essay.

**LO5** Edit the essay.

**LO6** Reflect on the experience.

# LO1 Reviewing a Comparison Essay

A **comparison-contrast** essay shows the similarities and differences between two subjects. In the following essay, a writer compares his bedroom to his sister's.

**Read/React**  Read the following essay. Then complete the analysis on the next page.

## Life in a War Zone

The **opening** catches the reader's interest and leads to the thesis statement.

"How do you ever find anything in here?" my sister asks. We're looking for her cell phone, which I borrowed last night, and which I left in my room. "It's like a bomb went off." She's right. Compared to Amaya's room, mine is a disaster. Maybe that's because I'm a guy. Maybe that's because I only sleep there. The differences between my room and Amaya's tell a lot about who we are.  *1*

The first **middle paragraph** describes one subject.

I couldn't survive in my sister's room. For one thing, it's pink. She's three years younger than me, and she's still into pink, though the princess posters are down and posters of pop stars cover everything. It's like a hundred people staring at you. Amaya has three chests of drawers, neatly closed, and a closet full of clothes, some of which belong to her friends. She's also got Grandma's old vanity, with three big mirrors and little drawers for makeup. Weirdest of all, she manages to get dirty clothes in the hamper, which means I can see the floor.  *10*  *15*

The second **middle paragraph** describes the other subject.

Now, Amaya couldn't survive in my room, either. The walls are black. I painted them that way in protest when Amaya painted hers pink. I've got no posters on the walls, only some old high-school art projects I did and never took down. There's just one chest of drawers, and the drawers are never closed, and the clothes are hanging out or stacked on top. I don't have a hamper, so my floor is the hamper. The only important thing in my room is my bed, because that's where I crash. Of course, the bed is never made.  *20*

The **closing** sums up the comparison and contrast, providing an additional perspective.

Our two different rooms show our different personalities. Amaya thinks a lot about how she looks and what people think of her. She also spends a lot of time in her room. I don't care about my looks. Engines are my thing, building them and fixing them, which means grease, which means fashion can't be a priority. Amaya might think my room is a health hazard, but I'd die in her room. (By the way, we did find her cell phone, not because I knew where I put it, but because I decided to call it.)  *25*  *30*

# A Closer Look

This essay used a **subject-by-subject pattern of organization**, describing one subject before moving to the other. This organizational pattern works best when focusing on the contrasts between two subjects.

**Analyze**  Reread the essay on the facing page. As you do, use the following T-chart to analyze the essay. In the first column, write details that describe the author's room. In the second column, write details that describe his sister's room.

**Vocabulary**

**subject-by-subject pattern of organization**
a pattern in which one subject is described before moving on to the other

| Author's Room | Sister's Room |
|---|---|
| Answers will vary. | |

**Explain**  The writer of the essay creates a parallel description of his sister's room and his own room. What do you think a "parallel description" is?

Answers will vary.

_____

_____

_____

_____

# LO2 Prewriting: Planning

In your own essay, you, too, will compare and contrast two places that you know well. Because you will be using subject-by-subject organization, choose two places with interesting contrasts. The activity below will help you select two places to write about.

## Selecting a Topic

**Select** After each general heading, write the names of two specific places you know enough about to compare and contrast. Then select the two places you would most like to write about in your essay.

| | | |
|---|---|---|
| Buildings | 1. Answers will vary. | 2. _____ |
| Businesses | 1. _____ | 2. _____ |
| Natural wonders | 1. _____ | 2. _____ |
| Neighborhoods | 1. _____ | 2. _____ |
| Restaurants | 1. _____ | 2. _____ |
| Rooms | 1. _____ | 2. _____ |

## Describing the Places

**Describe** Answer each question below, jotting down details about the two places.

1. What three adjectives best describe this place?

   Place 1: _____Answers will vary._____

   Place 2: _____

2. What is the main feature of this place?

   Place 1: _____

   Place 2: _____

3. What is the feeling you get in this place?

   Place 1: _____

   Place 2: _____

4. Why do you want to write about this place?

   Place 1: _____

   Place 2: _____

# Gathering Details

A Venn diagram will help you gather more details as you plan your comparison-contrast essay. The following diagram compares and contrasts two restaurants, listing unique details about each as well as similarities.

**Venn Diagram**

Similarities

**Bejing Cafe**
Chinese food
paper lanterns
Formica tables
booths
bright
lunchtime
carryout
loud
TV playing
cheap

good food
friendly people
clean space
strong spices
fortune cookies
chopsticks

**Bangkok Garden**
Thai food
paintings
tablecloths
chairs/tables
dark
nighttime
dine in
quiet
fountain
expensive

**Gather** Complete the Venn diagram below. Write the name of one place in one circle and the name of the other place in the other. Next, list the details specific to each place. In the overlapping part, write the things that the two places have in common. Answers will vary.

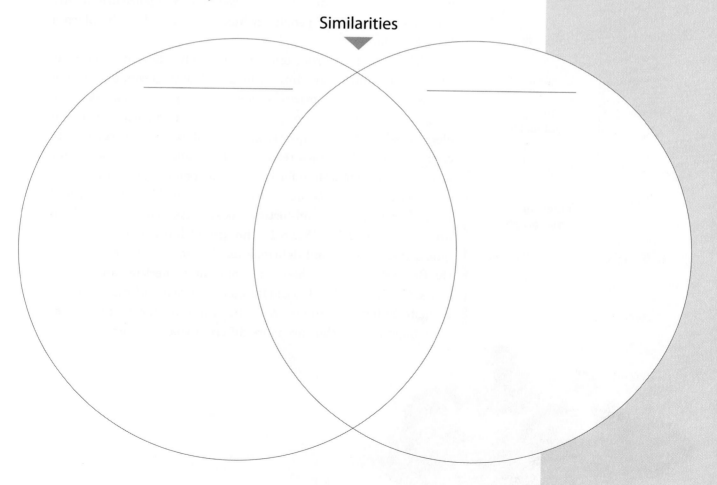

Similarities

# LO3 Writing: Creating a First Draft

Creating a first draft puts all of your planning and gathering into concrete form. Provided below is a sample essay that is organized subject by subject.

**Read/React** Read the essay, noting how the writer created an effective opening and closing for the subject-by-subject comparison.

## Two Tastes of Asia

**Opening paragraph**

What's the difference between Chinese and Thai food? That's _1_ what I wondered when a Thai restaurant opened just down the street from my favorite Chinese restaurant. Soon, I had two favorites. <u>The difference between Chinese and Thai cuisine is only the start of the differences between the Beijing Café and the _5_ Bangkok Garden.</u>

**Thesis statement**

**Subject 1**

The Beijing Café has been my favorite because of its inexpensive food and bright, busy atmosphere. The food is excellent, from the sizzling Chairman Mao's chicken to the extra spicy Szechuan vegetables, and lunch portions are priced below $5. _10_ Such prices mean the restaurant has basic decorations like paper lanterns and a utilitarian interior, with Formica tables and plastic booths. The fluorescent lights overhead make the place bright, and the constant traffic of people on lunch break makes the place a loud, busy hangout. _15_

**Subject 2**

The Bangkok Garden offers a completely different experience. The food is similar to Chinese food, but with coconut milk and different spices. The prices, though, are higher, partly because Bangkok Garden is more of a dinner place. The walls are covered in elegant paintings and tapestries, and candles give a warm glow to _20_ cloth-covered tables. As a result, the Bangkok Garden is a quieter spot, more for dates than for high-schoolers on a lunch break.

**Closing paragraph**

Both restaurants have great food and friendly staff, and both offer chopsticks and fortune cookies. As I've said, they both are favorites of mine. When I'm hungry at lunchtime and need a _25_ quick, inexpensive, and delicious meal, I go with friends over to the Beijing Café. And when I'm hungry at dinnertime and want a romantic dinner, I head to the Bangkok Garden. At first, it seemed a waste to have a Chinese restaurant and a Thai restaurant so close together, but they are more different than they are alike. _30_

# Creating an Opening Paragraph

The opening paragraph needs to capture the reader's attention and introduce your thesis statement. Here are some strategies for beginning your essay.

**Opening Strategies:**

- **Start with a surprising statement.**
  My two favorite restaurants feature food from the other side of the world.
- **Begin with a question.**
  What's the difference between Chinese and Thai food?
- **Use a quotation.**
  "You will soon have two favorites," read the fortune cookie.
- **Share an anecdote.**
  The first time I walked into Bangkok Garden, I was nervous. . . .

# Writing a Thesis Statement

To create a thesis statement for your essay, follow this formula.

| Topic | + | Compare/Contrast | = | Thesis Statement |
|---|---|---|---|---|
| Two places, Beijing Café and Bangkok Garden | + | The difference in cuisine is only the start | = | The difference between Chinese and Thai cuisine is only the start of the differences between the Beijing Café and the Bangkok Garden. |

**Write** Create your opening paragraph. Start with a sentence that uses one of the strategies above. Then write sentences that build to your thesis statement.

Answers will vary.

# Creating Middle Paragraphs

**Write** Refer to the Venn diagram you completed on page 185 as you develop the middle two paragraphs of your essay. Use one paragraph to describe the first place and another to describe the second place, creating topic sentences for each. Use the transitional words at the left to make your writing flow.

PeppPic, 2010/used under license from www.shutterstock.com

Answers will vary.

## Traits

**Transitions that compare:**

as / as well / also / both / in the same way / much as / much like / one way / like / likewise / similarly

**Transitions that contrast:**

although / even though / by contrast / but / however / on the other hand / otherwise / though / still / while / yet

# Creating a Closing Paragraph

The closing paragraph of your essay should sum up the comparison and contrast and provide a final thought for the reader.

**Write** Answer the following questions to help you sum up your essay.

1. What key similarity do the two places exhibit?

   Answers will vary.

   _____

2. What is the key difference between the two places?

   _____

   _____

3. What have I learned from writing this essay?

   _____

   _____

**Write** Create the closing paragraph for your comparison-contrast essay.

Answers will vary.

_____

_____

_____

_____

_____

_____

_____

_____

_____

_____

_____

_____

_____

**Speaking & Listening**

Have your partner read your essay aloud. Then complete the response sheet together.

# LO4 Revising: Improving the Writing

Revising your first draft involves adding, deleting, rearranging, and reworking parts of your writing. Revision begins with a peer review.

## Peer Review

Sharing your writing at various stages is important, especially when you review and revise a first draft. The feedback that you receive will help you change and improve your essay.

**Respond** Complete this response sheet after reading the first draft of a classmate's essay. Then share the sheet with the writer. (Keep your comments helpful and positive.) **Answers will vary.**

Essay title: _____

Writer: _____ Reviewer: _____

1. Which part of the essay seems to work best—opening, middle, or closing? Why?

   _____

   _____

   _____

   _____

2. Which part of the essay needs work—opening, middle, or closing? Why? _____

   _____

   _____

3. Which contrasting points about the two subjects caught your attention? Name three.

   a. _____

   b. _____

   c. _____

4. Name two favorite details.

   a. _____

   b. _____

5. Identify a phrase or two that shows the writer's level of interest.

   _____

   _____

   _____

# Adding Sensory Details

Your essay will be stronger if you show similarities and differences, not just tell about them. Consider the sensory details listed below and used to describe one of the restaurants in the essay on page 186. Build your own chart of sensory details to enhance your writing.

| Senses | Sensory Detail |
|---|---|
| Sight | paper lanterns, bright, fluorescents |
| Hearing | sizzle, loud, traffic |
| Smell | chicken, szechuan vegetables |
| Taste | extra spicy |
| Touch | plastic booths |

**Revising in Action**

Read aloud the unrevised and revised version of the following excerpt. Note how adding sensory details makes the description much richer.

The food is excellent, from the *sizzling* Chairman Mao's chicken to the *extra spicy* Szechuan

vegetables, and lunch portions are priced below $5. Such prices mean the

restaurant has basic decorations *like paper lanterns* and a utilitarian interior, with *Formica* tables

*plastic* and booths. . . .

**Revise** Improve your writing, using the following checklist and your partner's comments on the response sheet. Continue revising until you can check off each item in the list.

**Ideas**

☐ **1.** Do I compare two places?

☐ **2.** Do I include sensory details that make the places come to life?

**Organization**

☐ **3.** Does my opening capture the reader's interest and present a thesis statement?

☐ **4.** Have I used a subject-by-subject pattern in the middle part?

☐ **5.** Have I used transitions to connect my sentences?

☐ **6.** Does my closing sum up the comparison and contrast effectively?

**Voice**

☐ **7.** Do I sound knowledgeable about my subjects?

☐ **8.** Is my interest obvious to the reader?

**Insight**

Note that plural nouns often end in *s*, but plural verbs usually do not. Also note that only present tense verbs and *be* verbs have both singular and plural forms.

# LO5 Editing: Correcting Your Writing

The main work of editing is correcting your revised first draft.

## Correcting Subject-Verb Agreement

A verb must agree in number with the subject of the sentence. If the subject is singular, the verb must be singular. If the subject is plural, the verb must be plural. When a sentence has two or more subjects joined by *and,* the verb should be plural. When a sentence has two or more subjects joined by *or* or *nor,* the verb should agree with the last subject.

**Agreement Practice**   In the following sentences, correct the subject-verb agreement errors by deleting the wrong verb forms and writing the correct verbs above.

1. My old car ~~have~~ has a stick shift and ~~are~~ is really loud above 55 m.p.h.

2. My new car ~~are~~ is an automatic.

3. Both the new car and the old car ~~is~~ are ice blue.

4. The new one ~~are~~ is a Prius, but the old one ~~are~~ is a Taurus.

5. The Prius ~~have~~ has four speakers, but the Taurus ~~have~~ has just two.

6. Either the Prius or the Taurus ~~were~~ was built in the United States.

7. The Prius and the Taurus ~~has~~ have front-wheel drive.

8. My brother want the Prius, but either he or my sister ~~get~~ gets the Taurus.

9. A car ~~become~~ becomes your best friend when you commute.

10. Both my brother and my sister ~~needs~~ need a car for their jobs.

**Apply**   Read your comparison-contrast essay and watch for agreement errors. If you find any, correct them. (For more information, see page 282.)

# Agreement with *I* and *You*

The pronouns *I* and *you* sometimes take plural-form verbs, even though they are singular. Review the examples below.

**Agreement Formulas**

Correct: Plural verbs agree with *I* and *you*.

I look and see you. You smile at me.

Incorrect: Most singular verbs do not agree with *I* and *you*.

I looks and sees you. You smiles at me.

**Note:** The pronoun *I* takes the singular verbs *am* and *was*. Do not use *I* with *be* or *is*.

Correct: The singular verbs *am* and *was* agree with *I*.

I am happy. I was wanting to help. I am eager to lend a hand.

Incorrect: The verbs *are, is,* or *were* do not agree with *I*.

I are happy. I were wanting to help. I is eager to lend a hand.

**Agreement Practice** In the following sentences, correct the subject-verb agreement errors by deleting the wrong forms and writing the correct verbs above.

1. I ~~keeps~~ keep a balcony garden at my apartment.
2. You ~~is~~ are tasting some of the fruits I ~~grows~~ grow in my garden.
3. I ~~be~~ am especially good at growing tomatoes.
4. You ~~looks~~ look surprised that I ~~grows~~ grow tomatoes on a balcony.
5. I ~~has~~ have pots for scallions, carrots, and radishes, too.
6. I ~~thinks~~ think you ~~is~~ are the first person, besides me, to eat from my garden.
7. You ~~has~~ have never tasted such tomatoes, ~~has~~ have you?
8. I ~~be~~ am proud of this garden, as you ~~knows~~ know from my expression.
9. You ~~seems~~ seem amazed that I ~~raises~~ raise such good produce on a balcony!
10. I ~~works~~ work hard, but I ~~enjoys~~ enjoy it.

**Apply** Read your comparison-contrast essay and watch for agreement errors with *I* and *you*. If you find any, correct them. (For more information, see page 286.)

## Marking an Essay

Before you finish editing your revised essay, practice editing the following model.

**Editing Practice** Read this comparison-contrast essay, looking for problems listed in the checklist on the facing page. Also refer to the list of common errors on page 80. Correct the model using the marks listed to the left. One correction has been done for you.

### Correction Marks

| | |
|---|---|
| ⌿ | delete |
| d | capitalize |
| ⌀ | lowercase |
| ∧ | insert |
| ⌃ | add comma |
| ? | add question mark |
| *word* ∧ | add word |
| ⊙ | add period |
| ◯ | spelling |
| ∼ | switch |

### A Commuter's Best Friend

I ~~spends~~ *spend* much of my day in my car, an ice-blue Toyota Prius. Its a hybrid   1

which means it's much better for my commute to school than my old Taurus.

Still, I loved that old beater. It carried me safely and faithfully, Through many

winters. Aside from being the same color, my new Prius and my old Taurus

couldn't be more different.   5

The Taurus was a fifteen-year-old workhorse it had four doors, room for

six, and a trunk to hold all their stuff. The interior *was* is no-frills, with manual

windows, a stereo and tape deck, and two speakers. Nothing *was* is digital. In its

*was* last years, the Taurus ~~been~~ leaking every fluid I put in it, but still it soldiered

on—getting probably twenty miles to the gallon.   10

The Prius is brand new and a little delicate. It weighs about half as

much as the Taurus, and though it has four doors, it really has room only for

four people. It has power everything and a GPS ◯navagation◯ system. As I back

up the Prius, the digital console even shows me a picture of what's behind me.

*T* this hybrid is super quiet in the city and gets about twice the mileage of the   15

Taurus.

I think cars have souls, and my *T* taurus was a good friend to me. It read

me a lot of books on tape, and it never left me stranded when I needed it. I'm

still getting used to this Prius, and I hope we'll be friends, too. Heaven knows,

we spend plenty of time together.   20

# Correcting Your Essay

Now it's time to correct your own essay.

**Edit** Prepare a clean copy of your essay and use the following checklist to look for errors. Continue working until you can check off each item in the list.

---

**Words**

- ☐ **1.** Have I used specific nouns and verbs? (See page 74.)
- ☐ **2.** Have I used more action verbs than "be" verbs? (See page 348.)

**Sentences**

- ☐ **3.** Have I used sentences with varying beginnings and lengths? (See pages 264, 266.)
- ☐ **4.** Have I combined short choppy sentences? (See page 262.)
- ☐ **5.** Have I avoided improper shifts in sentences? (See pages 314–315.)
- ☐ **6.** Have I avoided fragments and run-ons? (See pages 297–302, 306–307.)

**Conventions**

- ☐ **7.** Do I use correct verb forms (*he saw,* not *he seen*)? (See page 356.)
- ☐ **8.** Do my subjects and verbs agree (*she speaks,* not *she speak*)? (See pages 282–291.)
- ☐ **9.** Have I used the right words (*their, there, they're*)?
- ☐ **10.** Have I capitalized first words and proper nouns and adjectives? (See page 414.)
- ☐ **11.** Have I used commas after long introductory word groups and to set off extra information? (See page 396.)
- ☐ **12.** Have I carefully checked my spelling?

---

**WAC**

You can use this checklist for editing your writing in any class.

# Adding a Title

Make sure to add an attention-getting title. Here are three simple strategies for creating one.

- ■ **Use a phrase from the essay:** Cars Have Souls
- ■ **Point to a similarity or difference:** Great Food, Worlds Apart
- ■ **Use the word "versus":** Pink Versus Black

**Create** Prepare a clean final copy of your essay and proofread it.

# L○6 Reviewing Comparison Writing

Complete these activities as needed to help you better understand how to write comparison-contrast essays.

**Compare/Contrast** Consider the woman and child in this photograph. How are they alike? How are they different? Fill in the following Venn diagram, describing the two people. **Answers will vary.**

Paul Matthew Photography 2010/used under license from www.shutterstock.com

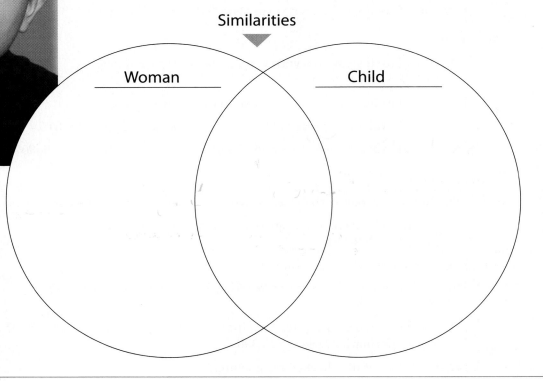

Similarities

Woman          Child

**Match** For each organizational pattern below, draw a line to connect it to its description.

1. Similarities-differences

2. Point-by-point

3. Subject-by-subject

- an organizational pattern focusing first on one subject and then on the other

- a pattern in which one point of comparison is discussed for both subjects before moving on to the next point

- an organizational pattern dealing with how subjects are alike and how they are different

**Sort** Circle transitions that *contrast*:

(although)    as well    like    much as    (otherwise)    (while)    similarly

"The cause is hidden. The effect is visible to all."

—Ovid

Julia Christe/fstop/Corbis

# 18

# Cause-Effect Essay

*Why?* It's such a simple word, but it digs into the deepest questions. When you ask *why,* you are searching for the cause of something. And there are different causes. A mom who asks why her son has cancer likely needs a different answer than a researcher who asks the same question.

This chapter is all about asking *why* in the form of an essay. You'll read essays that explore the causes and effects of phenomena in the world, and you'll write a similar essay yourself. All the while, keep asking *why?*

## Learning Outcomes

**LO1** Understand cause-effect essays.

**LO2** Plan a cause-effect essay.

**LO3** Write the first draft.

**LO4** Revise the essay.

**LO5** Edit the essay.

**LO6** Reflect on the experience.

### What do you think?

What are the possible causes of the fire above? What are the likely effects?

Answers will vary.

# L◯1 Reviewing a Cause-Effect Essay

A cause-effect essay shows indicates why something happens (the causes) and what results (the effects). In the following essay, a writer looks at the causes and effects of a spicy diet.

**Read/React** Read the following essay. Then complete the analysis on the next page.

## Why Eat That Stuff?

The **opening** catches the reader's attention and leads to the thesis.

I love spicy food. In fact, I have a theory that food gets better the closer you get to the equator. At the poles, people eat seal blubber and lutefisk, but at the equator, people eat tacos and teriyaki, curry and jalapenos. People who don't like spicy foods wonder what all the fuss is about. There are many reasons people use spices in their foods, and many benefits from doing so.   1   5

The first **middle paragraph** discusses causes.

The main reasons for using spice are to make food taste better and to help preserve it. Without salt, pepper, and other basic spices, foods taste bland. In the Middle Ages, explorers like Marco Polo set up trade routes to get desperately needed spices for European foods. Some spices were worth their weight in gold. These spices didn't grow in northern climates, and they weren't needed as much for food preservation as in the equatorial regions, but people still wanted them for taste.   10

The second **middle paragraph** discusses effects.

New studies show that spicy foods also have surprising health benefits. A recent study published in the *British Journal of Medicine* showed that women who added hot peppers to their food ate fewer calories in later meals than women who didn't. At the University of California, Los Angeles, scientists found that the substance curcumin, which makes tumeric yellow, clears plaque out of brains, helping stop Alzheimer's disease. And at the State University of New York, researchers found that capsaicin—what makes hot peppers hot—causes endorphins to be released, making the eater feel happy. Other studies show that capsaicin might even help kill off cancer cells in the digestive tract.   15   20   25

The **closing** sums up the causes and ties them back to the opening.

So, when I order a Szechuan chicken lunch special, extra hot, why do I do it? Well, partly it's because of the taste—I've grown to really love hot food. Partly it's for the health benefits that I'm getting eating it. But, to be honest, partly it's because I like to see the look of horror on my friends' faces when I start sweating but keep shoveling it in.   30

**Vocabulary**

**lutefisk**
pickled fish; traditional Norwegian dish

**teriyaki**
sweet soy sauce used on many Japanese foods

**curry**
hot spice for Indian and Middle-Eastern foods

**curcumin**
coloring agent in tumeric

**plaque**
unhealthy buildup of material

**capsaicin**
substance that makes hot peppers hot

**endorphins**
natural pain killer released by the body

**Szechuan**
spicy type of food from the Szechuan region of China

# A Closer Look

This essay first looks at causes of eating spicy foods, and then looks at effects. This pattern works best for an essay that focuses equally on both—cause and effect.

**Analyze** Reread the essay on the facing page. As you do, fill in the cause-effect chart below. On the left, write causes of eating spicy food and draw lines to connect them. On the right, write effects of eating spicy foods. Start with the causes and effects in the essay, but feel free to add causes and effects of your own.

| Causes | Effects |
|---|---|
| Answers may include . . . <br> • Improved taste <br> • Food preservation <br> • *And student thoughts* | Answers may include . . . <br> • Reduce calorie intake <br> • Clear plaque from the brain to combat Alzheimer's <br> • Release endorphins for pleasure <br> • Kill cancer cells in the digestive tract <br> • *And student thoughts* |

**Explain** Do you like to eat spicy foods or not? Explain why you do or do not like to eat spicy foods. Describe the effects you experience if you eat something spicy.

Answers will vary.

# LO2 Prewriting: Planning

You will also be writing a cause-effect essay about some lifestyle choice. You need a topic that interests you and that you know a good deal about—or are willing to find out about. You also need a topic that has specific causes and effects.

## Selecting a Topic

**Brainstorm** In each column below, brainstorm possible topics for your cause-effect essay. Sample topics have been provided in each category. Try to think of three or four more topics in each. Then select one topic that you would like to explore, tracing causes and effects. Answers will vary.

**Lifestyle Choices**

| Eating | Activities | Style | Pastimes | Habits |
|---|---|---|---|---|
| vegetarianism | rock climbing | dreadlocks | suduko | smoking |
| going w/out breakfast | line-dancing | bald-head | zumba | drinking |
| not eating after 6PM | online dating Chatting | shave / bright colors /- | line dancing Salsa bowling exercising | |

**Freewrite** After you select a topic that you would like to write a cause-effect essay about, freewrite about the topic. Write about causes of it and effects from it. Then review your freewriting to make sure this is a topic you want to explore. Otherwise, choose a new topic and freewrite about it.

Answers will vary.

# Gathering Details

As you gather details about your topic, think of what you already know and what you need to find out. Do whatever research it takes for you to find out about your topic. Then complete a cause-effect chart, like the one below, listing the causes and effects of your topic.

---

**Cause-Effect Chart**

**Topic:** *Vegetarianism*

| Causes | Effects |
|--------|---------|
| Concern for animals | Vegans vs. ovo-lacto |
| Opposition to "factory farming" | Greater awareness |
| Healthful lifestyle | Greater health |
| Home-grown food | More sustainable lifestyle |
| Personal preference | Need for proteins |
| Peer pressure/social reasons | Struggles in society |

---

**Gather** Complete the following cause-effect chart by writing your topic at the top and listing causes and effects in their columns. Answers will vary.

---

**Cause-Effect Chart**

**Topic:** _____

| Causes | Effects |
|--------|---------|
|        |         |

---

# LO3 Writing: Creating a First Draft

Creating a first draft puts all of your planning and gathering into concrete form. Provided below is a sample essay that is organized subject by subject.

**Read/React** Read the essay, noting how the writer created an effective opening and closing for the cause-effect essay.

## Herbivore, Carnivore, or Omnivore?

**Opening paragraph**

**Thesis statement**

"We've spent thousands of years getting to the top of the food chain, so why go back to eating leaves?" That's what people sometimes ask vegans and vegetarians, wondering why anyone would choose that kind of diet. <u>Vegetarians have many reasons for choosing a meat-free diet, but the diet results in the same basic benefits.</u>

**Causes**

Every vegetarian is unique, with unique reasons for eating what they eat. Many see animals as more than meat—creatures with intelligence and feelings. These vegetarians don't like the idea of killing animals for food, especially not in the overcrowded and inhumane factory farms of today. Other vegetarians reject modern American eating habits, with too much meat and too few vegetables. The US Department of Agriculture recommends that people "go lean on protein" and eat even less fat. However, the average American eats 16 percent of calories in proteins and 44 percent in fat. Vegetarians seek a better diet and a more sustainable lifestyle. And for some, it's just a matter of personal preference. They just would rather have a salad.

**Effects**

For most vegetarians, their choice has very positive effects. Vegetarians have to think about what they eat and where it comes from, and therefore they tend to eat better quality food and less of it. As a result, vegetarians are often slimmer than omnivores and less prone to arteriosclerosis and colon cancer—caused by fatty red meats. Vegetarians feel they live a more sustainable lifestyle, with less impact on the natural world. Still, vegans and vegetarians have their struggles. Many restaurants have meat in just about every dish, including soups and salads, making it a challenge to eat out. Ads and consumer culture also push vegetarians to eat meat. And vegetarians have to be careful to find proteins that can replace those that others get from eating meat.

**Closing paragraph**

The vegetarian lifestyle offers numerous benefits physically and spiritually to a person who chooses it. But the lifestyle isn't for everyone. People with poor impulse control will have a hard time resisting the flow of society at large. And growing children and adolescents must be careful to get enough of the proteins and fats they need to keep growing. The lifestyle doesn't work for everyone, but some people wouldn't have it any other way.

# Creating an Opening Paragraph

The opening paragraph needs to capture the reader's attention and introduce your thesis statement. Here are some strategies.

**Opening Strategies:**

- **Start with an interesting quotation:**
  "We've spent thousands of years getting to the top of the food chain, so why go back to eating leaves?"

- **Begin with a startling fact:**
  For more than four millennia, the "meat of the Orient" hasn't been meat at all, but soybeans.

- **Share an anecdote:**
  When I decided to become a vegetarian, my friends looked at me as if I had joined a cult.

- **Begin with a question:**
  How many animals does the average American eat in a year?

**Writing a Thesis Statement:**

To create a thesis statement for your essay, follow this formula.

| **Topic** $+$ | **Compare/Contrast** $=$ | **Thesis Statement** |
|---|---|---|
| vegetarianism | different reasons for choosing it, but the same benefits | Vegetarians have many reasons for choosing a meat-free diet, but the diet results in the same basic benefits. |

**Traits**

Using a variety of details strengthens your ideas and broadens your thinking.

**Write** Create your opening paragraph. Start with a sentence that uses one of the strategies above. Then write sentences that build to your thesis statement.

Answers will vary.

# Creating Middle Paragraphs

**Write** Refer to the cause-effect chart you created on page 201 as you develop the middle two paragraphs of your essay. Use one paragraph to describe the causes of the lifestyle choice and another to describe the effects of it. Create a topic sentence for each paragraph. Use transitional words at the left to make your writing flow.

Answers will vary.

# Creating a Closing Paragraph

The closing paragraph of your essay should revisit the causes and effects of the topic and connect to the ideas in the introduction.

**Write** Answer the following questions to help you sum up the causes and effects. Answers will vary.

1. What is the most important cause of the lifestyle choice?

   _____

   _____

2. What is the most important effect?

   _____

   _____

3. What final point could you leave your reader with?

   _____

   _____

**Write** Create the closing paragraph for your cause-effect essay.

Answers will vary.

_____

_____

_____

_____

_____

_____

_____

_____

_____

_____

_____

_____

_____

_____

**Speaking & Listening**

Have your partner read your essay aloud. Then complete the response sheet together.

# LO4 Revising: Improving the Writing

Revising your first draft involves adding, deleting, rearranging, and reworking parts of your writing. Revision begins with a peer review.

## Peer Review

Sharing your writing at various stages is important, especially when you review and revise a first draft. The feedback that you receive will help you change and improve your essay.

**Respond** Complete this response sheet after reading the first draft of a classmate's essay. Then share the sheet with the writer. (Keep your comments helpful and positive.)  Answers will vary.

Essay title: _____

Writer: _____ Reviewer: _____

1. Which part of the essay seems to work best—opening, middle, or closing? Why?

   _____

   _____

   _____

   _____

2. Which part of the essay needs work—opening, middle, or closing? Why? _____

   _____

   _____

3. Which cause-effect details caught your attention? Name three.

   a. _____

   b. _____

   c. _____

4. Write two other details that might be included.

   a. _____

   b. _____

5. Identify a phrase or two that shows the writer's level of interest.

   _____

   _____

   _____

# Using a Variety of Details

Your essay will be stronger if you use a variety of details to support your point. Different types of details provide different types of support.

**Facts** ground your essay in reality.

> The US Department of Agriculture recommends that people "go lean on protein" and eat even less fat.

**Statistics** quantify facts.

> However, the average American eats 16 percent of calories in proteins and 44 percent in fat.

**Quotations** from an expert lend support to your point.

> Chris Woolston of the Consumer Health interactive says, "Fatty, unbalanced, and oversized: That, in a nutshell, is the American diet."

**Anecdotes** share an experience from real life.

> After a week without meat, some vegetarians report that the smell of cooking hamburger makes them sick.

**Revising in Action**

Read aloud the unrevised and revised version of the following excerpt. Note how adding in facts and statistics makes the essay much stronger.

Other vegetarians reject modern American eating habits, with too much meat and too few vegetables. Vegetarians seek a better diet and a more sustainable lifestyle.

The US Department of Agriculture recommends that people "go lean on protein" and eat even less fat. However, the average American eats 16 percent of calories in proteins and 44 percent in fat.

**Revise**  Improve your writing, using your partner's comments on the response sheet and including sensory details. Continue revising until you can answer *yes* to each question in the following checklist.

---

## Revising Checklist

**Ideas:**

1. Do I focus on an interesting lifestyle choice?
2. Do I trace the causes and effects of the lifestyle choice?

**Organization:**

3. Do I have an effective opening, middle, and closing?
4. Have I used one paragraph for causes and the other for effects?
5. Have I used transitions to connect my sentences?

**Voice:**

6. Do I sound knowledgeable about and interested in my topic?

---

**Traits**

Using a variety of details strengthens your ideas and broadens your thinking.

## Correction Marks

 ⌿ delete

d ≡ capitalize

⌀ lowercase

∧ insert

 add comma

? add question

∧ mark

word ∧ add word

⊙ add period

�⌎ spelling

∿ switch

# LO5 Editing: Correcting Your Writing

The main work of editing is correcting your revised first draft.

## Correcting Comma Splices and Run-On Sentences

When you join two sentences together, you need to connect them with a comma and a coordinating conjunction (*and, but, or, nor, for, so, yet*). If you leave out the conjunction, you have an error called a comma splice. If you leave out both the comma and conjunction, you have a run-on sentence. Fix either one by using a comma **and** a coordinating conjunction.

> **Comma Splice:** Video games are fun, they shouldn't take over your life.
>
> **Run-On:** Video games are fun they shouldn't take over your life.
>
> **Corrected:** Video games are fun, but they shouldn't take over your life.

**Correct** Correct the following comma splices and run-on sentences by making sure both a comma and a coordinating conjunction are used.

1. I enjoy many types of video games,∧ *and* my friends and I play together.

2. Sometimes we are in the same room,∧ *but (or yet)* often we play together online.

3. We like first-person shooters mostly,∧ *yet (or but)* online role-playing games are also fun.

4. Some games are designed to be addictive,∧ *so* it's important to keep perspective.

5. A balance of life and games is crucial,∧ *for* you can't just live in the game.

6. Game technology is always changing,∧ *so (or and)* it's exciting to see what they invent next.

7. Motion-capture games get you moving,∧ *and* some people exercise to them.

8. Other games have social aspects,∧ *so* we talk to each other over the Internet.

9. Games are like other aspects of life,∧ *for* too much of a good thing is too much.

10. Games should be social,∧ *but (or yet)* they should not replace having friends.

**Apply** Read your comparison-contrast essay and watch for comma errors. If you find any, correct them. (For more information, see pages 304–307.)

# Correcting Sentence Fragments

A complete sentence has a subject and a verb and expresses a complete thought. If a group of words is missing a subject or a verb (or both) or does not express a complete thought, it is a fragment. Fix fragments by supplying what is missing.

| | |
|---|---|
| **Missing a Subject:** | Love to play video games. |
| **Complete Sentence:** | **My friends and I** love to play video games. |
| **Missing a Verb:** | Bill and I especially. |
| **Complete Sentence:** | Bill and I especially **are game fanatics.** |
| **Missing Subject and Verb:** | Every weekend for hours at a time. |
| **Complete Sentence:** | **We play games** every weekend for hours at a time. |
| **Incomplete Thought:** | When we should be studying. |
| **Complete Sentence:** | When we should be studying, **the temptation is greatest.** |

**Correct** Fix each fragment below by rewriting it and supplying what is missing. Use your imagination to provide details.  Answers will vary.

1. The best game ever

_____

_____

2. After we've played all afternoon

_____

_____

3. Until two in the morning

_____

_____

4. Everyone, including my little brother

_____

_____

5. Whenever somebody wants to quit

_____

_____

**Apply** Read your essay, watching for sentence fragments. Fix them by providing what is missing—a subject, a verb, a subject and verb, or a complete thought.

# Marking an Essay

Before you finish editing your revised essay, you can practice by editing the following model.

**Correct** Read the following cause-effect essay, looking for problems. Correct the model using the marks listed to the left. One correction has been done for you.

## Correction Marks

| | |
|---|---|
| ℑ | delete |
| d̲ | capitalize |
| Ø | lowercase |
| ∧ | insert |
| ˆ | add comma |
| ? | add question |
| ∧ | mark |
| word ∧ | add word |
| ⊙ | add period |
| ◯ | spelling |
| ∿ | switch |

## Staying in Step

People have many different ways to stay in shape, from jogging to    *1*
swimming to bike riding. Different people gravitate toward different types of
exercise. Recently, when I was trying to ~~chose~~ *choose* a type of exercise, I decided on
walking. Many factors made me choose walking over other forms of exercise⊙
walking has changed my life in a number of ways.    *5*

Walking appealed because of its simplicity, safety, cost, and sociability.
While other types of exercise require special equipment or special training∧
walking is an activity I do every day anyway. I've been walking since I was
*one* 1 year old. It requires only normal (cloths) comfortable shoes, and a sidewalk.
Walking also ~~ain't~~ *isn't* dangerous like swimming, and walking isn't hard on the    *10*
knees like (joging) To walk, I don't have to belong to a special club or rent any
special equipment. And when I walk, I walk with friends, and we talk.

Walking regularly has helped me a lot. First of all, I've dropped ten
pounds⊙ I also toned up my legs and the most important muscle of all, my
heart. Beyond these benefits, walking has ~~gave~~ *given* me a chance to talk with best    *15*
friends about all kinds of things. It has ~~brung~~ *brought* us closer. Walking also connects
me to my community. Many people stop me and say they see me walking and
feel they know me. I also like the way that walking connects me to N̄ature and
W̄eather. Rain or shine, I feel it when I'm walking.

So you can keep your fancy weight machines and thigh busters. I choose    *20*
walking because it is simple, safe, cheap, and fun. Walking has rewarded
me with health and happiness⊙ walking is a habit that many people should
learn.

# Correcting Your Essay

Now it's time to correct your own essay. Use the checklist below.

**Apply** Create a clean copy of your essay and use the following checklist to search for errors. When you can answer *yes* to a question, check it off. Continue working until all items are checked.

---

### Editing Checklist

**Words**

☐ **1.** Have I used specific nouns and verbs? (See page 74.)

☐ **2.** Have I used more action verbs than "be" verbs? (See page 348.)

**Sentences**

☐ **3.** Have I varied the beginnings and lengths of sentences? (See pages 264, 266.)

☐ **4.** Have I combined short choppy sentences? (See page 262.)

☐ **5.** Have I avoided improper shifts in sentences? (See pages 314–315.)

☐ **6.** Have I avoided fragments and run-ons? (See pages 297–302, 306–307.)

**Conventions**

☐ **7.** Do I use correct verb forms (*he saw,* not *he seen*)? (See page 356.)

☐ **8.** Do my subjects and verbs agree (*she speaks,* not *she speak*)? (See pages 282–291.)

☐ **9.** Have I used the right words (*their, there, they're*)?

☐ **10.** Have I capitalized first words and proper nouns and adjectives? (See page 414.)

☐ **11.** Have I used commas after long introductory word groups? (See page 396.)

☐ **12.** Have I punctuated dialogue correctly? (See pages 144–145.)

☐ **13.** Have I carefully checked my spelling?

---

# Adding a Title

Make sure to add an attention-getting title. Here are three simple strategies for writing titles.

- **Ask a question:** Why eat that stuff?
- **Use the word "or":** Herbivore or Carnivore
- **Repeat the sounds of letters:** Staying in Step

**Create** Prepare a clean final copy of your essay and proofread it.

# LO6 Reviewing Cause-Effect Writing

Complete these activities as needed to help you better understand how to write cause-effect essays.

Henglein and Steets/Cultura/Getty Images

**Analyze** Look at the photograph to the left. Think about the causes and effects shown in it. Fill in the following cause-effect chart with your observations. **Answers will vary.**

**Cause-Effect Chart**

**Topic:** _____

| Causes | Effects |
|--------|---------|
|        |         |
|        |         |
|        |         |
|        |         |
|        |         |
|        |         |
|        |         |
|        |         |

**Freewrite** Using your answers in the cause-effect chart above, freewrite about the reason the man is riding the child's car and what is likely to result.

Answers will vary.

_____

_____

_____

_____

_____

_____

_____

"Nothing is as frustrating as arguing with someone who knows what he's talking about."

—Sam Ewing

Charlene Key,2010/Used under license from Shutterstock.com

# Argument Essay

Have you ever dismissed a political ad for its over-the-top bias? Or left a lecture shaking your head because you just weren't convinced? Building a persuasive argument is difficult. Convincing others to buy into an argument is even more challenging.

Abraham Lincoln believed the best way to persuade was to present the facts and let logic run its course: "I am a firm believer in the people. If given the truth, they can be depended upon to meet any national crisis. The great point is to bring them the real facts."

In this chapter you will write an essay of argumentation that takes a position on a debatable topic and defends that position with logical and factual supporting details. Along the way you will learn strategies to motivate your audience to side with your argument.

## Learning Outcomes

**LO1** Understand argument essays.

**LO2** Plan an argument essay.

**LO3** Write the first draft.

**LO4** Revise the essay.

**LO5** Edit the essay.

**LO6** Reflect on the experience.

### What do you think?

In what ways do you defend your point of view during an argument? Give examples.

Answers will vary.

# LO1 Reviewing an Argument Essay

In an argument essay, a writer takes a stance on a debatable position. In the example below, the writer makes a pitch for preserving America's farmland.

**Read/React**  Read the following essay. Then complete the analysis on the next page.

## America the Developed

The **opening** raises concern for the issue with an attention-grabbing story and leads to the thesis (underlined).

Oh beautiful for spacious skies, for amber waves of grain, for purple mountain majesties, above the fruited plain. Sound familiar? These words begin the American classic, "America the Beautiful." Unfortunately, a portion of the American landscape spoken of so eloquently in this song is in danger of vanishing. Strip malls, housing developments, and transportation services are overrunning America's lush farmland, including those amber waves of grain and abundant fruited plains. An American Farmland Trust study estimates two acres of farm and ranch land is lost to development every minute of every day. Beyond the aesthetic loss, the loss of farmland is putting our economy and food supply at risk for future generations. The American public must take greater measures to preserve the country's farmland.

The first **middle paragraph** gives reasons to support the thesis.

From the years 2002 through 2007, America lost more than four million acres of active farmland to development. Much of that development has taken place in the proximity of big cities—areas where land is often most fertile. Studies show that farms closest to cities produce 83 percent of America's fruits and vegetables and 63 percent of its dairy. When development replaces this prime farmland, farmers are forced onto nonfertile land. The result is less production and higher costs for irrigation and transportation. Furthermore, cities lose out on quality of life factors, such as fresh produce, natural flood barriers, and scenic landscapes.

The second **middle paragraph** gives the best reasons to support the thesis.

The most critical case for preserving America's farmland, though, comes down to the nutritional and economic value of food. Food not only feeds bodies but it also supplies jobs. The U.S. food and farming system accounts for nearly $1 trillion of the national economy and employs 17 percent of the national workforce. By some estimates, the world's population will nearly double by 2050, which will greatly increase the demand for food here and abroad. By preserving its farmland, the United States will be able to safely feed itself while gaining a major economic boost from food exports.

The **closing** clarifies the writer's position and outlines what should be done.

It is critical that the United States takes greater steps toward preserving its farmland. By doing so, we will boost our economy and ensure our food supply is safe for future generations. We must build around, not on, farms on the urban edge. Furthermore, we must be more judicious with growth by making already-developed areas more livable. If we don't make it a priority now, the land spoken of in "America the Beautiful" will seem foreign to future generations.

# A Closer Look

This argument essay takes a defensible position on farmland and development. The writer's position on farmland is debatable, but it is supported by the details in the middle paragraphs.

**Identify** The argument essay on the facing page makes a pitch for the preservation of farmland and gives reasons to support it. In the chart below, identify three different reasons that support the thesis statement.

---

**Thesis Statement**

Beyond the aesthetic loss, the loss of farmland is putting our economy and food supply at risk for future generations. The American public must take greater measures to preserve the country's farmland.

**Reason 1**

Development around cities takes the most fertile land, pushing farmers to poorer land.

**Reason 2**

This drives up food prices and decreases quality of life factors like fresh food, flood barriers, and scenic landscapes.

**Reason 3**

It also results in fewer jobs and reduced food for expanding populations.

---

**Explain** Is the writer's argument convincing? Why or why not? Provide reasons.

Answers will vary.

# LO2 Prewriting: Planning

There is no sense in debating a topic about which everyone agrees. In your own essay, you will take a position on a debatable issue. You should pick an issue that you care about and choose the side you want to defend.

## Selecting a Topic

If you can't think of a topic, browse newspapers, magazines, and the Internet for current issues that people have strong feelings about.

**Select**  In the space below, list three or four debatable issues you could write about in an essay. Circle your favorite topic.

Answers will vary.

### Traits

Consider using one of the following verbs to strengthen the conviction of your position statement:
*should, must, ought to, need, needs*

## Selecting a Position

Whether in writing or speaking, a convincing argument starts with a strong position on a debatable topic. Once you decide on a topic, consider your initial position on the issue.

**Write**  Write down a defensible **position statement** that introduces the issue and expresses your opinion about it.

Answers will vary.

## Refining a Position

With your initial position written, use the following position strategies to develop and refine your opinion of the issue:

- Research all possible positions on your issue of debate. Who supports it and why? Who opposes it and why?
- Gather solid evidence regarding your issue. Does the most compelling evidence support or oppose your position?
- Refine your position. At this point you may have sharpened or changed your mind about your position. Before you are ready to write, clarify your position statement.

**Write**  On the lines below, write your refined position statement.

Answers will vary.

# Gathering Details

When you take a stand on an issue, you must gather convincing support to defend your position. You can use four different types of details to support your position: facts, statistics, testimonials, and predictions.

**Support Chart**

| Fact | Statistic | Testimony | Prediction |
|---|---|---|---|
| A shield law is a law that gives reporters protection from being forced to reveal confidential information or anonymous sources in a courtroom. | Currently 49 states, including California, offer shield laws of varying degrees. | "We definitely need to have a shield law, but we also need to have a balance." Senator Tom Coburn | Sources may fear being identified and decide against leaking a story of corruption or scandal. |

**Gather** Fill in the support chart below with the research you have gathered about your issue. If you have not found supporting details to fit each category, consider doing additional research.  Answers will vary.

| Fact | Statistic | Testimony | Prediction |
|---|---|---|---|
|  |  |  |  |

# LO3 Writing: Creating a First Draft

Creating a first draft puts all your planning and gathering into concrete form. Provided below is a sample argument essay about journalistic shield laws.

**Read/React**  Read the essay, noting the writer's position statement and supporting details.

## A Necessary Protection

**Opening paragraph**

Back in the summer of 2006, investigative journalists Lance   1
Williams and Mark Fainaru-Wada of the *San Francisco Chronicle*
faced a dilemma: either reveal the source who leaked confidential
information for their story about steroid use in professional
baseball or refuse to name names and be found in contempt of   5
court, a punishment carrying 18 months in prison. At the heart
of the matter were shield laws. A shield law is a law that gives
reporters protection from being forced to reveal confidential
information or anonymous sources in a courtroom. Currently 49
states, including California, offer shield laws of varying degrees.   10
However, Williams and Fainaru-Wada's source was involved in
a federal investigation, and no shield laws protect journalists in
federal court. This fact must change. <u>Passing a federal shield law
is a necessary step to ensure the general public's right to know.</u>

**Thesis statement**

**Support paragraph 1**

Some of the most consequential stories in American history   15
have surfaced due to anonymous whistleblowers, including the
Watergate and Enron scandals. Without a federal shield law,
future stories like these may never come to light for two reasons.
First, sources may fear being identified and decide against leaking
a story of corruption or scandal. Second, news organizations may   20
hold back from supporting their confidential-sources agreements
due to the financial responsibility of fighting a case in court. The
result is a chilling effect on breaking news.

**Support paragraph 2**

Furthermore, a federal shield law provides journalists with
the basic protections to fulfill their job as watchdogs for the general   25
public. It's the responsibility of a free press to provide a check
on government corruption, corporate misconduct, and threats
to public health and safety by unearthing stories. But what if a
journalist decides against running an important story with an
unnamed source out of fear of a subpoena?   30

**Closing paragraph**

To be certain, a federal shield law should not provide
journalists with unlimited protections. If an unnamed source is an
imminent threat to national security or bodily harm, the journalist
should be compelled to reveal the source. However, in cases where
an unnamed source is absolutely necessary, reporters shouldn't   35
have to fear incarceration for honoring a confidentiality agreement.
Trust is the foundation of a source-reporter relationship. Williams
and Fainaru-Wada knew this. They decided against revealing
their source and would have served jail time if the source had not
confessed. But the next journalist might not be so lucky. It's time   40
to pass a federal shield law.

# Creating an Opening Paragraph

The opening paragraph of your argument essay needs to capture the reader's interest, raise concern for the issue of debate, and establish your position on the topic.

Consider these attention-grabbing strategies for your opening paragraph.

- **Start with a brief dramatic story.**
  Back in the summer of 2006, investigative journalists Lance Williams and Mark Fainaru-Wada of the *San Francisco Chronicle* faced a dilemma: either reveal the source who leaked confidential information for their story about steroid use in professional baseball or refuse to name names and be found in contempt of court.

- **Ask a thought-provoking question.**
  How would you feel if you were wrongly convicted of a crime?

- **Offer a surprising statistic.**
  An American Farmland Trust study estimates two acres of farm and ranch land is lost to development every minute of every day.

- **Make a personal confession.**
  I can't stand cigarette smoke, but I believe adults should have the freedom to smoke in public.

**Speaking & Listening**

Imagine that you are giving a speech about your topic. What strategy would you use to get listeners' attention? Try a similar strategy in your writing.

**Write**  Create the opening paragraph for your argument essay.

Answers will vary.

# Creating Middle Paragraphs

The middle paragraphs should make a persuasive case for your position. Here is where your supporting details become so important. Each paragraph should use facts, statistics, testimonials, or predictions to deepen, clarify, and build upon your position statement. Address any objections to your position with a clear, well-reasoned defense.

**Write** Create the two middle paragraphs of your essay.

Answers will vary.

# Creating an End Paragraph

The closing paragraph should reaffirm your stance on the issue. If appropriate, make a direct or indirect plea to the reader to adopt your position.

- If the United States wants to maintain its fragile southern ecosystem, it should take a hard look at making the importation of Burmese pythons illegal.
- We must build around, not on, farms on the urban edge. Furthermore, we must be more judicious with growth by making already-developed areas more livable.
- It's time to pass a federal shield law.

**Write** Create the closing paragraph for your argument essay.

Answers will vary.

**Learning Outcome**

Revise the essay.

**Speaking & Listening**

Have your partner read your essay aloud. Then complete the response sheet together.

# LO4 Revising: Improving the Writing

Revising your first draft involves adding, deleting, rearranging, and reworking parts of your writing. Revision begins with a peer review.

## Peer Review

Sharing your writing at various stages—whether it is with a friend, classmate, or tutor—is an important step to improving your essay.

**Respond** Complete this response sheet after reading the first draft of a classmate's essay. Then share the sheet with the writer. (Keep your comments helpful and positive.)   Answers will vary.

---

Essay title: _____

Writer: _____     Reviewer: _____

1. Which part of the essay seems to work best—opening, middle, or closing? Why?

   _____

   _____

   _____

2. Which part of the essay needs work—opening, middle, or closing? Why? _____

   _____

   _____

   _____

3. Do the middle paragraphs support the writer's position statement? How so?

   _____

   _____

   _____

4. Does the writer use a variety of support details? Are more needed? Why or why not?

   _____

   _____

   _____

5. Does the writer build a convincing argument? Why or why not?

   _____

   _____

   _____

---

# Looking Out for Logical Fallacies

A **logical fallacy** is a false assertion that weakens an argument by distorting an issue, drawing faulty conclusions, misusing evidence, or misusing language. Below are four common logical fallacies that should be removed from your writing.

**Straw Man** This logical fallacy distorts an issue by exaggerating or misinterpreting an opponent's position.

> Those who consider themselves pro-choice don't value human life.

**Bandwagon Mentality** Such a logical fallacy appeals to "popular opinion," by implying that a claim cannot be true because most people oppose it, or must be true because most support it.

> It's obvious to everyone that cockroaches live only in the apartments of dirty people.

**Broad Generalization** This logical fallacy makes an all-or-nothing claim based on little evidence. The claim will often include an intensifier, such as *all, every,* or *never*.

> All athletes are driven by money.

**Impressing with Numbers** In this case, a writer attempts to overwhelm the reader with a deluge of statistics, some of which are unrelated to the issue at hand.

> At 35 ppm, CO levels factory-wide are only 10ppm above the OSHA recommendation, which is 25 ppm. Clearly, that 10 ppm is insignificant in the big picture.

**Revise** Improve your writing using your partner's comments on the response sheet and the following checklist. Continue working until you can answer *yes* to each question.

---

## Revising Checklist

**Ideas:**

1. Do I take a stance on a debatable issue?
2. Do I support my position with a variety of supporting details?
3. Do I avoid errors in logic?

**Organization:**

4. Do I have topic, middle, and closing paragraphs?
5. Have I used transitions to connect my sentences?

**Voice:**

6. Do I sound knowledgeable and passionate about the issue?

---

**Vocabulary**

**logical fallacy**
a false assertion that may distort an issue, sabotage an argument, draw faulty conclusions, misuse evidence, or misuse language

**Insight**

For more practice with correcting ambiguous wording, see pages 294–295.

# LO5 Editing: Correcting Your Writing

The main work of editing is correcting your revised first draft.

## Correcting Ambiguous Wording

Ambiguous wording creates uncertainty among readers. Such wording results in sentences that have multiple meanings. Avoid indefinite pronoun references, incomplete comparisons, and unclear wording.

**Indefinite Pronoun Reference**

When it is unclear which word or phrase a pronoun refers to, the wording is ambiguous.

**Ambiguous:**  When Mike moved the lamp on to the wobbly chair, **it** fell on the floor.

**Clear:**  When Mike moved the lamp on to the wobbly chair, **the lamp** fell on the floor.

**Ambiguous:**  Monica reminded Misha that **she** needed to buy a new black dress for the party. (*Who needed to buy a black dress—Monica or Misha?*)

**Clear:**  Monica reminded Misha to buy a new black dress for the party.

**Practice**  Rewrite each sentence so that it does not contain any ambiguous pronoun references.

1. When Andy placed the box of macaroni back on the shelf, it tipped over.

   When Andy placed the box of macaroni back on the shelf, the box

   tipped over.

2. The professor told Tim that he needed to pursue the research opportunity.

   The professor told Tim that Tim needed to pursue the research

   opportunity.

3. As Brad drove his motorcycle into the garage, it shook.

   As Brad drove his motorcycle into the garage, the garage shook.

**Apply**  Read your argument essay and watch for indefinite pronoun references. If you find any, correct them.

## Incomplete Comparisons

Don't confuse readers by leaving out a word or words that are necessary to complete a comparison.

**Ambiguous:** The head chef said the Kobe steak is tastier. (*The Kobe is tastier than what?*)

**Clear:** The head chef said the Kobe steak is tastier **than the porterhouse.**

## Unclear Wording

Avoid writing a statement that can have two or more meanings.

**Ambiguous:** Jill decided to take her sister to a movie, which turned out to be a real bummer. (*It is unclear what was a real bummer—taking her sister to the movie or the movie itself.*)

**Clear:** Jill decided to take her sister to a movie, **but the film turned out to be a real bummer.**

**Practice** Rewrite each of the following sentences so that it does not contain incomplete comparisons or unclear wording. Answers will vary.

1. Going bowling is more fun.

2. I can handle Mel's personality better.

3. Vera wanted to complete her economics report after reading the latest research, but she didn't.

4. Bryan planned to attend the ice cream social after he registered for class, but he didn't.

**Apply** Read your argument essay and watch for incomplete comparisons or unclear wording. If you find any problems, correct them.

# Marking an Essay

Before you finish editing your revised essay, you can practice by editing the following model.

**Editing Practice** Read the following argument essay, looking for problems listed in the checklist on the facing page. Correct the model using the marks to the left. The first one has been done for you.

## Ban Burmese Pythons

An invasive species ~~are~~ *is* taking the southern tip of Florida by storm. 1
Thousands of Burmese pythons—giant snakes native to Southern asia—are
thriving in the tropical-like environment of Everglades National Park. Their
presence in the park is a product of irresponsible pet owners, who intentionally
release the snakes into the wild when they become too difficult to care for. as a 5
result, Florida lawmakers have passed a law making it (illigal) for individuals
to own burmese pythons. In order to protect native wildlife and treasured
ecosystems of the southern United States, this law should expand nationally.

Reports show some 144,000 pythons have been imported into the United
States, many of which end up in homes of irresponsible pet owners. "All of the 10
Burmese pythons that we see in the park are a product of the international
pet trade" said Skip Snow, a wildlife biologist at Everglades National Park.
The problem is many pet owners ~~doesn't~~ *don't* fully understand the responsibility
of taking care of a python often the python, which grow up to between 10 and
20 feet becomes too big and (to) expensive to be kept in a home. In the end, the 15
owner releases the pet into the wild.

It is in the wild where Burmese pythons ~~is~~ *are* causing havoc. The tropical
environment of the Everglades provides perfect conditions for the pythons to
breed and feed. With no natural competitor the strong and stealthy python is
feeding at will on native Everglades species Scientists worry the ecological 20
effects could be devastating. Second to habitat loss, invasive species are the
leading cause of species endangerment.

To be fair, there are no doubt thousands of responsible pet owners across
the United States. But the drawbacks of owning Burmese pythons outweigh
the benefits. These species are not meant to be pets. If the United States 25
wants to maintain its fragile southern ecosystem, it should take a hard look
at making the importation of Burmese pythons illegal.

# Correcting Your Essay

Now it's time to edit your own essay.

**Apply** Create a clean copy of your essay and use the following checklist to check for errors. When you can answer *yes* to a question, check it off. Continue working until all items are checked off.

---

### Editing Checklist

**Words**

- ☐ **1.** Have I used specific nouns and verbs? (See page 74.)
- ☐ **2.** Have I used more action verbs than "be" verbs? (See page 348.)

**Sentences**

- ☐ **3.** Have I varied the beginnings and lengths of sentences? (See pages 264, 266.)
- ☐ **4.** Have I combined short choppy sentences? (See page 262.)
- ☐ **5.** Have I avoided improper shifts in sentences? (See pages 314–315.)
- ☐ **6.** Have I avoided fragments and run-ons? (See pages 297–302, 306–307.)

**Conventions**

- ☐ **7.** Do I use correct verb forms *(he saw,* not *he seen)*? (See page 356.)
- ☐ **8.** Do my subjects and verbs agree *(she speaks,* not *she speak)*? (See pages 282–291.)
- ☐ **9.** Have I used the right words *(their, there, they're)*?
- ☐ **10.** Have I capitalized first words and proper nouns and adjectives? (See page 414.)
- ☐ **11.** Have I used commas after long introductory word groups? (See page 396.)
- ☐ **12.** Have I punctuated dialogue correctly? (See pages 144–145.)
- ☐ **13.** Have I carefully checked my spelling?

---

# Adding a Title

Make sure to add an attention-getting title. Here are three simple strategies for writing titles

- **Use a play on words:** America the Developed
- **Sum up your argument:** A Necessary Protection
- **Create a slogan:** Ban Burmese Pythons

# LO6 Reviewing Argument Writing

Complete these activities as needed to help you further understand how to write argument essays.

**Describe** A convincing argument essay requires a logical defense, based on supporting details. Describe the four types of supporting details illustrated in this chapter.

---

_Answers will vary._

---

**Match** Draw a line to connect each logical fallacy with a claim that best demonstrates that fallacy.

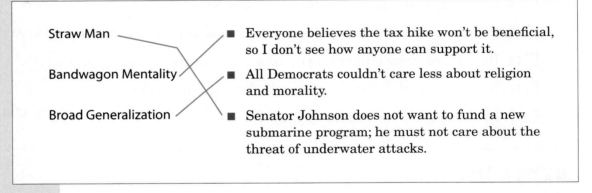

Straw Man

Bandwagon Mentality

Broad Generalization

■ Everyone believes the tax hike won't be beneficial, so I don't see how anyone can support it.

■ All Democrats couldn't care less about religion and morality.

■ Senator Johnson does not want to fund a new submarine program; he must not care about the threat of underwater attacks.

**Correct** The following sentence contains an indefinite pronoun reference. Rewrite the sentence so it becomes clear what word or phrase the pronoun refers to.

Krunal reminded Reid that he should arrive at the party at half past nine.

_Example answers:  Krunal reminded Reid to arrive at the party at half past nine._

_Krunal reminded Reid that Reid should arrive at the party at half past nine._

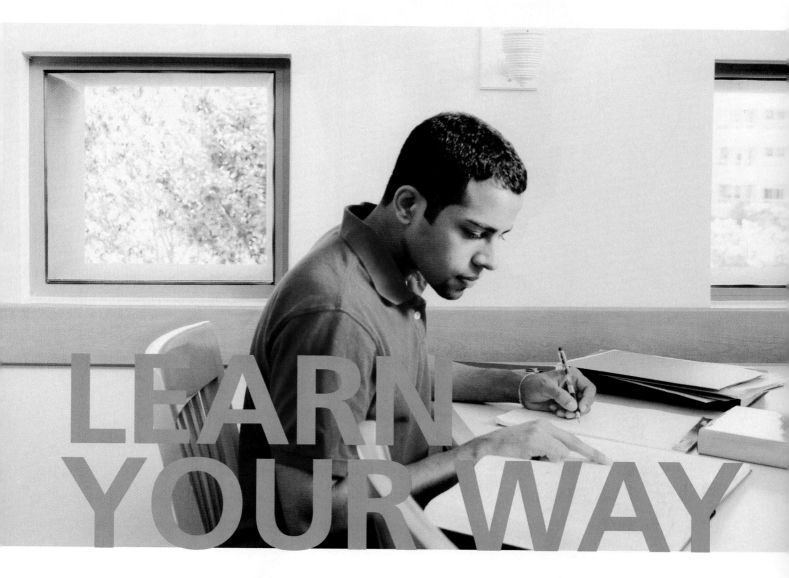

# LEARN YOUR WAY

We know that no two students are alike. **WRITE 2** was developed to help you improve your writing skills in a way that works for you.

Not only is the format fresh and contemporary, it's also concise and focused. **WRITE 2** is loaded with a variety of supplements like portable **In Review** cards, interactive online quizzes, vocabulary flashcards, videos, and more.

At **login.cengagebrain.com**, you'll find plenty of resources to help you become a more successful writer no matter what your learning style!

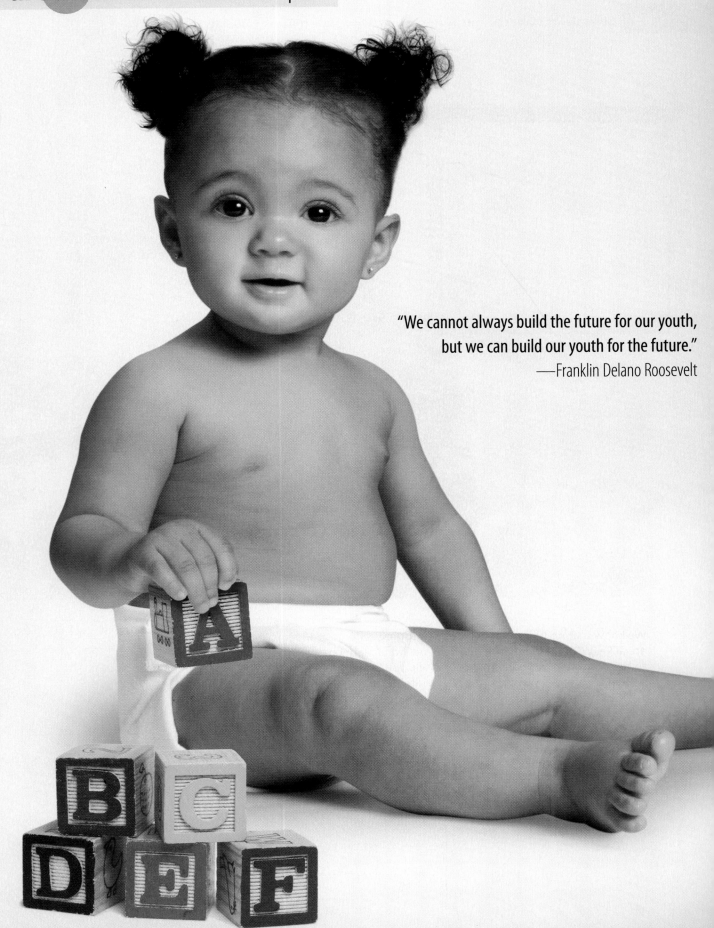

"We cannot always build the future for our youth,
but we can build our youth for the future."

—Franklin Delano Roosevelt

# Sentence Basics

As you know, sentences are built from some very simple parts—nouns, verbs, and modifiers. Every sentence has, at its base, the pairing of a noun and a verb, or a few of them. The other words in the sentence merely modify the noun and verb.

These are sentence basics—the building blocks of thought. With these blocks, you can build tiny towers or magnificent mansions. It all comes down to understanding how to put the pieces together and deciding what you want to create. This chapter can help.

John Lund/Annabelle Breakey/Blend Images/Getty Images

## What do you think?

How do we "build our youth for the future," as Roosevelt suggests in the quotation on the facing page? What part do language and writing have to do with building our youth?

Answers will vary.

## Learning Outcomes

**LO1** Understand subjects and predicates.

**LO2** Work with special subjects.

**LO3** Work with special predicates.

**LO4** Understand adjectives.

**LO5** Understand adverbs.

**LO6** Use prepositional phrases.

**LO7** Use clauses.

**LO8** Apply sentence basics in a real-world context.

# LO1 Subjects and Verbs (Predicates)

The subject of a sentence tells what the sentence is about. The verb (predicate) of a sentence tells what the subject does or is.

Dogs bark.

└ Subject: what the sentence is about    └ Predicate: what the subject does

Eric Isselee,2010 / Used under license from Shutterstock.com

## Simple Subject and Simple Predicate

The **simple subject** is the subject without any modifiers, and the **simple predicate** is the predicate without modifiers or objects.

The black and white Schnauzer barked all day long.
                    simple subject   simple predicate

## Complete Subject and Complete Predicate

The **complete subject** is the subject with modifiers, and the **complete predicate** is the predicate with modifiers and objects.

The black and white Schnauzer barked all day long.
        complete subject              complete predicate

## Implied Subject

In commands, the subject *you* is implied. Commands are the only type of sentence in English that can have an **implied subject**.

(You)                              Stop barking!
implied subject                    complete predicate

## Inverted Order

Most often in English, the subject comes before the predicate. However, in questions and sentences that begin with *here* or *there*, the subject comes after the predicate.

                 subject                        subject
Why are you so loud?         Here is a biscuit.
     predicate                    predicate

**Vocabulary**

**simple subject**
the subject without any modifiers

**simple predicate**
the predicate without modifiers or objects

**complete subject**
the subject with modifiers

**complete predicate**
the predicate with modifiers and objects

**implied subject**
the word *you* implied in command sentences

# Creating Subjects and Verbs (Predicates)

**Identify/Write**  For each sentence below, underline and label the simple subject (SS) and simple predicate (SP). Then write a similar sentence of your own and identify the simple subject and simple predicate in the same way.

> 1. For thousands of years, <u>humans</u> (SS) <u>have bred</u> (SP) dogs.
>
>    Answers will vary.
> _____
>
> 2. All dog <u>breeds</u> (SS) <u>descended</u> (SP) from wolf ancestors.
>
>    Answers will vary.
> _____
>
> 3. At the end of the Ice Age, <u>humans</u> (SS) <u>lived</u> (SP) nomadically with their dogs.
>
>    Answers will vary.
> _____
>
> 4. Ever since that time, <u>dogs</u> (SS) <u>have enjoyed</u> (SP) going for walks.
>
>    Answers will vary.
> _____

**Identify/Write**  For each sentence below, underline and label the complete subject (CS) and complete predicate (CP). Then write a similar sentence of your own and identify the complete subject and complete predicate in the same way.

> 1. <u>An Irish wolfhound</u> (CS) <u>stands as tall as a small pony.</u> (CP)
>
>    Answers will vary.
> _____
>
> 2. <u>Wolfhounds</u> (CS) <u>were bred to hunt their ancestors.</u> (CP)
>
>    Answers will vary.
> _____
>
> 3. <u>Wolfhounds</u> (CS) <u>also were used for hunting boar.</u> (CP)
>
>    Answers will vary.
> _____
>
> 4. <u>Is</u> (CP) <u>that</u> (CS) <u>why boars are extinct in Ireland?</u> (CP)
>
>    Answers will vary.
>
> 5. <u>There is</u> (CP) <u>little doubt.</u> (CS)
>
>    Answers will vary.
> _____

# LO2 Special Types of Subjects

As you work with subjects, watch for these special types.

## Compound Subjects

A **compound subject** is two or more subjects connected by *and* or *or*.

My <u>sister and I</u> like to hike. <u>Terri, Josh, and I</u> love the outdoors.
compound subject        compound subject

## "To" Words (Infinitives) as Subjects

An **infinitive** can function as a subject. An infinitive is a verbal form that begins with *to* and may be followed by objects or modifiers.

<u>To become a park ranger</u> is my dream.
infinitive subject

## "Ing" Words (Gerunds) as Subjects

A **gerund** can function as a subject. A gerund is a verb form that ends in *ing* and may be followed by objects or modifiers.

<u>Hiking</u> builds strong calves.      <u>Hiking the Appalachian Trail</u> is amazing.
gerund subject           gerund subject

## Noun Clause as Subject

A **noun clause** can function as a subject. The clause itself has a subject and a verb but cannot stand alone as a sentence. Noun clauses are introduced by words like *what, that, when, why, how, whatever,* or *whichever*.

<u>Whoever hikes the trail</u> should bring replacement boots.
noun clause subject

<u>Whatever you need</u> must be carried on your back.
noun clause subject

**Traits**

Note that each of these special subjects still functions as a noun or a group of nouns. A sentence is still, at root, the connection between a noun and a verb.

**Vocabulary**

**compound subject**
two or more subjects connected by *and* or *or*

**infinitive**
a verb form that begins with *to* and can be used as a noun (or as an adjective or adverb)

**gerund**
a verb form that ends in *ing* and is used as a noun

**noun clause**
a group of words beginning with words like *that, what, whoever,* and so on; containing a subject and a verb but unable to function as a sentence

### Say It

Pair up with a partner and read each sentence aloud. Take turns identifying the type of subject—compound subject, infinitive subject, gerund subject, or noun-clause subject. Discuss your answers.

1. You and I should go hiking sometime.

2. To reach the peak of Mount Rainier would be amazing.

3. Whoever wants to go should train with mountaineering.

4. Hiking the Rockies at altitude is challenging.

# Creating Special Subjects

**Identify/Write** For each sentence below, underline and label the complete subject: compound subject (CS), infinitive (I), gerund (G), or noun clause (NC). Then write a similar sentence of your own and identify the complete subject in the same way.

---

          G
1. <u>Planning for success</u> is the key to success.

   Answers will vary.

               I
2. <u>To complete the course in two years</u> is my main goal.

   Answers will vary.

            CS
3. <u>The fan and the air conditioner</u> are running.

   Answers will vary.

           G
4. <u>Working through our differences</u> won't be easy.

   Answers will vary.

            CS
5. <u>A donut, a cup of coffee, and good conversation</u> make my morning.

   Answers will vary.

          G
6. <u>Lifting the ban on street parking</u> will help the neighborhood.

   Answers will vary.

        I
7. <u>To live life to its fullest</u> is not as easy as it sounds.

   Answers will vary.

         NC
8. <u>Whoever finds the money</u> will keep it.

   Answers will vary.

          CS
9. Are <u>Hannah, Michelle, and Sharissa</u> going?

   Answers will vary.

        NC
10. <u>Whenever he arrives</u> is the starting time.

   Answers will vary.

Tony Campbell,2010 / Used under license from Shutterstock.com

# LO3 Special Verbs (Predicates)

As you work with predicates, watch for these special types.

## Compound Predicates

A **compound predicate** consists of two or more predicates joined by *and* or *or*.

> I <u>watched and laughed</u>. My cat <u>stalked, pounced, and tumbled</u>.
>    compound predicate                    compound predicate

## Predicates with Direct Objects

A **direct object** follows a transitive verb and tells what or who receives the action of the verb.

> I pointed the <u>laser</u>. My cat got the <u>spot</u>. He batted <u>it</u> and nipped the <u>ground</u>.
>       direct object           direct object          direct objects

## Predicates with Indirect Objects

An **indirect object** comes between a transitive verb and a direct object and tells to whom or for whom an action was done.

> I gave <u>him</u> a rest. My cat shot <u>me</u> a puzzled look.
>    indirect object           indirect object

## Passive Predicates

When a predicate is **passive**, the subject of the sentence is being acted upon rather than acting. Often, the actor is the object of the preposition in a phrase that starts with *by*. Using that object as the subject, the sentence can be rewritten to be **active**.

| **Passive** | **Active** |
|---|---|
| My <u>cat</u> <u>was exhausted</u> by the <u>game</u>. | The <u>game</u> <u>exhausted</u> <u>my cat</u>. |
| subject  passive verb  object of the preposition | subject  active verb  direct object |

> **Say It**
>
> Pair up with a partner and read each sentence aloud. Take turns identifying the sentence as active or passive. If the sentence is passive, speak the active version out loud.
>
> 1. My cat was mesmerized by the laser.
>
> 2. The light danced in his paws.
>
> 3. The laser glowed red on the wall.
>
> 4. The light was chased all down the hallway.

# Creating Special Predicates

**Identify/Write** For each sentence below, underline and label any compound predicate (CP), direct object (DO), and indirect object (IO). Then write a similar sentence of your own and identify the compound predicate and direct or indirect object in the same way.

1. Our pet rabbits <u>hopped and thumped</u>.     *CP*

   Answers will vary.

2. The lop-ear leaped the <u>gate</u>.     *DO*

   Answers will vary.

3. I gave <u>her</u> a <u>carrot</u>.     *IO* *DO*

   Answers will vary.

4. She <u>crouched and nibbled</u>.     *CP*

   Answers will vary.

5. The lionhead <u>sniffed and bounded</u>.     *CP*

   Answers will vary.

6. I gave <u>him</u> some dried <u>banana</u>.     *IO* *DO*

   Answers will vary.

7. Those rabbits give <u>me</u> <u>hours</u> of entertainment.     *IO* *DO*

   Answers will vary.

**Identify/Write** For each passive sentence below, underline and label the simple subject (SS), the simple predicate (SP), and the object of the preposition *by* (O). Then rewrite each sentence, making it active. (See "Passive Predicates" on the previous page.)

1. The <u>rabbits</u> <u>are fed</u> and watered by my <u>sister</u>.     *SS* *SP* *O*

   Answers will vary.

2. Their <u>cages</u> <u>are cleaned</u> by <u>her</u> as well.     *SS* *SP* *O*

   Answers will vary.

3. <u>She</u> <u>is seen</u> by <u>them</u> as their food goddess.     *SS* *SP* *O*

   Answers will vary.

Nice One Productions/Flame/Corbis

# LO4 Adjectives

To modify a noun, use an adjective or a phrase or clause acting as an adjective.

## Adjectives

Adjectives answer these basic questions: *which, what kind of, how many, how much.*

To modify the noun **athletes,** ask . . .

*Which* athletes? ⟶ college athletes

*What kind of* athletes? ⟶ female athletes

*How many* athletes? ⟶ ten athletes

| ten female college athletes |
| --- |

## Adjective Phrases and Clauses

Phrases and clauses can also act as adjectives to modify nouns.

To modify the noun **athletes,** ask . . .

*Which* athletes? ⟶ athletes who are taking at least 12 credit hours

*What kind of* athletes? ⟶ athletes with a 3.0 average

| The administration will approve loans for athletes with a 3.0 average who are taking at least 12 credit hours. |
| --- |

### Say It

Pair up with a classmate to find adjectives—words, phrases, or clauses—that modify the nouns below. Take turns asking the questions while the other person answers.

1. **Sports**
   *Which* sports?
   *What kind of* sports?
   *How many* sports?

2. **Classes**
   *Which* classes?
   *What kind of* classes?
   *How many* classes?

# Using Adjectives

**Answer/Write** For each noun, answer the questions using adjectives—words, phrases, or clauses. Then write a sentence using two or more of your answers.

Answers will vary.

1. **Tournaments**

   *Which* tournaments? _____

   *What kind of* tournaments? _____

   *How many* tournaments? _____

   Sentence: _____

   _____

   _____

   _____

2. **Opponents**

   *Which* opponents? _____

   *What kind of* opponents? _____

   *How many* opponents? _____

   Sentence: _____

   _____

   _____

   _____

3. **Victories**

   *Which* victories? _____

   *What kind of* victories? _____

   *How many* victories? _____

   Sentence: _____

   _____

   _____

   _____

# LO5 Adverbs

To modify a verb, use an adverb or a phrase or clause acting as an adverb.

## Adverbs

Adverbs answer these basic questions: *how, when, where, why, how long,* and *how often*.

To modify the verb **dance,** ask . . .

| | |
|---|---|
| *How* did they dance? ⟶ | danced vigorously |
| *When* did they dance? ⟶ | danced yesterday |
| *Where* did they dance? ⟶ | danced there |
| *How often* did they dance? ⟶ | danced often |

> Yesterday, the bride and groom often vigorously danced, there in the middle of the floor.

## Adverb Phrases and Clauses

Phrases and clauses can also act as adverbs to modify verbs.

To modify the verb **dance,** ask . . .

| | |
|---|---|
| *How* did they dance? ⟶ | danced grinning and laughing |
| *When* did they dance? ⟶ | danced from the first song |
| *Where* did they dance? ⟶ | danced all around the room |
| *Why* did they dance? ⟶ | danced to celebrate their wedding |
| *How long* did they dance? ⟶ | danced until the last song |

> Grinning and laughing, **the bride and groom danced** all around the room from the first song until the last song to celebrate their wedding.

**Speaking & Listening**

Read the last two sentences aloud. Though they may look imposing on the page, they sound completely natural, probably because adverbs and adjectives are a common part of our speech. Experiment with these modifiers in your writing as well.

Ned Frisk/Blend Images/Getty Images

# Using Adverbs

**Answer/Write** For each verb, answer the questions using adverbs—words, phrases, or clauses. Then write a sentence using three or more of your answers.

Answers will vary.

**1. Ran**

*How* did they run? _____

*When* did they run? _____

*Where* did they run? _____

*Why* did they run? _____

*How long* did they run? _____

*How often* did they run? _____

Sentence: _____

_____

_____

_____

_____

**2. Jumped**

*How* did they jump? _____

*When* did they jump? _____

*Where* did they jump? _____

*Why* did they jump? _____

*How long* did they jump? _____

*How often* did they jump? _____

Sentence: _____

_____

_____

_____

_____

# LO6 Prepositional Phrases

One of the simplest and most versatile types of phrases in English is the **prepositional phrase**. A prepositional phrase can function as an adjective or an adverb.

## Building Prepositional Phrases

A prepositional phrase is a preposition followed by an object (a noun or pronoun) and any modifiers.

| Preposition | + | Object | = | Prepositional Phrase |
|---|---|---|---|---|
| at | | noon | | at noon |
| in | | an hour | | in an hour |
| beside | | the green clock | | beside the green clock |
| in front of | | my aunt's vinyl purse | | in front of my aunt's vinyl purse |

As you can see, a prepositional phrase can be just two words long, or many words long. As you can also see, some prepositions are themselves made up of more than one word. Here is a list of common prepositions.

## Prepositions

| | | | | |
|---|---|---|---|---|
| aboard | back of | except for | near to | round |
| about | because of | excepting | notwithstanding | save |
| above | before | for | of | since |
| according to | behind | from | off | subsequent to |
| across | below | from among | on | through |
| across from | beneath | from between | on account of | throughout |
| after | beside | from under | on behalf of | 'til |
| against | besides | in | onto | to |
| along | between | in addition to | on top of | together with |
| alongside | beyond | in behalf of | opposite | toward |
| alongside of | but | in front of | out | under |
| along with | by | in place of | out of | underneath |
| amid | by means of | in regard to | outside | until |
| among | concerning | inside | outside of | unto |
| apart from | considering | inside of | over | up |
| around | despite | in spite of | over to | upon |
| as far as | down | instead of | owing to | up to |
| aside from | down from | into | past | with |
| at | during | like | prior to | within |
| away from | except | near | regarding | without |

# Using Phrases

**Create** For each item below, create a prepositional phrase by writing a preposition in the first box and an object (and any modifiers) in the second box. Then write a sentence using the prepositional phrase. Answers will vary.

1. | Preposition | **+** | Object (and any modifiers) |

Sentence: _____

_____

2. | Preposition | **+** | Object (and any modifiers) |

Sentence: _____

_____

3. | Preposition | **+** | Object (and any modifiers) |

Sentence: _____

_____

4. | Preposition | **+** | Object (and any modifiers) |

Sentence: _____

_____

5. | Preposition | **+** | Object (and any modifiers) |

Sentence: _____

_____

# LO7 Clauses

A clause is a group of words with a subject and a predicate. If a clause can stand on its own as a sentence, it is an **independent clause**, but if it cannot, it is a **dependent clause**.

## Independent Clause

An independent clause has a subject and a predicate and expresses a complete thought. It is the same as a simple sentence.

> Clouds piled up in the stormy sky.

## Dependent Clause

A dependent clause has a subject and a predicate but does not express a complete thought. Instead, it is used as an **adverb clause**, an **adjective clause**, or a **noun clause**.

**An adverb clause** begins with a subordinating conjunction (see below) and functions as an adverb, so it must be connected to an independent clause to be complete.

| | | | |
|---|---|---|---|
| after | before | since | when |
| although | even though | so that | whenever |
| as | given that | that | where |
| as if | if | though | whereas |
| as long as | in order that | unless | while |
| because | provided that | until | |

> Even though the forecast said clear skies, the storms rolled in.

**An adjective clause** begins with a relative pronoun *(which, that, who)* and functions as an adjective, so it must be connected to an independent clause to be complete.

> I don't like a meteorologist who often gets the forecast wrong.

**A noun clause** begins with words like those below and functions as a noun. It is used as a subject or an object in a sentence.

| | | | |
|---|---|---|---|
| how | what | whoever | whomever |
| that | whatever | whom | why |

> I wish he had known what the weather would be.

**Speaking & Listening**

In each example, read the dependent clause out loud. (The dependent clause is in red.) Can you hear how each dependent clause sounds incomplete? Read it to another person, and the listener will probably say, "What about it?" These clauses depend on a complete thought to make sense.

**Vocabulary**

**independent clause**
a group of words with a subject and predicate that expresses a complete thought

**dependent clause**
a group of words with a subject and predicate that does not express a complete thought

**adverb clause**
a dependent clause beginning with a subordinating conjunction and functioning as an adverb

**adjective clause**
a dependent clause beginning with a relative pronoun and functioning as an adjective

**noun clause**
a dependent clause beginning with a subordinating word and functioning as a noun

# Using Clauses

**Identify/Write** For each sentence below, underline and label any adverb clauses (ADVC), adjective clauses (ADJC), or noun clauses (NC). Then write a similar sentence of your own and identify the clauses.

1. I wonder why weather is so unpredictable. **[NC]**

   Answers will vary.

2. Though we have satellites, storms still surprise us. **[ADVC]**

   Answers will vary.

3. Many different factors determine what will happen in the sky. **[NC]**

   Answers will vary.

4. Until we can track all factors, we can't predict perfectly. **[ADVC]**

   Answers will vary.

5. Whoever gives a forecast is making a guess. **[NC]**

   Answers will vary.

6. Since weather is so uncertain, predictions have percentages. **[ADVC]**

   Answers will vary.

7. A 50 percent chance of rain means that there is a 50 percent chance of fair weather. **[NC]**

   Answers will vary.

8. When air crosses a large lake, it picks up moisture. **[ADVC]**

   Answers will vary.

9. Because of lake-effect rain, Valparaiso is called "Vapor Rain Snow." **[ADVC]**

   Answers will vary.

10. Buffalo gets as snow whatever moisture Lake Erie dishes up. **[NC]**

    Answers will vary.

# LO8 Real-World Application

**Identify** In the e-mail below, underline simple subjects once and simple predicates twice. Circle dependent clauses.

| Send | Attach | Fonts | Colors | Save As Draft |

To: Teri Bell

Subject: Revision Suggestions

Hi, Teri:

I enjoyed your article, "What Is New in *BattleTown 2*," submitted for publication on MMORPNews2.com. We are very interested in publishing your article but would like to request a few revisions before we send contracts.

This is a quick rundown of our revision suggestions:

1. The opening could be more gripping. The title works well to grab the reader's interest, but the opening feels flat. Perhaps you could provide a glimpse of new features of game play, or even give a scenario that wasn't possible in *BattleTown 1*.

2. A direct quotation from Todd Allen would strengthen the center section. Though you allude to your interview on many occasions, Todd never gets to speak for himself, and he is a definite name in the industry.

3. Can you get permission to use the visuals? AssemblyArts would love the free publicity, but you need written permission to include the screenshots.

If you could make these changes, we would be very interested in publishing your article. Once I see the revised piece, I can send a contract for you to sign.

Thanks,
Richard Prince

**Expand** Answer the adjective and adverb questions below. Then expand the sentence using some of the words, phrases, and clauses you have created.

**The agent called.** Answers will vary.

*Which* agent? _____

*What kind of* agent? _____

Called *when*? _____

Called *how*? _____

Sentence: _____

> "A complex system that works is invariably found to have evolved from a simple system that works."
>
> —John Gaule

# 21

# Simple, Compound, and Complex Sentences

Most leaves have a central stem with veins extending from it. Sometime this structure forms a simple oval, but at other times, two or more ovals connect to form a compound leaf. And the shape of some leaves is complex, as if a number of leaves were fused together.

Sentences are similar. All have a noun and a verb, but some stop at this simple structure. In other cases, two or more sentences combine to make a compound sentence. And when a sentence has one or more dependent clauses fused to it, it becomes complex.

This chapter shows how to create simple, compound, and complex sentences. As with leaves, variety makes sentences beautiful.

## Learning Outcomes

**LO1** Create simple sentences.

**LO2** Create simple sentences with compound subjects.

**LO3** Create simple sentences with compound verbs (predicates).

**LO4** Create compound sentences.

**LO5** Create complex sentences.

**LO6** Create complex sentences with relative clauses.

**LO7** Apply simple, compound, and complex sentences in a real-world document.

## What do you think?

Which type of leaf is most beautiful—a simple, compound, or complex leaf? Why?

Answers will vary.

*raresirimie,2010 / Used under license from Shutterstock.com*

# LO1 Simple Sentences

A **simple sentence** consists of a subject and a verb. The subject is a noun or pronoun that names what the sentence is about. The verb tells what the subject does or is.

Rachel sang.
subject  verb

## Modifiers

Other words can be added to modify the subject. Words that modify the subject answer the adjective questions: *which, what kind of, how many, how much.*

> **My new roommate** Rachel sang.
> *(Which Rachel do you mean?)*

Other words can also modify the verb. These words and phrases answer the adverb questions: *how, when, where, why, to what degree,* and *how often.*

> Rachel sang **in the shower at the top of her lungs.**
> *(Where and how did Rachel sing?)*

## Direct and Indirect Objects

The verb might also be followed by a noun or pronoun that receives the action of the verb. Such a word is called the **direct object,** and it answers the question *what* or *whom?*

> Rachel sang **"I Need a Hero."**
> *(What did Rachel sing?)*

Another noun or pronoun could come between the verb and the direct object, telling *to whom* or *for whom* an action is done. Such a word is the **indirect object.**

> I gave **her** a picture of Chuck Norris.
> *(I gave a picture of Chuck Norris to whom?)*

**Vocabulary**

**simple sentence**
a subject and a verb that together form a complete thought

**direct object**
a noun or pronoun that follows a verb and receives its action

**indirect object**
a noun or pronoun that comes between a verb and a direct object, telling *to whom* or *for whom* an action is done

**Insight**

In item 1, you are adding modifiers to the verb and in item 2, you are adding modifiers to the subject. In item 3, you are adding a direct object, and in item 4, you are adding an indirect object.

### Say It

Team up with a partner and follow these steps: One of you speaks the sentence aloud, and the other asks the question in italics. Then the first person says the sentence again, inserting an answer.

1. We sang songs. (*Where did you sing songs?*)

2. The song was our favorite. (*Which song was your favorite?*)

3. Rachel sang. (*What did Rachel sing?*)

4. I sang a song. (*To whom did you sing a song?*)

# Creating Simple Sentences

**Create** Provide a noun for a subject and a verb for a predicate. Then write a sentence with the noun and verb, adding details that answer the questions asked.

Answers will vary.

1. | Subject | | Verb |
   |---|---|---|

   Which?

   _____

   _____

2. | Subject | | Verb |
   |---|---|---|

   What kind of?

   _____

   _____

3. | Subject | | Verb |
   |---|---|---|

   When?

   _____

   _____

4. | Subject | | Verb |
   |---|---|---|

   Where?

   _____

   _____

5. | Subject | | Verb |
   |---|---|---|

   How?

   _____

   _____

# LO2 Simple Sentences with Compound Subjects

A simple sentence can have a **compound subject** (two or more subjects)

## A Simple Sentence with Two Subjects

To write a simple sentence with two subjects, join them using *and* or *or*.

**One Subject:** Lee worked on the Rube Goldberg machine.
**Two Subjects:** Lee **and** Jerome will add the lever arm that tips the bucket.
Lee **or** Jerome will add the lever arm that tips the bucket.

**One Subject:** Ms. Claymore will help them attach the flywheel.
**Two Subjects:** Ms. Claymore **and** her aide will help them attach the flywheel.
Either Ms. Claymore **or** her aide will help them attach the flywheel.

**Traits**

A compound subject does not make the sentence compound. As long as both (or all) of the subjects connect to the same verb or verbs, the sentence is still considered simple.

## A Simple Sentence with Three or More Subjects

To write a simple sentence with three or more subjects, create a series. List each subject, placing a comma after all but the last, and place an *and* or *or* before the last.

**Three Subjects:** Jerome, Lee, and Sandra are finishing the machine soon.
**Five Subjects:** Jerome, Lee, Sandra, Ms. Claymore, **and** her aide will enter the machine in a contest.

*Note:* When a compound subject is joined by *and*, the subject is plural and requires a plural verb. When a compound subject is joined by *or*, the verb should match the last subject.

**Ms. Claymore and her aide need** to submit the entry form.
**Ms. Claymore or her aide needs** to submit the entry form.

> ### Say It
>
> Speak each of the following sentences out loud.
>
> 1. Jerome *loves* the Rube Goldberg project.
> 2. Jerome *and* Sandra *love* the Rube Goldberg project.
> 3. Jerome *or* Sandra *works* on it every day after school.
> 4. Jerome, Sandra, *and* Lee *have* contributed most.
> 5. Jerome, Sandra, *or* Lee *has* contributed most.

# Using Compound Subjects

**Create** Write subjects in each of the boxes provided. Then write a sentence that includes the subjects as a compound subject using *and* or *or*.

Answers will vary.

1. | Subject | | Subject |

_____

_____

2. | Subject | | Subject |

_____

_____

3. | Subject | | Subject | | Subject |

_____

_____

4. | Subject | | Subject | | Subject |

_____

_____

5. | Subject | | Subject | | Subject | | Subject |

_____

_____

6. | Subject | | Subject | | Subject | | Subject |

_____

_____

# LO3 Simple Sentences with Compound Verbs

A simple sentence can also have two or more verbs (predicates). Remember that the predicate tells what the subject is doing or being, so as long as both predicates connect to the same subject, the sentence is still a simple sentence.

## Two Verbs

To create a **compound predicate** with two parts, join two verbs using *and* or *or*.

> **One Verb:** The band rocked.
> **Two Verbs:** The band rocked **and** danced.

Remember that the predicate includes not just the verbs, but also words that modify or complete the verbs.

> **One Predicate:** The band played their hit single.
> **Two Predicates:** The band played their hit single **and** covered other songs.

## Three or More Verbs

To create a compound predicate with three or more parts, list the verbs in a series, with a comma after each except the last, and the word *and* or *or* before the last.

> **Three Verbs:** The singer crooned, wailed, **and** roared.
> **Five Verbs:** The fans clapped, screamed, danced, cheered, **and** swayed.

If each verb also includes modifiers or completing words (direct and indirect objects), place the commas after each complete predicate.

> The crowd members got to their feet, waved their hands back and forth, and sang along with the band.

Ant Strack/Corbis Yellow/Corbis

# Using Compound Predicates

**Write** For each subject below, create predicates in the boxes provided. Then write a simple sentence that joins the compound predicates with *and* or *or*.

Answers will vary.

1. The reporters

| Predicate |
| --- |

| Predicate |
| --- |

_____

_____

2. The police

| Predicate |
| --- |

| Predicate |
| --- |

_____

_____

3. The manager

| Predicate |
| --- |

| Predicate |
| --- |

_____

_____

4. The bouncer

| Predicate |
| --- |

| Predicate |
| --- |

| Predicate |
| --- |

_____

_____

_____

# LO4 Compound Sentences

A **compound sentence** is made out of simple sentences joined by a coordinating conjunction: *and, but, or, nor, for, so,* or *yet*.

## Compound of Two Sentences

### Insight

The word *and* indicates that the second clause provides additional information. The words *but, or, nor,* and *yet* create a contrast. The words *for* and *so* indicate that one clause is the cause of the other.

Most compound sentences connect two simple sentences, which are also called independent clauses. Connect the sentences by placing a comma after the first sentence and using a coordinating conjunction after the comma.

> **Two Sentences:** We ordered pizza. I got just one piece.
> **Compound Sentence:** We ordered pizza, **but** I got just one piece.

## Compound of Three or More Sentences

Sometimes, you might want to join three or more short sentences in a compound sentence.

> **Two Sentences:** Tim likes cheese. Jan likes veggie. I like pepperoni.
> **Compound Sentence:** Tim likes cheese, Jan likes veggie, **and** I like pepperoni.

You can also join the sentences using semicolons. Authors sometimes use this approach to describe a long, involved process or a flurry of activity.

> Tim ate the cheese pizza; Jan ate the veggie pizza; Ray showed up and ate the pepperoni pizza; I got back in time for the last slice.

*Note:* Remember that a compound sentence is made of two or more complete sentences. Each part needs to have its own subject and verb.

Radius Images/Radius/Corbis

# Creating Compound Sentences

**Write** Write a simple sentence for each prompt; then combine them as a compound sentence.

Answers will vary.

1. What pizza do you like? _____

   What pizza does a friend like? _____

   Compound Sentence: _____

   _____

2. Where do you go for pizza? _____

   What other place do people go? _____

   Compound Sentence: _____

   _____

3. Who likes thin crust pizza? _____

   Who likes pan pizza? _____

   Who likes stuffed pizza? _____

   Compound Sentence: _____

   _____

4. What is the weirdest pizza? _____

   What is the grossest pizza? _____

   What is the stinkiest pizza? _____

   Compound Sentence: _____

   _____

   _____

5. When do you eat pizza? _____

   When do your friends eat pizza? _____

   When does your family eat pizza? _____

   Compound Sentence: _____

   _____

   _____

# LO5 Complex Sentences

A **complex sentence** shows a special relationship between two ideas. Instead of connecting two sentences as equal ideas (as in a compound sentence), a complex sentence shows that one idea depends on the other.

## Using a Subordinating Conjunction

You can create a complex sentence by placing a subordinating conjunction before the sentence that is less important. Here are common subordinating conjunctions:

| | | | |
|---|---|---|---|
| after | before | so that | when |
| although | even though | that | where |
| as | if | though | whereas |
| as if | in order that | till | while |
| as long as | provided that | 'til | |
| because | since | until | |

## Speaking & Listening

Read the example complex and compound-complex sentences aloud. Despite their daunting names, these sentences aren't that complicated. You use them all the time in speech. Experiment with them in your writing.

The subordinating conjunction shows that this sentence depends on the other sentence and can't stand without it.

**Two Sentences:** We played strong offense. We won the football game.

**Complex Sentence:** **Because** we played strong offense, we won the football game.

We won the football game **because** we played strong offense.

*Note:* The subordinating conjunction goes at the beginning of the less important clause, but the two clauses could go in either order. When the dependent clause comes second, it usually isn't set off with a comma.

## Compound-Complex

You can also create a **compound-complex sentence** by placing a subordinating conjunction before a simple sentence and connecting it to a compound sentence.

**Simple Sentence:** I threw two touchdowns.

**Compound Sentence:** Jake kicked the extra points and the other team couldn't catch up.

**Compound-Complex:** **After I threw two touchdowns,** Jake kicked the extra points, and the other team couldn't catch up.

# Creating Complex Sentences

**Write** Write a simple sentence after each prompt. Then select a subordinating conjunction from the facing page, place it at the beginning of one sentence, and combine the two sentences into a single complex sentence.

Answers will vary.

1. What did you play? _____

   Did you win or lose? _____

   Complex sentence: _____

2. Who did you play? _____

   Why did you play the opponent? _____

   Complex sentence: _____

3. Who won the game? _____

   Why did that side win? _____

   Complex sentence: _____

4. Where did you play? _____

   Where else could you have played? _____

   Complex sentence: _____

5. What surprised you? _____

   Why did it surprise you? _____

   Complex sentence: _____

6. How long did you play? _____

   When did you stop? _____

   Complex sentence: _____

# LO6 Complex Sentences with Relative Clauses

In a complex sentence, one idea depends on the other. You've seen how a dependent clause can start with a subordinating conjunction. Another type of dependent clause starts with a relative pronoun.

## Relative Clauses

A **relative clause** is a group of words that begins with a **relative pronoun** (*that, which, who, whom*) and includes a verb and any words that modify or complete it:

> **Relative Clauses:** that leads into the garden
> which usually leans against the shed
> who planted the scallions
> whom I asked to help me weed

Each relative clause above has a subject and a verb, but none of the clauses is a complete sentence. All need to be connected to a complete sentence.

> **Complex Sentences:** I followed the path that leads into the garden.
> I looked for the shovel, which usually leans against the shed.
> We have many onions thanks to a friend who planted the scallions.
> I worked with Tina, whom I asked to help me weed.

**Insight**

In some languages, if the relative pronoun is the object of the clause it introduces, another pronoun is inserted in the clause: *I liked the gift that my boss gave* it *to me.* In English, no additional pronoun is inserted: *I liked the gift that my boss gave to me.*

## *That* and *Which*

The pronoun *that* signals that the information after it is necessary to the sentence. The pronoun *which* signals that the information is not necessary, so the clause is set off with a comma.

> **That:** The scallions **that** we planted this spring taste strongest. (*That* defines the scallions.)
> **Which:** I love scallions, **which** I eat raw or fried. (*Which* does not define the scallions but just adds more information about them.)

## *Who* and *Whom*

The pronoun *who* is the subject of the relative clause that it introduces. The pronoun *whom* is a direct object of a clause it introduces.

> **Who:** I helped the woman **who** harvested scallions. (*Who* is the subject.)
> **Whom:** I thanked the woman **whom** I helped. (*Whom* is the direct object.)

**Vocabulary**

**relative clause**
a group of words that begins with a relative pronoun and includes a verb but cannot stand alone as a sentence

**relative pronoun**
a word *(that, which, who, whom)* that relates a relative clause with another word in the sentence

# Using Relative Clauses

**Create** For each item, write a relative clause beginning with the pronoun provided. Then write a complex sentence that includes the relative clause. In case you need a topic idea, think of a party you have attended or one that you would like to attend.

Answers will vary.

1. Relative clause: _that_____

   Complex sentence: _____

   _____

   _____

2. Relative clause: _who_____

   Complex sentence: _____

   _____

   _____

3. Relative clause: _which_____

   Complex sentence: _____

   _____

   _____

4. Relative clause: _whom_____

   Complex sentence: _____

   _____

   _____

5. Relative clause: _that_____

   Complex sentence: _____

   _____

   _____

6. Relative clause: _which_____

   Complex sentence: _____

   _____

   _____

**Learning Outcome**

Apply simple, compound, and complex sentences in a real-world document.

# LO6 Real-World Application

**Rewrite** Read the following message about a meeting. Note how every sentence is a simple sentence. Rewrite the message, combining sentences into some compound or complex sentences and improving the flow.

**Workplace**

Using a variety of sentences in workplace writing will help ideas flow and will present a polished image.

Dear Mr. Lindau:

You asked about the Monday production meeting. I will summarize it. The production staff met with the editors. The writers explained their new project. It focuses on twenty-first century skills. The writers presented two chapters. They will become a prototype.

The new project needs to be visual. It should appeal to students and teachers. The design needs to make text accessible. The writing has an open quality. It still feels academic. The book should be available for sale in the fall. A teacher's edition will follow.

The designers are beginning work on a prototype. The writers continue to create chapters.

**Dear Mr. Lindau:** Answers will vary.

> "Never offend people with style when you can
> offend them with substance."
> —Sam Brown

Aurelie and Morgan David de Lossy/cultura/cultura/Corbis

# 22

# Sentence Style

The purpose of makeup is to accentuate a person's natural beauty. Mascara that thickens lashes, blush that lends color to cheeks, lipstick that tastefully outlines the contours of one's lips—these are the appropriate uses of makeup.

Curly mustaches and goatees are not.

In the same way, sentence style is not about putting on a false face or making elaborate curlicues in your writing. It's about saying what you want to say and expressing who you really are. This chapter will help you create effective sentence style.

## Learning Outcomes

**LO1** Vary sentence lengths.

**LO2** Vary sentence beginnings.

**LO3** Combine with coordination.

**LO4** Combine with subordination.

**LO5** Combine by moving parts.

**LO6** Combine by deleting.

**LO7** Expand sentences.

**LO8** Model professional sentences.

**LO9** Revise a real-world document for sentence style.

## What do you think?

What will this young man think of his makeup? What do others think? What do readers think of a sentence style that is equally fake and "dressed up"?

Answers will vary.

261

# L◯1 Varying Sentence Lengths

To create a smooth flow of thought, use a variety of sentence lengths.

## Short Sentences

Short sentences are powerful. They make a point. In dramatic circumstances, a series of short sentences can create a staccato effect:

> I like pigs. Dogs look up to us. Cats look down on us. Pigs treat us as equals.
>
> —Sir Winston Churchill

Sometimes a series of short sentences will start to sound choppy. In such situations, use short sentences in combination with longer sentences.

**WAC**

Read an article or a speech in your major, noting the lengths of the sentences. Count the words in each. What effect does the variety of sentences (or lack of variety) have on readability?

## Medium Sentences

Medium-length sentences do most of the work in everyday writing. They are not overly punchy or overly complicated, and so they communicate well.

> I look to the future because that's where I'm going to spend the rest of my life.
>
> —George Burns

## Long Sentences

Long sentences express complex ideas and create an expansive feeling. The long sentence may be the hardest type to pull off because it needs to have a clear sense of direction. Otherwise, it may begin to ramble.

> I write entirely to find out what I'm thinking, what I'm looking at, what I see and what it means, what I want and what I fear.
>
> —Joan Didion

## Varying Lengths

The most effective writing includes sentences of different lengths, serving different purposes. Read this call to action, noting the different lengths of sentences and their effect on the whole.

> You're alive. Do something. The directive in life, the moral imperative was so uncomplicated. It could be expressed in single words, not complete sentences. It sounded like this: Look. Listen. Choose. Act.
>
> —Barbara Hall

# Varying Sentence Lengths

**Create** Write the types of sentences requested below.

Answers will vary.

**1.** Write a short sentence naming your favorite food.

_____

**2.** Write a medium sentence describing your favorite food.

_____

_____

**3.** Write a long sentence indicating what you like most about this food.

_____

_____

_____

**4.** Write a medium sentence providing a final thought about the food.

_____

_____


**Create** Write the types of sentences requested below.

Answers will vary.

**1.** Write a short sentence indicating your course of study.

_____

**2.** Write a medium sentence describing your course of study.

_____

_____

**3.** Write a long sentence explaining why you chose to follow this course.

_____

_____

_____

**4.** Write a medium sentence providing a final thought about the course of study.

_____

_____

**Test Taking**

It is more important to be
able to use prepositional
phrases and infinitive
phrases than to be able to
identify them. However,
some tests require the
ability to identify phrases.
For more practice, see
pages 242–243 and
386–387.

# LO2 New Beginnings 1

If every sentence begins with the subject, writing can become monotonous. Vary
sentence beginnings by starting in these different ways.

## Prepositional Phrase

A **prepositional phrase** is formed from a preposition (*in, at, through*) followed
by an object (a noun and any modifiers). (For more prepositions, see page
386.)

PR = Preposition
O = Object

| After the game . . . | For that matter . . . | With a renewed interest . . . |
|---|---|---|
| PR     O | PR     O | PR       O |

A prepositional phrase functions as an adjective or an adverb. That means that
a prepositional phrase can answer any of the adjective or adverb questions:

| Adjective Questions | Adverb Questions |
|---|---|
| Which? | How? |
| What kind of? | When? |
| How many? | Where? |
| How much? | Why? |
| | How often? |
| | To what degree? |

## Infinitive Phrase

An **infinitive phrase** is formed from the word *to* followed by a verb and any
objects and modifiers.

V = Verb
O = Object

| To prove my point . . . | To complete the comparison . . . | To be specific . . . |
|---|---|---|
| V    O | V     O | V   O |

An infinitive phrase functions as a noun, an adjective, or an adverb. It can
answer any of the adjective and adverb questions above, but it can also serve
as the subject of the sentence:

**To complete my degree** is my goal.
(*To complete my degree* functions as the subject of the sentence.)

**Vocabulary**

**prepositional phrase**
phrase formed from a
preposition followed by an
object and any modifiers;
functioning as an adjective or
adverb

**infinitive phrase**
verbal phrase that begins
with *to* followed by a verb and
any objects; functioning as a
noun, an adjective, or
an adverb

# Varying with Prepositional and Infinitive Phrases

**Vary** For each sentence below, add the requested type of beginning.

Answers will vary.

**1.** (Prepositional phrase):

_____

we decided to go out for ice cream.

**2.** (Infinitive phrase):

_____

we bought homemade frozen custard instead.

**3.** (Prepositional phrase):

_____

the custard was richer and creamier.

**4.** (Infinitive phrase):

_____

an occasional treat like this helps keep life in balance.

**Create** Write the types of sentences requested below.

Answers will vary.

**1.** Write a short sentence about a treat you like. (Begin with a prepositional phrase.)

_____

**2.** Write a medium sentence about the treat. (Begin with an infinitive phrase.)

_____

_____

**3.** Write a long sentence about the treat. (Begin with a prepositional phrase.)

_____

_____

_____

**4.** Write a medium sentence about the treat. (Begin with an infinitive phrase.)

_____

_____

# LO2 New Beginnings II

If sentences still sound repetitive, you can start with two other constructions—participial phrases and adverb clauses.

## Participial Phrase

A **participial phrase** is formed from a participle (verb ending in *ing* or *ed*) and any objects and modifiers. (For more on participles, see page 362.)

PA = Participle
O = Object

| Expecting the best . . . | Considering the source . . . | Concerning the plan . . . |
|:---:|:---:|:---:|
| PA         O | PA         O | PA         O |

A participial phrase functions as an adjective. That means that the phrase answers one of the adjective questions.

| Adjective Questions | |
|---|---|
| Which? | How many? |
| What kind of? | How much? |

## Adverb Clause

An **adverb clause** is formed from a subordinating conjunction followed by a noun (or pronoun) and verb (and any objects and modifiers).

SC = Subordinating Conjunction        N = Noun        V = Verb

| When Bill arrived . . . | Because Jan climbed so high . . . | While Ted watched . . . |
|:---:|:---:|:---:|
| SC    N    V | SC    N    V | SC    N    V |

| Subordinating Conjunctions | | | |
|---|---|---|---|
| after | before | since | when |
| although | even though | so that | whenever |
| as | given that | that | where |
| as if | if | though | whereas |
| as long as | in order that | unless | while |
| because | provided that | until | |

An adverb clause functions as an adverb, answering one of the adverb questions.

| Adverb Questions | |
|---|---|
| How? | Why? |
| When? | How often? |
| Where? | To what degree? |

# Varying with Participial Phrases and Adverb Clauses

**Vary** For each sentence below, add the requested type of beginning.

Answers will vary.

**1.** (Participial phrase):

_____

we worked all through the evening.

**2.** (Adverb clause):

_____

the lights from our office shone out on the people passing by.

**3.** (Participial phrase):

_____

I smiled at my colleagues and shook their hands.

**4.** (Adverb clause):

_____

the project was finished, and we could at last go home.

**Create** Write the types of sentences requested below.

Answers will vary.

**1.** Write a short sentence about working. (Begin with a participial phrase.)

_____

**2.** Write a medium sentence about working. (Begin with an adverb clause.)

_____

_____

**3.** Write a long sentence about working. (Begin with an adverb clause.)

_____

_____

_____

**4.** Write a medium sentence about working. (Begin with a participial phrase.)

_____

_____

# LO3 Using Coordination

When you have too many short sentences, writing begins to sound choppy. Look for sentences that have related ideas and combine them.

## Coordination

### Insight

The word *coordinate* means "to place together." A *coordinating conjunction,* then, is a word that connects ideas in an equal way, placing them together.

If two sentences express ideas of equal importance, you can combine the sentences by connecting them with a **coordinating conjunction**. (See the box below.)

| Coordinating Conjunctions | | | | | | |
|---|---|---|---|---|---|---|
| and | but | or | nor | for | so | yet |

**Choppy:** Human beings are self-aware. Animals may or may not be.

**Combined:** Human beings are self-aware**, but** animals may or may not be.

*Note:* Remember to place a comma before the conjunction.

The different coordinating conjunctions make different connections between ideas:

**Comparison** ⟶ and
**Contrast** ⟶ but, yet
**Options** ⟶ or, nor
**Cause** ⟶ so, for

Human beings recognize themselves in mirrors**, and** great apes can as well.
Dolphins recognize themselves in mirrors**, so** they must be self-aware.
Dogs, cats, and babies do not**, so** their self-awareness is in question.

Scorpp.2010 / Used under license from Shutterstock.com

# Combining Using Coordination

**Coordinate** Mark the sentences below to show what coordinating conjunction you would insert to combine them. Use the correction marks as needed to add words and change punctuation and capitalization.

| Correction Marks | |
|---|---|
| ℒ | delete |
| d̲̲ | capitalize |
| Ø | lowercase |
| ∧ | insert |
| ⌃̓ | add comma |
| ? ∧ | add question mark |
| word ∧ | add word |
| ⊙ | add period |
| ⬭ | spelling |
| ∿ | switch |

1. Gordon Gallup created the mirror test. He was testing self-awareness. ^for

2. Gallup put odorless dye on an animal. Spots were in front and in back. ^and

3. The animal looked in a mirror. Some animals noticed the front spot. ^and

4. The animal shifted to see better. Pawing the body part showed awareness. ^and

5. Other animals did not notice the spot. The mirror image seemed another animal. ^for

6. Great apes, dolphins and orcas, and elephants passed. Monkeys did not. ^but (or yet)

7. Pigeons could be trained to pass. Magpies passed without training. ^yet (or but)

8. A sticker was under the magpie's beak. The bird tried to pull it off. ^so

9. The other passing creatures had big brains. Magpies have small brains. ^but

10. Magpies are visual creatures. Shiny things attract them. ^so

11. Dogs are more olfactory. Smell is used to identify themselves and others. ^so

12. Dogs might need an olfactory test. Smell is a better indicator for them. ^for

13. Humans would fail an olfactory test. We don't want to smell ourselves. ^for

14. Pigs passed a modified test. Food was reflected in a mirror. ^for

15. Most pigs turned around to find the food. One in eight looked behind the mirror. ^yet (or but)

16. Pigs may not be self-aware. Food-aware is a different story. ^but

17. Squid are very intelligent. Perhaps the mirror test would work for them. ^so

18. Squid have big eyes and brains. Both are needed to succeed on the mirror test. ^and

# LO4 Using Subordination

If sentences sound choppy, you can combine them using subordination.

## Subordination

If one sentence is more important than the other, you can combine the sentences by connecting them with a **subordinating conjunction**. (See the box below). Place the subordinating conjunction before the less important part.

| Subordinating Conjunctions | | | |
|---|---|---|---|
| after | before | since | when |
| although | even though | so that | whenever |
| as | given that | that | where |
| as if | if | though | whereas |
| as long as | in order that | unless | while |
| because | provided that | until | |

**Choppy:** Every culture has music. Music is an innate part of being human.
**Combined:** **Because** every culture has music, music is an innate part of being human.

**Choppy:** Music is a language of emotion. It first touches one's feelings.
**Combined:** Music is a language of emotion **because** it first touches one's feelings.

*Note:* If the subordinate clause comes first, put a comma between the clauses.

Different subordinating conjunctions show different kinds of connections:

**Time** ⟶ after, as, as long as, before, since, until, when, whenever, while

**Cause** ⟶ because, given that, if, in order that, provided that, since, so that

**Contrast** ⟶ although, as if, even though, though, unless, whereas, while

sextoacto,2010 / Used under license from Shutterstock.com

# Combining Using Subordination

**Subordinate** Mark the sentences below to show what subordinating conjunction you would use to combine them. Use the correction marks as needed to add words and add and delete punctuation.

Example answers:

1. A note can be high or low. *because* The pitch is the frequency of wavelength.

2. A note can be short or long. *since* The duration is its length in time.

3. Changes in duration make rhythm. *whereas* Changes in pitch make melodies.

4. Sound is waves. *given that* Waves move through air, water, and other substances.

5. *While* We use sound to communicate in speech. Music is the cousin of speech.

6. A spoken sentence can become a melody. *given that* The program Autotune can do it.

7. *Though* Language communicates emotion. Music communicates emotion even more.

8. Music is also mathematical. *given that* It measures pitch and time.

9. *Though* Mathematical patterns repeat throughout. Music makes the math emotional.

10. *Although* Science designs instruments. Musicians make science into art.

---

**Write** For each prompt, write a simple sentence, with a subject and predicate. Then combine the sentences, using subordination.   Answers will vary.

1. What music do you like most? _____

   What music do your friends like? _____

   Combine: _____

   _____

2. Where do you get your music? _____

   Where do your friends get their music? _____

   Combine: _____

   _____

# LO5 Combining by Moving Parts

Sometimes sentences need to be combined because they cover the same material. The way to combine such sentences is to move one part of one sentence into the other sentence.

### Moving a Word

**Before:** Chinese New Year lasts for 15 days. Each day is festive.

**After:** Chinese New Year lasts for 15 festive days.

### Moving a Phrase

**Before:** Red lanterns scare off the monster Nien. Children dressed in red scare him, too.

**After:** Red lanterns and children dressed in red scare off the monster Nien.

**Before:** People clean their houses. They try to sweep away bad luck.

**After:** People clean their houses to sweep away bad luck.

### Reworking Sentences

**Before:** Chinese New Year changes each year. It falls between January 21 and February 20. The date is usually on the second new moon after the winter solstice.

**After:** Chinese New Year falls between January 21 and February 20, usually on the second new moon after the winter solstice.

Image Source/Image Source/Corbis

# Combining by Moving Parts

**Combine** Combine each pair of sentences below by moving a word or phrase or by reworking the sentences.

1. Nien used to stalk villages. The monster would devour animals, plants, and people.
   The monster Nien used to stalk villages, devouring animals, plants, and people.

2. Villagers left food offerings. The offerings would satisfy Nien's hunger.
   Villagers left food offerings to satisfy Nien's hunger.

3. A child wearing red confronted Nien. The child in red scared the monster.
   A child wearing red confronted Nien and scared the monster.

4. Red became a lucky color. It was used with lanterns and spring scrolls.
   Red, used with lanterns and spring scrolls, became a lucky color.

5. Firecrackers also scared him. They were loud and bright.
   Loud and bright firecrackers also scared him.

6. Nien was driven off. The monster was tamed by a Taoist monk.
   Tamed by a Taoist monk, Nien was driven off.

7. The monk rode Nien. The monster never bothered anyone again.
   The monk rode Nien, and the monster never bothered anyone again.

8. People cleaned house. They wanted to get rid of bad luck.
   People cleaned house to get rid of bad luck.

9. The clean houses were ready. Good luck could come into them.
   The clean houses were ready for good luck to come into them.

10. Villagers gave each other red envelopes. The envelopes had money inside.
    Villagers gave each other red envelopes with money inside.

# LO6 Combining by Deleting

When writing is wordy or repetitious, the best way to combine sentences is by finding the key pieces of information, deleting the rest, and writing new sentences from what is left.

## Finding the Key Pieces

Read the following paragraph, noting how wordy and repetitious it is. Afterward, note the important ideas that the writer underlined.

What is the difference between science fiction and fantasy? Well, it seems when you look at it at first that the main difference is that science fiction is about technology while fantasy is about magic. That definition might seem pretty good at first, but when you think about it, the difference between science fiction and fantasy goes deeper. Science fiction is all about achieving the new. In a science fiction story, usually the world is changed by what happens in the story and it will never be the same again. Fantasy is just the opposite. In a fantasy story, the whole point is to get things back to the way they used to be, for example restoring a king or rediscovering an ancient and lost treasure or artifact. When you think of it that way, science fiction is revolutionary and fantasy is reactionary. So, though it is true that science fiction features technology and fantasy features magic, the deeper difference is that science fiction looks to the future and change while fantasy looks to the past and continuity.

## Rewriting and Combining

Now read the much shorter and more effective sentences that the writer wrote from the main ideas.

What is the difference between science fiction and fantasy? Some say science fiction is about technology while fantasy is about magic, but the difference goes deeper. Science fiction is all about achieving the new, while fantasy is about returning to what is old. In that way, science fiction is revolutionary and fantasy is reactionary.

# Combining by Deleting

**Underline** Read the following wordy, repetitive paragraph. Afterward, go back through and reread the paragraph, looking for important details. Underline them.

Let's look at <u>two classic films,</u> <u>one from science fiction</u> and <u>the other from fantasy.</u> <u>The science fiction film is</u> *2001: A Space Odyssey*. The film shows a lot of <u>technology,</u> which may or may not look really impressive now because the film was made in the '60s. The main point of the film is to show the <u>conflict between the human astronauts and their thinking computer, HAL, who tries to take over the ship.</u> <u>The astronauts manage to shut down the computer,</u> but they and the computer <u>are drawn into connection with</u> <u>a mysterious object</u> in space and <u>the people and computer fuse to become a new life form.</u> The world will never be the same. <u>Now think of</u> *The Lord of the Rings*. In it, the whole <u>point is to stop an ancient evil from rising</u> and <u>save the world from being destroyed.</u> This film is all about trying to save something that is important, and even <u>the last part—</u>*The Return of the King*—<u>tells about restoring the ancient lineage of human beings</u> to return their age of glory. The world is renewed. Note how *2001: A Space Odyssey* focuses on <u>plunging headlong into an unknowable future,</u> while *The Lord of the Rings* focuses on <u>returning to a better past.</u>

**Combine** Rewrite the paragraph above without unimportant details, combining important details into new sentences. Make the new paragraph concise and smooth.

Answers will vary.

# LO7 Sentence Expanding

Sometimes a sentence does not say enough, or it is too general. When that happens, the sentence needs to be expanded. Sentence expanding simply means adding details. The best way to expand a sentence is to answer the 5 W's about the topic.

**Speaking & Listening**

Imagine each sentence-expanding activity on the facing page as a conversation you are having with a friend. You might even read the sentence aloud and have a friend ask you each of the questions beneath. Then roll some of your answers into a single, more-informative sentence.

**Original Sentence:** My friend likes extreme sports.

*Who* likes extreme sports? my friend Liam

*What* sports does he like? He likes BMX biking and jumping.

*Where* does he train? He trains in a field beside his yard.

*When* did he start? about eight years ago

*Why* does he do it? He loves the adrenaline rush.

**Expanded Sentence:** My friend Liam likes the extreme sport of BMX biking and jumping, and he trains in a field beside his house.

*Note:* The expanded sentence does not use all of the answers to the 5 W's, but a second sentence could cover the other details:

He started BMX jumping about eight years ago and says he loves the adrenaline rush.

# Expanding Sentences

**Expand** Expand the sentences below by answering the questions provided.

Answers will vary.

1. **Short Sentence:** My friend needs help.

   **a.** Who is your friend?_____

   **b.** What help does the person need?_____

   **c.** Where does the friend need help?_____

   **d.** When does the person need help?_____

   **e.** Why does the person need help?_____

   **Expanded Sentence:** _____

   _____

   _____

   _____

   _____

   _____

2. **Short Sentence:** My friend got hurt.

   **a.** Who is your friend?_____

   **b.** What happened to the person?_____

   **c.** Where did the person get hurt?_____

   **d.** When did the person get hurt?_____

   **e.** Why did the person get hurt?_____

   **Expanded Sentence:** _____

   _____

   _____

   _____

   _____

   _____

# LO8 Sentence Modeling

Sentence modeling helps you see new ways to put sentences together. Modeling involves reading a well-written sentence and then writing a similar sentence by substituting words. Here is an example original sentence and a sentence modeled after it.

**Original Sentence:** It seemed the world was divided into good and bad people. The good ones slept better, while the bad ones seemed to enjoy the waking hours much more.

—Woody Allen

**Modeled Sentence:** I figured the school was divided into talkers and listeners. The talkers dominated in class, while the listeners got better grades on the tests.

***Note:*** The new sentence doesn't *exactly* match the model. The writer made adjustments to make the sentence work.

**Original Sentence:** Storms are sensual feasts—the cold wet touch of rain, the smell of damp soil, the percussive crack of thunder, the brilliant flashes of lightning.

—Eli King

**Modeled Sentence:** Morning on the lake was a languid treat—the soft wet slap of oars, the coils of rising mist, the watery murmur of waves, the dark, welling depths.

***Note:*** In the sentence above, the writer chose words that had an opposite feeling from the ones in the original and created a passage with a very different impact. Notice, however, that the sentence still works and makes sense.

**WAC**

Instead of modeling sentences taken from literature, you can model well-constructed sentences from your academic discipline. When you find a great sentence in one of your books, try to craft a similar sentence. You'll be learning the way professionals write in your field of study.

Richard Bowden, 2010 / Used under license from Shutterstock.com

# Modeling Sentences

**Model** Create sentences that model the ones below.

Answers will vary.

1. Thanks to the Interstate Highway System, it is now possible to travel from coast to coast without seeing anything.

—Charles Kuralt

2. It was a bright cold day in April, and the clocks were striking thirteen.

—George Orwell

3. The average, healthy, well-adjusted adult gets up at seven-thirty in the morning feeling just plain terrible.

—Jean Kerr

4. Arranging a bowl of flowers in the morning can give a sense of quiet in a crowded day—like writing a poem, or saying a prayer.

—Anne Morrow Lindberg

5. The secret of staying young is to live honestly, eat slowly, and lie about your age.

—Lucille Ball

6. A boy can learn a lot from a dog: obedience, loyalty, and the importance of turning around three times before lying down.

—Robert Benchley

7. My mother used to say that there are no strangers, only friends you haven't met yet. She's now in a maximum security twilight home in Australia.

—Dame Edna Everage

# LO9 Real-World Application

**Expand** Read the following cover letter, written to present a résumé for a job. Note how the writer uses a lot of short, say-nothing sentences that could refer to anyone. Then rewrite the letter below, expanding the sentences with details you either make up or take from your own life. Make the letter interesting, informative, and engaging by improving the sentences style and enriching the content.

**Workplace**

As you can see from this exercise, bland sentences can cost you a job, and great sentences can land you one.

Dear Mr. Dawson:

Do you need a good worker? I need a good employer. My education is good. I have work experience.

Many traits make me a good worker. I do well with many things.

Do you need a good worker? If so, please contact me.

I look forward to hearing from you.

Sincerely,

**Dear Mr. Dawson:**

Answers will vary.

"My idea of an agreeable person is a person who agrees with me."

—Benjamin Disraeli

# 23 Agreement

When two people agree, they can work together. They have the same goals and outlook, and they can become a team.

Subjects and verbs are much the same. If the subject is plural, the verb needs to be as well, or they can't work together. Pronouns also need to agree with their antecedents in terms of number. Without agreement, these words fight each other, and instead of conveying ideas, they disrupt communication.

This chapter focuses on the agreement between subjects and verbs and between pronouns and antecedents. It also tackles other pronoun problems. After you work through the exercises here, you'll find it easy to write agreeable sentences.

## Learning Outcomes

**LO1** Make subjects and verbs agree.

**LO2** Make two subjects agree with verbs.

**LO3** Practice agreement with *I* and *you.*

**LO4** Practice agreement with indefinite pronouns.

**LO5** Practice pronoun-antecedent agreement.

**LO6** Correct other pronoun problems.

**LO7** Check agreement in a real-world context.

## What do you think?

What makes a person agreeable? What makes subjects and verbs agreeable?

Answers will vary.

Bernd Vogel/Fancy/Corbis

281

# LO1 Subject-Verb Agreement

A verb must **agree in number** with the subject of the sentence. If the subject is singular, the verb must be singular. If the subject is plural, the verb must be plural.

| singular subject | + | singular verb | = agreement | | plural subject | + | plural verb | = agreement |

The truck needs a tune-up.          The trucks need tune-ups.

Note how plural subjects often end in *s*, but plural verbs usually do not. Also note that only present tense verbs and certain *be* verbs have separate singular and plural forms.

| Present: | singular | plural | | Past: | singular | plural |
|---|---|---|---|---|---|---|
| | walks | walk | | | walked | walked |
| | sees | see | | | saw | saw |
| | eats | eat | | | ate | ate |
| | is/am | are | | | was | were |

To make most verbs singular, add just an *s*.

run—runs          write—writes          stay—stays

The verbs *do* and *go* are made singular by adding an *es*.

do—does          go—goes

When a verb ends in *ch, sh, x,* or *z,* make it singular by adding *es*.

latch—latches          wish—wishes          fix—fixes          buzz—buzzes

When a verb ends in a consonant followed by a *y,* change the *y* to *i* and add *es*.

try—tries          fly—flies          cry—cries          quantify—quantifies

**Insight**

The "Say It" activity below will help you become familiar with the subject-verb agreement patterns in English. Practice it aloud, and for added practice, write the sentences as well.

> ## Say It
>
> Read the following sentences aloud, emphasizing the words in *italics*.
>
> 1. The bird *sings*. The birds *sing*. The phone *rings*. The phones *ring*.
> 2. The person *is*. The people *are*. The child *is*. The children *are*.
> 3. He *works*. They *work*. She *learns*. They *learn*.
> 4. The woman *does*. The women *do*. The man *goes*. The men *go*.
> 5. She *wishes*. They *wish*. He *boxes*. They *box*.

# Correcting Basic Subject-Verb Agreement

Speaking & Listening

**Write**  In each sentence below, write the correct form of the verb in parentheses.

After completing the sentences in the first activity, say them aloud, emphasizing the underlined verbs.

1. A philosophy major _____knows_____ about thinking. (know)

2. A philosopher _____tries_____ to find philosophical work. (try)

3. An employer rarely _____wishes_____ to hire philosophers. (wish)

4. But such students _____are_____ able to think (is).

5. My roommate _____studies_____ philosophy. (study)

6. He also _____needs_____ to study the want ads for jobs. (need)

7. He _____says_____ employers need thinkers. (say)

8. That idea _____makes_____ sense. (make)

9. But that idea doesn't _____make_____ people hire him. (make)

10. At his job, he _____fixes_____ lawn mowers very philosophically. (fix)

**Correct**  Read the following paragraph. Correct any agreement errors you find by crossing out the incorrect verb and writing the correct present tense verb above.

      The philosopher Plato ~~say~~ *says* the material world ~~aren't~~ *isn't* the real world. He ~~say~~ *says* we ~~sees~~ *see* shadows on a cave wall. Plato ~~believe~~ *believes* in eternal forms of perfection. Every real table in the world ~~are~~ *is* patterned after the perfect form of a table. In that way, people too ~~is~~ *are* patterned after the perfect form of people. Though Plato ~~live~~ *lives* more than three hundred years before Jesus, many Christian thinkers ~~likes~~ *like* his concept of eternal forms. The idea ~~fit~~ *fits* well with the ideas of a soul and a creator. Many modern thinkers, though, ~~has~~ *have* the opposite idea. They ~~says~~ *say* that only physical things ~~is~~ *are* real. Plato, of course, ~~disagree~~ *disagrees*.

**Write**  For each plural verb below, write one sentence using the verb in its singular form.  Answers will vary.

1. fly _____

2. do _____

3. fish _____

4. wax _____

5. go _____

6. deny _____

**Test Taking**

For more practice with
compound subjects, see
pages 250–251.

# LO2 Agreement with Two Subjects

Sentences with **compound subjects** have special rules to make sure that they
agree.

## Two or More Subjects

When a sentence has two or more subjects
joined by *and,* the verb should be plural.

plural
subject **+** plural
verb **=** agreement

Jumbo and Dumbo **march.**

When a sentence has two or more subjects
joined by *or, nor,* or *but also,* the verb should
agree with the last subject.

**or**

singular
subject **+** singular
verb **=** agreement

Either Jumbo or Dumbo trumpets.

Not only Jumbo but also Dumbo trumpets.

Radius Images/Radius/Corbis

---

### Say It

Read the following sentences aloud, emphasizing the words in *italics*.

1. Jumbo *and* Dumbo *perform*. Jumbo *or* Dumbo *performs*.

2. The man *and* woman *dance*. The man *or* woman *dances*.

3. The Democrat *and* the Republican *agree*. The Democrat *or* the
   Republican *agrees*.

4. Not only Dave *but also* Tim *writes*.

5. The dog, cat, *and* guinea pig *greet* me. The dog, cat, *or* guinea
   pig *greets* me.

**Vocabulary**

**compound subject**
two or more subjects that
share the same verb or verbs

# Fixing Agreement with Two Subjects

**Write** In each sentence below, write the correct form of the verb in parentheses.

1. The acrobat and clown _____ entertain _____ the crowd. (entertain)
2. The acrobat or clown _____ gets _____ a pie in the face. (get)
3. A trapeze artist and a tightrope walker _____ receive _____ an ovation. (receive)
4. Not only the acrobat but also the clown _____ is _____ highly paid. (are)
5. Neither the lion tamer nor the sword swallower _____ has _____ insurance. (have)
6. The human cannonball or the lion tamer _____ has _____ the scariest job. (have)
7. Either Todd or Lewis _____ plans _____ to join the circus. (plan)
8. Thrills and hard work _____ await _____ Todd or Lewis. (await)
9. Not only Todd but also Lewis _____ is _____ a daredevil. (are)
10. The clowns or the ringmaster _____ introduces _____ each act. (introduce)

**Correct** Read the following paragraph. Correct any agreement errors you find by crossing out the incorrect verb and writing the correct present tense verb above.

Childhood dreams and fantasies rarely ~~comes~~ come true. A firefighter or police officer ~~are~~ is what many children dream of being. Imagine a world filled with firefighters and police! Neither the accountant nor the landscaper ~~figure~~ figures big in childhood plans. A princess or a wizard ~~are~~ is also a popular choice for kids. Job openings and pay for both careers ~~is~~ are pretty slim. Even the job of astronaut or explorer ~~have~~ has become scarce. The trials of joblessness and the responsibilities of adulthood ~~conspires~~ conspire to convince people to seek other careers. Childhood stars sometimes get "real" jobs, too. Johnny Whitaker and Wil Wheaton ~~works~~ work with computers. They traded childhood dreams for adult ones.

**Write** Write a sentence with a compound subject joined by *and*. Write a sentence with a compound subject joined by *or*. Check subject-verb agreement.

Answers will vary.

# LO3 Agreement with *I* and *You*

The pronouns *I* and *you* usually take plural verbs, even though they are singular.

plural verb

**Correct:** I go to Great America and ride roller coasters. You do too..

singular verb

**Incorrect:** I goes to Great America and rides roller coasters. You does too.

**Note:** The pronoun *I* takes the singular verbs *am* and *was*. **Do not** use *I* with *be* or *is*.

**Correct:** I am excited. I was nervous. I am eager to ride the roller coaster.

**Incorrect:** I are happy. I were nervous. I is eager to ride the roller coaster.

**Insight**

The word *am* exists for one reason only, to go along with the word *I*. There is no other subject for the verb *am*. In academic or formal writing, *I* should never be used with *be* or *is*. Think of René Descartes saying, "I think, therefore I am."

## Quick Guide
Using *am, is, are, was,* and *were*

|  | Singular | Plural |
|---|---|---|
| **Present Tense** | I *am*<br>you *are*<br>he *is*<br>she *is*<br>it *is* | we *are*<br>you *are*<br>they *are* |
| **Past Tense** | I *was*<br>you *were*<br>he *was*<br>she *was*<br>it *was* | we *were*<br>you *were*<br>they *were* |

**Say It**

Read the following word groups aloud, emphasizing the words in *italics*.

1. I *laugh*  /  You *laugh*  /  She *laughs*  /  They *laugh*

2. I *work*  /  You *work*  /  He *works*  /  They *work*

3. I *do*  /  You *do*  /  He *does*  /  They *do*

4. I *am*  /  You *are*  /  She *is*  /  They *are*

5. I *was*  /  You *were*  /  He *was*  /  They *were*

# Correcting Agreement with *I* and *You*

**Speaking & Listening**

After completing the sentences in the first exercise, say them aloud, emphasizing the underlined verbs.

**Write** In each sentence below, write the correct forms of the verb in parentheses. (Do not change the tense.)

1. I ___laugh___ louder than he ___laughs___ . (laugh)
2. You ___climb___ as well as she ___climbs___ . (climb)
3. We ___work___ together, or you ___work___ alone. (work)
4. Stan ___washes___ silverware while I ___wash___ pans. (wash)
5. I ___help___ often, but he ___helps___ rarely. (help)
6. The group ___watches___ on Sunday, but I ___watch___ later. (watch)
7. I ___eat___ first and she ___eats___ after. (eat)
8. You ___are___ tired, and I ___am___ too. (is)
9. Last year, I ___was___ short, but you ___were___ tall. (was)
10. You ___are___ helpful; I hope I ___am___ also. (is)

**Correct** Read the following paragraphs. Correct any agreement errors you find by crossing out the incorrect verb and writing the correct verb above.

I ~~is~~ *am* starting a class in astronomy, and I ~~wonders~~ *wonder* if I can borrow your ₁ telescope. You rarely ~~uses~~ *use* it anymore, and I ~~needs~~ *need* it to be able to look at the moons of Jupiter. My professor says that even a moderate-size telescope will show the moons. She ~~have~~ *has* instructions for finding Jupiter. I ~~knows~~ *know* how to use the telescope, but if you ~~is~~ *are* afraid I would break it, you could set it up for me. ₅

Another idea would be for us to stargaze together. I ~~has~~ *have* a place away from city lights, and I ~~has~~ *have* lawn chairs and blankets we could use. If you ~~agrees~~ *agree* to come along and set up the telescope, I ~~agrees~~ *agree* to bring snacks for us.

What do you think? I ~~hopes~~ *hope* I'm not asking too much and that you ~~isn't~~ *aren't* mad about the request. I just ~~is~~ *am* excited to see Jupiter's moons, and I ~~thinks~~ *think* you might ₁₀ like to see them, too.

**Write** Write two sentences using "I" as the subject. Then write two more using "you" as the subject. Check your subject-verb agreement.

Answers will vary.

# LO4 Agreement with Singular Indefinite Pronouns

An **indefinite pronoun** is intentionally vague. Instead of referring to a specific person, place, or thing, it refers to something general or unknown.

## Singular Indefinite Pronouns

| Singular |
| --- |
| someone |
| somebody |
| something |
| anyone |
| anybody |
| anything |
| no one |
| nobody |
| nothing |
| everyone |
| everybody |
| everything |
| one |
| each |
| either |
| neither |

Singular **indefinite pronouns** take singular verbs:

Someone cooks every night.
No one gets out of kitchen duty.
Everyone benefits from the chore schedule.

Note that indefinite pronouns that end in *one, body,* or *thing* are singular, just as these words themselves are singular. Just as you would write, "That thing is missing," so you would write "Something is missing." The words *one, each, either,* and *neither* can be tricky because they are often followed by a prepositional phrase that contains a plural noun. The verb should still be singular.

One of my friends is a great cook.

Each of us wants to cook as well as he does.

Remember that a compound subject joined with *and* needs a plural verb, and a compound subject joined with *or* needs a verb that matches the last subject.

Anything and everything taste terrific in his meals.
No one or nothing keeps him from making a wonderful meal.

"Everybody needs somebody to love."

—Solomon Burke

### Say It

Read the following word groups aloud, emphasizing the words in *italics*.

1. No one *is*  /  Nobody *has*  /  Nothing *does*

2. Everyone *is*  /  Everybody *has*  /  Everything *does*

3. One of my friends *is*  /  Each of my friends *has*  /  Either of my friends *does*

Vocabulary

**indefinite pronoun**
a special type of pronoun that does not refer to a specific person or thing

Lew Robertson/Corbis Yellow/Corbis

# Correcting Indefinite Pronoun Agreement I

**Write** In each sentence below, write the correct form of the verb in parentheses. (Do not change the tense.)

1. Everyone _____ completes _____ an application. (complete)

2. Somebody _____ has _____ to get the job. (have)

3. Each of the jobs _____ is _____ available. (are)

4. Neither of the applicants _____ is _____ qualified. (are)

5. Either of the prospects _____ hopes _____ to be trained. (hope)

6. Nobody _____ wants _____ to go home empty-handed. (want)

7. Everybody _____ has _____ bills to pay. (have)

8. Someone or something _____ has _____ to give. (have)

9. Either of the positions _____ pays _____ well. (pay)

10. One of my friends _____ waits _____ for word on the job. (wait)

**Write** Write sentences using each indefinite pronoun as a subject. Choose present tense verbs and check subject-verb agreement.   Answers will vary.

1. Someone _____

   _____

2. Nothing _____

   _____

3. Neither _____

   _____

4. Everyone _____

   _____

5. Each _____

   _____

6. Anybody _____

   _____

# Agreement with Other Indefinite Pronouns

Other indefinite pronouns are always plural, or have a singular or plural form, depending on how they are used.

## Plural Indefinite Pronouns

| Plural |
| --- |
| both |
| few |
| many |
| several |

Plural indefinite pronouns take plural verbs:

Many of us follow classical music.
Several are big fans.

## Singular or Plural Indefinite Pronouns

| Singular or Plural |
| --- |
| all |
| any |
| half |
| part |
| most |
| none |
| some |

Some indefinite pronouns or quantity words are singular or plural. If the object of the preposition in the phrase following the pronoun is singular, the pronoun takes a singular verb; if the object is plural, the pronoun takes a plural verb.

Most of the song thrills us.
Most of the songs thrill us.

Notice the shift in meaning, depending on the prepositional phrase. "Most of the song" means that one song is mostly thrilling. "Most of the songs" means that all but a few of many songs are thrilling. Here's another startling difference.

Half of the concert features Tchaikovsky.
Half of the concerts feature Tchaikovsky.

In the first example, half of one concert features the Russian master. In the second, half of a number of concerts features Tchaikovsky's music. What a difference one *s* can make!

**Speaking & Listening**

The "Say It" activity below will help you become familiar with subject-verb agreement patterns with indefinite pronouns.

## Say It

Read the following word groups aloud, emphasizing the words in *italics*.

1. Both *are*  /  Few *have*  /  Many *do*  /  Several *were*

2. All of the piece *is*  /  Any of the pieces *are*  /  Half of the piece *does*

3. Part of the song *is*  /  Most of the songs *are*  /
   None of the instruments *are*  /  Part of the instrument *is*

# Correcting Indefinite Pronoun Agreement II

**Speaking & Listening**

After completing the sentences in the first exercise, say them aloud, emphasizing the underlined verbs.

**Write** In each sentence below, write the correct forms of the verb in parentheses. (Do not change the tense.) See also page 314.

1. Several ___are___ attending, but all of us ___are___ listening. (are)

2. All of the songs ___are___ dramatic, but all of the drama ___is___ intentional. (is)

3. Some of my friends ___have___ the music on MP3, and some of my player ___has___ the selections. (have)

4. Everyone ___likes___ Tchaikovsky, but few ___like___ only him. (likes)

5. One of my friends ___listens___ to classical radio; several ___listen___ to MP3's. (listen)

6. Half of the album ___features___ symphonies, and half of the symphonies ___feature___ brass fanfares. (feature)

7. Most of us ___read___ about music, and some of us ___read___ music, too. (read)

8. Of the music fans, several ___are___ hard core, but none of them ___is___ a composer. (is)

9. One of my friends ___plays___ trombone, and some of my friends ___play___ piano. (play)

10. Few ___have___ played in an orchestra, but one of us ___has___ played in a band. (has)

**Write** Write sentences using each indefinite pronoun as a subject. Choose present tense verbs and check subject-verb agreement.  Answers will vary.

1. Part _____

_____

2. Most _____

_____

3. Few _____

_____

4. Several _____

_____

5. Both _____

_____

6. All _____

_____

# LO5 Pronoun-Antecedent Agreement

A pronoun must agree in **person**, **number**, and **gender** with its **antecedent**. (The antecedent is the word the pronoun replaces.)

The woman brought her briefcase but forgot her computer.

antecedent (third person singular feminine) **+** pronoun (third person singular feminine) **=** agreement

## Quick Guide

| | Singular | Plural |
|---|---|---|
| **First Person:** | I, me (my, mine) | we, us (our, ours) |
| **Second Person:** | you (your, yours) | you (your, yours) |
| **Third Person:**<br>masculine<br>feminine<br>neuter | <br>he, him (his)<br>she, her (her, hers)<br>it (its) | <br>they, them (their, theirs)<br>they, them (their, theirs)<br>they, them (their, theirs) |

## Two or More Antecedents

When two or more antecedents are joined by *and*, the pronoun should be plural.

Kali and Teri **filled** their baskets with eggs.

When two or more singular antecedents are joined by *or, nor,* or *but also,* the pronoun or pronouns should be singular.

Kali or Teri **filled** her basket with eggs.

Not only Kali but also Teri **filled** her basket with eggs.

Ada Summer/Fancy/Corbis

**Note:** Avoid sexism when choosing pronouns that agree in number.

**Sexist:** Each child should bring his basket.

**Correct:** Each child should bring her or his basket.

**Correct:** Children should bring their baskets.

# Correcting Pronoun-Antecedent Agreement

**Write** In each sentence below, write the pronoun that agrees with the underlined word.

1. <u>Ted</u> has written a patriotic poem and ____he____ will read ____his____ poem at the Fourth of July festival.

2. <u>Shandra</u> and <u>Shelli</u> will bring ____their____ lawn chairs to the fireworks display.

3. Either <u>John</u> or <u>Grace</u> will play ____his____ or ____her____ favorite marches over the sound system.

4. Not only <u>John</u> but also <u>Dave</u> plays trombone and will bring ____his____ instrument to play with the band.

5. Each <u>person</u> should bring ____his____ or ____her____ own flag.

6. <u>Mayor Jenny White</u> or <u>Congressperson Mark Russell</u> will give the invocation, and then ____she____ or ____he____ will introduce the main speaker.

7. <u>Rick</u> and <u>Linda</u> will sing ____their____ rendition of the national anthem.

8. <u>Acrobats</u> will stroll through the park on ____their____ ten-foot-tall stilts.

9. Each <u>acrobat</u> will have to keep ____his____ or ____her____ balance on uneven ground among running children.

10. <u>Ducks</u> and <u>ducklings</u> in the lake will have to make ____their____ way to quieter waters when the fireworks begin.

**Revise** Rewrite each of the following sentences to avoid sexism. Answers will vary.

1. Every acrobat should check his equipment.

   _____

   _____

2. Each acrobat must keep her balance.

   _____

   _____

3. One of the acrobats left his stilts at the park.

   _____

   _____

---

**Insight**

Different languages treat gender differently. For example, Romance languages have masculine and feminine forms for nonliving things. In English, gender is reserved for people and animals.

# LO6 Other Pronoun Problems

## Missing Antecedent

If no clear antecedent is provided, the reader doesn't know what or whom the pronoun refers to.

**Confusing:** In Illinois, they claim Lincoln as their own.

(Who does "they" refer to?)

**Clear:** In Illinois, the citizens claim Lincoln as their own.

## Vague Pronoun

If the pronoun could refer to two or more words, the passage is **ambiguous**.

**Indefinite:** Sheila told her daughter to use her new tennis racket.

(To whom does the pronoun "her" refer, Sheila or her daughter?)

**Clumsy:** Sheila told her daughter to use Sheila's new tennis racket.

**Clear:** Sheila lent her new tennis racket to her daughter.

## Double Subject

If a pronoun is used right after the subject, an error called a double subject occurs.

**Incorrect:** Your father, he is good at poker.

**Correct:** Your father is good at poker

## Insight

Use *my* before the thing possessed and use *mine* afterward: *my cat,* but *that cat is mine.* Do the same with *our/ours, your/yours,* and *her/hers.*

## Incorrect Case

Personal pronouns can function as subjects, objects, or possessives. If the wrong case is used, an error occurs.

**Incorrect:** Them are funny videos.

**Correct:** They are funny videos.

The list below tells you which pronouns to use in each case.

| Subject | Object | Possessive |
|---|---|---|
| I | me | my, mine |
| we | us | our, ours |
| you | you | your, yours |
| he | him | his |
| she | her | her, hers |
| it | it | its |
| they | them | their, theirs |

# Correcting Other Pronoun Problems

**Write** In each blank below, write the correct pronoun from the choices in parentheses.

1. ___I___ need to help ___you___ with the taxes.
   (I, me, my, mine)   (you, your, yours)

2. ___You___ should help ___her___ and see what ___she___ needs.
   (you, your, yours)   (she, her, hers)   (she, her, hers)

3. ___He___ can show ___me___ that account of ___yours___ .
   (he, him, his)   (I, me, my, mine)   (you, your, yours)

4. ___You___ gave ___your___ permission for ___me___ to see.
   (you, your, yours)   (you, your, yours)   (I, me, my, mine)

5. ___We___ asked ___our___ accountant to help ___us___ .
   (we, us, our, ours)   (we, us, our, ours)   (we, us, our, ours)

**Revise** Rewrite each sentence below, correcting the pronoun problems.

1. Bob and Josh took his assignment to class.

   Answers will vary.

2. Lupita needed to visit with Kelly, but she had no time.

3. Before climbing in, it broke.

4. They say that a cure for cancer is coming.

5. Trina and Lois, they bought frozen custard.

6. Carl asked Tim to cook his lunch.

# LO7 Real-World Application

**Correct** In the letter below, correct the agreement errors. Use the correction marks to the left.

## Correction Marks

⌐ delete

d̲ capitalize

∅ lowercase

∧ insert

⋏ add comma

? add question mark
∧

word add word
∧

⊙ add period

◯ spelling

⌐⌐ switch

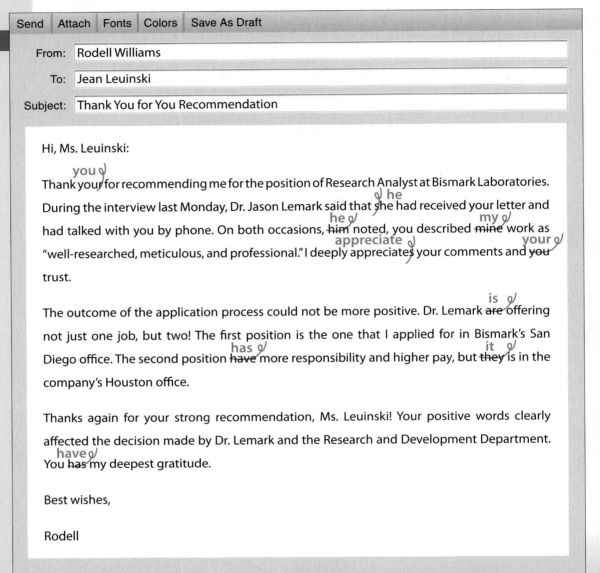

| Send | Attach | Fonts | Colors | Save As Draft |

From: Rodell Williams

To: Jean Leuinski

Subject: Thank You for You Recommendation

Hi, Ms. Leuinski:

Thank your *you* for recommending me for the position of Research Analyst at Bismark Laboratories. During the interview last Monday, Dr. Jason Lemark said that she *he* had received your letter and had talked with you by phone. On both occasions, him *he* noted, you described mine *my* work as "well-researched, meticulous, and professional." I deeply appreciates *appreciate* your comments and you *your* trust.

The outcome of the application process could not be more positive. Dr. Lemark are *is* offering not just one job, but two! The first position is the one that I applied for in Bismark's San Diego office. The second position have *has* more responsibility and higher pay, but they *it* is in the company's Houston office.

Thanks again for your strong recommendation, Ms. Leuinski! Your positive words clearly affected the decision made by Dr. Lemark and the Research and Development Department. You has *have* my deepest gratitude.

Best wishes,

Rodell

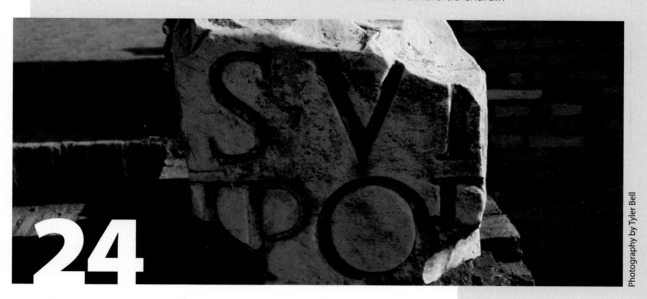

Photography by Tyler Bell

"The fragments of the world seek each other
so that the world may come into being."
——Pierre Teilhard de Chardin

# 24

# Sentence Fragments

Once upon a time, someone spent days carving letters the size of a man's head into a solid block of stone. What message would be important enough to inscribe in that way? A couple thousand years later, we don't know. All that remains is a fragment of the stone, and of the meaning.

Sometimes in writing, sentences get broken into fragments as well. The subject gets knocked away, or the verb drops out, or some other important part goes missing. The reader then has to puzzle out the meaning—or just skips it entirely.

This chapter focuses on sentence fragments, on recognizing them and repairing them. The exercises here will help you to put the pieces back together.

## Learning Outcomes

**LO1** Correct common fragments.

**LO2** Correct tricky fragments.

**LO3** Check for fragments in a real-world context.

### What do you think?

Read the quotation above. Explain why the fragments of a sentence might "seek each other."

Answers will vary.

# LO1 Common Fragments

In spoken communication and informal writing, sentence fragments are occasionally used and understood. In formal writing, fragments should be avoided.

## Missing Parts

A sentence requires a subject and a predicate. If one or the other or both are missing, the sentence is a **fragment**. Such fragments can be fixed by supplying the missing part.

| | |
|---|---|
| **Fragment:** | Went to the concert. |
| **Fragment + Subject:** | We went to the concert. |
| | |
| **Fragment:** | Everyone from Westville Community College. |
| **Fragment + Predicate:** | Everyone from Westville Community College may participate. |
| | |
| **Fragment:** | For the sake of student safety. |
| **Fragment + Subject and Predicate:** | The president set up a curfew for the sake of student safety. |

## Incomplete Thoughts

A sentence also must express a complete thought. Some fragments have a subject and a verb but do not express a complete thought. These fragments can be corrected by providing words that complete the thought.

| | |
|---|---|
| **Fragment:** | The concert will include. |
| **Completing Thought:** | The concert will include an amazing light show. |
| | |
| **Fragment:** | If we arrive in time. |
| **Completing Thought:** | If we arrive in time, we'll get front-row seats. |
| | |
| **Fragment:** | That opened the concert. |
| **Completing Thought:** | I liked the band that opened the concert. |

*Zibedik, 2010/used under license from www.shutterstock.com*

### Say It
*Answers will vary.*

Read these fragments aloud. Then read each one again, but this time supply the necessary words to form a complete thought.

1. The student union building.

2. Where you can buy used books.

3. Walked to class every morning.

4. When the instructor is sick.

5. The cop was.

**Vocabulary**

**fragment**
a group of words that is missing a subject or a predicate (or both) or that does not express a complete thought

**Correct** Add words to correct each fragment below. Write the complete sentence on the lines provided. Answers will vary.

1. Went to the office. _____

_____

2. The photographer, standing at the door. _____

_____

3. Will debate the pros and cons of tanning. _____

_____

4. Native Americans. _____

_____

5. Is one of the benefits of art class. _____

_____

**Correct** The following paragraph contains numerous fragments. Either add what is missing or combine fragments with other sentences to make them complete. Use the correction marks shown to the right. Answers will vary.

> Some people are good at memorizing facts. They piece things together. Like the inside of a jigsaw puzzle. Slowly build a big picture. Others are better at grasping overall shapes. Then filling in the middle with facts. Either way, have to finish the puzzle.

**Correction Marks**

| | |
|---|---|
| ✄ | delete |
| d̲̲ | capitalize |
| ∅ | lowercase |
| ∧ | insert |
| ⌃ | add comma |
| ? ∧ | add question mark |
| word ∧ | add word |
| ⊙ | add period |
| ⬭ | spelling |
| ∿ | switch |

**Correct** On your own paper or orally, correct the following fragments by supplying the missing parts. Use your imagination. Answers will vary.

1. In the newspaper.
2. We bought.
3. The purpose of sociology class.
4. Somewhere above the clouds tonight.
5. Was the reason.

# LO2 Tricky Fragments

Some fragments are more difficult to find and correct. They creep into our writing because they are often part of the way we communicate in our speaking.

## Absolute Phrases

An **absolute phrase** looks like a sentence that is missing its helping verb. An absolute phrase can be made into a sentence by adding the helping verb or by connecting the phrase to a complete sentence.

| | |
|---|---|
| **Absolute Phrase (Fragment):** | Our legs trembling from the hike. |
| **Absolute Phrase + Helping Verb:** | Our legs were trembling from the hike. |
| **Absolute Phrase + Complete Sentence:** | We collapsed on the couch, our legs trembling from the hike. |

## Informal Fragments

Fragments that are commonly used in speech should be eliminated from formal writing. Avoid the following types of fragments unless you are writing dialogue.

| | |
|---|---|
| **Interjections:** | Hey! Yeah! |
| **Exclamations:** | What a nuisance! How fun! |
| **Greetings:** | Hi, everybody. Good afternoon. |
| **Questions:** | How come? Why not? What? |
| **Answers:** | About three or four. As soon as possible. |

**Note:** Sentences that begin with *here* or *there* have a **delayed subject**, which appears after the verb. Other sentences (commands) have an **implied subject** (*you*). Such sentences are not fragments.

| | |
|---|---|
| **Delayed Subject:** | Here are some crazy fans wearing wild hats. |
| **Implied Subject:** | Tackle him! Bring him down! |

**Vocabulary**

**absolute phrase**
a group of words with a noun and a participle (a word ending in *ing* or *ed*) and the words that modify them

**delayed subject**
a subject that appears after the verb, as in a sentence that begins with *here* or *there* or a sentence that asks a question

**implied subject**
the word *you*, assumed to begin command sentences

**Say It**   Answers will vary.

Read these fragments aloud. Then read each one again, but this time supply the necessary words to form a complete thought.

1. Are three types of laptop computers.

2. Our instructor explaining the assignment.

3. About three in the morning.

4. Is my favorite Web site.

5. My friend working at a half-priced disk shop.

**Complete** Rewrite each tricky fragment below, making it a sentence.

1. Our boisterous behavior announcing our approach.

Answers will vary.

2. A tidy hedge surrounding the trimmed lawn.

3. The owner's gaze tracking us from the front porch.

4. His dogs barking loudly from the backyard.

5. Our welcome feeling less likely with each step.

**Delete** The following paragraph contains a number of informal fragments. Identify and delete each one. Reread the paragraph and listen for the difference.

~~Wow!~~ It's amazing what archaeologists can discover from bones. Did you know that Cro-Magnon (our ancestors) and Neanderthal tribes sometimes lived side by side? ~~Sure did!~~ In other places, when climate change drove our ancestors south, Neanderthals took their place. Neanderthals were tough and had stronger arms and hands than Cro-Magnons had. Neanderthal brains were bigger, too. ~~What?~~ So why aren't there any Neanderthals around now? ~~Huh?~~ Well, although Neanderthal tribes used spears and stone tools, our ancestors were much better toolmakers. ~~Yeah!~~ Also, Neanderthals mainly ate big animals, while Cro-Magnon ate anything from fish to pigs to roots and berries. So in the long run, Cro-Magnon hominids prospered while Neanderthal tribes dwindled away.

# LO1 Comma Splices

Comma splices occur when two sentences are connected with only a comma. A comma splice can be fixed by adding a coordinating conjunction (*and, but, or, nor, for, so,* or *yet*) or a subordinating conjunction (*while, after, when,* and so on). The two sentences could also be joined by a semicolon (;) or separated by a period.

**Comma Splice:** The Eiffel Tower was a main attraction at the Paris Exposition, the Ferris wheel was its equivalent at the Chicago Exposition.

| | |
|---|---|
| **Corrected by adding a coordinating conjunction:** | The Eiffel Tower was a main attraction at the Paris Exposition, and the Ferris wheel was its equivalent at the Chicago Exposition. |
| **Corrected by adding a subordinating conjunction:** | While the Eiffel Tower was a main attraction at the Paris Exposition, the Ferris wheel was its equivalent at the Chicago Exposition. |
| **Corrected by replacing the comma with a semicolon:** | The Eiffel Tower was a main attraction at the Paris Exposition; the Ferris wheel was its equivalent at the Chicago Exposition. |

**Comma Splice:** An engineer named George Washington Gale Ferris planned the first Ferris wheel, many people thought he was crazy.

| | |
|---|---|
| **Corrected by adding a coordinating conjunction:** | An engineer named George Washington Gale Ferris planned the first Ferris wheel, but many people thought he was crazy. |
| **Corrected by adding a subordinating conjunction:** | When an engineer named George Washington Gale Ferris planned the first Ferris wheel, many people thought he was crazy. |
| **Corrected by replacing the comma with a period:** | An engineer named George Washington Gale Ferris planned the first Ferris wheel. Many people thought he was crazy. |

# Correcting Comma Splices

**Practice A**  Correct the following comma splices by adding a coordinating conjunction *(and, but, yet, or, nor, for, so)*, adding a subordinating conjunction *(when, while, because,* and so on), or replacing the comma with a semicolon or period. Use the approach that makes the sentence read most smoothly. (The first one has been done for you.)

1. We set out for a morning hike, *but* it was raining.

2. The weather cleared by the afternoon, *so* we hit the trail.

3. Both Jill and I were expecting wonderful scenery, *and* we were not disappointed.

4. The view of the valley was spectacular, *for* it was like a portrait.

5. We snacked on granola bars and apples, *and* we enjoyed the view.

6. Then we strapped on our backpacks, *for* the final leg of the hike awaited us.

7. The trail became rockier, *so (and)* we had to watch our step.

8. We reached the end of our hike, *for* the sun was setting.

9. We're on the lookout for a new trail, *but (yet)* it will be tough to beat this one.

10. We're done with our physical activities, *so (and, for)* it is time to watch a movie.

**Practice B**  Correct any comma splices in the following e-mail message.

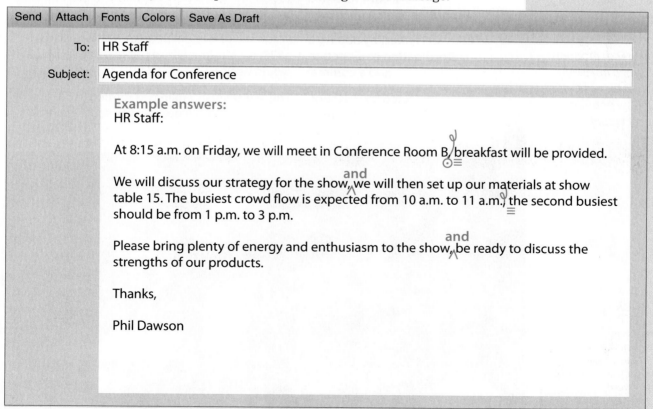

| Send | Attach | Fonts | Colors | Save As Draft |

To: HR Staff

Subject: Agenda for Conference

Example answers:
HR Staff:

At 8:15 a.m. on Friday, we will meet in Conference Room B; breakfast will be provided.

We will discuss our strategy for the show, *and* we will then set up our materials at show table 15. The busiest crowd flow is expected from 10 a.m. to 11 a.m.; the second busiest should be from 1 p.m. to 3 p.m.

Please bring plenty of energy and enthusiasm to the show, *and* be ready to discuss the strengths of our products.

Thanks,

Phil Dawson

# LO2 Run-On Sentences

A **run-on sentence** occurs when two sentences are joined without punctuation or a connecting word. A run-on can be corrected by adding a comma and a conjunction or by inserting a semicolon or period between the two sentences.

**Run-On:** Horace Wilson taught in Tokyo in 1872 he introduced the Japanese to baseball.

| | |
|---|---|
| **Corrected by adding a comma and coordinating conjunction:** | Horace Wilson taught in Tokyo in 1872, and he introduced the Japanese to baseball. |
| **Corrected by adding a subordinating conjunction and a comma:** | While Horace Wilson taught in Tokyo in 1872, he introduced the Japanese to baseball. |
| **Corrected by inserting a semicolon:** | Horace Wilson taught in Tokyo in 1872; he introduced the Japanese to baseball. |

**Run-On:** The first team in Japan was formed in 1878 no one knew how popular the sport would become.

| | |
|---|---|
| **Corrected by adding a comma and a coordinating conjunction:** | The first team in Japan was formed in 1878, yet no one knew how popular the sport would become. |
| **Corrected by adding a subordinating conjunction and a comma:** | When the first team in Japan was formed in 1878, no one knew how popular the sport would become. |
| **Corrected by inserting a period:** | The first team in Japan was formed in 1878. No one knew how popular the sport would become. |

Alan C. Heison, 2010 / Used under license from Shutterstock.com

**Traits**

Here's an additional way to correct a run-on sentence: Turn one of the sentences into a phrase or series of phrases; then combine it with the other sentence.

*The first team in Japan was formed in 1878 without a thought about how popular the sport would become.*

**Vocabulary**

**run-on sentence**
a sentence error that occurs when two sentences are joined without punctuation or a connecting word

306

# Correcting Run-On Sentences

**Correct**   Correct the following run-on sentences. Use the approach that makes the sentence read most smoothly. The first one has been done for you.

1. In 1767 English scientist Joseph Priestley discovered a way to infuse water with carbon dioxide⊙ this invention led to carbonated water.

2. Carbonated water is one of the main components of soft drinks⊙ it gives soft drinks the fizz and bubbles we enjoy.

3. The first soft drinks in America were dispensed out of soda fountains⊙ they were most often found at drug stores and ice-cream parlors.

4. Interestingly, soda was sold at drug stores⌃because it promised healing properties.

5. Most of the formulas for American soft drinks were invented by pharmacists⊙ the idea was to create nonalcoholic alternatives to traditional medicines.

6. The first carbonated drink bottles could not keep bubbles from escaping⌃so it was more popular to buy a soda from a soda fountain.

7. A successful method of keeping bubbles in a bottle was not invented until 1892⊙ it was called a crowned bottle cap.

8. The first diet soda to be sold was known as "No-Cal Beverage"⊙ in 1959 the first diet cola hit the stores.

---

**Rewrite**   Rewrite the following paragraph, correcting any run-on sentences that you find.

    Arbor Day is an undervalued holiday in America. On this holiday, people are encouraged to plant trees it is celebrated on the fourth Friday of April. It was created by J. Sterling Morton he was President Grover Cleveland's Secretary of Agriculture. The holiday is now observed in a number of other countries.

Example rewrite:

Arbor Day is an undervalued holiday in America. On this holiday, people are encouraged to

plant trees. It is celebrated on the fourth Friday of April. It was created by J. Sterling Morton,

President Grover Cleveland's Secretary of Agriculture. The holiday is now observed in a

number of other countries.

# LO3 Rambling Sentences

A **rambling sentence** occurs when a long series of separate ideas are connected by one *and, but,* or *so* after another. The result is an unfocused sentence that goes on and on. To correct a rambling sentence, break it into smaller units, adding and cutting words as needed.

**Rambling:** When we signed up for the two-on-two tournament, I had no thoughts about winning, but then my brother started talking about spending his prize money and he asked me how I would spend my share so we were counting on winning when we really had little chance and as it turned out, we lost in the second round.

**Corrected:** When we signed up for the two-on-two tournament, I had no thoughts about winning. Then my brother started talking about spending the prize money. He even asked me how I would spend my share. Soon, we were counting on winning when we really had little chance. As it turned out, we lost in the second round.

## Say It

Read the following rambling sentences aloud. Afterward, circle all of the connecting words (*and, but, so*), and be prepared to suggest different ways to break each rambling idea into more manageable units.

1. I enjoyed touring the hospital and I would enjoy joining the nursing staff and I believe that my prior work experience will be an asset but I also know that I have a lot more to learn.

2. The electronics store claims to offer "one-stop shopping" and they can take care of all of a customer's computer needs and they have a fully trained staff to answer questions and solve problems so there is really no need to go anywhere else.

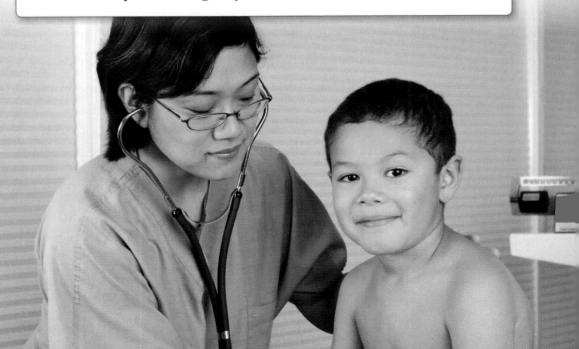

forestpath 2010/used under license from www.shutterstock.com

# Correcting Rambling Sentences

**Correct**  Correct the following rambling sentences by dividing them into separate sentences. Afterward, share your corrections with a classmate. Did you change each rambling sentence in the same way?  Answers will vary.

1. The dancer entered gracefully onto the stage and she twirled around twice and then tiptoed to the front of the stage and the crowd applauded.

_____

_____

_____

2. I went to the movies last night and when I got to the theater, I had to wait in a superslow line and when I finally got to the front, the show I wanted to see was sold out.

_____

_____

_____

3. I like to listen to music everywhere but I especially like to rock out in my car so I scream and dance and I don't care if anyone sees me through the windows.

_____

_____

_____

**Answer**  Answer the following questions about rambling sentences.

1. How can you recognize a rambling sentence?

   Answers will vary.

   _____

   _____

2. Why is a rambling sentence a problem?

   _____

   _____

   _____

3. How can you correct one?

   _____

   _____

   _____

**Extend**

Share your corrections with a classmate. Did you change each rambling sentence in the same way?

# LO4 Real-World Application

**Correct** Correct any comma splices or run-on sentences in the following e-mail message.

| Send | Attach | Fonts | Colors | Save As Draft |

**To:** StaplePro Employees

**Subject:** Agenda for Personnel Meeting

Example corrections:
Good morning:

This Saturday, from 8:00 a.m. to noon, StaplePro will conduct its quarterly inventory check the warehouse supervisors and I will lead the inventory teams. Please provide any assistance the inventory teams require of you.

After this check, the paper inventory forms will be discontinued, *and* all shipments in and out must be inventoried using the hand scanners. There should be fewer errors when using StaplePro's electronic system, the supervisors will schedule training for their employees who are unfamiliar with the scanners.

Thanks for your cooperation, StaplePro's new system will help us store and ship staples more effectively and provide better service for our customers.

Best regards,

Kevin Dooley

Warehouse Director

**Reflect** Reflect on what you have learned about comma splices and run-on sentences by answering the following questions.

1. What is the difference between a comma splice and a run-on sentence?

   Answers will vary.

2. How can you correct comma splices and run-on sentences? (Name at least three ways.)

3. What are three common coordinating conjunctions that you can use to connect two sentences?

Tim Pannell/Corbis Yellow/Corbis

# 26

# Additional Sentence Problems

Cars are great when they go, but when a car breaks down, it is a huge headache. There's going to be a look under the hood, a bit of scrabbling beneath the thing, maybe a push, maybe a jack, and probably a tow truck and a big bill.

Sentences also are great until they break down. But you don't have to be a skilled mechanic to fix sentences. This chapter outlines a few common sentence problems and shows how to fix them. You'll be on your way in no time!

## What do you think?

Which can carry you farther, a car or a sentence?

Answers will vary.

## Learning Outcomes

**LO1** Correct misplaced and dangling modifiers.

**LO2** Correct shifts in sentence construction.

**LO3** Correct sentence problems in a real-world context.

## Dangling Modifiers

A modifier is a word, phrase, or clause that functions as an adjective or adverb. When the modifier does not clearly modify another word in the sentence, it is called a **dangling modifier**. This error can be corrected by inserting the missing word and/or rewriting the sentence.

**Dangling Modifier:** After strapping the toy cowboy to his back, my cat stalked sullenly around the house.
*(The cat could strap the toy cowboy to his own back?)*

**Corrected:** After I strapped the toy cowboy to his back, my cat stalked sullenly around the house.

**Dangling Modifier:** Trying to get the cowboy off, the bowl got knocked off the shelf. *(The bowl was trying to get the cowboy off?)*

**Corrected:** Trying to get the cowboy off, the cat knocked the bowl off the shelf.

## Misplaced Modifiers

When a modifier is placed beside a word that it does not modify, the modifier is misplaced and often results in an amusing or **illogical** statement. A **misplaced modifier** can be corrected by moving it next to the word that it modifies.

**Misplaced Modifier:** My cat was diagnosed by the vet with fleas.
*(The vet has fleas?)*

**Corrected:** The vet diagnosed my cat with fleas.

**Misplaced Modifier:** The vet gave a pill to my cat tasting like fish.
*(The cat tastes like fish?)*

**Corrected:** The vet gave my cat a pill tasting like fish.

### Say It

Read the following sentences aloud, noting the dangling or misplaced modifier in each one. Then tell a classmate how you would correct each error.

1. The climbing tower on the front porch is the place to find my cat called Feline Paradise.

2. You will often see him climbing up the shag-carpeted towers and ramps with sharp claws.

3. Though just three months old, I have taught my cat his name.

4. After tearing up the couch, I decided to get my cat a scratching post.

5. I have worked to teach my cat to beg for three weeks.

# Correcting Dangling and Misplaced Modifiers

**Rewrite** Rewrite each of the sentences below, correcting the misplaced and dangling modifiers. Sample answers:

1. I bought a hound dog for my brother named Rover.

   I bought a hound dog named Rover for my brother.

2. The doctor diagnosed me and referred me to a specialist with scoliosis.

   The doctor diagnosed me with scoliosis and referred me to a specialist.

3. The man was reported murdered by the coroner.

   The coroner reported that the man was murdered.

4. Please present the recommendation that is attached to Mrs. Burble.

   Please present the attached recommendation to Mrs. Burble.

5. Jack drove me to our home in a Chevy.

   Jack drove me in a Chevy to our home.

6. I couldn't believe my brother would hire a disco DJ who hates disco.

   I couldn't believe my brother, who hates disco, would hire a disco DJ.

7. We saw a fox and a vixen on the way to the psychiatrist.

   On the way to the psychiatrist, we saw a fox and a vixen.

8. I gave the secretary my phone number that works in reception.

   I gave the secretary who works in reception my phone number.

9. I found a pair of underwear in the drawer that doesn't belong to me.

   I found a pair of underwear that doesn't belong to me in my drawer.

10. We offer jackets for trendy teens with gold piping.

    We offer jackets with gold piping for trendy teens.

**Correct** For each sentence, correct the placement of the adverb.

1. Give quickly the report to your boss.

   Quickly give the report to your boss.

   *put ontext /*

2. We will provide immediately an explanation.

   We will immediately provide an explanation.

3. Fill completely out the test sheet.

   Completely fill out the test sheet.

> **Insight**
>
> When a modifier comes at the beginning of the sentence or the end of the sentence, make sure it modifies the word or phrase closest to it. Ask yourself, "Who or what is being described?"

David Peta,2010 / Used under license from Shutterstock.com

# LO2 Shifts in Sentences

## Shift in Person

A **shift in person** is an error that occurs when first, second, and/or third person are improperly mixed in a sentence.

**Shift in person:** If you exercise and eat right, an individual can lose weight.
(The sentence improperly shifts from second person—*you*—to third person—*individual*.)

**Corrected:** If you exercise and eat right, you can lose weight.

## Shift in Tense

A **shift in tense** is an error that occurs when more than one verb tense is improperly used in a sentence. (See pages 354–361 for more about tense.)

**Shift in tense:** He tried every other option before he agree to do it my way.
(The sentence improperly shifts from past tense—*tried*—to present tense—*agree*.)

**Corrected:** He tried every other option before he agreed to do it my way.

## Shift in Voice

A **shift in voice** is an error that occurs when active voice and passive voice are mixed in a sentence.

**Shift in voice:** When she fixes the radiator, other repairs may be suggested.
(The sentence improperly shifts from active voice—*fixes*—to passive voice—*may be suggested*.)

**Corrected:** When she fixes the radiator, she may suggest other repairs.

**Vocabulary**

**person**
first person (*I* or *we*—the person speaking), second person (*you*—the person spoken to), or third person (*he, she, it,* or *they*—the person or thing spoken about)

**voice of verb**
whether the subject is doing the action of the verb (active voice) or is being acted upon (passive voice) (See page 352.)

**shift in person**
an error that occurs when first, second, and third person are improperly mixed in a sentence

**shift in tense**
an error that occurs when more than one verb tense is improperly used in a sentence

**shift in voice**
an error that occurs when active voice and passive voice are mixed in a sentence

### Say It

Read the following sentences aloud, paying careful attention to the improper shift each one contains. Then tell a classmate how you would correct each error.

1. David exercises daily and ate well.
2. Marianne goes running each morning and new friends might be met.
3. After you choose an exercise routine, a person should stick to it.
4. Lamar swam every morning and does ten laps.
5. The personal trainer made a schedule for me, and a diet was suggested by her.

# Correcting Improper Shifts in Sentences

**Rewrite** Rewrite each sentence below, correcting any improper shifts in construction.  *Sample answers:*

1. You should be ready for each class in a person's schedule.

   *You should be ready for each class in your schedule.*

2. I work for my brother most days and classes are attended by me at night.

   *I work for my brother most days and attend classes at night.*

3. When you give me a review, can he also give me a raise?

   *When you give me a review, can you also give me a raise?*

4. As we walked to school, last night's football game was discussed by us.

   *As we walked to school, we discussed last night's football game.*

5. I hoped to catch the bus until I see it leave.

   *I hoped to catch the bus until I saw it leave.*

**Correct** Correct the improper shifts in person, tense, or voice in the following paragraph. Use the correction marks to the right when you make your changes.  *Example corrections:*

Some people are early adopters, which means ^they adopt^ technology ~~is adopted~~  *1*
~~by them~~ when it is new. Other people are technophobes because ^they^ ~~you~~ are
afraid of technology, period. I am not an early adopter or a technophobe,
but ^I have^ ~~a person has~~ to see the value in technology before I use it. Technology
has to be cheap, intuitive, reliable, and truly helpful before ^I^ ~~you~~ start using  *5*
it. I let others work out the bugs and pay the high prices before ^I adopt^ a piece
of technology ~~is adopted by me.~~ But when I decide it is time to get a new
gadget or program, ^I~~you~~ buy it and use it until it is worn out. Then I look
for something else that is even cheaper and more intuitive, reliable, and
helpful, which ^I^ is then ^buy~~bought by me.~~  *10*

### Correction Marks

- ℐ delete
- d̲̲ capitalize
- ⱷ lowercase
- ∧ insert
- ⩞ add comma
- ? add question
- ∧ mark
- word∧ add word
- ⊙ add period
- ⟳ spelling
- ∿ switch

# LO3 Real-World Application

**Correct** Correct any dangling modifiers, misplaced modifiers, or shifts in construction in the following message. Use the correction marks to the left.

| Send | Attach | Fonts | Colors | Save As Draft |

From: Julia Armstrong

To: Human Resources Staff

Cc: Richard Montgomery

Subject: Monthly Human Resources Staff Meeting with President Smith

## Correction Marks

| | |
|---|---|
| ℐ | delete |
| d̲ | capitalize |
| ∅ | lowercase |
| ∧ | insert |
| ∧̂ | add comma |
| ⌄? | add question mark |
| word ∧ | add word |
| ⊙ | add period |
| ◯ | spelling |
| ⌢ | switch |

Dear HR Team:

Monday, September 12, will be the Human Resources staff meeting with the ~~first~~ ^first monthly^ ~~monthly~~ president. ~~A person~~ ^You^ should plan to attend these meetings on the second Monday of each month from 8:30 to 9:30 a.m., and you should go to the Human Resources conference room.

To help make these meetings productive, ~~a staff member~~ ^you^ can prepare in two ways:

1. You should review and bring any periodic reports that are generated by you—hiring stats, exit interviews, medical or worker's comp claims, and so on. ~~He or she~~ ^You^ should bring 11 copies and an electronic file of each document.

2. You should bring any questions or concerns. However, if an issue is significant, ~~the person~~ ^you^ should review it with Richard before you bring it to a monthly meeting.

This monthly meeting is a big commitment of time from everyone ~~needing~~ ^and needs^ regular attendance. If you can't make the meeting, send an e-mail and attach ~~to~~ ^to^ Richard a note.

Thanks for your cooperation. If you have questions or suggestions about the meeting, Richard or ~~I should be contacted by you~~ ^contact^ ^me^.

Thanks,

Julia

316

**Rewrite** The sentences that follow come from church bulletins and are amusing due to misplaced or dangling modifiers or other sentence problems. Rewrite each sentence to remove these problems. Answers will vary.

1. Remember in prayer the many who are sick of our church and community.

   _____

   _____

   _____

2. For those of you who have children and don't know it, we have a nursery downstairs.

   _____

   _____

   _____

3. The ladies of the church have cast off clothing of every kind. They can be seen in the church basement Saturday.

   _____

   _____

   _____

4. The third verse of "Blessed Assurance" will be sung without musical accomplishment.

   _____

   _____

   _____

**Workplace**

Journalists and publishers need to be especially careful to avoid mistakes in their writing. But errors in writing reflect badly on all professionals.

**Write** Write the first draft of a personal narrative (true story) in which you share a time when you misplaced or lost something important to you or to someone else. Here are some tips for adding interest to your story:

- Start right in the middle of the action.    Answers will vary.
- Build suspense to keep the reader's interest.
- Use dialogue.
- Use sensory details (what you heard, saw, felt, and so on).

Afterward, exchange your writing with a classmate. Read each other's narrative first for enjoyment and a second time to check it for the sentence errors discussed in this chapter.

"If you want to make an apple pie from scratch,
you must first create the universe."

—Carl Sagan

# 27 Noun

Astrophysicists tell us that the universe is made up of two things—matter and energy. Matter is the stuff, and energy is the movement or heat of the stuff.

Grammarians tell us that thoughts are made up of two things—nouns and verbs. Nouns name the stuff, and verbs capture the energy. In that way, the sentence reflects the universe itself. You can't express a complete thought unless you are talking about matter and energy. Each sentence, then, is the basic particle of thought.

This chapter focuses on nouns, which describe not just things you can see—such as people, places, or objects—but also things you can't see—such as love, justice, and democracy. The exercises in this chapter will help you sort out the stuff of thinking.

StockTrek/Digital Vision/Getty Images

## What do you think?

What is the most beautiful noun? What is the ugliest one? What makes a noun beautiful or ugly?

Answers will vary.

## Learning Outcomes

**LO1** Understand classes of nouns.

**LO2** Use singular and plural nouns.

**LO3** Form tricky plurals.

**LO4** Use count and noncount nouns.

**LO5** Use articles.

**LO6** Use other noun markers.

**LO7** Use nouns correctly in a real-world context.

# LO1 Classes of Nouns

All nouns are either *common* or *proper*. They can also be *individual* or *collective*, *concrete* or *abstract*.

## Common or Proper Nouns

**Common nouns** name a general person, place, thing, or idea. They are not capitalized as names. **Proper nouns** name a specific person, place, thing, or idea, and they are capitalized as names.

|  | **Common Nouns** | **Proper Nouns** |
|---|---|---|
| **Person:** | politician | Barack Obama |
| **Place:** | park | Yellowstone |
| **Thing:** | marker | Sharpie |
| **Idea:** | religion | Hinduism |

## Individual or Collective Nouns

Most nouns are **individual**: They refer to one person or thing. Other nouns are **collective**, referring most commonly to a group of people or animals.

|  | **Individual Nouns** | **Collective Nouns** |
|---|---|---|
| **Person:** | secretary | staff |
|  | catcher | team |
|  | student | class |
|  | daughter | family |
| **Animal:** | lamb | herd |
|  | locust | swarm |
|  | wolf | pack |
|  | kitten | litter |
|  | goose | gaggle |

## Concrete or Abstract

If a noun refers to something that can be seen, heard, smelled, tasted, or touched, it is a **concrete noun**. If a noun refers to something that can't be sensed, it is an **abstract noun**. Abstract nouns name ideas, conditions, or feelings.

| **Concrete Nouns** | **Abstract Nouns** |
|---|---|
| judge | impartiality |
| brain | mind |
| heart | courage |
| train | transportation |

**Vocabulary**

**common noun**
noun referring to a general person, place, thing, or idea; not capitalized as a name

**proper noun**
noun referring to a specific person, place, thing, or idea; capitalized as a name

**individual noun**
noun referring to one person or thing

**collective noun**
noun referring to a group of people or animals

**concrete noun**
noun referring to something that can be sensed

**abstract noun**
noun referring to an idea, a condition, or a feeling—something that cannot be sensed

# Using Different Classes of Nouns

**Identify** In each sentence below, identify the underlined nouns as common (C) or proper (P).

1. <u>William Faulkner</u> wrote about the <u>death</u> of the <u>Old South</u>.
        P               C       P

2. His novel *<u>The Unvanquished</u>* tells about the <u>aftermath</u> of the <u>Civil War</u>.
        P               C     P

3. He chronicles the <u>end</u> of <u>slavery</u> but also of the genteel class in the <u>South</u>.
        C   C                        P

4. His novel *<u>Absalom, Absalom!</u>* describes the <u>creation</u> and end of a <u>plantation</u>.
        P               C        C

**Identify** In each sentence below, identify the underlined nouns as individual (I) or collective (CL).

1. <u>Quentin Compson</u> appears often in the collected <u>works</u> of Faulkner.
        I                      CL

2. The Compson <u>family</u> is the <u>centerpiece</u> of Yoknapatawpha County.
        CL        I

3. The novel *<u>The Sound and the Fury</u>* tells of the plight of the <u>Compsons'</u>.
        I                CL

4. <u>Benjamin Compson</u> watches a <u>group</u> golf in what was once their farm field.
        I            CL

**Identify** In each sentence below, identify the underlined nouns as concrete (CT) or abstract (A).

1. The <u>Compsons</u> become a <u>symbol</u> of the decline of the South.
        CT         A

2. <u>Faulkner</u> depicts the family with <u>compassion</u> and <u>humor</u>.
        CT            A     A

3. Other <u>novels</u> tell of other denizens of Faulkner's <u>imagination</u>.
        CT              A

4. Faulkner won the <u>Pulitzer Prize</u> for his novel *A Fable,* set outside the <u>county</u>.
        CT                    CT

# LO2 Singular or Plural

The **number** of a noun indicates whether it is singular or plural. A **singular** noun refers to one person, place, thing, or idea. A **plural** noun refers to more than one person, place, thing or idea. For most words, the plural is formed by adding *s*. For nouns ending in *ch, s, sh, x,* or *z,* add an *es*.

| | Most Nouns Add *s* | | Nouns Ending in *ch, s, sh, x,* or *z* Add *es* | |
|---|---|---|---|---|
| | **Singular** | **Plural** | **Singular** | **Plural** |
| **Person:** | sister | sisters | coach | coaches |
| **Place:** | park | parks | church | churches |
| **Thing:** | spoon | spoons | kiss | kisses |
| **Idea:** | solution | solutions | wish | wishes |

## Same in Both Forms or Usually Plural

Some nouns are the same in both forms, and others are usually plural:

| Same in Both Forms | | Usually Plural | |
|---|---|---|---|
| **Singular** | **Plural** | **Plural** | |
| deer | deer | clothes | series |
| fish | fish | glasses | shears |
| moose | moose | pants | shorts |
| salmon | salmon | proceeds | species |
| sheep | sheep | savings | tongs |
| swine | swine | scissors | trousers |

## Irregular Plurals

**Irregular plurals** are formed by changing the words themselves. That is because the plural form comes from Old English or Latin.

| From Old English | | From Latin | |
|---|---|---|---|
| **Singular** | **Plural** | **Singular** | **Plural** |
| child | children | alumnus | alumni |
| foot | feet | axis | axes |
| goose | geese | crisis | crises |
| man | men | datum | data |
| mouse | mice | millennium | millennia |
| person | people | medium | media |
| tooth | teeth | nucleus | nuclei |
| woman | women | phenomenon | phenomena |

# Using Singular and Plural Nouns

**Identify**  For each word, fill in the blank with either the singular or plural form, whichever is missing. If the word usually uses the plural form, write an X on the line.

1. crisis      crises

2. x      species

3. child      children

4. automobile      automobiles

5. x      shears

6. tooth      teeth

7. x      clothes

8. deer      deer

9. swine      swine

10. phenomenon      phenomena

11. girl      girls

12. millennium      millennia

13. man      men

14. fish      fish

15. x      pants

16. moose      moose

17. axis      axes

18. boy      boys

19. mouse      mice

20. goose      geese

21. datum      data

22. alumnus      alumni

23. x      savings

24. tree      trees

25. woman      women

Anthony DiChello,2010 / Used under license from Shutterstock.com

# L○3 Tricky Plurals

Some plural nouns are more challenging to form. Words ending in *y, f,* or *fe* and certain compound nouns require special consideration.

## Nouns Ending in *y*

If a common noun ends in *y* after a consonant, change the *y* to *i* and add *es*. If the noun ends in *y* after a vowel, leave the *y* and add *s*.

| *y* After a Consonant | | *y* After a Vowel | |
|---|---|---|---|
| **Singular** | **Plural** | **Singular** | **Plural** |
| fly | flies | bay | bays |
| lady | ladies | key | keys |
| penny | pennies | toy | toys |
| story | stories | tray | trays |

## Nouns Ending in *f* or *fe*

If a common noun ends in *f* or *fe,* change the *f* or *fe* to a *v* and add *es*—unless the *f* sound remains in the plural form. Then just add an *s*.

| *v* Sound in Plural | | *f* Sound in Plural | |
|---|---|---|---|
| **Singular** | **Plural** | **Singular** | **Plural** |
| calf | calves | belief | beliefs |
| life | lives | chef | chefs |
| self | selves | proof | proofs |
| shelf | shelves | safe | safes |

## Compound Nouns

A **compound noun** is made up of two or more words that function together as a single noun. Whether the compound is hyphenated or not, make it plural by placing the *s* or *es* on the most important word in the compound.

| Important Word First | | Important Word Last | |
|---|---|---|---|
| **Singular** | **Plural** | **Singular** | **Plural** |
| editor in chief | editors in chief | bird-watcher | bird-watchers |
| mother-in-law | mothers-in-law | human being | human beings |
| professor emeritus | professors emeritus | test tube | test tubes |
| secretary of state | secretaries of state | well-wisher | well-wishers |

# Forming Tricky Plurals

**Form Plurals** For each word below, create the correct plural form.

1. day _____ days _____
2. shelf _____ shelves _____
3. middle school _____ middle schools _____
4. pony _____ ponies _____
5. bay _____ bays _____
6. life _____ lives _____
7. chief _____ chiefs _____
8. loaf _____ loaves _____
9. tray _____ trays _____
10. compact car _____ compact cars _____

11. mother-in-law _____ mothers-in-law _____
12. ray _____ rays _____
13. lady _____ ladies _____
14. carafe _____ carafes _____
15. stepsister _____ step sisters _____
16. poof _____ poofs _____
17. nose tackle _____ nose tackles _____
18. party _____ parties _____
19. son-in-law _____ sons-in-law _____
20. baby _____ babies _____

**Form Plurals** In the sentences below, correct the plural errors by circling them and writing the correct forms above.

1. If I give you two ~~pennys~~ *pennies* for your thoughts, will you give me two cents' ~~worths~~ *worth*?

2. Have you read *The Secret* ~~*Lifes*~~ *Lives* *of* ~~*Cheves*~~ *Chefs*?

3. The ~~professor emerituses~~ *professors emeritus* are working on two mathematical ~~prooves~~ *proofs*.

4. I won't question your ~~believes~~ *beliefs* or insult your ~~wells-wisher~~ *well-wishers*.

5. The ~~ladys~~ *ladies* tried to quiet their screaming ~~babys~~ *babies*.

6. Time is sure fun when you're having ~~flys~~ *flies*.

7. The ~~compacts car~~ *compact cars* are equipped with remote-access ~~keis~~ *keys*.

8. I like chicken ~~pattys~~ *patties* but don't like ~~salmons patty~~ *salmon patties*.

9. I read about ~~dwarves~~ *dwarfs* and ~~elfs~~ *elves*.

10. Stack those books on the ~~shelfs~~ *shelves* above the ~~saves~~ *safes*.

# LO4 Count and Noncount Nouns

Some nouns name things that can be counted, and other nouns name things that cannot. Different rules apply to each type.

## Count Nouns

**Count nouns** name things that can be counted—*pens, people, votes, cats,* and so forth. They can be singular or plural, and they can be preceded by numbers or articles (*a, an,* or *the*).

| Singular | Plural |
| --- | --- |
| apple | apples |
| iguana | iguanas |
| thought | thoughts |
| room | rooms |

think4aphotop.2010 / Used under license from Shutterstock.com

## Noncount Nouns

**Noncount nouns** name things that cannot be counted. They are used in singular form, and they can be preceded by *the*, but not by *a* or *an*.

This semester, I'm taking **mathematics** and **biology** as well as **Spanish**.

| Substances | Foods | Activities | Science | Languages | Abstractions |
| --- | --- | --- | --- | --- | --- |
| wood | water | reading | oxygen | Spanish | experience |
| cloth | milk | boating | weather | English | harm |
| ice | wine | smoking | heat | Mandarin | publicity |
| plastic | sugar | dancing | sunshine | Farsi | advice |
| wool | rice | swimming | electricity | Greek | happiness |
| steel | meat | soccer | lightning | Latin | health |
| aluminum | cheese | hockey | biology | French | joy |
| metal | flour | photography | history | Japanese | love |
| leather | pasta | writing | mathematics | Afrikaans | anger |
| porcelain | gravy | homework | economics | German | fame |

## Two-Way Nouns

**Two-way nouns** can function as count or noncount nouns, depending on their context.

Please set a **glass** in front of each place mat. (count noun)

The display case was made of tempered **glass**. (noncount noun)

# Using Count and Noncount Nouns

**Sort** Read the list of nouns below and sort the words into columns of count and noncount nouns.

| | | | | |
|---|---|---|---|---|
| window | aluminum | holiday | health | rain |
| English | shoe | tricycle | poetry | ice |
| bowling | plum | Japanese | lawyer | teaspoon |

| Count Nouns | Noncount Nouns |
|---|---|
| window | English |
| shoe | bowling |
| plum | aluminum |
| holiday | Japanese |
| tricycle | health |
| lawyer | poetry |
| teaspoon | rain |
| | ice |

**Correct** Read the following paragraph and correct the noun errors. The first sentence has been corrected for you.

Our kitchen redesign involved tearing out the plastic that covered the counter and removing the flashing around the edges. We installed [1] new aluminum to replace the old metal. Also, the cupboard doors, which used to be made of wood, were replaced by doors made of glass. We have a new jar for holding flour and a new refrigerator with a special place for milk and a dispenser for water. Everything is illuminated by [5] new lighting, and a larger window lets more sunlight in.

## Correction Marks

- ⌐ delete
- d̲ capitalize
- Ø lowercase
- ∧ insert
- ⌃ add comma
- ? add question
- ∧ mark
- word
- ∧ add word
- ⊙ add period
- ◯ spelling
- ∿ switch

# LO5 Articles

**Articles** help you to know if a noun refers to a specific thing or to a general thing. There are two basic types of articles—definite and indefinite.

## Definite Article

The **definite article** is the word *the*. It signals that the noun refers to one specific person, place, thing, or idea.

Look at the rainbow.
(Look at a specific rainbow.)

**Note:** *The* can be used with most nouns, but usually not with proper nouns.

**Incorrect:** The Joe looked at the rainbow.

**Correct:** Joe looked at the rainbow.

## Indefinite Articles

The **indefinite articles** are the words *a* and *an*. They signal that the noun refers to a general person, place, thing, or idea. The word *a* is used before nouns that begin with consonant sounds, and the word *an* is used before nouns that begin with vowel sounds.

I enjoy seeing a rainbow.
(I enjoy seeing any rainbow.)

**Note:** Don't use *a* or *an* with plural count nouns or noncount nouns.

**Incorrect:** I love a sunshine.

**Correct:** I love the sunshine

**Note:** If a word begins with an *h* that is pronounced, use *a*. If the *h* is silent, use *an*.

**Incorrect:** I stared for a hour.

**Correct:** I stared for an hour.

## Insight

If your heritage language does not use articles, pay close attention to the way native English speakers use *the* when referring to a specific thing. Note, however, that *the* is not usually used with proper nouns naming people or animals.

## Vocabulary

**article**
the most common type of noun marker (*a, an,* or *the*)

**definite article**
the word *the*, used to mark a noun that refers to a specific person, place, or thing

**indefinite article**
the words *a* or *an*, used to mark a noun that refers to a general person, place, or thing

# Using Articles

**Identify** Add the appropriate indefinite article (*a* or *an*) to each of the words below. The first one has been done for you.

1. _____ *an* _____ orchard
2. _____ a _____ petunia
3. _____ a _____ hose
4. _____ an _____ honor
5. _____ an _____ avocado

6. _____ an _____ evening
7. _____ a _____ house
8. _____ an _____ hour
9. _____ a _____ shark
10. _____ an _____ eye

11. _____ an _____ error
12. _____ an _____ opportunity
13. _____ an _____ honest mistake
14. _____ an _____ emblem
15. _____ a _____ handkerchief

**Correct** Either delete or replace any articles that are incorrectly used in the following paragraph. The first sentence has been done for you.

Climate scientists see a shift in ~~a~~ *the* weather. With ~~a~~ *an* increase in the *1* levels of carbon dioxide, the atmosphere traps ~~a~~ *the* heat of the sun. More heat in ~~an~~ *the* air means more heat in the oceans. If ~~a~~ *an* ocean gets warmer, the storms it creates are more intense. ~~An~~ *A* hurricane could develop to ~~an~~ *a* higher category, with stronger winds and ~~a~~ *an* increase in ~~a~~ lightning. ~~A~~ *5* Earth is already ~~an~~ *a* storm world, but with a rise in global temperatures, ~~a~~ *the* weather could become more extreme.

Steve Nagy/Design Pics/Corbis

**Correction Marks**

| | |
|---|---|
| ℐ | delete |
| d̳ | capitalize |
| ∅ | lowercase |
| ∧ | insert |
| ⌃ | add comma |
| ? | add question |
| ∧ | mark |
| word ∧ | add word |
| ⊙ | add period |
| ◯ | spelling |
| ∿ | switch |

## Traits

These noun markers show if a noun is owned, if it is very general, if it is very specific, or if it is numerous or plentiful.

# LO6 Other Noun Markers

Other words help provide information about nouns.

## Possessive Adjective

A **possessive adjective** is the possessive form of a noun or pronoun. Possessive adjectives can be formed by adding *'s* to singular nouns and *'* to plural nouns.

**Paul's** car is in the shop, but **Taylor's** is fixed.

**Florida's** coast is beautiful.

The **King's** porch has screens.

That is **my** pen. This pen is **mine**.

It's **your** choice. The choice is **yours**.

**Possessive Pronouns**

|  | Singular | | Plural | |
|---|---|---|---|---|
|  | Before | After | Before | After |
| First Person | my | mine | our | ours |
| Second Person | your | yours | your | yours |
| Third Person | his | his | their | theirs |
|  | her | hers | their | theirs |
|  | its | its | their | theirs |

**Note:** One form of a possessive pronoun is used before the noun, and a different form is used after.

## Indefinite Adjectives

An **indefinite adjective** signals that the noun it marks refers to a general person, place, thing, or idea. Some indefinite adjectives mark count nouns and others mark noncount nouns.

**Each** person brought food. **Much** food was set out.

| With Count Nouns | | | With Noncount Nouns | With Count or Noncount | | |
|---|---|---|---|---|---|---|
| each | either | every | much | all | any | more |
| few | many | neither | | most | some | |
| several | | | | | | |

## Demonstrative Adjectives

A **demonstrative adjective** marks a specific noun. The words *this* and *that* (singular) or *these* and *those* (plural) demonstrate exactly which one is meant.

**These** pickles are from **that** jar.     **This** taste comes from **those** spices.

## Quantifiers

A **quantifier** tells *how many* or *how much* there is of something.

| With Count Nouns | | With Noncount Nouns | | With Count or Noncount | | |
|---|---|---|---|---|---|---|
| each | a couple of | a bag of | a little | no | a lot of | most |
| several | every | a bowl of | much | not any | lots of | all |
| a number of | many | a piece of | a great deal of | some | plenty of | |
| both | a few | | | | | |
| nine | | | | | | |

## Vocabulary

**possessive adjective**
the possessive form of a noun or pronoun, showing ownership of another noun

**indefinite adjective**
an indefinite pronoun (*many, much, some*) used as an adjective to mark a nonspecific noun

**demonstrative adjective**
a demonstrative pronoun (*this, that, those*) used as an adjective to mark a specific noun

**quantifier**
a modifier that tells *how many* or *how much*

# Using Noun Markers

**Identify** Circle the appropriate noun marker in parentheses for each sentence.

1. I brought one of (*my*, *mine*) favorite recipes, and you brought one of (*your*, *yours*).

2. Is this (*her*, *hers*) recipe, or is it (*their*, *theirs*)?

3. How (*many*, *much*) sugar should I add to the batter?

4. I can't believe the recipe does not use (*any*, *each*) flour.

5. Next, we should make (*this*, *these*) casserole.

6. Your face tells me you don't like (*that*, *those*) idea.

7. After making the dough, we had (*several*, *a little*) butter left over.

8. We liked (*a number of*, *much*) the recipes.

9. The best pie of all was (*her*, *hers*).

10. Let's make sure everyone has a copy in (*their*, *theirs*) recipe files.

**Correct** Delete and replace any incorrectly used noun markers in the following paragraph. The first one has been done for you.

    An omelet can contain as few or as ~~much~~ (many) ingredients as you wish. *1* Of course, a good omelet starts with three or four eggs. Blend the eggs in ~~yours~~ (your) biggest bowl and add a ~~couple of~~ (little) milk. Next, you can include ~~much~~ (some) vegetables. Try fresh ingredients from ~~yours~~ (your) garden. Add a cup of chopped scallions, fresh tomatoes, or green peppers. And ~~a number of~~ (some) spinach can *5* give the omelet a savory flavor. You can also add ~~several~~ (some) meat. Mix in a ~~couple of~~ (little) bacon or ~~many~~ ham. Or you might include ~~several~~ (some) sausage. Fry the omelet, fold it, sprinkle it with a ~~couple of~~ (little) cheese, and enjoy!

## Correction Marks

| Mark | Meaning |
| --- | --- |
| ℐ | delete |
| d̲̲ | capitalize |
| Ø | lowercase |
| ∧ | insert |
| ̂ | add comma |
| ? | add question mark |
| word ∧ | add word |
| ⊙ | add period |
| ⬭ | spelling |
| ∿ | switch |

# LO7 Real-World Application

**Correct** In the letter that follows, correct any errors with nouns, articles, or other noun markers. Use the correction marks to the left.

| Send | Attach | Fonts | Colors | Save As Draft |

| | |
|---|---|
| From: | Melissa St. James |
| To: | Design and Printing Staff |
| Cc: | |
| Subject: | Internship Program for University Students |

Hi, Team:

Could you use a assistant—a extra pair of hands at little cost?

The head of the Graphic Arts Department at Northwestern College has asked us if we'd be interested in developing internships for third-year students in a university's four-year graphic-arts program.

Internships could be the real win-win proposition because internes would
• work on tasks that you assign.
• give you 20 hours of work per week for 15 weeks.
• get excellent professional experience by working with you.
• allow us an opportunity to work with potential employees.

Please consider working with an student intern during the fall semester. If you are interested, let me know before January 28.

Thanks for considering these invitation to help future member of a graphic arts profession.

Melissa

"Clothes make the man. Naked people have little or no influence on society."

—Mark Twain

# 28

# Pronoun

An old saying goes that clothes make the man. Well, not quite. Just because a suit is sitting there with a laptop on its, well, lap doesn't mean that a living, breathing and thinking person is in the room. The clothes are just temporary stand-ins.

Pronouns, similarly, are stand-ins for nouns. They aren't nouns, but they suggest nouns or refer back to them. That's why it's especially important for the pronouns to clearly connect to whatever it is replacing.

This chapter will help you make sure your pronoun stand-ins work well.

## Learning Outcomes

**LO1** Understand personal pronouns.

**LO2** Create pronoun-antecedent agreement.

**LO3** Correct other pronoun problems.

**LO4** Create agreement with indefinite pronouns.

**LO5** Use relative pronouns.

**LO6** Use other pronouns.

**LO7** Use pronouns correctly in a real-world context.

## What do you think?

How could clothes make the man (or woman)? How do pronouns help nouns?

Answers will vary.

# LO1 Personal Pronouns

A **pronoun** is a word that takes the place of a noun or another pronoun. The most common type of pronoun is the **personal pronoun**. Personal pronouns indicate whether the person is speaking, is being spoken to, or is being spoken about.

| Person | Singular | | | Plural | | |
|---|---|---|---|---|---|---|
| | **Nom.** | **Obj.** | **Poss.** | **Nom.** | **Obj.** | **Poss.** |
| First (speaking) | I | me | my/mine | we | us | our/ours |
| Second (spoken to) | you | you | your/yours | you | you | your/yours |
| Third (spoken about) masculine | he | him | his | they | them | their/theirs |
| feminine | she | her | her/hers | they | them | their/theirs |
| neuter | it | it | its | they | them | their/theirs |

**Nom.**=nominative case  /  **Obj**=objective case  /  **Poss.**=possessive case

## Case of Pronouns

The **case** of a personal pronoun indicates how it can be used.

- **Nominative** pronouns are used as the subjects of sentences or as subject complements (following the linking verbs *am, is, are, was, were, be, being,* or *been*).

  > **He** applied for the job, but the person hired was **she**.

- **Objective** pronouns are used as direct objects, indirect objects, or objects of prepositions.

  > The police officer warned **us** about **them**.

- **Possessive** pronouns show ownership and function as adjectives.

  > **Her** lawn looks much greener than **mine**.

## Gender

Pronouns can be **masculine**, **feminine**, or **neuter**.

> **He** showed **her** how to fix **it**.

**Vocabulary**

**pronoun**
a word that takes the place of
a noun or other pronoun

**personal pronoun**
a pronoun that indicates
whether the person is
speaking, is spoken to, or is
spoken about

**case**
whether a pronoun is used
as a subject, an object, or a
possessive

**nominative**
used as a subject or subject
complement

**objective**
used as a direct object, an
indirect object, or an object of
a preposition

**possessive**
used to show ownership

**masculine**
male

**feminine**
female

**neuter**
neither male nor female

> **Say It**
>
> Read the following aloud.
>
> 1. *I* am / *You* are / *He* is / *She* is / *It* is / *We* are / *They* are
>
> 2. Show *me* / Show *you* / Show *him* / Show *her* / Show *them* / Show *us*
>
> 3. *My* car / *Your* car / *His* car / *Her* car / *Their* car
>
> 4. The car is *mine.* / The car is *yours.* / The car is *his.* / The car is *hers.* / The car is *theirs.*

# Using Personal Pronouns

**Select** For each sentence below, circle the correct personal pronoun in parentheses.

1. (*I*, me, my) love to hang out at the corner coffee shop.

2. (I, Me, *My*) friends and I gather there on Saturday morning.

3. One friend, Zach, is making a film, and (*he*, him, his) asked me to be in it.

4. We read over the lines, and other patrons listened to (we, *us*, our).

5. (We, Us, *Our*) friend Rachel is also in the film.

6. At one point, I have to give (she, *her*, hers) a kiss.

7. The other people in the coffee shop applauded (we, *us*, our.)

8. Rachel and (*I*, me, my) blushed and stared into (we, us, *our*) lattes.

9. Zach thought it was great, and (*he*, him, his) set up a shooting schedule.

10. Whoever comes to the coffee shop that day will be (we, us, *our*) extras.

**Correct** In the following paragraph, correct the pronouns by crossing out the incorrect forms and writing the correct forms above.

Zach, Rachel, and ~~me~~ **I** went to the coffee shop on Saturday afternoon, when ~~them~~ **they** are usually closed. The owners agreed to let ~~we~~ **us** film there. Zach rearranged the tables a little to make room for the camera, and ~~him~~ **he** and ~~me~~ **I** set up the equipment. The camera rolled, and Rachel and ~~me~~ **I** started into our lines. A couple of times, we had to stop because the owners were laughing so much ~~them~~ **they** couldn't hold a straight face. Rachel and ~~me~~ **I** had a hard time being straight when it came to ~~ours~~ **our** kissing scene. It went well, and ~~her~~ **she** and ~~me~~ **I** got through it in one take. Zach took the footage away, and he told us he would send a disk of the rough cut to ~~she~~ **her** and ~~I~~ **me**.

# LO2 Pronoun-Antecedent Agreement

The **antecedent** is the word that a pronoun refers to or replaces. A pronoun must have the same person, number, and gender as the antecedent, which is called **pronoun-antecedent agreement**.

> **third-person**     **singular feminine**     **singular feminine**
>
> **Colleen** thought **she** would need a lift, but **her** car started.

## Agreement in Person

A pronoun needs to match its antecedent in **person** (first, second, or third).

> **third person**     **second person**
>
> Incorrect:  If **people** keep going, **you** can usually reach the goal.
> Correct:  If **you** keep going, **you** can usually reach the goal.
> Correct:  If **people** keep going, **they** can usually reach the goal.

## Agreement in Number

A pronoun needs to match its antecedent in **number** (singular or plural).

> **singular**     **plural**
>
> Incorrect:  Each **lifeguard** must buy **their** own uniform.
> Correct:  **Lifeguards** must buy **their** own uniforms.
> Correct:  Each **lifeguard** must buy **her** or **his** own uniform.

## Agreement in Gender

A pronoun needs to match its antecedent in **gender** (masculine, feminine, or neuter).

> **feminine**     **masculine**
>
> Incorrect:  **Mrs. Miller** will present **his** speech.
> Correct:  **Mrs. Miller** will present **her** speech.

> **Say It**
>
> Speak the following words aloud.
>
> 1. First person: *I, me, my, mine; we, us, our, ours*
> 2. Second person: *you, your, yours*
> 3. Third person feminine: *she, her, hers; they, them, their, theirs*
> 4. Third person masculine: *he, him, his; they, them, their, theirs*
> 5. Third person neuter: *it, its; they, them, their, theirs*

# Correcting Agreement Errors

**Correct Person**  Rewrite each sentence to correct the person error.

Sample answers:

1. When you go to the multiplex, a person has a lot of movies to choose from.

   When you go to the multiplex, you have a lot of movies to choose from.

2. Each of us has to buy their own ticket and snacks.

   Each of us has to buy our own ticket and snacks.

3. If the viewer arrives early enough, you can see a triple feature.

   If the viewer arrives early enough, he or she can see a triple feature.

4. One can be overwhelmed by how many movies you can see.

   One can be overwhelmed by how many movies one can see.

**Correct Number**  Rewrite each sentence to correct the number error.

Sample answers:

5. Each moviegoer chooses what movies they want to see.

   Each moviegoer chooses what movies he or she wants to see.

6. A snack-counter attendant serves treats, and they also clean up messes.

   A snack-counter attendant serves treats, and he or she also cleans up messes.

7. Movie critics give his opinion about different films.

   Movie critics give their opinions about different films.

8. A critic shouldn't give away the ending because they would ruin the movie.

   A critic shouldn't give away the ending because he or she would ruin the movie.

**Correct Gender**  Rewrite each sentence to correct the gender error.

Sample answers:

9. A critic shouldn't give away the ending because he would ruin the movie.

   A critic shouldn't give away the ending because he or she would ruin the movie.

10. When Roger Ebert critiques a film, she's right most of the time.

    When Roger Ebert critiques a film, he's right most of the time.

11. Anita accidentally left his purse at the theater.

    Anita accidentally left her purse at the theater.

12. The multiplex sits on a hilltop, and she looks like a palace.

    The multiplex sits on a hilltop, and it looks like a palace.

# LO3 Other Pronoun Problems

Pronouns are very useful parts of speech, but if they are mishandled, they can cause problems.

## Vague Pronoun

Do not use a pronoun that could refer to more than one antecedent.

> **Unclear:** Raul played baseball with his friend and **his** brother.
> **Clear:** Raul played baseball with his friend and **his friend's** brother.

## Missing Antecedent

Avoid using *it* or *they* without clear antecedents.

> **Unclear:** **They** say humans share 97 percent of DNA with chimps.
> **Clear:** **Scientists** say humans share 97 percent of DNA with chimps.

> **Unclear:** **It** says in the *Times* that the Democrats back the bill.
> **Clear:** The *Times* says that the Democrats back the bill.

## Double Subjects

Do not place a pronoun right after the subject. Doing so creates an error called a **double subject**, which is not a standard construction.

> **Nonstandard:** Rudy and Charlie, **they** went fishing.
> **Standard:** Rudy and Charlie went fishing.

## Usage Errors *(They're, You're, It's)*

Do not confuse possessive pronouns *(your, their, its)* with contractions *(you're, they're, it's)*. Remember that the contractions use apostrophes in place of missing letters.

> **Incorrect:** Keep **you're** car in **it's** own lane.
> **Correct:** Keep **your** car in **its** own lane.

George Fairbairn,2010 / Used under license from Shutterstock.com

# Correcting Other Pronoun Problems

**Rewrite** Rewrite each sentence to correct the pronoun-reference problems.

Answers will vary.

1. Sarah asked her sister and her friend to help her move.

_____

2. It said on the news that the accident will cost billions to fix.

_____

3. They say that dark energy takes up 75 percent of the universe.

_____

4. Dan wants his father and his friend to help.

_____

5. They have found a way to make deep-water drilling safer.

_____

6. It says on the parking ticket that I have to pay $50.

_____

**Correct** In the following paragraph, correct the pronoun errors. Use the correction marks to the right.

Answers will vary.

For 28 years, it reported in the *Weekly World News* all kinds of outlandish

stories. Often the paper reported about Elvis or the Loch Ness Monster being

spotted and his impromptu concerts for die-hard fans. A bat-human hybrid

named Bat Boy and an alien named P'lod appeared repeatedly in the tabloid,

and he even supposedly had an affair with Hillary Clinton. Since this was during

the Monica Lewinski scandal, maybe she was getting back at him. The writers

and editors of the *Weekly World News*, they rarely publicly acknowledged that

their stories were jokes, but said that he or she had to "suspend disbelief for the

sake of enjoyment."

| Correction Marks | |
|---|---|
| ◡ | delete |
| d̲ | capitalize |
| ⌀ | lowercase |
| ∧ | insert |
| ⌄ | add comma |
| ? ∧ | add question mark |
| word ∧ | add word |
| ⊙ | add period |
| ◯ | spelling |
| ∿ | switch |

# LO4 Indefinite Pronouns

An **indefinite pronoun** does not have an antecedent, and it does not refer to a specific person, place, thing, or idea. These pronouns pose unique issues with subject-verb and pronoun-antecedent agreement.

## Singular Indefinite Pronouns

Some indefinite pronouns are singular. When they are used as subjects, they require a singular verb. As antecedents, they must be matched to singular pronouns.

| | | | |
|---|---|---|---|
| each | anyone | anybody | anything |
| either | someone | somebody | something |
| neither | everyone | everybody | everything |
| another | no one | nobody | nothing |
| one | | | |

> **Nobody is** expecting to see Bigfoot on our camping trip.
>
> **Someone** used **his** or **her** own money to buy a Bigfoot detector at a novelty shop.

## Plural Indefinite Pronouns

Some indefinite pronouns are plural. As subjects, they require a plural verb, and as antecedents, they require a plural pronoun.

| both | few | several | many |
|---|---|---|---|

> **A few** of the campers **hear** thumps in the night.
>
> **Several** of my friends swear **they** can see eyes glowing eight feet off the ground.

## Singular or Plural Indefinite Pronouns

Some indefinite pronouns can be singular or plural, depending on the object of the preposition in the phrase that follows them.

| all | any | most | none | some |
|---|---|---|---|---|

> **Most** of **us are** too frightened to sleep.
>
> **Most** of the **night is** over already anyway.

## Insight

For more practice with indefinite pronouns, see pages 288–290.

## Vocabulary

**indefinite pronoun**
a pronoun that does not refer to a specific person, place, thing, or idea

aquariagirl1970,2010 / Used under license from Shutterstock.com

# Correcting Agreement

**Correct** Rewrite each sentence to correct the agreement errors. (Hint: the sentences are about a group of female campers.)

1. Everyone needs to set up their own tent.

   Everyone needs to set up her own tent.

2. No one are getting out of work.

   No one is getting out of work.

3. Anyone who wants to be dry should make sure they have a rain fly.

   Anyone who wants to be dry should make sure she has a rain fly.

4. Nothing are more miserable than a wet sleeping bag.

   Nothing is more miserable than a wet sleeping bag.

5. Few is wanting to end up drenched.

   Few are wanting to end up drenched.

6. Several wants to go hiking to look for Bigfoot.

   Several want to go hiking to look for Bigfoot.

7. Many has doubts that he exists.

   Many have doubts that he exists.

8. A few says they might have dated him in high school.

   A few say they might have dated him in high school.

9. A Bigfoot hunter should make sure they have a camera along.

   A Bigfoot hunter should make sure she has a camera along.

10. Most of the hunters is also going to carry a big stick.

    Most of the hunters are also going to carry a big stick.

11. Most of the afternoon are available for different activities.

    Most of the afternoon is available for different activities.

12. None of the girls is planning to hike after dark.

    None of the girls are planning to hike after dark.

13. None of the food are to be left out to attract animals or Bigfoot.

    None of the food is to be left out to attract animals or Bigfoot.

# LO5 Relative Pronouns

A **relative pronoun** introduces a dependent clause and relates it to the rest of the sentence.

| who | whom | which | whose |
|-----|------|-------|-------|
| whoever | whomever | that | |

**relative clause**

I would like to meet the woman **who** discovered dark matter.

## Who/Whoever and Whom/Whomever

*Who, whoever, whom,* and *whomever* refer to people. *Who* or *whoever* functions as the subject of the relative clause, while *whom* or *whomever* functions as the object of the clause.

**relative clause**

I am amazed by a person **who** could imagine matter that can't be seen.
The woman **whom** I met was named Vera Rubin.

**relative clause**

**Note:** In the second relative clause, *whom* introduces the clause even though it is the direct object, not the subject *(I thanked whom).*

## That and Which

*That* and *which* usually refer to things. When *that* introduces the clause, the clause **is not** set off with commas. When *which* introduces the clause, the clause **is** set off with commas.

**relative clause**

I saw a documentary **that** explained about dark matter and dark energy.
The show is *Into the Wormhole,* **which** is on the Science Channel.

**relative clause**

**Note:** In the first example, the *that* clause is restrictive, or essential to the meaning of the sentence. In the second example, the *which* clause is nonrestrictive, or unnecessary to the meaning of the sentence.

## Whose

*Whose* shows ownership or connection.

**relative clause**

Morgan Freeman, **whose** voice is soothing, hosts the show.

**Note:** Do not confuse *whose* with the contraction *who's* (who is).

# Using Relative Pronouns

**Select** For each sentence, circle the correct relative pronoun.

1. Vera Rubin, (*who*, *whom*) first discovered dark matter, wasn't seeking fame.

2. In the 1960s, she avoided black holes, (*that*, *which*) were a hot topic.

3. Instead, Rubin focused on the rotation of spiral galaxies, (*that*, *which*) few other people studied.

4. She expected stars (*that*, *which*) were on the outside of galaxies would move faster than stars (*that*, *which*) were near the center.

5. Instead, Rubin discovered the same speed for stars (*that*, *which*) were in different parts of the galaxy.

6. The only way for the galaxy to move that way would be if it had ten times the mass (*that*, *which*) was visible.

7. Rubin, (*who*, *whom*, *whose*) had never courted fame, became a very controversial figure when she presented her findings about dark matter.

8. Other astrophysicists (*who*, *whom*) disbelieved her did similar observations and calculations and confirmed her findings.

9. Rubin, (*who*, *whom*, *whose*) theory once was radical, became one of the great contributors to modern science.

10. (*Whoever*, *Whomever*) wrestles with the idea of dark matter should remember that over fifty years ago, one woman was the first to wrestle with the idea.

Stocktrek Images/Alloy/Corbis

**Write** On your own paper, write a relative clause for each of these relative pronouns: Answers will vary.

1. who        3. whom        5. which        7. whose
2. whoever    4. whomever    6. that

Write a sentence including one of your clauses.

# LO6 Other Pronoun Types

Other types of pronouns have specific uses in your writing: asking questions, pointing to specific things, reflecting back on a noun (or pronoun), or intensifying a noun (or pronoun).

## Interrogative Pronoun

An **interrogative pronoun** asks a question—*who, whose, whom, which, what.*

> **What** should we call our band? **Who** will be in it?

## Demonstrative Pronoun

A **demonstrative pronoun** points to a specific thing—*this, that, these, those.*

> **That** is a great name! **This** will look terrific on a cover!

## Reflexive Pronoun

A **reflexive pronoun** reflects back to the subject of a sentence or clause—*myself, ourselves, yourself, yourselves, himself, herself, itself, themselves.*

> I credit **myself** for the name. You can credit **yourself** for the logo.

## Intensive Pronoun

An **intensive pronoun** emphasizes the noun or pronoun it refers to—*myself, ourselves, yourself, yourselves, himself, herself, itself, themselves.*

> You **yourself** love the name Psycho Drummer. I **myself** couldn't be happier.

## Reciprocal Pronoun

A **reciprocal pronoun** refers to two things in an equal way—*each other, one another.*

> We shouldn't fight with **each other**. We should support **one another**.

### Say It

Speak the following words aloud.

1. Interrogative: *Who* is? / *Whose* is? / *Which* is? / *What* is? / *Whom* do you see?
2. Demonstrative: *This* is / *That* is / *These* are / *Those* are
3. Reflexive: I helped *myself.* / You helped *yourself.* / They helped *themselves*
4. Intensive: I *myself* / You *yourself* / She *herself* / He *himself* / They *themselves*
5. Reciprocal: We helped *each other*. / We helped *one another*.

# Using Other Types of Pronouns

**Identify** Indicate the type of each underlined pronoun: *interrogative, demonstrative, reflexive, intensive,* or *reciprocal.*

1. That is why this band needs a road crew.  demonstrative

2. What are we supposed to do without power cords?  interrogative

3. I myself would not mind playing unplugged.  intensive

4. You need to remind yourself that we don't have acoustic guitars.  reflexive

5. That is the whole problem.  demonstrative

6. The guitars themselves prevent us from playing unplugged.  intensive

7. Who could hear an unplugged electric guitar?  interrogative

8. What person will stand a foot away to listen?  interrogative

9. This is ridiculous.  demonstrative

10. That won't work as a power cord.  demonstrative

11. I myself am about to quit this band.  intensive

12. We should be ashamed of ourselves.  reflexive

13. We shouldn't blame each other.  reciprocal

14. As a band, we should help one another get through this.  reciprocal

15. Let's buy ourselves another set of cords.  reflexive

**Write** Create a sentence using *myself* as a reflexive pronoun, and a second using *myself* as an intensive pronoun. **Answers will vary.**

1. _____

_____

_____

2. _____

_____

_____

# LO7 Real-World Application

**Correct** In the letter that follows, correct any pronoun errors. Use the correction marks to the left.

**Correction Marks**

ℐ delete

d̲ capitalize

∅ lowercase

∧ insert

⌄ add comma

? add question
∧ mark

word
∧ add word

⊙ add period

⬭ spelling

∿ switch

---

✗ **Psycho Drummer**
12185 W. 22nd Avenue, Elkhorn, WI 53100 ▪ Ph: 262.555.7188

July 30, 2011

Ms. Marcia Schwamps, Manager
Piedog Studios
350 South Jackson Street
Elkhorn, WI 53100

Dear Ms. Schwamps:

One of your recording technicians says that you are looking for session musicians
who
~~whom~~ could play instruments for other artists. My band-mate Jerome and ~~me~~ I
our
would like to offer ~~ours~~ services.

I                      who
Jerome and ~~me~~ are the power duo ~~whom~~ are called Psycho Drummer, a name that
himself                                     he            himself
refers to Jerome ~~hisself~~. He is a master percussionist, and ~~him~~ has trained ~~hisself~~
in many styles from heavy metal to rock, pop, jazz, blues, and even classical.

I am the guitarist in Psycho Drummer. I play electric and acoustic (six- and 12-
string) guitars as well as electric bass, and I too have trained myself in them.

our                                              we
Attached, you will find ~~ours~~ résumés, a list of recent gigs ~~us~~ have played, and a
us
review of ~~we~~ from the *Walworth County Week*.

me
Please consider Jerome and ~~I~~ for work as session musicians at Piedog Studios.
you
We look forward to hearing from ~~yous~~ and would very much appreciate an
interview/audition.

Sincerely,

*Terrance "Tear-It-Up" Clark*

Terrance "Tear-It-Up" Clark
Guitarist
Enclosures 3

**Workplace**

In workplace documents, correct grammar is critical to creating a strong impression.

"There are 350 varieties of shark, not counting loan and pool."

—L. M. Boyd

Image Source/Image Source/Corbis

# 29
# Verb

You've probably heard that a shark has to keep swimming or it suffocates. That's not entirely true. Yes, sharks breathe by moving water across their gills, but they can also lie on the bottom and push water through their gills or let currents do the work. Still, most sharks stay on the move, and when a shark is still, it has to work harder to breathe.

Verbs are much the same way. They like to stay on the move. Most verbs are action words, describing what is happening. Some verbs describe states of being—much like sharks sitting on the bottom, breathing. Either way, though, the verb gives life to the sentence, and often it is a word with big teeth. This chapter gives a view into the compelling world of verbs.

## What do you think?

Do you prefer doing or being? Why?

Answers will vary.

## Learning Outcomes

**LO1** Understand and use verb classes.

**LO2** Work with number and person.

**LO3** Work with voice.

**LO4** Form basic verb tenses.

**LO5** Form progressive tense.

**LO6** Form perfect tense.

**LO7** Understand verbals.

**LO8** Use verbals as objects.

**LO9** Apply learning to real-world examples.

# LO1 Verb Classes

Verbs show action or states of being. Different classes of verbs do these jobs.

## Action Verbs

Verbs that show action are called **action verbs**. Some action verbs are **transitive**, which means that they transfer action to a direct object.

> Trina **hurled** the softball.
> (The verb *hurled* transfers action to the direct object *softball*.)

Others are **intransitive**: They don't transfer action to a direct object.

> Trina **pitches**.
> (The verb *pitches* does not transfer action to a direct object.)

## Linking Verbs

Verbs that link the subject to a noun, a pronoun, or an adjective are **linking verbs**. Predicates with linking verbs express a state of being.

> Trina **is** a pitcher.
> (The linking verb *is* connects *Trina* to the noun *pitcher*.)
> She **seems** unbeatable.
> (The linking verb *seems* connects *She* to the adjective *unbeatable*.)

**Linking Verbs**

| is | am | are | was | were | be | being | been | become |
|------|------|------|------|------|------|------|------|------|
| grow | feel | seem | look | smell | taste | sound | appear | remain |

**Note:** The bottom-row words are linking verbs if they don't show action.

## Helping Verbs

A verb that works with an action or linking verb is a **helping** (or auxiliary) verb. A helping verb helps the main verb form tense, mood, and voice.

> Trina **has** pitched two shut-out games, and today she **may be** pitching her third.
> (The helping verb *has* works with the main verb *pitched*; the helping verbs *may be* work with *pitching*. Both form special tenses.)

**Note:** Helping verbs work with verbs ending in *ing* or in past tense form.

**Helping Verbs**

| am | been | could | does | have | might | should | will |
|-----|-------|-------|------|------|-------|--------|-------|
| are | being | did | had | is | must | was | would |
| be | can | do | has | may | shall | were | |

# Using Verb Classes

**Identify/Write** For each sentence below, identify the underlined verbs as transitive action verbs (T), intransitive action verbs (I), linking verbs (L), or helping verbs (H). Then write your own sentence using the same class of verb.

1. I <u>love</u> [T] fast-pitch softball, but I rarely <u>pitch</u> [I].

_____

_____

2. I <u>play</u> [T] first base; it <u>is</u> [L] a pressure-filled position.

_____

_____

3. Runners <u>charge</u> [T] first base, and I <u>tag</u> [T] them out.

_____

_____

4. Double-plays <u>require</u> [T] on-target throws, clean catches, and timing.

_____

_____

5. If a runner <u>steals</u> [I], the pitcher and second baseperson <u>work</u> [I] with me.

_____

_____

6. We <u>catch</u> [T] the runner in a "pickle" and <u>tag</u> [T] her out.

_____

_____

7. Softball <u>is</u> [L] exciting, and I <u>will</u> [H] play all summer.

_____

_____

8. I <u>look</u> [L] worn out after a game, but I <u>feel</u> [L] completely exhilarated.

_____

_____

# LO2 Number and Person of Verb

Verbs reflect number (singular or plural) and person (first person, second person, or third person).

## Number

The **number** of the verb indicates whether the subject is singular or plural. Note that most present tense singular verbs end in *s*, while most present tense plural verbs do not.

**Singular:** A civil war re-enactment **involves** infantry, cavalry, and artillery units.

**Plural:** Civil war re-enactors **stage** amazing battle scenes from the war.

## Person

The **person** of the verb indicates whether the subject is speaking, being spoken to, or being spoken about.

|  | **Singular** | **Plural** |
|---|---|---|
| **First Person:** | (I) am | (we) are |
| **Second Person:** | (you) are | (you) are |
| **Third Person:** | (she) is | (they) are |

Note that the pronoun *I* takes a special form of the *be* verb—*am*.

**Correct:** I am eager to see the cannons fire.
**Incorrect:** I is eager to see the cannons fire.

The pronoun *I* also is paired with plural present tense verbs.

**Correct:** I hope to see a bayonet charge.
**Incorrect:** I hopes to see a bayonet charge.

In a similar way, the singular pronoun *you* takes the plural form of the *be* verb—*are, were*.

**Correct:** You are in for a treat when the battle begins.
**Incorrect:** You is in for a treat when the battle begins.
**Correct:** You were surprised at how steady the horses were in combat.
**Incorrect:** You was surprised at how steady the horses were in combat.

Uwe Bumann,2010 / Used under license from Shutterstock.com

**Vocabulary**

**number**
singular or plural

**person**
whether the subject is speaking *(I, we)*, is being spoken to *(you)*, or is being spoken about *(he, she, it, they)*

# Using Number and Person

Provide For each sentence below, provide the correct person and number of present tense *be* verb *(is, am, are)*.

1. We ___are___ at the Civil War encampment.

2. It ___is___ a gathering of Union and Confederate regiments.

3. You ___are___ in a uniform of Union blue.

4. I ___am___ in the gray of the Confederacy.

5. A light artillery brigade ___is___ a group of mobile cannon.

6. A cavalry regiment ___is___ a group of mounted soldiers.

7. The camp doctors ___are___ equipped to do amputations.

8. The medicine they use ___is___ sometimes worse than the disease.

9. I ___am___ amazed by all of the tent encampments.

10. You ___are___ interested in becoming a re-enactor.

**Rewrite** Rewrite each sentence below to fix the errors in the number and person of the verb.

1. I jumps the first time a cannon goes off.

   I jump the first time a cannon goes off.

2. The guns blows huge white smoke rings whirling into the air.

   The guns blow huge white smoke rings whirling into the air.

3. The cavalry regiments charges together and battles with sabers.

   The cavalry regiments charge together and battle with sabers.

4. In the fray, one cavalry officer fall from his horse.

   In the fray, one cavalry officer falls from his horse.

5. The infantry soldiers lines up in two rows and sends out volleys of bullets.

   The infantry soldiers line up in two rows and send out volleys of bullets.

6. After the battle, President Lincoln deliver a solemn address.

   After the battle, President Lincoln delivers a solemn address.

# LO3 Voice of the Verb

The **voice** of the verb indicates whether the subject is acting or being acted upon.

## Voice

An **active voice** means that the subject is acting. A **passive voice** means that the subject is acted on.

> **Active:** The cast **sang** the song "Our State Fair."
> **Passive:** The song "Our State Fair" **was sung** by the cast.

| | **Active Voice** | | **Passive Voice** | |
|---|---|---|---|---|
| | Singular | Plural | Singular | Plural |
| **Present Tense** | I see<br>you see<br>he/she/it sees | we see<br>you see<br>they see | I am seen<br>you are seen<br>he/she/it is seen | we are seen<br>you are seen<br>they are seen |
| **Past Tense** | I saw<br>you saw<br>he saw | we saw<br>you saw<br>they saw | I was seen<br>you were seen<br>it was seen | we were seen<br>you were seen<br>they were seen |
| **Future Tense** | I will see<br>you will see<br>he will see | we will see<br>you will see<br>they will see | I will be seen<br>you will be seen<br>it will be seen | we will be seen<br>you will be seen<br>they will be seen |
| **Present Perfect Tense** | I have seen<br>you have seen<br>he has seen | we have seen<br>you have seen<br>they have seen | I have been seen<br>you have been seen<br>it has been seen | we have been seen<br>you have been seen<br>they have been seen |
| **Past Perfect Tense** | I had seen<br>you had seen<br>he had seen | we had seen<br>you had seen<br>they had seen | I had been seen<br>you had been seen<br>it had been seen | we had been seen<br>you had been seen<br>they had been seen |
| **Future Perfect Tense** | I will have seen<br>you will have seen<br>he will have seen | we will have seen<br>you will have seen<br>they will have seen | I will have been seen<br>you will have been seen<br>it will have been seen | we will have been seen<br>you will have been seen<br>they will have been seen |

Active voice is preferred for most writing because it is direct and energetic.

> **Active:** The crowd gave the cast a standing ovation.
> **Passive:** The cast was given a standing ovation by the crowd.

Passive voice is preferred when the focus is on the receiver of the action or when the subject is unknown.

> **Passive:** A donation was left at the ticket office.
> **Active:** Someone left a donation at the ticket office.

**Workplace**

In workplace writing, use active voice for most messages. Use passive voice to deliver bad news.

**Vocabulary**

**voice**
active or passive

**active voice**
voice created when the subject is performing the action of the verb

**passive voice**
voice created when the subject is receiving the action of the verb

# Using Voice of a Verb

**Rewrite** Read each passive sentence below and rewrite it to be active. Think about what is performing the action and make that the subject. The first one is done for you.

1. *State Fair* was put on by the community theater group.
   *The community theater group put on State Fair.*

2. The Frake family was featured in the musical.
   *The musical featured the Frake family.*

3. Many songs were sung and danced by the cast.
   *The cast sang and danced many songs.*

4. Pickles and mincemeat were rated by judges at the fair.
   *The judges at the fair rated pickles and mincemeat.*

5. Mrs. Frake's mincement was spiked with too much brandy.
   *Mrs. Frake spiked her mincemeat with too much brandy.*

6. The judges of the contest were overcome by the strength of the mincemeat.
   *The strength of the mincemeat overcame the judges of the contest.*

7. Two couples were shown falling in love at the fair.
   *Two couples fell in love at the fair.*

8. The singers were assisted by a stalwart piano player in the orchestra pit.
   *A stalwart piano player in the pit assisted the singers.*

9. The song "It's a Grand Night for Singing" was the climax of the first half.
   *The song "It's a Grand Night for Singing" climaxed the first half.*

10. The cast was applauded gratefully by the crowd.
    *The crowd gratefully applauded the cast.*

**Write** Using the chart on the facing page, write a sentence for each situation below.   Answers will vary.

1. (A present tense singular active sentence) _____

2. (A past tense plural passive sentence) _____

# LO4 Present and Future Tense Verbs

Basic verb tenses tell whether action happens in the past, in the present, or in the future.

## Present Tense

Present tense verbs indicate that action is happening right now.

> Master musicians and new professionals **gather** at the Marlboro Music Festival.

Present tense verbs also can indicate that action happens routinely or continually.

> Every summer, they **spend** seven weeks together learning music.

## Present Tense in Academic Writing

Use present tense verbs to describe current conditions.

> Pianist Richard Goode **plays** beside talented young artists.

Use present tense verbs also to discuss the ideas in literature or to use historical quotations in a modern context. This use is called the "historical present," which allows writers to continue speaking.

> The audiences at Marlboro **rave** about the quality of the music, or as the *New York Times* **says**, "No matter what is played . . . the performances at Marlboro are usually extraordinary."

**Note:** It is important to write a paragraph or an essay in one tense. Avoid shifting needlessly from tense to tense as you write. (See also page 314.)

## Future Tense

Future tense verbs indicate that action will happen later on.

> Marlboro music **will launch** the careers of many more young stars.

Kokhanchikov, 2010 / Used under license from Shutterstock.com

# Using Present and Future Verb Tenses

**Write** For each sentence below, fill in the blank with the present tense form of the verb indicated in parentheses.

1. Young musicians _____come_____ to Marlboro Music by special invitation. (came)

2. Seasoned professionals _____treat_____ them like colleagues, not students. (treated)

3. Musicians _____work_____ side by side for weeks before performing. (worked)

4. The town of Marlboro, New Hampshire, _____has_____ only 987 citizens. (had)

5. Many times that number _____come_____ to the concerts each summer. (came)

**Change** Cross out and replace the verbs in the following paragraph, making them all present tense.

A sixteen-year-old cellist named Yo Yo Ma ~~arrived~~ *arrives* at Marlboro Music. He ~~couldn't~~ *can't* believe his fortune to be surrounded by such great musicians. He ~~began~~ *begins* to play and soon ~~fell~~ *falls* in love with music. A festival administrator named Jill Hornor also ~~caught~~ *catches* his eye, and he ~~fell~~ *falls* in love with her as well. They ~~were~~ *are* married.

**Write** Write a sentence of your own, using each word below in the form indicated in parentheses. Answers will vary.

1. thought (present) _____

_____

2. lived (future) _____

_____

3. hoped (present) _____

_____

4. cooperated (future) _____

_____

# Past Tense Verbs

Past tense verbs indicate that action happened in the past.

> When referring to his campaign in England, Julius Caesar **reported**, "I **came**. I **saw**. I **conquered**."

## Forming Past Tense

Most verbs form their past tense by adding *ed*. If the word ends in a silent *e*, drop the *e* before adding *ed*.

help ➡ helped          love ➡ loved
look ➡ looked          hope ➡ hoped

If the word ends in a consonant before a single vowel and the last syllable is stressed, double the final consonant before adding *ed*.

stop ➡ stopped          occur ➡ occurred
plan ➡ planned          refer ➡ referred

If the word ends in a *y* preceded by a consonant, change the *y* to *i* before adding *ed*.

study ➡ studied          hurry ➡ hurried
worry ➡ worried          carry ➡ carried

## Irregular Verbs

Some of the most commonly used verbs form past tense by changing the verb itself. See the chart below:

| Present | Past | Present | Past | Present | Past |
|---------|------|---------|------|---------|------|
| am | was, were | fly | flew | see | saw |
| become | became | forget | forgot | shake | shook |
| begin | began | freeze | froze | shine | shone |
| blow | blew | get | got | show | showed |
| break | broke | give | gave | shrink | shrank |
| bring | brought | go | went | sing | sang |
| buy | bought | grow | grew | sink | sank |
| catch | caught | hang | hung | sit | sat |
| choose | chose | have | had | sleep | slept |
| come | came | hear | heard | speak | spoke |
| dig | dug | hide | hid | stand | stood |
| do | did | keep | kept | steal | stole |
| draw | drew | know | knew | swim | swam |
| drink | drank | lead | led | swing | swung |
| drive | drove | pay | paid | take | took |
| eat | ate | prove | proved | teach | taught |
| fall | fell | ride | rode | tear | tore |
| feel | felt | ring | rang | throw | threw |
| fight | fought | rise | rose | wear | wore |
| find | found | run | ran | write | wrote |

## Traits

Note that the irregular verbs at the bottom of the page are some of the oldest verbs in the English language. That's why they are irregular. Sadly, they are used quite often because they describe the everyday tasks that English speakers have been doing for more than a thousand years.

## Vocabulary

**past tense**
verb tense indicating that action happened previously

# Using Past Tense Verbs

**Write** For each verb, write the correct past tense form.

1. swing ___swung___
2. think ___thought___
3. slip ___slipped___
4. reply ___replied___
5. teach ___taught___
6. cry ___cried___
7. sing ___sang___
8. give ___gave___
9. cap ___capped___
10. fly ___flew___
11. type ___typed___
12. cope ___coped___
13. shop ___shopped___
14. grip ___gripped___
15. gripe ___griped___
16. pour ___poured___
17. soap ___soaped___
18. trick ___tricked___
19. try ___tried___
20. tip ___tipped___

**Edit** Make changes to the following paragraph, converting it from present tense to past tense. Use the correction marks to the right.

When I ~~am~~ [was] fresh out of college, I ~~get~~ [got] my first job as an assistant editor at a sports publisher. At this company, acquisitions editors ~~follow~~ [followed] trends, ~~talk~~ [talked] with authors, and ~~work~~ [worked] with them to create a manuscript. Developmental editors then ~~work~~ [worked] with the manuscript to develop it into a worthwhile book. Assistant editors ~~help~~ [helped] with all stages of production. They ~~edit~~ [edited] manuscripts and ~~typemark~~ [typemarked] them. Then they ~~check~~ [checked] the galleys—or long sheets of printout film that paste-up artists cut and ~~wax~~ [waxed] to create pages. Those ~~are~~ [were] the days of manual layout. Assistant editors ~~have~~ [had] to check the paste-up pages for dropped copy. They also proofread and ~~enter~~ [entered] changes, and ~~check~~ [checked] bluelines. Publishing is completely different now, but back then, I ~~get~~ [got] my first experience in real-world work. I ~~am~~ [was] glad just to have an office of my own.

**Correction Marks**

- ˗ɔ delete
- d̲ capitalize
- ꟼ lowercase
- ∧ insert
- ˆ add comma
- ? add question mark
- ⊙ add period
- ◯ spelling
- ∽ switch
- word ∧ add word

# LO5 Progressive Tense Verbs

The basic tenses of past, present, and future tell when action takes place. The progressive tense or aspect tells that action is ongoing.

## Progressive Tense

**Progressive tense** indicates that action is ongoing. Progressive tense is formed by using a helping verb along with the *ing* form of the main verb.

> Work habits **were changing** rapidly.

There are past, present, and future progressive tenses. Each uses a helping verb in the appropriate tense.

> For thousands of years, most humans **were working** in agriculture.
> Currently in the West, most humans **are working** in nonagricultural jobs.
> In the future, people **will be making** their living in unimaginable ways.

### Forming Progressive Tense

| | | | | | | |
|---|---|---|---|---|---|---|
| **Past:** | was/were | + | main verb | + | ing |
| **Present:** | am/is/are | + | main verb | + | ing |
| **Future:** | will be | + | main verb | + | ing |

**Insight**

**Avoid** using progressive tense with the following:

- Verbs that express thoughts, attitudes, and desires: *know, understand, want, prefer*

- Verbs that describe appearances: *seem, resemble*

- Verbs that indicate possession: *belong, have own, possess*

- Verbs that signify inclusion: *contain, hold*

  I **know** your name, not I **am knowing** your name.

**Vocabulary**

**progressive tense**
verb tense that expresses ongoing action

# Using Progressive Tense

**Form** Rewrite each sentence three times, changing the tenses as requested in parentheses.

Humans need food, but agribusiness makes food production very efficient.

1. (present progressive) Humans are needing food, but agribusiness is making food production very efficient.

2. (past progressive) Humans were needing food, but agribusiness was making food production very efficient.

3. (future progressive) Humans will be needing food, but agribusiness will be making food production very efficient.

People provide a product or service, and others pay for it.

4. (present progressive) People are providing a product or service, and others are paying for it.

5. (past progressive) People were providing a product or service, and others were paying for it.

6. (future progressive) People will be providing a product or service, and others will be paying for it.

The products and services in greatest demand produce the most wealth.

7. (present progressive) The products and services in greatest demand are producing the greatest wealth.

8. (past progressive) The products and services in greatest demand were producing the greatest wealth.

9. (future progressive) The products and services in greatest demand will be producing the greatest wealth.

# LO6 Perfect Tense Verbs

The perfect tense tells that action is not ongoing, but is finished, whether in the past, present, or future.

## Perfect Tense

**Perfect tense** indicates that action is completed. Perfect tense is formed by using a helping verb along with the past tense form of the main verb.

Each year of my career, I **have learned** something new.

There are past, present, and future perfect tenses. These tenses are formed by using helping verbs in past, present, and future tenses.

In my first year, I **had learned** to get along in a corporate structure.
This year, I **have learned** new technology skills.
By this time next year, I **will have learned** how to be an effective salesperson.

| | **Forming Perfect Tense** | | |
|---|---|---|---|
| **Past:** | had | + | past tense main verb |
| **Present:** | has/have | + | past tense main verb |
| **Future:** | will have | + | past tense main verb |

## Perfect Tense with Irregular Verbs

**Insight**

For the simple past tense form of these irregular verbs, see page 356.

To form perfect tense with irregular verbs, use the past participle form instead of the past tense form. Here are the past participles of common irregular verbs.

| Present | Past Part. | Present | Past Part. | Present | Past Part. |
|---|---|---|---|---|---|
| am, be | been | fly | flown | see | seen |
| become | become | forget | forgotten | shake | shaken |
| begin | begun | freeze | frozen | shine | shone |
| blow | blown | get | gotten | show | shown |
| break | broken | give | given | shrink | shrunk |
| bring | brought | go | gone | sing | sung |
| buy | bought | grow | grown | sink | sunk |
| catch | caught | hang | hung | sit | sat |
| choose | chosen | have | had | sleep | slept |
| come | come | hear | heard | speak | spoken |
| dig | dug | hide | hidden | stand | stood |
| do | done | keep | kept | steal | stolen |
| draw | drawn | know | known | swim | swum |
| drink | drunk | lead | led | swing | swung |
| drive | driven | pay | paid | take | taken |
| eat | eaten | prove | proven | teach | taught |
| fall | fallen | ride | ridden | tear | torn |
| feel | felt | ring | rung | throw | thrown |
| fight | fought | rise | risen | wear | worn |
| find | found | run | run | write | written |

# Using Perfect Tense

**Form** Rewrite each sentence three times, changing the tenses as requested in parentheses.

> I work hard and listen carefully.

**1.** (past perfect) _____ I had worked hard and had listened carefully. _____

_____

**2.** (present perfect) _____ I have worked hard and have listened carefully. _____

_____

**3.** (future perfect) _____ I will have worked hard and will have listened carefully. _____

_____

> I gain my position by being helpful, and I keep it the same way.

**4.** (past perfect) _____ I had gained my position by being helpful, and I had kept it the

_____ same way. _____

**5.** (present perfect) _____ I have gained my position by being helpful, and I have kept it the

_____ same way. _____

**6.** (future perfect) _____ I will have gained my position by being helpful, and I will have kept it

_____ the same way. _____

> My colleagues depend on me, and I deliver what they need.

**7.** (past perfect) _____ My colleagues had depended on me, and I had delivered what

_____ they need. _____

**8.** (present perfect) _____ My colleagues have depended on me, and I have delivered what

_____ they need. _____

**9.** (future perfect) _____ My colleagues will have depended on me, and I will have delivered

_____ what they need. _____

# LO7 Verbals

A **verbal** is formed from a verb but functions as a noun, an adjective, or an adverb. Each type of verbal—gerund, participle, and infinitive—can appear alone or can begin a **verbal phrase**.

## Gerund

A **gerund** is formed from a verb ending in *ing*, and it functions as a noun.

> **Kayaking** is a fun type of exercise. (subject)
>
> I love **kayaking**. (direct object)

A **gerund phrase** begins with the gerund and includes any objects and modifiers.

> **Running rapids in a kayak** is exhilarating. (subject)
>
> I enjoy **paddling a kayak through white water**. (direct object)

## Participle

A **participle** is formed from a verb ending in *ing* or *ed*, and it functions as an adjective.

> **Exhilarated**, I ran my first rapids at age 15. (*exhilarated* modifies *I*)
>
> That was an **exhilarating** ride! (*exhilarating* modifies *ride*)

A **participial phrase** begins with the participle and includes any objects and modifiers.

> **Shocking my parents**, I said I wanted to go again.

## Infinitive

An **infinitive** is formed from *to* and a present tense verb, and it functions as a noun, an adjective, or an adverb.

> **To kayak** is to live. (noun)
>
> I will schedule more time **to kayak**. (adjective)
>
> You need courage and a little craziness **to kayak**. (adverb)

An **infinitive phrase** begins with an infinitive and includes any objects or modifiers.

> I want **to kayak the Colorado River through the Grand Canyon**.

**Vocabulary**

**verbal**
gerund, participle, or infinitive; a construction formed from a verb but functioning as a noun, an adjective, or an adverb

**verbal phrase**
phrase beginning with a gerund, a participle, or an infinitive

**gerund**
verbal ending in *ing* and functioning as a noun

**gerund phrase**
phrase beginning with a gerund and including objects and modifiers

**participle**
verbal ending in *ing* or *ed* and functioning as an adjective

**participial phrase**
phrase beginning with a participle and including objects and modifiers

**infinitive**
verbal beginning with *to* and functioning as a noun, an adjective, or an adverb

**infinitive phrase**
phrase beginning with an infinitive and including objects and modifiers

# Using Verbals

Identify each underlined verbal by circling the correct choice in parentheses (gerund, participle, infinitive).

1. <u>Rock climbing</u> is an extreme sport. (**gerund**, participle, infinitive)

2. I'd like <u>to climb</u> El Capitan one day. (gerund, participle, **infinitive**).

3. <u>Rappelling down a cliff in Arizona</u>, I almost slipped. (gerund, **participle**, infinitive).

4. <u>Catching myself</u>, I checked my lines and carabiners. (gerund, **participle**, infinitive).

5. <u>To fall while climbing</u> could be fatal. (gerund, participle, **infinitive**).

6. I keep my equipment in top shape <u>to avoid a mishap</u>. (gerund, participle, **infinitive**).

**Form** Complete each sentence below by supplying the type of verbal requested in parentheses.   Answers will vary.

1. My favorite exercise is _____. (gerund)

2. _____ would get me into shape. (gerund)

3. _____, I could stay in shape (participle)

4. Perhaps I will also try _____. (gerund)

5. When exercising, remember _____. (infinitive)

6. _____, I'll lose weight. (participle)

**Write** For each verbal phrase below, write a sentence that correctly uses it.

Answers will vary.

1. to work out _____

_____

2. choosing a type of exercise _____

_____

3. excited by the idea _____

_____

# LO8 Verbals as Objects

Though both infinitives and gerunds can function as nouns, they can't be used interchangeably as direct objects. Some verbs take infinitives and not gerunds. Other verbs take only gerunds and not infinitives.

## Gerunds as Objects

Verbs that express facts are followed by **gerunds**.

| | | | | |
|---|---|---|---|---|
| admit | deny | enjoy | miss | recommend |
| avoid | discuss | finish | quit | regret |
| consider | dislike | imagine | recall | |

> I miss **walking** along the beach.
> **not** I miss to walk along the beach.
>
> I regret **cutting** our vacation short.
> **not** I regret to cut our vacation short.

## Infinitives as Objects

Verbs that express intentions, hopes, and desires are followed by **infinitives**.

| | | | | |
|---|---|---|---|---|
| agree | demand | hope | prepare | volunteer |
| appear | deserve | intend | promise | want |
| attempt | endeavor | need | refuse | wish |
| consent | fail | offer | seem | |
| decide | hesitate | plan | tend | |

> We should plan **to go** back to the ocean.
> **not** We should plan going back to the ocean.
>
> We will endeavor **to save** money for the trip.
> **not** We will endeavor saving money for the trip.

## Gerunds or Infinitives as Objects

Some verbs can be followed by either a gerund or an infinitive.

| | | | | |
|---|---|---|---|---|
| begin | hate | love | remember | stop |
| continue | like | prefer | start | try |

> I love **walking** by the ocean.
> **or** I love **to walk** by the ocean.

# Using Verbals as Objects

**Select** For each sentence below, circle the appropriate verbal in parentheses.

1. I imagine (walking, to walk) along the Pacific Coast.

2. We want (seeing, to see) whales or dolphins when we are there.

3. I hope (getting, to get) some beautiful shots of the ocean.

4. We should avoid (getting, to get) sunburned when we are on the beach.

5. I enjoy (getting, to get) sand between my toes.

6. Maybe a surfer will offer (showing, to show) me how to surf.

7. We deserve (going, to go) on vacation more often.

8. Later, we will regret not (taking, to take) the time for ourselves.

9. I have never regretted (taking, to take) a vacation.

10. I wish (having, to have) a vacation right now.

**Write** For each verb below, write your own sentence using the verb and following it with a gerund or an infinitive, as appropriate. Answers will vary.

1. quit _____

_____

2. recall _____

_____

3. tend _____

_____

4. volunteer _____

_____

5. discuss _____

_____

6. decide _____

_____

# LO9 Real-World Application

**Revise** Rewrite the following paragraph, changing passive verbs to active verbs. (See page 352.)

Bedford's school music program should be supported by Grohling Music Suppliers. Our instrument rentals and our sheet-music services have been used extensively by the school system. In these tough economic times, the school should be assisted by us.

> Grohling Music Suppliers should support Bedford's school music program. The
> school system has extensively used our instrument rentals and our sheet-music
> services. In these tough economic times, we should assist the school.

**Revise** In the following paragraph, change future perfect verbs into past perfect verbs by crossing out helping verbs and writing new helping verbs. (See page 360.)

We ~~will have~~ *had* provided reduced-cost sheet music to the school system and ~~will have~~ *had* added used and refurbished instrument rentals. In addition, we ~~will have~~ *had* provided best-customer discounts to schools that ~~will have~~ *had* rented and bought in volume.

**Revise** In the following paragraph, correct misused verbals by crossing out the gerund or infinitive and replacing it with the correct verbal form. (See page 364.)

I hope ~~exploring~~ *to explore* these possibilities with you. We could recommend ~~to make~~ *making* some of these changes the first year. I admit ~~to have~~ *having* a soft spot for student performers. I recall ~~to get~~ *getting* my first flute as a student and ~~to begin~~ *beginning* with music then.

"Where lipstick is concerned, the important thing is not color,
but to accept God's final word on where your lips end."

—Jerry Seinfeld

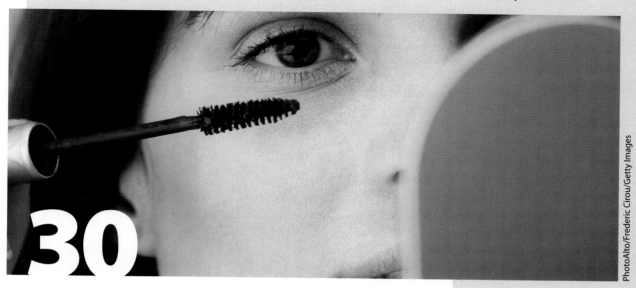

PhotoAlto/Frederic Cirou/Getty Images

# 30
# Adjective and Adverb

The purpose of makeup is to accentuate the beauty that is already in your face. The focus should be on you, not on the mascara, lipstick, foundation, or blush you use.

In the same way, the real beauty of a sentence lies in the nouns and verbs. Adjectives and adverbs can modify those nouns and verbs, bringing out their true beauty, but these modifiers should not overwhelm the sentence. Use them sparingly to make your meaning clear, not to distract with flash. This chapter will show you how to get the most out of those few adjectives and adverbs.

## What do you think?

What effect is created when lipstick overwhelms lips? What effect is created when adjectives overload nouns?

Answers will vary.

## Learning Outcomes

**LO1** Understand adjective basics.

**LO2** Put adjectives in order.

**LO3** Use adjectivals.

**LO4** Understand adverb basics.

**LO5** Place adverbs well.

**LO6** Use adverbials.

**LO7** Apply adjectives and adverbs in real-world contexts.

# LO1 Adjective Basics

An **adjective** is a word that modifies a noun or pronoun. Even **articles** such as *a, an,* and *the* are adjectives, because they indicate whether you mean a general or specific thing. Adjectives answer these basic questions: *which, what kind of, how many / how much.*

**Speaking & Listening**

Read the first example sentence aloud. Then read it without the adjectives. Note how adjectives add spice to the description. Like spice, though, adjectives should be used sparingly, to "season" nouns, not to overwhelm them.

Adjectives often appear before the word they modify.

> I saw a **beautiful gray tabby** cat.

A **predicate adjective** appears after the noun it modifies and is linked to the word by a linking verb.

> The cat was **beautiful** and **gray**.

Proper adjectives come from proper nouns and are capitalized.

> I also saw a **Persian** cat.

## Forms of Adjectives

Adjectives come in three forms: positive, comparative, and superlative.

- **Positive adjectives** describe one thing without making any comparisons.

> Fred is a **graceful** cat.

- **Comparative adjectives** compare the thing to something else.

> Fred is **more graceful** than our dog, Barney.

- **Superlative adjectives** compare the thing to two or more other things

> He is the **most graceful** cat you will ever see.

**Vocabulary**

**adjective**
word that modifies a noun or pronoun

**articles**
the adjectives *a, an,* and *the*

**predicate adjective**
adjective that appears after a linking verb and describes the subject

**positive adjective**
word that modifies a noun or pronoun without comparing it

**comparative adjective**
word that modifies a noun or pronoun by comparing it to something else

**superlative adjective**
word that modifies a noun or pronoun by comparing it to two or more things

**Note:** For one- and two-syllable words, create the comparative form by adding *er*, and create the superlative form by added *est*. For words of three syllables or more, use *more* (or *less*) for comparatives and *most* (or *least*) for superlatives. Also note that *good* and *bad* have special superlative forms:

| Positive | Comparative | Superlative |
|---|---|---|
| good | better | best |
| bad | worse | worst |
| big | bigger | biggest |
| happy | happier | happiest |
| wonderful | more wonderful | most wonderful |

# Using the Forms of Adjectives

**Identify/Write** In each sentence below, identify the underlined adjectives as positive (P), comparative (C), or superlative (S). Then write a new sentence about a different topic, but use the same adjectives.

1. The shelter had a <u>Siamese</u> (P) cat with <u>crossed</u> (P) eyes and <u>black</u> (P) feet.

_____

_____

2. She was <u>more inquisitive</u> (C) than the other cats.

_____

_____

3. Her eyes were the <u>bluest</u> (S) I had ever seen on a cat.

_____

_____

4. Her <u>surprising</u> (P) meow was <u>loud</u> (P) and <u>insistent</u> (P).

_____

_____

5. But her name—Monkey—was the <u>most surprising</u> (S) fact of all.

_____

_____

**Correct** Read the paragraph below and correct adjective errors, using the correction marks to the right. The first one has been done for you.

Some people say dogs are ~~more~~ tamer than cats, but cats have a ~~more great~~ *greater* place in some people's hearts. Cats were probably first attracted to human civilizations during the ~~most early~~ *earliest* days of the agricultural revolution. The sudden surplus of grains attracted many mice, which in turn attracted cats. Cats that were the ~~most~~ best mousers were welcomed by humans. In time, ~~more cute~~ *cuter* and ~~more cuddly~~ *cuddlier* cats became pets. But cats have never given up their wildness. Even now, a barn cat that is not used to human touch can be ~~feraler~~ *more feral* than a dog.

## Correction Marks

- ℐ delete
- d̲ capitalize
- Ɑ lowercase
- ∧ insert
- ⌄ add comma
- ? add question mark
- ∧ word add word
- ⊙ add period
- ⬭ spelling
- ∿ switch

# LO2 Adjective Order

Adjectives aren't all created equally. Native English speakers use a specific order when putting multiple adjectives before a noun, and all speakers of English can benefit from understanding this order.

## Begin with . . .

| 1. articles | a, an, the |
|---|---|
| demonstrative adjectives | that, this, these, those |
| possessives | my, our, her, their, Kayla's |

## Then position adjectives that tell . . .

| 2. time | first, second, next, last |
|---|---|
| 3. how many | three, few, some, many |
| 4. value | important, prized, fine |
| 5. size | giant, puny, hulking |
| 6. shape | spiky, blocky, square |
| 7. condition | clean, tattered, repaired |
| 8. age | old, new, classic |
| 9. color | blue, scarlet, salmon |
| 10. nationality | French, Chinese, Cuban |
| 11. religion | Baptist, Buddhist, Hindu |
| 12. material | cloth, stone, wood, bronze |

## Finally place . . .

| 13. nouns used as adjectives | baby [seat], shoe [lace] |
|---|---|

### Example:

> that ruined ancient stone temple
>
> (1  +  7  +  8  +  12  +  **noun**)

**Note:** Avoid using too many adjectives before a noun. An article and one or two adjectives are usually enough. More adjectives may overload the noun.

| **Too many:** | their first few expensive delicious French bread appetizers |
|---|---|

| **Effective:** | their first French bread appetizers |
|---|---|

Kelly Cheng Travel Photography/Flickr/Getty Images

# Placing Adjectives in Order

**Order** Rearrange each set of adjectives and articles so that they are in the correct order. The first one has been done for you.

1. blue       square       that

     _that square blue_       button

2. my       Scottish       rugged

     my rugged Scottish       kilt

3. plastic       brand-new       few

     few brand-new plastic       beads

4. worthless       a       brass

     a worthless brass       tack

5. classic       many       Kenyan

     many classic Kenyan       masks

6. aluminum       soda       Ted's

     Ted's aluminum soda       can

7. key       Catholic       my

     my Catholic key       chain

8. dilapidated       this       old

     this dilapidated old       shack

9. wool       her       woven

     her woven wool       cardigan

10. identical       seven       music

     seven identical music       stands

11. young       the       bright

     the bright young       faces

12. last       real       our

     our last real       option

# LO3 Adjective Questions and Adjectivals

Reggie Casagrande/Photodisc/Getty Images

Adjectives answer four basic questions: *which, what kind of, how many / how much.*

| | Guy |
|---|---|
| **Which?** | that guy |
| **What kind of?** | cool tattooed guy |
| **How many/how much?** | one guy |

that one cool tattooed guy

**Insight**

Instead of trying to memorize the names of different types of phrases and clauses, just remember the adjective questions. Turn them into a cheer—*which, what kind of, how many/ how much.*

## Adjectivals

A single word that answers one of these questions is called an adjective. If a phrase or clause answers one of these questions, it is an **adjectival** phrase or clause.

| | Guy |
|---|---|
| **Which?** | guy leaning on the Mustang |
| **What kind of?** | guy who exudes attitude |

Look at that guy, **who exudes attitude, leaning on the Mustang.**

The following types of phrases and clauses can be adjectivals:

| | |
|---|---|
| **Prepositional phrase:** | with his arms crossed |
| **Participial phrase:** | staring at something |
| **Adjective clause:** | who doesn't even own the Mustang |

**Vocabulary**

**adjectival**
phrase or clause that answers one of the adjective questions and modifies a noun or pronoun

**prepositional phrase**
phrase that starts with a preposition and includes an object and modifiers

**participial phrase**
phrase beginning with a participle (*ing* or *ed* form of verb) plus objects and modifiers; used as an adjective

**adjective clause**
clause beginning with a relative pronoun and including a verb, but not able to stand alone; functioning as an adjective

### Say It

Partner with a classmate. One of you should say the noun, and the other should ask the adjective questions. Then the first person should answer each question with adjectives or adjectivals.

1. **convertibles**

   Which convertibles?

   What kind of convertibles?

   How many convertibles?

2. **detergent**

   Which detergent?

   What kind of detergent?

   How much detergent?

# Using Adjectives and Adjectivals

**Answer/Write** For each word, answer the adjective questions using adjectives and adjectivals. Then write a sentence using two or more of your answers.

Answers will vary.

**1. Dogs**

Which dogs? _____

What kind of dogs? _____

How many dogs? _____

Sentence: _____

_____

_____

_____

**2. Sports**

Which sports? _____

What kind of sports? _____

How many sports? _____

Sentence: _____

_____

_____

_____

**3. Proposals**

Which proposals? _____

What kind of proposals? _____

How many proposals? _____

Sentence: _____

_____

_____

_____

# LO4 Adverb Basics

An **adverb** modifies a verb, a **verbal**, an adjective, an adverb, or a whole sentence. An adverb answers five basic questions: *how, when, where, why, to what degree, how often.*

Sheri leaped **fearlessly**.
(*Fearlessly* modifies the verb *leaped*.)

Sheri leaped **quite readily**.
(*Quite* modifies *readily*, which modifies *leaped*.)

**Obviously,** she wants to fly.
(*Obviously* modifies the whole sentence.)

**Note:** Most adverbs end in *ly*. Some can be written with or without the *ly*, but when in doubt, use the *ly* form.

loud ⟶ loud**ly**          tight ⟶ tight**ly**          deep ⟶ deep**ly**

## Forms of Adverbs

Adverbs have three forms: positive, comparative, and superlative.

- **Positive adverbs** describe without comparing.

  Sheri leaped **high** and **fearlessly**.

- **Comparative adverbs** (*-er, more,* or *less*) describe by comparing with one other action.

  She leaped **higher** and **more fearlessly** than I did.

- **Superlative adverbs** (*-est, most,* or *least*) describe by comparing with more than one action.

  She leaped **highest** and **most fearlessly** of any of us.

**Note:** Some adjectives change form to create comparative or superlative forms.

well ⟶ better ⟶ best          badly ⟶ worse ⟶ worst

**Insight**

In the United States, intensifying adverbs such as *very* and *really* are used sparingly. Also, in academic writing, it is considered better to find a precise, vivid verb than to prop up an imprecise verb with an adverb.

**Vocabulary**

**adverb**
word that modifies a verb, a verbal, an adjective, an adverb, or a whole sentence

**verbal**
word formed from a verb but functioning as a noun, an adjective, or an adverb

**positive adverb**
adverb that modifies without comparing

**comparative adverb**
adverb that modifies by comparing with one other thing

**superlative adverb**
adverb that modifies by comparing to two or more things

# Using the Forms of Adverbs

**Provide** In each sentence below, provide the correct form of the adverb in parentheses—positive, comparative, or superlative.

1. My friend likes to eat _____quickly_____ (quickly).

2. She eats _____more quickly_____ (quickly) than I do.

3. She eats _____most quickly_____ (quickly) of anyone I know.

4. My brother eats _____reluctantly_____ . (reluctantly)

5. He eats _____more reluctantly_____ (reluctantly) than a spoiled child.

6. He eats _____most reluctantly_____ (reluctantly) of anyone on Earth.

7. I eat _____slowly_____ . (slowly)

8. I eat _____more slowly_____ (slowly) than I used to.

9. I eat _____most slowly_____ (slowly) of anytime in my life.

10. I suppose the three of us eat pretty _____ (badly).

**Choose** In each sentence, circle the correct word in parentheses. If the word modifies a noun or pronoun, choose the adjective form (good, bad). If the word modifies a verb, a verbal, an adjective, or an adverb, choose the adverb form (well, badly.)

1. My brother went to a (*good*, well) play.

2. He said the actors did (good, *well*), and that the plot was (*good*, well).

3. He even got a (*good*, well) deal on tickets for (*good*, well) seats.

4. He wanted (bad, *badly*) to see this play.

5. The problem was that one patron behaved (bad, *badly*).

6. He had a (*bad*, badly) attitude and once even booed.

7. My brother told him to stop, but the guy took it (bad, *badly*).

8. The ushers did (good, *well*) when they removed the guy.

9. The audience even gave them a (*good*, well) ovation.

10. My brother says the overall evening went (good, *well*).

Kapu,2010 / Used under license from Shutterstock.com

# LO5 Placement of Adverbs

Adverbs should be placed in different places in sentences, depending on their use.

## *How* Adverbs

Adverbs that tell *how* can appear anywhere except between a verb and a direct object.

> **Steadily** we hiked the trail.
> We **steadily** hiked the trail.
> We hiked the trail **steadily**.
> **not** We hiked **steadily** the trail.

## *When* Adverbs

Adverbs that tell *when* should go at the beginning or end of the sentence.

> We hiked to base camp **yesterday**. **Today** we'll reach the peak.

## *Where* Adverbs

Adverbs that tell *where* should follow the verb they modify, but should not come between the verb and the direct object. (**Note:** Prepositional phrases often function as *where* adverbs.)

> The trail wound **uphill** and passed **through rockslide debris**.
> We avoided falling rocks **throughout our journey**.
> **not** We avoided **throughout our journey** falling rocks.

## *To What Degree* Adverbs

Adverbs that tell *to what degree* go right before the adverb they modify.

> I learned **very** definitely the value of good hiking boots.

## *How Often* Adverbs

Adverbs that tell *how often* should go right before an action verb, even if the verb has a helping verb.

> I **often** remember that wonderful hike.
> I will **never** forget the sights I saw.

# Placing Adverbs Well

**Place** For each sentence below, insert the adverb (in parentheses) in the most appropriate position. The first one has been done for you.

1. In order to scare off bears, we *occasionally* made noise. (occasionally)

2. Bears *usually* avoid contact with human beings. (usually)

3. A bear surprised or cornered by people will *often* turn to attack. (often)

4. A mother bear with cubs is *very* likely to attack. (very)

5. If a bear approaches, playing dead may *sometimes* work. (sometimes)

6. Climbing a tree is not *usually* the best idea. (usually)

7. Black bears *often* climb trees. (often)

8. Grizzly bears *usually* just knock the tree down. (usually)

9. Another defense is to open your coat to look *especially* large. (especially)

10. At the same time, try to make a *very* loud noise. (very)

**Revise** In the paragraph below, use the transpose mark ( ⁀ ) to move adverbs into their correct positions.

Spotting wildlife is one often of the highlights of a hiking trip. Deer appear in fields occasionally, and lucky hikers might glimpse a bear sometimes in the distance. Porcupines, raccoons, and other creatures amble out of the woods curiously. Not usually hikers will see mountain lions because the cats are ambush predators. Mountain lions attack groups of people rarely and usually avoid human contact. Do keep children from behind straggling.

# LO6 Adverb Questions and Adverbials

Adverbs answer six basic questions: *how, when, where, why, to what degree,* and *how often.*

| | **Children splashed.** |
|---|---|
| **How?** | splashed barefoot |
| **When?** | splashed today |
| **Where?** | splashed outside |
| **Why?** | splashed excitedly |
| **To what degree?** | splashed very excitedly |
| **How often?** | splashed repeatedly |

**Today,** the children **repeatedly** and **very excitedly** splashed **barefoot outside**.

**Note:** Avoid this sort of adverb overload in your sentences.

Don Smith/Flickr/Getty Images

## Adverbials

Often, the adverb questions are answered by **adverbial** phrases and clauses, which answer the same six questions.

| | **Children splashed.** |
|---|---|
| **How?** | splashed jumping up and down |
| **When?** | splashed during the downpour |
| **Where?** | splashed in the puddles in the driveway |
| **Why?** | splashed for the joy of being wet |
| **To what degree?** | splashed until they were drenched |
| **How often?** | splashed throughout the storm |

**During the downpour** and **throughout the storm**, the children splashed, **jumping up and down in the puddles in the driveway for the joy of being wet** and **until they were drenched**.

**Note:** Again, avoid this sort of adverbial overload in your sentences.

The following types of phrases and clauses can be adverbials:

| | |
|---|---|
| **Prepositional phrase:** | in the puddles in the driveway |
| **Participial phrase:** | jumping up and down |
| **Dependent clause:** | until they were drenched |

# Using Adverbials

**Answer/Write** For each sentence, answer the adverb questions using adverbs and adverbials. Then write a sentence using three or more of your answers.

Answers will vary.

**1. They danced.**

How did they dance? _____

When did they dance? _____

Where did they dance? _____

Why did they dance? _____

To what degree did they dance? _____

How often did they dance? _____

Sentence: _____

_____

_____

_____

**2. They sang.**

How did they sing? _____

When did they sing? _____

Where did they sing? _____

Why did they sing? _____

To what degree did they sing? _____

How often did they sing? _____

Sentence: _____

_____

_____

_____

**Correct** In the following document, correct the use of adjectives and adverbs. Use the correction marks to the left.

## ● Clowning Around

1328 West Mound Road
Waukesha, Wi 53100
262-555-8180 ●

January 6, 2011

Mrs. Judy Bednar
38115 North Bayfield Drive
Waukesha, WI 53100

Dear Ms. Bednar:

It's time for a party birthday! You've thought of everything—balloons, decorations, cake . . . But what about ~~awesomely~~ *awesome,* entertainment? How many kids are coming and how much time do you have to keep them entertained?

Fear not. At Clowning Around, we specialize in making every birthday the ~~funnest~~ *most fun* and ~~memorablest~~ *most memorable* it can be. For young kids, we offer balloon colorful animals, ~~magic~~ *magic* amazing tricks, and backyard goofy games. For older kids, we have water wild games and magic street illusions. And for kids of all ages, we have the ~~most funny~~ *funniest* clowns, the ~~most~~ bravest superheroes, and most ~~amazingest~~ *amazing* impressionists.

That's right. You can throw a terrific party for your loved one worrying without about the entertainment—and paying without a lot either. See the enclosed brochure for our services and rates. Then give us a call at Clowning Around, and we'll make your party next an event to remember.

Let's talk soon!

*Dave Jenkins*

Dave Jenkins
CEO, Clowning Around

Enclosure: Brochure

> "A family is a unit composed not only of children but of men, women, an occasional animal, and the common cold."
>
> —Ogden Nash

Alistair Berg/Digital Vision/Getty Images

# 31

# Conjunction and Preposition

A family is a network of relationships. Some people have an equal relationship, like wives and husbands or brothers and sisters. Some people have unequal relationships, like mothers and daughters or fathers and sons. And the very young or very old are often considered dependent on those in their middle age.

Ideas also have relationships, and conjunctions and prepositions show those relationships. When two ideas are equal, a coordinating conjunction connects them. When two ideas are not equal, a subordinating conjunction makes one idea depend on the other. And prepositions create special relationships between nouns and other words.

Conjunctions and prepositions help you connect ideas and build whole families of thought.

## Learning Outcomes

**LO1** Use coordinating and correlative conjunctions.

**LO2** Use subordinating conjunctions.

**LO3** Understand common prepositions.

**LO4** Use *by, at, on,* and *in.*

**LO5** Use conjunctions and prepositions in real-world documents.

### What do you think?

What equal relationships do you have? What dependent relationships do you have?

Answers will vary.

# LO1 Coordinating and Correlative Conjunctions

A **conjunction** is a word or word group that joins parts of a sentence—words, phrases, or clauses.

## Coordinating Conjunctions

A **coordinating conjunction** joins grammatically equal parts—a word to a word, a phrase to a phrase, or a clause to a clause. (A clause is basically a sentence.)

Stockbyte/Getty Images

### Coordinating Conjunctions

| and | but | or | nor | for | so | yet |
|-----|-----|-----|-----|-----|-----|-----|

**Equal importance:** A coordinating conjunction shows that the two things joined are of equal importance.

Rachel and Lydia enjoy arts and crafts..
(*And* joins words in an equal way.)

They have knitted sweaters and pieced quilts.
(*And* joins the phrases *knitted sweaters* and *pieced quilts*.)

I tried to knit a sweater, but the thing unraveled.
(*But* joins the two clauses, with a comma after the first.)

**Items in a series:** A coordinating conjunction can also join more than two equal things in a series.

Rachel, Lydia, and I will take a class on making mosaics.
(*And* joins *Rachel, Lydia,* and *I*. A comma follows each word except the last.)

We will take the class, design a mosaic, and complete it together.
(*And* joins three parts of a compound verb.)

## Correlative Conjunctions

**Correlative conjunctions** consist of a coordinating conjunction paired with another word. They also join equal grammatical parts: word to word, phrase to phrase, or clause to clause.

### Correlative Conjunctions

| either/or | neither/nor | whether/or | both/and | not only/but also |
|-----------|-------------|------------|----------|-------------------|

**Stressing equality:** Correlative conjunctions stress the equality of parts.

Not only Rachel but also Lydia has made beautiful quilts.
(*Not only / but also* stresses the equality of *Rachel* and *Lydia*.)

Either I will learn quilting, or I will die trying.
(*Either / or* joins the two clauses, with a comma after the first.)

# Using Coordinating and Correlative Conjunctions

**Traits**

When two ideas correlate, they work together. They co-relate. Thinking in this way can help you remember the term *correlative conjunctions*.

**Correct** In each sentence below, circle the best coordinating conjunction in parentheses.

1. I would like to learn knitting (but, for, (or)) crocheting.

2. Lydia, Rachel, ((and), nor, yet) I enjoy making cloth with our hands.

3. We have different talents, (or, (so), yet) we teach each other what we know.

4. Lydia is best at knitting, (nor, (but), for) I am best at tatting.

5. Rachel is our weaver, (but, yet, (so)) she is the loom master.

6. Each week, Lydia, Rachel, ((and), but, or) I meet to share our works.

7. We want to broaden our skills, (and, or, (yet)) it's hard to learn something new.

8. I like needlepoint, Rachel likes quilting, ((and), nor, so) Lydia likes construction.

9. Come join us one day, (and, (for), so) we love to teach beginners.

10. We'll show you our work, ((but), nor, for) you'll decide what you want to learn.

**Write** Create sentences of your own, using a coordinating conjunction (*and, but, or, nor, for, so, yet*) as requested in each. Answers will vary.

1. joining two words: _____

   _____

2. joining two phrases: _____

   _____

3. creating a series: _____

   _____

4. joining two clauses (place a comma after the first clause, before the conjunction): _____

   _____

   _____

   _____

**Write** Create a sentence using a pair of correlative conjunctions:

Answers will vary.

_____

_____

_____

# LO2 Subordinating Conjunctions

A **subordinating conjunction** is a word or word group that connects two clauses of different importance. (A clause is basically a sentence.)

## Subordinating Conjunctions

| | | | | | |
|---|---|---|---|---|---|
| after | as long as | if | so that | till | whenever |
| although | because | in order that | than | unless | where |
| as | before | provided that | that | until | whereas |
| as if | even though | since | though | when | while |

**Subordinate clause:** The subordinating conjunction comes at the beginning of the less-important clause, making it subordinate (it can't stand on its own). The **subordinate clause** can come before or after the more important clause (the **independent clause**).

> Summer is too hot to cook inside. I often barbecue.
> (two clauses)
>
> Because summer is too hot to cook inside, I often barbecue.
> (*Because* introduces the subordinate clause, which is followed by a comma.)
>
> I often barbecue because summer is too hot to cook inside.
> (If the subordinate clause comes second, a comma usually isn't needed.)

**Special relationship:** A subordinating conjunction shows a special relationship between ideas. Here are the relationships that subordinating conjunctions show:

| | |
|---|---|
| **Time** | after, as, before, since, till, until, when, whenever, while |
| **Cause** | as, as long as, because, before, if, in order that, provided that, since, so that, that, till, until, when, whenever |
| **Contrast** | although, as if, even though, though, unless, whereas |

> Whenever the temperature climbs, I cook on the grill.
> (time)
>
> I grill because I don't want to heat up the house.
> (cause)
>
> Even though it is hot outside, I feel cool in the shade as I cook.
> (contrast)

# Using Subordinating Conjunctions

**Write** Fill in the blank in each sentence with an appropriate subordinating conjunction. Then circle what type of relationship it shows.

Example answers:

1. _____**After**_____ I marinated the chicken, I put it on the grill.
   ((time), cause, contrast)

2. Grilling bratwurst is tough _____**because**_____ the grease causes big flames.
   (time, (cause), contrast)

3. _____**Because**_____ of trichinosis, pork should not be pink inside.
   (time, (cause), contrast)

4. I like grilling chicken _____**even though**_____ my favorite food is steak.
   (time, cause, (contrast))

5. I grill my steak rare _____**although**_____ the FDA recommends well-done.
   (time, cause, (contrast))

6. Some people use barbecue sauce _____**whereas**_____ I prefer marinades.
   (time, cause, (contrast))

7. I use a gas grill _____**since**_____ it is fast and convenient.
   (time, (cause), contrast)

8. Purists use only charcoal _____**because**_____ it creates a nice flavor.
   (time, (cause), contrast)

9. _____**When**_____ I was in Texas, I had magnificent brisket.
   ((time), cause, contrast)

10. _____**Although**_____ brisket can be tough, this was totally tender.
    (time, cause, (contrast))

**Write** Create three of your own sentences, one for each type of relationship.

Answers will vary.

1. time: _____

_____

_____

2. cause: _____

_____

_____

3. contrast: _____

_____

_____

# LO3 Common Prepositions

A **preposition** is a word or word group that shows a relationship between a noun or pronoun and another word. Here are common prepositions:

**Prepositions**

| | | | | |
|---|---|---|---|---|
| aboard | back of | except for | near to | round |
| about | because of | excepting | notwithstanding | save |
| above | before | for | of | since |
| according to | behind | from | off | subsequent to |
| across | below | from among | on | through |
| across from | beneath | from between | on account of | throughout |
| after | beside | from under | on behalf of | 'til |
| against | besides | in | onto | to |
| along | between | in addition to | on top of | together with |
| alongside | beyond | in behalf of | opposite | toward |
| alongside of | but | in front of | out | under |
| along with | by | in place of | out of | underneath |
| amid | by means of | in regard to | outside | until |
| among | concerning | inside | outside of | unto |
| apart from | considering | inside of | over | up |
| around | despite | in spite of | over to | upon |
| as far as | down | instead of | owing to | up to |
| aside from | down from | into | past | with |
| at | during | like | prior to | within |
| away from | except | near | regarding | without |

## Prepositional Phrases

A **prepositional phrase** starts with a preposition and includes an object of the preposition (a noun or pronoun) and any modifiers. A prepositional phrase functions as an adjective or adverb.

> The Basset hound flopped on his side on the rug.
> (*On his side* and *on the rug* modify the verb *flopped*.)
>
> He slept on the rug in the middle of the hallway.
> (*On the rug* modifies *slept; in the middle* modifies *rug;* and *of the hallway* modifies *middle.*)

Comstock/Getty Images

# Using Common Prepositions

**Create** In each sentence, fill in the blanks with prepositional phrases. Create them from the prepositions on page 386 and nouns or pronouns of your own choosing. Be creative! Answers will vary.

1. Yesterday, I ran _____ .

2. Another runner _____ waved at me.

3. I was so distracted, I ran _____ .

4. The other runner then ran _____ .

5. We both had looks of surprise _____ .

6. I leaped _____ .

7. The other runner jogged _____ .

8. Then we both were _____ .

9. The incident _____ was a lesson.

10. The lesson was not to run _____ .

**Model** Read each sentence below and write another sentence modeled on it. Note how the writer uses prepositional phrases to create specific effects.

Answers will vary.

1. The coupe shot between the semis, around the limousine, down the tunnel, and up into bright sunlight.

   _____

   _____

2. I will look for you, but I also look to you.

   _____

   _____

3. Before the freedom of the road and the fun of the trip, I have finals.

   _____

   _____

4. Walk through the hallway, down the stairs, through the door, and into the pantry.

   _____

   _____

# LO4 *By, At, On,* and *In*

Prepositions often show the physical position of things—above, below, beside, around, and so on. Four specific prepositions show position but also get a lot of other use in English.

## Uses for *By, At, On,* and *In*

in a boat
on the Seinne
by the roadway
in Paris
at dusk
on May 30

*Proframe Photography/Flickr/Getty Images*

**By** means "beside" or "up to a certain place or time."

> by the creek, by the garage
>
> by noon, by August 16

**At** refers to a specific place or time.

> at the edge, at the coffe shop
>
> at 6:45 p.m., at midnight

**On** refers to a surface, a day or date, or an electronic medium.

> on the table, on the T-shirt
>
> on July 22, on Wednesday
>
> on the computer, on the DVD

**In** refers to an enclosed space; a geographical location; an hour, a month, or a year; or a print medium.

> in the hall, in the bathroom
>
> in Madison, in France
>
> in a minute, in December, in 2014
>
> in the magazine, in the book

## Say It

Team up with a partner. Have the first person read one of the words below, and have the second person use it in a prepositional phrase beginning with *by, at, on,* or *in.* The first person should check if the form is correct. (Some have more than one correct answer.) Then you should switch roles.

1. the den
2. June 23
3. 9:33 p.m.
4. the MP3 player
5. the corner

6. Pittsburgh
7. the counter
8. the diner
9. sunset
10. the newspaper

# Using *By, At, On,* and *In*

**Provide** In each sentence, circle the correct preposition in parentheses.

1. The guests arrived (**by**, on, in) 7:30 p.m., so we could eat (**at**, on, in) 8:00 p.m.

2. Put your suitcase (by, at, on, **in**) the trunk or (by, at, **on**) the rooftop luggage rack.

3. I looked for the new album (by, at, on, **in**) a music store, but could find it only (by, at, **on**, in) the Internet.

4. We waited (by, at, on, **in**) the lobby for a half hour, but Jerry didn't show up or even call (by, at, **on**, in) his cell phone.

5. Three people standing (by, **at**, in) the corner saw a traffic accident (by, **at**, on) the intersection of 45th and Monroe.

6. (By, At, **On**, In) April 1 of 2012, many pranksters may post apocalypse hoaxes (by, at, **on**, in) the Internet.

7. Let's meet (by, **at**, on) the convenience store (**at**, on, in) 7:00 p.m.

8. Place your order form (by, at, on, **in**) the postage-paid envelope, write your return address (by, at, **on**, in) the envelope, and post it.

9. A cat lay (by, at, **on**) the windowsill and looked me (by, at, on, **in**) the eye.

10. (**At**, On, In) noon of January 7, the school's pipes (at, on, **in**) the basement froze and caused flooding.

**Write** Write a sentence that uses all four of these prepositions in phrases: *by, at, on, in.*     Answers will vary.

# LO7 Real-World Application

**Revise** Read the following e-mail, noting how choppy it sounds because all of the sentences are short. Connect some of the sentences using a coordinating conjunction and a comma, and connect others using a subordinating conjunction. You can also change other words as needed. (Use the correction symbols to the left.) Reread the e-mail to make sure it sounds smooth.

**Coordinating Conjunctions**

| | | | |
|---|---|---|---|
| and | but | or | nor |
| for | so | yet | |

**Subordinating Conjunctions**

| | | | | | |
|---|---|---|---|---|---|
| after | as long as | if | so that | till | whenever |
| although | because | in order that | than | unless | where |
| as | before | provided that | that | until | whereas |
| as if | even though | since | though | when | while |

**Correction Marks**

⌿ delete

d̳ capitalize

∅ lowercase

∧ insert

⌃ add comma

? add question
∧ mark

word
∧ add word

⊙ add period

⬭ spelling

∿ switch

**Update on Book Revision**

Send  Attach  Format

From: rhaverson@haversonpublishing.com

To: dkraitsman@delafordandco.com

Subject: Completed Photo Log

**Example corrections:**

Dear Deirdra:

Attached, please find the photo log. <del>The log</del> /that shows all photos on the Website. Some photos are from Getty Images. <del>Others</del> are from Shutterstock. <del>A</del> few are from Corbis. /and All photos have been downloaded. <del>The downloads</del> /and have the right resolution.

I hope you are pleased with the log. It includes permissions details. <del>It also shows</del> the resolution. <del>I included</del> /and a description of each photo.

I am available for more work. I could compile another photo log. <del>I could also</del> /or do the permissions work on these photos. I do writing and editing as well.

Thank you for this project. I look forward to hearing from you.

Thanks,

Roger Haverson
Photo Editor

**Workplace**

Correct use of *by, at, on,* and *in* will mark you as a writer comfortable with English.

**Correct** Read the following party invitation, noting the incorrect use of the prepositions *by, at, on,* and *in*. (See pages 388.) Correct the errors by deleting the prepositions and replacing them. Use the correction marks on the facing page.

---

Rankin Technology Annual Picnic

| ✉ Send | 📎 Attach | *f* Format |
|---|---|---|

| From: | Leanna Cartwright |
|---|---|
| To: | Running Man Press Staff |
| Subject: | Annual Running Man Holiday Party |

Dear Staff:

It's time for the Running Man Press Holiday Party!

**Who?** All employees and their significant others

**What?** Should come for dinner

**Where?** ~~By~~ [At] the Hilton ~~in~~ [on] Grand Avenue ~~on~~ [in] Ballroom B

**When?** ~~At~~ [On] December 12, beginning ~~on~~ [at] 7:00 p.m. and going until 11:00 p.m.

**Why?** We're celebrating a great year ~~on~~ [at] Running Man Press

The event is full of fun, including drinks ~~in~~ [at] 7:00 p.m., dinner ~~on~~ [at] 8:00 p.m., awards ~~in~~ [at] 9:00 p.m., and dancing ~~on~~ [at] 9:30 p.m. Prime rib, roast chicken, and vegetarian selections are ~~at~~ [on] the menu, and beverages of all sorts will be available ~~in~~ [at] the bar.

Please RSVP ~~at~~ [by] December 2 to let us know how many people will join us ~~on~~ [at] the Hilton. We look forward to having a great night with everyone ~~at~~ [on] December 12.

Sincerely,

Leanna Cartwright
Human Resources

"The writer who neglects punctuation, or mispunctuates, is liable to be misunderstood for the want of merely a comma. "
—Edgar Allan Poe

*Jozef Sedmak, 2010 / Used under license from Shutterstock.com*

# 32 Comma

When you speak, you communicate with much more than words. You pause, raise or lower your pitch, change your tone or volume, and use facial expressions and body language to get your point across.

When you write, you can forget about pitch or volume, facial expressions or body language. You're left with the tone of your words and with the pauses that you put in them. Commas give you one way to create a soft pause. They help to show which words belong together, which should be separated, and which line up in parallel. Commas are key to being understood.

In this chapter you will learn about the conventional use of commas. Understanding the correct comma usage is an important step in becoming a college-level writer.

## What do you think?

Imagine reading a book or newspaper without punctuation. What difficulties may you encounter? Explain.

> Answers will vary.

## Learning Outcomes

**LO1** Use commas in compound sentences.

**LO2** Use commas with introductory phrases and equal adjectives.

**LO3** Use commas between items in a series.

**LO4** Use commas with appositives and nonrestrictive modifiers.

**LO5** Use commas in real-world writing.

**Traits**

Make sure to use both a comma and a coordinating conjunction in a compound sentence, or you will create a comma splice or a run-on. For more information, see pages 303–310.

# LO1 In Compound Sentences and After Introductory Clauses

The following principles will guide the conventional use of commas in your writing.

## In Compound Sentences

Use a comma before the coordinating conjunction *(and, but, or, nor, for, yet, so)* in a compound sentence.

> Heath Ledger completed his brilliant portrayal as the Joker in *The Dark Knight,* **but** he died before the film was released.

**Note:** Do not confuse a compound verb with a compound sentence.

> Ledger's Joker became instantly iconic and won him the Oscar for best supporting actor. (compound verb)
>
> His death resulted from the abuse of prescription drugs, but it was ruled an accident. (compound sentence)

## After Introductory Clauses

Use a comma after most introductory clauses.

> **Although Charlemagne was a great patron of learning,** he never learned to write properly. (adverb dependent clause)

When the clause follows the independent clause and is not essential to the meaning of the sentence, use a comma. This comma use generally applies to clauses beginning with *even though, although, while,* or some other conjunction expressing a contrast.

> Charlemagne never learned to write properly, **even though he continued to practice**.

**Note:** A comma is *not* used if the dependent clause following the independent clause is needed.

# Correcting Comma Errors

**Correct** For each sentence below, add a comma (∧) before the coordinating conjunction (*and, but, or, nor, for, so, yet*) if the clause on each side could stand alone as a sentence. Write "correct" if the conjunction separates word groups that can't stand alone.

1. Catherine had questions about her class schedule, so she set up an appointment with her academic adviser. _____

2. I was going to play in the sand volleyball league, but it conflicted with my work schedule. _____

3. Trisha picked up some groceries and stopped by the bank. _____correct_____

4. I normally don't listen to jazz music, yet I love going to summer jazz concerts in the park. _____

5. Should I finish my essay a day early, or should I go to my friend's house party? _____

6. Kevin has a job interview at the advertisement agency, and he hopes he can make a good impression. _____

7. Creativity is his best quality, but leadership is not far behind. _____

**Correct** For each sentence below, add a comma after any introductory clauses. If no comma is needed, write "correct" next to the sentence.

1. Even though digital books are the craze, I prefer paperbacks. _____

2. Although the crab dip appetizer was delicious, my entrée left something to be desired. _____

3. Because I'm starved for time, online shopping is a convenient alternative to mall shopping. _____

4. I toggled through radio stations while I waited at the tollbooth. _____correct_____

5. Erin worried about giving her speech, even though she had practiced for weeks. _____

**Learning Outcome**

Use commas with
introductory words and
equal adjectives.

# LO2 With Introductory Words and Equal Adjectives

## After Introductory Phrases

Use a comma after introductory phrases.

> **In spite of his friend's prodding,** Jared decided to stay home and study.

A comma is usually omitted if the phrase follows an independent clause.

> Jared decided to stay home and study **in spite of his friend's prodding.**

You may omit a comma after a short (four or fewer words) introductory phrase unless it is needed to ensure clarity.

> **At 10:30 p.m.** he would quit and go to sleep.

**Speaking & Listening**

Try the strategies below
by speaking the words
aloud. If it sounds strange
to switch the order of the
adjectives or to insert an
*and* between them, do
not separate them with
a comma.

## To Separate Adjectives

Use commas to separate adjectives that equally modify the same noun. Notice in the examples below that no comma separates the last adjective from the noun.

> You should exercise regularly and follow a **sensible, healthful** diet.
>
> A good diet is one that includes lots of **high-protein, low-fat** foods.

## To Determine Equal Modifiers

To determine whether adjectives modify a noun equally, use these two tests.

1. Reverse the order of the adjectives; if the sentence is clear, the adjectives modify equally. (In the example below, *hot* and *crowded* can be switched, but *short* and *coffee* cannot.)

> Matt was tired of working in the **hot, crowded** lab and decided to take a **short coffee** break.

2. Insert *and* between the adjectives; if the sentence reads well, use a comma when *and* is omitted. (The word *and* can be inserted between *hot* and *crowded*, but *and* does not make sense between *short* and *coffee*.)

Brian K., 2010/used under license from www.shutterstock.com

# Correcting Comma Errors

**Correct** For each sentence below, insert a comma after the introductory phrase if it is needed. If no comma is needed, write "correct" next to the sentence.

1. Before you send the e-mail make sure you reread it for errors in clarity. _____

2. In accordance with the academic code plagiarism is deemed a major offense. _____

3. After hitting the 10-mile jogging plateau Heather felt a great rush of adrenaline. _____

4. Heather felt a great rush of adrenaline after hitting the 10-mile jogging plateau. _correct_

5. Thankfully DeMarcus stopped the leak before it could do any real damage. _correct_

6. Based on his past experience Wilson decided against going to the concert. _____

7. To train for the triathlon Brent altered his diet. _____

8. At the end of the day Erin recorded her favorite show. _____

**Correct** For each sentence below, determine whether or not a comma is needed to separate the adjectives that modify the same noun. Add any needed commas (⋀). Write "no" next to the sentence if a comma is not needed.

1. I'm expecting this to be a **rocking after** party. _no_

2. There's nothing like the **warm emerald** water off the Florida Gulf Coast. _____

3. The exercise program included a **calorie-burning cardio** session. _no_

4. My **surly economics** professor is one of a kind. _no_

5. I'm in desperate need of a **relaxing summer** vacation. _no_

6. Marathon runners favor **light comfortable** shorts. _____

# LO3 Between Items in a Series and Other Uses

## Between Items in Series

Use commas to separate individual words, phrases, or clauses in a series. (A series contains at least three items.)

> Many college students must balance studying with **taking care of a family, working, getting exercise, and finding time to relax**.

Do not use commas when all the items in a series are connected with *or, nor,* or *and*.

> Hmm . . . should I study **or** do laundry **or** go out?

## To Set Off Transitional Expressions

**Traits**

*Do not* use a comma before an indirect quotation.

**Incorrect:** My roommate said, that she doesn't understand the notes I took.

**Correct:** My roommate said that she doesn't understand the notes I took.

Use a comma to set off conjunctive adverbs and transitional phrases.

> Handwriting is not, **as a matter of fact,** easy to improve upon later in life; **however,** it can be done if you are determined enough.

If a transitional expression blends smoothly with the rest of the sentence, it does not need to be set off.

> If you are **in fact** coming, I'll see you there.

## To Set Off Dialogue

Use commas to set off the words of the speaker from the rest of the sentence.

> **"Never be afraid to ask for help,"** advised Ms. Kane
>
> **"With the evidence that we now have,"** Professor Thom said, **"many scientists believe there could be life on Mars."**

## To Enclose Explanatory Words

Use commas to enclose an explanatory word or phrase.

> Time management, **according to many professionals,** is an important skill that should be taught in college.

# Correcting Comma Errors

**Correct** Indicate where commas are needed in the following sentences.

1. I considered becoming a lawyer; however, law school wasn't for me.

2. "Don't give up, don't ever give up," advised the late Jim Valvano.

3. MGMT's music is infused with electronic beats, catchy lyrics, and a pop-friendly sound.

4. Western Wisconsin, as opposed to Illinois, is relatively hilly.

5. In Boston I visited Fenway Park, the U.S.S. *Constitution,* and Old North Church.

6. Thomas, as you may have noticed, is eager to share his vast knowledge of random facts.

7. In regard to public transportation, you may decide between the subway, buses, or taxicabs.

8. "While it certainly offers a convenient alternative to paper maps," said Emilie, "my car's navigational system more often gets me lost."

9. Avocados, the key ingredient of guacamole, are a good source of fiber.

10. Secondly, determine if weather, price, or transportation will factor into your decision.

**Correct** Indicate where commas are needed in the following paragraph.

On an early summer morning in July, I sat slumped in a terminal at JFK airport, reminiscing about my time in Washington, D.C. It had been a fun trip. I visited all the usual landmarks, including the Lincoln Memorial, Arlington National Cemetery, and the Smithsonian Institute. However, my favorite landmark was Mount Vernon, the home and former estate of President George Washington. It's easy to see why Washington adored the location. The estate, located in Alexandria, Virginia, is nestled above the Hudson River. Besides Washington's plantation home, the estate also included a distillery, a blacksmith shop, and acres of farmland. If you're ever in Washington, D.C., I highly recommend a trip to Mount Vernon.

# LO4 With Appositives and Other Word Groups

## To Set Off Some Appositives

A specific kind of explanatory word or phrase called an **appositive** identifies or renames a preceding noun or pronoun.

> Albert Einstein, **the famous mathematician and physicist,** developed the theory of relativity.

Do not use commas if the appositive is important to the basic meaning of the sentence.

> The famous physicist **Albert Einstein** developed the theory of relativity.

## With Some Clauses and Phrases

### Traits

*Do not* use commas to set off necessary clauses and phrases, which add information that the reader needs to understand the sentence.

**Example:** Only the professors **who run at noon** use the locker rooms in Swain Hall to shower. (necessary clause)

Use commas to enclose phrases or clauses that add information that is not necessary to the basic meaning of the sentence. For example, if the clause or phrase (in **boldface**) were left out of the two examples below, the meaning of the sentences would remain clear. Therefore, commas are used to set off the information.

> The locker rooms in Swain Hall, **which were painted and updated last summer,** give professors a place to shower. (nonrestrictive clause)
>
> Work-study programs, **offered on many campuses,** give students the opportunity to earn tuition money. (nonrestrictive phrase)

## Using "That" or "Which"

Use *that* to introduce necessary clauses; use *which* to introduce unnecessary clauses.

> Campus jobs **that are funded by the university** are awarded to students only. (necessary)
>
> The cafeteria, **which is run by an independent contractor,** can hire nonstudents. (unnecessary)

# Correcting Comma Errors

**Correct** Indicate where commas are needed in the following sentences. If no commas are needed, write "correct" next to the sentence.

1. The U.S.S. *Constitution*, a wooden-hulled ship named by George Washington, is the world's oldest, floating, commissioned naval vessel.  _____

2. Gordon Ramsay, the fiery chef and television star, specializes in French, Italian, and British cuisines.  _____

3. Hall of Fame baseball player and notable philanthropist Roberto Clemente died in a plane crash while en route to Nicaragua to deliver aid to earthquake victims.  _____

4. The concert hall, which is on the corner of Meridian Ave and 1st Street, is expected to revitalize the downtown district.  _____

5. Press passes that allow for backstage access are given out to special media members.  _____

6. John Quincy Adams, who later became the sixth president of the United States, authored the Monroe Doctrine in 1823.  _____

**Write** The following sentences contain clauses using *that*. Rewrite the sentences with clauses using *which*, and insert commas correctly. You may need to reword some parts.

Example answers:

1. The mechanical issue that delayed the flight should be corrected within 25 minutes.

   The mechanical issue, which delayed the flight, should be corrected
   within 25 minutes.

2. The wind farm that was built along I-95 is scheduled to double in size by 2013.

   The wind farm, which was built along I-95, is scheduled to double in size
   by 2013.

3. Scholarships that are sponsored by the Kiwanis Club are awarded to local high school students.

   Scholarships, which are sponsored by the Kiwanis Club, are awarded to
   local high school students.

# LO5 Real-World Application

**Correct** Indicate where commas are needed in the following e-mail message.

| | |
|---|---|
| Send | Attach | Format |

From:    Tru_Sha@shieldmarketing.com

To:    Michael_Green@shieldmarketing.com

Subject    Revised Agenda for Quarterly Update

Attach::    Meeting agenda 04-19-11.doc

Hi, Michael:

I've attached the agenda for the quarterly update with the marketing team. Daniel Gilchrest senior marketing coordinator will moderate the meeting but I want you to familiarize yourself with the material. Here are some highlights of the new agenda:

1. The advertising allowance for Gillette, Hillsboro Farms and Justice Inc. has increased by 5 percent.

2. The penetrated market which accounts for actual users of products declined in the health-care sector.

3. We will shift the focus of marketing efforts to meet the digital and social media demands of today's market.

Please review the agenda by the end of the day and let me know if you have any additions or corrections.

Thanks

Tru Sha

Marketing Associate

Pablo Eder, 2010/used under license from www.shutterstock.com

# 33

# Apostrophe

The position of an apostrophe makes a world of a difference to the meaning of a sentence. Take a close look at the following two examples:

- My brother's girlfriend is having a beach party.
- My brothers' girlfriend is having a beach party.

In the first sentence, an apostrophe and *s* is added to make the singular *brother* possessive. The meaning of the sentence is clear: the girlfriend of the writer's brother is having a beach party. In the second sentence, an apostrophe is positioned after the *s*, forming the plural possessive *brothers'*. In other words, the writer of the second example has more than one brother dating the same girl, who is throwing a beach party.

Apostrophes have two main uses: to form possessives and contractions. The rules and activities in this chapter will help you understand their usage.

## Learning Outcomes

**LO1** Use apostrophes for contractions and possessives.

**LO2** Apply apostrophes in real-world documents.

## What do you think?

Have you ever noticed a misplaced apostrophe? Where did you find it? Explain the situation.

Answers will vary.

# LO1 Contractions and Possessives

Apostrophes are used primarily to show that a letter or number has been left out, or that a noun is possessive.

## Contractions

When one or more letters are left out of a word, use an apostrophe to form the **contraction**.

| | | |
|---|---|---|
| don't<br>(*o* is left out) | he'd<br>(*woul* is left out) | would've<br>(*ha* is left out) |

### Missing Characters

Use an apostrophe to signal when one or more characters are left out.

| | | |
|---|---|---|
| class of '16<br>(*20* is left out) | rock 'n' roll<br>(*a* and *d* are left out) | good mornin'<br>(*g* is left out) |

Binkski, 2010/used under license from www.shutterstock.com

## Possessives

Form possessives of singular nouns by adding an apostrophe and an *s*.

| | | |
|---|---|---|
| Sharla's pen | the man's coat | *The Pilgrim's Progress* |

### Singular Noun Ending In *s* (One Syllable)

Form the possessive by adding an apostrophe and an *s*.

| | | |
|---|---|---|
| the boss's idea | the lass's purse | the bass's teeth |

### Singular Noun Ending In *s* (Two Or More Syllables)

Form the possessive by adding an apostrophe and an *s*—or by adding just an apostrophe.

| | | |
|---|---|---|
| Kansas's plains | *or* | Kansas' plains |

### Plural Noun Ending In *s*

Form the possessive by adding just an apostrophe.

| | |
|---|---|
| the bosses' preference | the Smiths' home |

**Note:** The word before the apostrophe is the owner.

| | |
|---|---|
| the girl's ball<br>(*girl* is the owner) | the girls' ball<br>(*girls* are the owners) |

### Plural Noun Not Ending In *s*

Form the possessive by adding an apostrophe and an *s*.

| | |
|---|---|
| the children's toys | the women's room |

# Forming Contractions and Possessives

**Write** For each contraction below, write the words that formed the contraction. For each set of words, write the contraction that would be formed.

1. you're _____ you are _____
2. John is _____ John's _____
3. would have _____ would've _____
4. she'd _____ she would _____
5. you would _____ you'd _____

6. shouldn't _____ should not _____
7. I had _____ I'd _____
8. they are _____ they're _____
9. we've _____ we have _____
10. it is _____ it's _____

**Rewrite** Rework the following sentences, replacing the "of" phrases with possessives using apostrophes.

1. I'm going to the house of Jeremy.

   I'm going to Jeremy's house.

2. The ice cream of the corner stand is amazing.

   The corner stand's ice cream is amazing.

3. The pace of the track star is impressive.

   The track star's pace is impressive.

4. I like the early work of the Rolling Stones.

   I like the Rolling Stones' early work.

5. The persona of Texas is well represented in the slogan "Everything is bigger in Texas."

   Texas' persona is well represented in the slogan "Everything is bigger in Texas."

6. The paintings of the artist were outstanding.

   The artist's paintings were outstanding.

7. I discovered the best pizza spot of Portland.

   I discovered Portland's best pizza spot.

8. She reviewed the notes of Kimbra.

   She reviewed Kimbra's notes.

9. The contractor assessed the structure of the house.

   The contractor assessed the house's structure.

10. The position of the politician on health care remained firm.

    The politician's position on health care remained firm.

# LO2 Real-World Application

**Correct** The following letter sounds too informal because it contains too many contractions. Cross out contractions and replace them with full forms of the words. Also, correct any errors with apostrophes. Use the correction marks to the left.

**Correction Marks**

ℒ delete

d̲ capitalize

Ð lowercase

∧ insert

⌄ add comma

? ∧ add question mark

ʷᵒʳᵈ ∧ add word

⊙ add period

◯ spelling

∿ switch

## ❦ REDLAND STATE BANK ❧

October 13, 2012

Phillip Jones
2398 10th Ave.
Westchester, NY 10959

Dear Mr. Jones:

    *letter is*
This ~~letter's~~ a response to your inquiry about financing your housing project. I enjoyed discussing your project and appreciated your honesty about your current loan.

    *we have*               *I have*
As of today, ~~we've~~ decided to make a commitment to your project. ~~I've~~ enclosed Redland State Bank**s'** commitment letter. Please take time to read the terms of agreement.

    *there is*    *do not*    *do not*        *We would*
If ~~there's~~ any part you ~~don't~~ understand, ~~don't~~ hesitate to call or e-mail us. ~~We'd~~ be happy to answer any questions. As always**s**, we look forward to serving you.

Sincerely,

*Melinda Erson*

Melinda Erson
Loan Officer

Enclosure: Commitment Letter

"Sometimes people give [book] titles to me,
and sometimes I see them on a billboard."

—Robert Penn Warren

Image Source/Getty Images

# 34

# Quotation Marks and Italics

Broadway is plastered with billboards five stories high and is jammed with marquees that flash in the night. They advertise plays and movies, books and magazines, albums and TV shows—all in spotlights or neon trying to make people take notice.

In writing, there are no spotlights, there is no neon. Instead of writing the names of plays, movies, books, and so forth in giant, flashing letters, writers set them off with  This chapter will show you how to correctly punctuate titles of works big and small and words used as words.

## Learning Outcomes

**LO1** Understand the use of quotation marks.

**LO2** Understand the use of italics.

**LO3** Apply quotation marks and italics in a real-world document.

## What do you think?

How are quotation marks and italics like flashing lights in writing? How are they different?

Answers will vary.

_____

_____

_____

_____

_____

_____

**407**

# LO1 Quotation Marks

## To Punctuate Titles (Smaller Works)

Use quotation marks to enclose the titles of smaller works, including speeches, short stories, songs, poems, episodes of audio or video programs, chapters or sections of books, unpublished works, and articles from magazines, journals, newspapers, or encyclopedias. (For other titles, see page 410.)

|  |  |
|---:|:---|
| Speech: | "Ain't I a Woman?" |
| Song: | "California Gurls" |
| Short Story: | "The Tell-Tale Heart" |
| Magazine Article: | "Is Google Making Us Stupid?" |
| Chapter in a Book: | "The Second Eve" |
| Television Episode: | "The Empty Child" |
| Encyclopedia Article: | "Autoban" |

## Placement of Periods and Commas

When quoted words end in a period or comma, always place that punctuation inside the quotation marks.

"When you leave the kitchen," Tim said, "turn out the light."

## Placement of Semicolons and Colons

When a quotation is followed by a semicolon or colon, always place that punctuation outside the quotation marks.

I finally read "The Celebrated Jumping Frog of Calaveras County"; it is a hoot!

## Placement of Exclamation Points and Question Marks

If an exclamation point or a question mark is part of the quotation, place it inside the quotation marks. Otherwise, place it outside.

Shawndra asked me, "Would you like to go to the movies?" What could I say except, "That sounds great"?

## For Special Words

Quotation marks can be used (1) to show that a word is being referred to as the word itself; (2) to indicate that it is jargon, slang, or a coined term; or (3) to show that it is used in an ironic or sarcastic sense.

(1) The word "chuffed" is British slang for "very excited."
(2) I'm "chuffed" about my new computer.
(3) I'm "chuffed" about my root canal.

**Insight**

In British English, a single quotation mark is used instead of double quotation marks. Also, British English has different rules for using other punctuation with quotation marks. When writing in a U.S. setting, use the rules on this page.

# Using Quotation Marks

**Correct** In the following sentences, insert quotation marks ("„") where needed.

1. Tim loves the short story "Cask of Amontillado" by Edgar Allan Poe.

2. Stephen King's short story "The Body" was made into a movie.

3. Anna Quindlen wrote the article "Uncle Sam and Aunt Samantha."

4. Lisa told Jennie, "Tonight is the pizza and pasta buffet."

5. Jennie asked, "Isn't it buy one, get one free?"

6. Was she thinking, "That's a lot better than cooking?"

7. Here is the main conflict of the story "To Build a Fire": man versus nature.

8. I read an article entitled "The Obese Fruit of Capitalism"; it suggested that our modern obesity epidemic demonstrates the tremendous achievements of fast food and agribusiness.

9. What does the word "hypertrophy" mean?

10. I was "thrilled" to receive the unexpected bill.

**Write** Write a sentence that indicates the actual meaning of each sentence below.

Sample answers:

1. The fully loaded logging truck "tiptoed" across the one-lane bridge.

   The fully loaded truck drove slowly and carefully across the one-lane bridge.

2. Enjoy our "fast" and "friendly" service.

   Enjoy our slow and unfriendly service.

3. We had a "fun" time at our IRS audit.

   We had an unpleasant time at our IRS audit.

**WAC**

As you write research reports in different classes, find out which style your discipline uses for reporting titles of larger and smaller works.

# LO2 Italics

## To Punctuate Titles (Larger Works)

Use italics to indicate the titles of larger works, including newspapers, magazines, journals, pamphlets, books, plays, films, radio and television programs, movies, ballets, operas, long musical compositions, CD's, DVD's, software programs, and legal cases, as well as the names of ships, trains, aircraft, and spacecraft. (For other titles, see page 408.)

| | |
|---|---|
| Magazine: *The Week* | Newspaper: *Chicago Tribune* |
| Play: *Cat on a Hot Tin Roof* | Journal: *Nature* |
| Film: *Casablanca* | Software Program: *Final Draft* |
| Book: *Death's Disciples* | Television Program: *Doctor Who* |

## For a Word, Letter, or Number Referred to as Itself

Use italics (or quotation marks—see page 408) to show that a word, letter, or number is being referred to as itself. If a definition follows a word used in this way, place that definition in quotation marks.

> The word *courage* comes from the French word *cour*, which means "heart."
>
> In the handwritten note, I couldn't distinguish an *N* from an *M*.

## For Foreign Words

Use italics to indicate a word that is being borrowed from a foreign language.

> The phrase *et cetera ad nauseum* is a Latin phrase meaning "and so on until vomiting."

## For Technical Terms

Use italics to introduce a technical term for the first time in a piece of writing. After that, the term may be used without italics.

> Particle physicists are seeking the elusive *Higgs boson*—a subatomic particle thought to provide mass to all other particles. The Higgs boson has become a sort of Holy Grail of quantum mechanics.

**Note:** If a technical term is being used within an organization or field of study where it is common, it may be used without italics even the first time in a piece of writing.

# Using Italics

**Correct** In the following sentences, underline words that should be in italics.

1. One of my favorite novels is <u>The Curious Incident of the Dog in the Night-Time</u> by Mark Haddon.

2. Have you seen the amazing movie <u>Memento</u>?

3. The name of the <u>paso doble</u> dance comes from the Spanish word for "double step."

4. In 1945, the bomber called the <u>Enola Gay</u> dropped the first atomic bomb, a weapon predicted in 1914 in the H. G. Wells novel <u>The World Set Free</u>.

5. She always has a real <u>joie de vivre</u>.

6. To look at the PDF, you need <u>Adobe Reader</u> or <u>Adobe Acrobat</u>.

7. In this context, the words <u>profane</u> and <u>profanity</u> do not refer to swearing but simply to things that are not divine.

8. The television show <u>Project Runway</u> pits fashion designers against each other.

9. In the musical <u>A Funny Thing Happened on the Way to the Forum</u>, the slave Pseudolus spells out his hope to be F – R – E – E.

10. The enlargement of muscles through weight lifting is known as <u>hypertrophy</u>.

**Write** Write three sentences, each demonstrating your understanding of one or more rules for using italics.  Answers will vary.

1. _____

_____

_____

_____

2. _____

_____

_____

_____

3. _____

_____

_____

_____

**Practice** In the following business letter, underline any words that should be italicized and add quotation marks (〝〞) where needed.

Send  Attach  *f* Format

From: John Metrameme

To: Will McMartin

Subject: Metrameme Author Bio

Hi, Will:

Here is the author bio you requested from me to be published in my next book, War Child:

John Metrameme has published over a dozen novels, most recently the historical epic Sons of Thunder and the romp Daddy Zeus. He has written articles also for The Atlantic and The New Yorker, and his short story 〝Me and the Mudman〞won the Rubel Prize. Metrameme is perhaps best known for his novel Darling Buds of May.

In his spare time, Metrameme enjoys acting in productions at his community theater. He played himself in the three-man show The Complete Works of William Shakespeare (Abridged). He also starred as Kit Gill in No Way to Treat a Lady and as Jonathan in Arsenic and Old Lace.

Will, please let me know if you need anything more from me.

Thanks,

John

> "Conventions are subject to the *vagaries* of time and fashion. . . .
> The writers of the Constitution capitalized words in the middle of sentences."
>
> —Mitchell Ivers

Richard Newstead/Flickr/

# 35

# Capitalization

Why is the word *mom* capitalized in "Did Mom call?" and not in "Did my mom call?" Why is *river* capitalized in "the Ohio River" but not in "the Ohio and Missouri rivers"? These are just two of the vagaries when it comes to proper capitalization in our language. As you page through this section, you will find others.

One of the best ways to learn about the unexpected changes in capitalization is to become a reader and writer yourself. Combine regular reading and writing with the practice in this chapter and you will be well on your way to mastering correct capitalization. You can also use this chapter as a reference whenever you have questions about capitalization. Each left-hand page provides an easy-to-use set of rules and examples.

## Learning Outcomes

**LO1** Understand basic capitalization rules.

**LO2** Understand advanced capitalization rules.

**LO3** Understand capitalization of titles, organizations, abbreviations, and letters.

**LO4** Understand capitalization of names, courses, and Web terms.

**LO5** Apply capitalization in real-world documents.

### Vocabulary

**vagaries**
unexpected changes

### What do you think?

Why do you suppose that we pay so much attention to the rules of capitalization? Why don't we capitalize words in the middle of sentences?

Answers will vary.

# LO1 Basic Capitalization

All first words, proper nouns, and proper adjectives must be capitalized. The following guidelines and examples will help explain these rules.

## Proper Nouns and Adjectives

Capitalize all proper nouns and all proper adjectives (adjectives derived from proper nouns). The chart below provides a quick overview of capitalization.

### Quick Guide: Capitalization at a Glance

| | |
|---|---|
| Days of the week | **Saturday, Sunday, Tuesday** |
| Months | **March, August, December** |
| Holidays, holy days | **Christmas, Hanukah, President's Day** |
| Periods, events in history | **the Renaissance, Middle Ages** |
| Special events | **Tate Memorial Dedication Ceremony** |
| Political parties | **Republican Party, Green Party** |
| Official documents | **Bill of Rights** |
| Trade names | **Frisbee disc, Heinz ketchup** |
| Formal epithets | **Alexander the Great** |
| Official titles | **Vice-President Al Gore, Senator Davis** |
| Official state nicknames | **the Garden State, the Beaver State** |
| Planets, heavenly bodies | **Earth, Mars, the Milky Way** |
| Continents | **Asia, Australia, Europe** |
| Countries | **France, Brazil, Japan, Pakistan** |
| States, provinces | **Montana, Nebraska, Alberta, Ontario** |
| Cities, towns, villages | **Portland, Brookfield, Broad Ripple** |
| Streets, roads, highways | **Rodeo Drive, Route 66, Interstate 55** |
| Sections of the United States and the world | **the West Coast, the Middle East** |
| Landforms | **Appalachian Mountains, Kalahari Desert** |
| Bodies of water | **Lake Erie, Tiber River, Atlantic Ocean** |
| Public areas | **Central Park, Rocky Mountain National Park** |

## First Words

Capitalize the first word in every sentence and the first word in a full-sentence direct quotation.

> **Professional** sports has become far too important in the United States.
>
> Yvonne asked, "**Why** do baseball players spit all of the time?"

# Correcting Capitalization

In each sentence below, place capitalization marks ( ≡ ) under any letters that should be capitalized.

1. Musician louis armstrong helped make jazz popular to american and european audiences.

2. Armstrong grew up in new Orleans in a rough neighborhood called the "battleground."

3. he was sent to reform school because he fired a gun in the air on new year's eve.

4. Upon his release, he visited music halls like funky butt hall to hear king oliver play.

5. Oliver gave armstrong his first real cornet, and he played with oliver's band in storyville, the red-light district in New orleans.

6. He also played with the allen brass band on the strekfus line of riverboats.

7. In 1919, Armstrong left new Orleans for Chicago and played with kid orv.

8. He really began to make a name for himself in the creole jazz band that played at Lincoln gardens in Chicago.

**Practice B** Read the following paragraph. Place capitalization marks ( ≡ ) under any letters that should be capitalized in proper nouns, proper adjectives, or first words.

My great-grandfather Erv grew up in Racine, Wisconsin, during the great depression. He lived in two different houses on villa street just south of the downtown area. Erv attended Holy Name Catholic school and Franklin school when he was a kid. His dad, my great-great-grandfather, came from Poland and started out by selling hot dogs at north beach. Because money was scarce, great-grandfather's family sometimes had only corn on the cob for dinner. After high school, he enlisted in the U.S. navy, but was turned down because of poor eyesight. He then joined the army and fought in Europe during world war II. when Erv returned to Racine, he went to work at massey harris, a company that made tractors.

# LO2 Advanced Capitalization

## Sentences in Parentheses

Capitalize the first word in a sentence that is enclosed in parentheses if that sentence is not combined within another complete sentence.

> I need to learn more about the health care system in Canada. (**Missy** just married a guy from Toronto.)

**Note:** Do *not* capitalize a sentence that is enclosed in parentheses and is located in the middle of another sentence.

> Missy's husband (his name is Andre) works in a family business.

## Sentences Following Colons

Capitalize a complete sentence that follows a colon when that sentence is a formal statement, a quotation, or a sentence that you want to emphasize.

> Seldom have I heard such encouraging words: **The** economy is on the rebound.

## Salutation and Complimentary Closing

In a letter, capitalize the first and all major words of the salutation. Capitalize only the first word of the complimentary closing.

> **Dear Governor Doyle:**        **Sincerely** yours,

## Sections of the Country

Words that indicate sections of the country are proper nouns and should be capitalized; words that simply indicate directions are not proper nouns.

> The **Southwest** is suffering from a drought. *(section of country)*
>
> I live a few blocks **southwest** of here. *(direction)*

## Languages, Ethnic Groups, Nationalities, and Religions

Capitalize languages, ethnic groups, nationalities, religions, Supreme Beings, and holy books.

> **African**    **Navajo**    **Islam**    **God**    **Allah**
>
> **Jehovah**    **the Koran**    **Exodus**    **the Bible**

### Insight

Some sections of different countries may be unfamiliar to you. For example, the Corn Belt and the Great Plains are sections of this county. The Lake District or The Lakes is a specific district in Great Britain.

# Correcting Capitalization

**Practice A** In each sentence below, place capitalization marks ( ≡ ) under any letters that should be capitalized.

1. The high plains is a subregion in the great plains.

2. Golda Meir once said this about women: "whether women are better than men I cannot say—but I can say they are certainly no worse."

3. The hopi indians come from a group of people called pueblo.

4. My dad is already planning for his retirement. (what will he do with so much free time?)

5. Many people from Mexico prefer Mexican American more than hispanic or latino.

6. Don't visit the deep south in August unless you like stifling heat and humidity.

7. The third largest religion, hinduism, does not have a single founder or a single sacred text.

8. My mechanic made a bad day even worse: he told me that my car needed four new tires.

**Practice B** Read the following paragraph. Place capitalization marks ( ≡ ) under any letters that should be capitalized.

From 1943-1954, the midwest was blessed with the All American Girls Professional Baseball League. There were teams in Racine, Kenosha, Rockford, south Bend, Fort Wayne, grand Rapids, and Minneapolis. The league filled an entertainment need created by World War II: many men, especially minor leaguers, were serving overseas. The women wore dress uniforms with knee-high woolen socks. (they must have been careful about sliding.) The women became heroines for young girls all across the country, from new England to the west coast.

**Practice C** Place capitalization marks ( ≡ ) under any letters that should be capitalized.

kleenex tissue　　the koran　　holiday　　asian　　forest

memorial day　　sherwood forest　　tissue paper　　the middle east

**WAC**

Note that the American Psychological Association has a different style for capitalizing the titles of smaller works. Be sure you know the style required for a specific class.

# LO3 Other Capitalization Rules I

## Titles

Capitalize the first word of a title, the last word, and every word in between except articles *(a, an, the)*, short prepositions, *to* in an infinitive, and coordinating conjunctions. Follow this rule for titles of books, newspapers, magazines, poems, plays, songs, articles, films, works of art, and stories.

| | |
|---|---|
| ***Knight** and **Day*** (movie) | ***Washington Post*** (newspaper) |
| **"What a Wonderful World"** (song) | **"Death Penalty's False Promise"** (essay) |
| ***Comedy** of **Errors** (play)* | ***Gulliver's Travels*** (novel) |

## Organizations

Capitalize the name of an organization or a team and its members.

| | |
|---|---|
| **Habitat** for **Humanity** | **Libertarian Party** |
| **The Bill & Melinda Gates Foundation** | **Chicago Cubs** |
| **Special Olympics** | **Phoenix Suns** |

## Abbreviations

Capitalize abbreviations of titles and organizations.

| | | | | | |
|---|---|---|---|---|---|
| **M.D.** | **Ph.D.** | **NAACP** | **C.E.** | **B.C.E.** | **GPA** |

## Letters

Capitalize letters used to indicate a form or shape.

| | | | |
|---|---|---|---|
| **S-curve** | **T-shirt** | **R-rated** | **C-section** |

# Correcting Capitalization

**Practice A** In each sentence below, place capitalization marks (≡) under any letters that should be capitalized.

1. To me, *a midsummer night's dream* is one of Shakespeare's best plays.

2. The San Francisco giants used to play in Candlestick park.

3. I enjoyed reading *city of thieves,* a novel by David Benioff.

4. Do you know the song "don't drink the water" by dave matthews?

5. My brother splattered some paint on my favorite Chicago white sox t-shirt.

6. Newman's own foundation donates to charities all net royalties and profits after taxes it receives from Newman's own products.

7. Javier Lopez, an old friend from the neighborhood, earned a ph.d in history.

8. Perhaps the least known of the beatles is George Harrison; I love his song "while my guitar gently weeps."

9. The current hit "the kids are all right" is r-rated according to the *Denver post*.

10. Anna Quindlen's article "uncle sam and aunt samantha" first appeared in *newsweek*.

11. People attend aa (alcoholics anonymous) meetings to support each other as they battle their alcoholism.

**Practice B** Read the paragraph below, placing capitalization marks (≡) under letters that should be capitalized.

An article in last week's *standard press* promoted the city's farmer's market. The market, held every Thursday afternoon, is sponsored by the Brighton chamber of commerce. The vendors, who must reside within the local area, sell everything from fresh produce to tie-dyed t-shirts. In addition, organizations such as the american red cross and Brighton little league have informational booths at the market. A special feature is the live entertainment supplied by rainbow road, a local folk rock band. They play a lot of Bob Dylan, singing favorites like "blowin' in the wind."

# LO4 Other Capitalization Rules II

## Words Used as Names

Capitalize words like father, mother, uncle, senator, and professor only when they are parts of titles that include a personal name or when they are substitutes for proper nouns (especially in direct address).

> Hello, **Representative** Baldwin. (*Representative* is part of the name.)
>
> It's good to meet you, **Representative**. (*Representative* is a substitute for the name.
>
> Our **representative** is a member of two important committees.
>
> Who was the volleyball **coach** last year?
>
> We had **Coach Snyder** for two years.
>
> I met **Coach** in the athletic office.

**Note:** To test whether a word is being substituted for a proper noun, simply read the sentence with a proper noun in place of the word. If the proper noun fits in the sentence, the word being tested should be capitalized. Usually the word is not capitalized if it follows a possessive—*my, his, our, your,* and so on.

> Did **Mom** (Yvonne) pick up the dry cleaning?
> (*Yvonne* works in the sentence.)
>
> Did your **mom** (Yvonne) pick up the dry cleaning?
> (*Yvonne* does not work in the sentence; the word *mom* follows *your*.)

## Titles of Courses

Words such as technology, history, and science are proper nouns when they are included in the titles of specific courses; they are common nouns when they name a field of study.

> The only course that fits my schedule is **Introduction to Oil Painting**.
> (title of a specific course)
>
> Judy Kenner advises anyone interested in **oil painting**.
> (a field of study)

## Internet and E-Mail

The words *Internet* and *World Wide Web* are capitalized because they are considered proper nouns. When your writing includes a Web address (URL), capitalize any letters that the site's owner does (on printed materials or on the site itself).

> When doing research on the **Internet**, be sure to record each site's **Web** address (URL) and each contact's **e-mail** address.

# Correcting Capitalization

**Practice A** In each sentence below, place capitalization marks ($\equiv$) under any words that should be capitalized.

1. Every summer, pastor Bachman leads the youth group on a hike around lake geneva.

2. Claude Dickert, our current mayor, writes blog entries on *About brighton,* the city's official web site.

3. At the celebration, dad asked senator ryan about health care.

4. The easiest course I ever took in high school was called leisure reading.

5. When I'm on the internet, I use google to answer all kinds of questions.

6. Whenever mom talks about politics, she eventually criticizes our local congressman.

7. My night course, contemporary history, is always packed because professor scharfenburg presents such interesting lectures.

8. When it comes to shopping for books, I often go to amazon.com for ideas and information.

9. Our instructor had us bookmark *grammar girl,* a web site that provides grammar tips and practice.

10. Make an appointment with the dean if you want to drop cultural geography.

**Practice B** Read the paragraph below, placing capitalization marks ($\equiv$) under any words or letters that should be capitalized.

Internet art does not consist of existing pieces of artwork digitized to be seen using a web browser. Instead, it is art that is created on or with the net, and it comes into being using web sites, e-mail options, virtual worlds such as *second life,* and so on. Steve Dietz, formerly the curator of the Walker art center, defines internet art as art that has "the internet as a necessary condition of viewing/participating/experiencing." Martin Wattenberg has created a Web site called *idea line,* which provides "a timeline of net artwork" to help people experience this type of art.

# LO5 Real-World Application

**Correct** In the following basic letter, place capitalization marks (≡) under letters that should be capitalized. If a letter is capitalized and shouldn't be put a lowercase editing mark ( / ) through the letter.

| Send | Attach | Fonts | Colors | Save As Draft |
|------|--------|-------|--------|---------------|

**From:** Rodell Williams  rodellwilliams2@earthlink.net

**To:** Professor Jean Leuinski

**Subject:** Thank You for Your Recommendation

Dear professor Leuinski,

Thank you for recommending me for the internship at Bismark laboratories.  During my interview last Monday, Dr. Lemark said that he had received your letter and had talked with you by phone. Apparently you said, "clearly Rodell has demonstrated meticulous and thorough lab techniques." I really appreciate this description of my work habits.

The outcome of the application and interviewing process could not have gone any better, because this morning Dr. Lemark offered me the position. I will be working at Conway science center, one of Bismark's newest labs, helping various chemists with their work.

I am so glad that I had you for biochemistry I. You made that course so interesting, and I learned so much. Dr. Lemark also was impressed that I had taken analytical chemistry I and II taught by professor Khan.

Again, I can't thank you enough, professor, for your help. I know I will be busy next semester with the internship, but I can't wait to get started. (you can expect to hear from me about my work.)

sincerely,

Rodell Williams

**Special Challenge** Write one sentence in which you use the same regional or directional word twice—with the word correctly capitalized in one case and correctly lowercase in the other case.

SPEAK UP!

**WRITE 2** was built on a simple principle: to create a new teaching and learning solution that reflects the way today's faculty teach and the way you learn.

Through conversations, focus groups, surveys, and interviews, we collected data that drove the creation of the current version of **WRITE 2** that you are using today. But it doesn't stop there. In order to make **WRITE 2** an even better learning experience, we'd like you to **SPEAK UP** and tell us how **WRITE 2** worked for you.

What did you like about it? What would you change? Are there additional ideas you have that would help us build a better product for next semester's students?

At **login.cengagebrain.com,** you'll find a survey form to send us your comments—in addition to all of the resources you need to become a confident and effective writer.

**Speak up!** Go to **login.cengagebrain.com** today.

"How we remember, what we remember, and why we remember form the most personal map of our individuality."
—Christina Baldwin

# 36 Narrative Essays

People have been telling stories since the dawn of time. And listeners have always had a fascination for the "true tale," especially when a speaker could say "I was there."

In relating a personal narrative, the speaker—or author—has an opportunity to revisit the events, choose the most important ones, order them effectively, discard the rest, and perhaps discover some meaning. The listener or reader gains from the tale not only entertainment but a chance to learn something without having to actually experience it.

## What do you think?

Study the image and quotation on the previous page; then answer the following question: What do your oldest memories say about you?

Answers will vary.

iofoto,2010 / Used under license from Shutterstock.com

## Learning Outcomes

**LO1** Understand, read, and analyze personal narratives.

**LO2** Write your own personal narrative.

# L○1 Understanding Narrative Essays

This chapter contains three example personal essays, along with questions to help analyze each reading. You'll also find writing guidelines for creating a personal essay of your own.

**SQ3R** When you read, become involved with the text by using the SQ3R approach.

- **Survey:** Prepare by reading "About the Author," skimming the essay, and noting any vocabulary words.
- **Question:** Ask yourself what the title and the author description might lead you to expect from the essay. List any questions that come to mind.
- **Read:** Read the essay for effect, allowing the story to carry you along.
- **Recite:** Recite especially effective or enjoyable sections aloud to better understand and remember them.
- **Review:** Scan the essay again, asking yourself what the author sought to accomplish and how successful you believe he or she was. Answer the questions provided to help you analyze the essay.

## Essay List:

**"Shark Bait":** In this narrative from the book *Dave Barry Is Not Making This Up,* Dave Barry tells of a day spent on a boat, off the shores of Miami, with five other men and four 10-year-olds. Things get interesting when a barracuda shows up where they have been swimming.

---

**"You've Got Hate Mail":** Freelance writer Lydie Raschka describes just how unsettling mail can be from an anonymous sender, especially spiteful messages that attack her personally rather than connecting with her work.

---

**"A Doctor's Dilemma":** James N. Dillard revisits a life-or-death decision he faced as a young doctor in training, and explains why he would choose differently facing the same situation today.

**About the Author**

Dave Barry is a book author and Pulitzer Prize-winning humor columnist whose work has appeared in over 500 newspapers.

Dave Berry, "Shark Bait," Dave Barry Is Not Making This Up, Random House, 2001.

## Shark Bait
## by Dave Barry

1    It began as a fun nautical outing, 10 of us in a motorboat off the coast of Miami. The weather was sunny and we saw no signs of danger, other than the risk of sliding overboard because every exposed surface on the boat was covered with a layer of snack-related grease. We had enough **cholesterol** on board to put 5 the entire U.S. Olympic team into **cardiac arrest**. This is because all 10 of us were guys.

I hate to engage in gender **stereotyping**, but when women plan the menu for a recreational outing, they usually come up with a nutritionally balanced menu featuring all the major food groups, including the Sliced Carrots Group, the Pieces 10 of Fruit Cut into Cubes Group, the Utensils Group, and the Plate Group. Whereas guys tend to focus on the Carbonated Malt Beverages Group and the Fatal Snacks Group. On this particular trip, our food supply consisted of about 14 bags of potato chips and one fast-food fried-chicken Giant Economy Tub o' Fat. Nobody brought, for example, napkins, the theory being that you could just wipe your hands on 15 your stomach. Then you could burp. This is what guys on all-guy boats are doing while women are thinking about their relationships.

The reason the grease got smeared everywhere was that four of the guys on the boat were 10-year-olds, who, because of the way their still-developing digestive systems work, cannot chew without punching. This results in a lot of 20 dropped and thrown food. On this boat, you regularly encountered semi-gnawed pieces of chicken skittering across the deck toward you like small but hostile alien creatures from the Kentucky Fried Planet. Periodically a man would yell "CUT THAT OUT!" at the boys, then burp to indicate the depth of his concern. Discipline is vital on a boat.

25    We motored through random-looking ocean until we found exactly what we were looking for: a patch of random-looking ocean. There we dropped anchor and dove for Florida lobsters, which protect themselves by using their tails to scoot backward really fast. They've been fooling **predators** with this move for millions of years, but the guys on our boat, being advanced life forms, including a 30 dentist, figured it out in under three hours. I myself did not participate, because I believe that lobsters are the result of a terrible **genetic** accident involving nuclear

**Vocabulary**

**cholesterol**
a waxy substance in animal cells, sometimes leading to clogged arteries, heart disease, and/or stroke

**cardiac arrest**
a heart stoppage, heart attack

**stereotyping**
applying an oversimplified mental attitude toward some group

**predators**
animals that survive by hunting and eating other animals

**genetic**
having to do with DNA, encoded in a creature's genes

radiation and cockroaches. I mostly sat around, watching guys lunge out of the water, heave lobsters into the boat, burp, and plunge back in. Meanwhile, the lobsters were scrabbling around in the chicken grease, frantically trying to shoot backward through the forest of legs belonging to 10-year-old boys squirting each other with gobs of the No. 197,000,000,000 Sun Block that their moms had sent along. It was a total Guy Day, very relaxing, until the arrival of the **barracuda**.

This occurred just after we'd all gotten out of the water. One of the men, Larry, was fishing, and he hooked a barracuda right where we had been swimming. This was **unsettling**. The books all say that barracuda rarely eat people, but very few barracuda can read, and they have far more teeth than would be necessary for a strictly seafood diet. Their mouths look like the entire $39.95 set of **Ginsu knives**, including the handy Arm Slicer.

We gathered around to watch Larry fight the barracuda. His plan was to catch it, weigh it, and release it with a warning. After 10 minutes he almost had it to the boat, and we were all pretty excited for him, when all of a sudden . . .

*Ba-DUMP . . . Ba-DUMP . . .*

Those of you who read music recognize this as the sound track from the motion picture *Jaws*. Sure enough, cruising right behind Larry's barracuda, thinking **sushi**, was a shark. And not just any shark. It was a hammerhead shark, **perennial** winner of the coveted Oscar for Ugliest Fish. It has a weird, T-shaped head with a big eyeball on each tip, so that it can see around both sides of a telephone pole. This ability is of course useless for a fish, but nobody would dare try to explain this to a hammerhead.

The hammerhead, its fin breaking the surface, zigzagged closer to Larry's barracuda, then surged forward.

"Oh \*\*\*\*!" went Larry, reeling furiously.

*CHOMP* went the hammerhead, and suddenly Larry's barracuda was in a new weight division.

*CHOMP* went the hammerhead again, and now Larry was competing in an entirely new category, Fish Consisting of Only a Head.

The boys were staring at the remainder of the barracuda, deeply impressed.

"This is your leg," said the dentist. "This is your leg on *Jaws*. Any questions?"

The boys, for the first time all day, were quiet.

**Summarize** In one or two sentences, sum up what happened in this narrative.

Answers will vary.

**Comment** Did you enjoy this story? Why or why not?

Answers will vary.

**About the Author**

Lydie Raschka is a freelance writer and part-time Montessori educator living in New York City.

Lydie Raschka, "You've Got Hate Mail," Salon.com, February 16, 2001.

## You've Got Hate Mail
## by Lydie Raschka

1  ***First I expected it; now I'm scared.***

Hate mail confirms a vague, nagging feeling that you've done something wrong. It's a firm tap on the shoulder that says, "The jig is up." So when the first letter came, it was expected. The second, however, was a shock. By the third I was

5  a wreck. How did he know it would take exactly and only three?

I started writing a few years ago, after I had a baby. I haven't completely figured out what led me to writing, but it was probably tied up with my son's birth and the attendant emotions that needed sorting.

I like the solitary work life. I write at a table in the bedroom. I send my ideas

10  out into the void. The bedroom seems a safe enough place. I have been told that I am an introvert. What on earth makes me want to communicate with strangers in this perilous way—standing naked in a field?

"You have to expect these things when you are a writer," my father says about the hate mail. "When you're in the public eye, anyone can read what you

15  write."

The letters are effective and unsettling, to say the least. I have an unusual name, so he thinks I'm foreign. He calls me "Eurotrash." It's a relief because it means he doesn't really know me—although he makes some pretty accurate guesses. He doesn't know that my parents simply like unusual names.

20  He spells my name correctly. I can only hope he's mispronouncing it. He uses it in ways I've never seen it used before—paired with obscenities and crooked thoughts.

It bothers me that he has written my name and my address three different times on three different envelopes. My name is next to the buzzer outside my

25  building so that people will have easier access to me. I am two doors and one buzzer away from danger. But the mail slips through, into the letter box, into my psyche.

I call the postal inspector but she never calls me back. One day I leave a message on her machine and I am in tears. Finally she calls. She tells me that

30  letters like these don't usually lead to violence. She says there's nothing we can

do; we have to wait until he makes a mistake.

My fingers shake when I open the mailbox. I pick through the stack. When a letter arrives I open it quickly. You read your mail. You do.

I spend most of a morning sitting in an old school chair at the police station, the kind with a desk attached. The police are standing around. They joke with one another. They drink coffee and ask me what I need in a **skeptical** way, as though there is nothing I can offer that will surprise them.

"I am getting anonymous hate mail," I say.

"Is it threatening?" they ask.

"Not specifically," I answer. "But the first one had feces in it." Sending feces is threatening, in my mind. At the very least it's a health hazard. The policewoman writes down what I say and photocopies the letters. She makes a file.

I am vulnerable to people's opinions of me. I partly believe what he says. When I tell my friends and family, I imagine that they partly believe what he says, too. They ask me what I wrote, what he wrote. "What does it matter what I wrote!?" I say. "Do you think I did something to deserve this?!" I can't yell at him, so I yell at them. I want unconditional support from everyone I know. I want protection. I have revealed too much about who I am.

I cling to his most obvious mistakes—Eurotrash—in the hope that he has gotten other things wrong, too. He is **sarcastic** and angry and a good speller. A person can be a good speller and be crazy, right? But still, it's hard that he's a good speller.

I try to have **rational** conversations with him in my mind, but it's hopeless. We get nowhere.

He owns a dog. It's his dog's feces he has sent. I always thought animal lovers were especially sensitive human beings. In my vulnerable state—in spite of this **blatant** example of insensitivity—dog ownership gives him stature.

He has decided I'm rich because I live in a certain neighborhood. He has decided I've stolen someone's job because I'm foreign. He attacks my writing and everything he can **eke** out about me from what I have written. But he reveals who he is in his writing, too. He has an aunt and a disabled sister. He doesn't know how much we have in common. He doesn't know that I have a sister and a disabled aunt.

I think about changing my **byline**. I will remove my address from the phone book. I will use only a first initial. I will give up writing.

But then he wins, says my editor.

I am unable to write for a month, two months. My editor calls. I say I'm not ready. He hires someone else to write on a topic I wanted to write about. I don't trust my motivations. Perhaps there's truth in what he says. I have been **flippant**. I have been **patronizing**. I have been biased.

At home I put the letters in a brown envelope and write "Anonymous Mail" in the top right-hand corner, avoiding the word "hate." I make a mental note to throw them away before my son can reach the shelf where I have put them. I don't want him to read these letters that have my name written all over them, with their inaccuracies and assumptions and possible wayward truths.

35

40

45

50

55

60

65

70

75

## Vocabulary

**skeptical**
suspiciously unbelieving

**sarcastic**
ridiculing ironically

**rational**
logical, sensible

**blatant**
glaringly obvious

**eke**
laboriously obtain

**byline**
name on published essays

**flippant**
lacking serious respect

**patronizing**
speaking to someone as to an inferior

The feces were wrapped in a piece of foil; they came in a small padded envelope. I threw the feces away, then fished them out again and put them in a baggie. I washed my hands with soap, and rubbed them red. I am afraid of contamination or disease. I am afraid I will pass on germs to my son.

80     "Here's a little present from my best friend," he writes. The way he uses language is **absurd**: little present, best friend. He writes in sentences, with periods and commas and capital letters. He ignores the typical friendly greeting—he does not say "Dear."

    I imagine him in a room, at a desk or a table. I imagine the light in the
85 room, and the clothes tossed on the bed. He has paper and a pen. He pulls up a chair. Something **compels** him to write. He doesn't know how much we have in common.

**Analyze**   Unlike Dave Barry's "Shark Bait," this narrative does not follow a linear timeline. Make a list of the main events from Raschka's story in the order she presents them. Then write a number next to each in the order you believe they actually happened.

Answers will vary.

_____

_____

_____

_____

_____

_____

_____

_____

**Comment**   Why do you believe Raschka ordered the events as she did?

Answers will vary.

_____

_____

_____

_____

_____

_____

_____

_____

## About the Author

Dr. Dillard served for 12 years as an assistant professor at Columbia University's College of Physicians and Surgeons, and as medical director for its Rosenthal Center for Complementary and Alternative Medicine. Since 2006 he has worked in private practice. He is also an author and television personality.

James Dillard, "A Doctor's Dilemma," Newsweek, June 12, 1995.

# A Doctor's Dilemma
## by James N. Dillard

***Helping an accident victim on the road could land you in court.***

It was a bright, clear February afternoon in Gettysburg. A strong sun and layers of **down** did little to ease the biting cold. Our climb to the crest of **Little Roundtop** wound past somber monuments, barren trees and polished cannon. From the top, we peered down on the wheat field where men had fallen so close together that one could not see the ground. Rifle balls had whined as thick as bee swarms through the trees, and cannon shots had torn limbs from the young men fighting there. A frozen wind whipped tears from our eyes. My friend Amy huddled close, using me as a wind breaker. Despite the cold, it was hard to leave this place. 1

Driving east out of Gettysburg on a country blacktop, the gray Bronco ahead of us passed through a rural crossroad just as a small pickup truck tried to take a left turn. The Bronco swerved, but slammed into the pickup on the passenger side. We immediately slowed to a crawl as we passed the scene. The Bronco's driver looked fine, but we couldn't see the driver of the pickup. I pulled over on the shoulder and got out to investigate. 10

The right side of the truck was smashed in, and the side window was shattered. The driver was partly out of the truck. His head hung forward over the edge of the passenger-side window, the front of his neck crushed on the shattered windowsill. He was unconscious and starting to turn a dusky blue. His chest slowly heaved against a blocked windpipe. 15

A young man ran out of a house at the crossroad. "Get an ambulance out here," I shouted against the wind. "Tell them a man is dying." 20

I looked down again at the driver hanging from the windowsill. There were six empty beer bottles on the floor of the truck. I could smell the beer through the window. I knew I had to move him, to open his airway. I had no idea what neck injuries he had sustained. He could easily end up a **quadriplegic**. But I thought: he'll be dead by the time the ambulance gets here if I don't move him and try to do something to help him. 25

An image flashed before my mind. I could see the courtroom and the driver of the truck sitting in a wheelchair. I could see his attorney pointing at me and 30 thundering at the jury: "This young doctor, with still a year left in his **residency training**, took it upon himself to play God. He took it upon himself to move this gravely injured man, condemning him forever to this wheelchair . . ." I imagined the millions of dollars in award money. And all the years of hard work lost. I'd be

35  paying him off for the rest of my life. Amy touched my shoulder. "What are you going to do?"

The automatic response from long hours in the emergency room kicked in. I pulled off my overcoat and rolled up my sleeves. The trick would be to keep enough **traction** straight up on his head while I moved his torso, so that his probable

40  broken neck and spinal-cord injury wouldn't be made worse. Amy came around the driver's side, climbed half in and grabbed his belt and shirt collar. Together we lifted him off the windowsill.

He was still out cold, limp as a rag doll. His throat was crushed and blood from the jugular vein was running down my arms. He still couldn't breathe. He

45  was deep blue-magenta now, his pulse was rapid and **thready**. The stench of alcohol turned my stomach, but I positioned his jaw and tried to blow air down into his lungs. It wouldn't go.

Amy had brought some supplies from my car. I opened an oversize intravenous needle and groped on the man's neck. My hands were numb, covered with freezing

50  blood and bits of broken glass. **Hyoid** bone—God, I can't even feel the thyroid cartilage, it's gone . . . OK, the **thyroid** gland is about there, **cricoid** rings are here . . . we'll go in right here . . .

It was a lucky first shot. Pink air sprayed through the IV needle. I placed a second needle next to the first. The air began whistling through it. Almost

55  immediately, the driver's face turned bright red. After a minute, his pulse slowed down and his eyes moved slightly. I stood up, took a step back and looked down. He was going to make it. He was going to live. A siren wailed in the distance. I turned and saw Amy holding my overcoat. I was shivering and my arms were turning white with cold.

60  The ambulance captain looked around and bellowed, "What the hell . . . who did this?" as his team scurried over to the man lying in the truck.

"I did," I replied. He took down my name and address for his reports. I had just destroyed my career. I would never be able to finish my residency with a massive lawsuit pending. My life was over.

65  The truck driver was strapped onto a **backboard**, his neck in a stiff collar. The ambulance crew had controlled the bleeding and started intravenous fluid. He was slowly waking up. As they loaded him into the ambulance, I saw him move his feet. Maybe my future wasn't lost.

A police sergeant called me from Pennsylvania three weeks later. Six days

70  after successful throat-reconstruction surgery, the driver had signed out, against medical advice, from the hospital because he couldn't get a drink on the ward. He was being **arraigned** on drunk-driving charges.

A few days later, I went into the office of one of my senior professors, to tell the story. He peered over his half glasses and his eyes narrowed. "Well, you did the

75  right thing medically of course. But, James, do you know what you put at risk by doing that?" he said sternly. "What was I supposed to do?" I asked.

**Vocabulary**

**residency training**
a period of specialty medical training after internship

**traction**
pull to straighten an injury and avoid pressure

**thready**
weak

**hyoid**
a small, U-shaped bone between the tongue and larynx

**thyroid**
a gland located near the base of the throat

**cricoid**
cartilage forming part of the larynx

**backboard**
a board designed for immobilizing and carrying people suspected to have a spinal injury

**arraigned**
called to a court to face criminal charges

"Drive on," he replied. "There is an army of lawyers out there who would stand in line to get a case like that. If that driver had turned out to be a quadriplegic, you might never have practiced medicine again. You were a very lucky young man." 80

The day I graduated from medical school, I took an oath to serve the sick and the injured. I remember truly believing I would be able to do just that. But I have found out it isn't so simple. I understand now what a foolish thing I did that day. Despite my oath, I know what I would do on that cold roadside near Gettysburg today. I would drive on. 85

**Map** Along the time line below, list the most important details of Dr. Dillard's story. Answers will vary.

**Start**

**End**

**Evaluate** What is the doctor's main point in this story? Do his chosen details effectively support that point? Why or why not?

Medical professionals are often forced to choose between providing

critical treatment and avoiding legal liability. (Explanations supporting

this point will vary.)

**WAC**

This essay focuses on an issue of medical ethics. What ethical considerations do you have in your area of study?

# L○2 Writing a Narrative Essay

**Prewrite** To begin writing a personal essay, you need to choose a memorable event from your life. One way to do this is with a life map. At the beginning of the map, write the day you were born. At the end, write today's date. Then begin listing memorable events along the way.

**Life Map**

**Date of birth:**   Answers will vary.

**Today's date:**

**Freewrite** Next, choose an event from your life map and ask yourself why it is important to you. How did that event shape you or illustrate who you are today? Spend at least 10 minutes writing whatever comes to mind in explanation.

**Prewrite** Next, you will need to gather details about the event you have chosen. Most stories occur in a linear fashion, from start to finish. To prepare for your story, begin listing details on a timeline. (Leave space between events to add new details as they occur to you.)

**Timeline**

Start    Answers will vary.

Finish

**Prewrite** A sensory chart is another good way to gather details to use in a personal narrative. As you recall the event, write details of sight, sound, smell, touch, and taste in the appropriate column.  Answers will vary.

**Sensory Chart**

| Sight | Sound | Smell | Touch | Taste |
|-------|-------|-------|-------|-------|
|       |       |       |       |       |

**Draft** Create a strong opening, middle, and closing for your essay. Use the supports below as you create each part. Answers will vary.

## Opening Paragraph

Capture your reader's attention in the first line of your personal essay. Use one of the following strategies:

■ **Begin with action:** "I was clocking out, sweaty and exhausted after a long shift waiting tables, when he walked in."

■ **Ask a question:** "What is it about some people—me for example—that makes travel such an adventure in wrong turns?"

■ **Connect to the reader:** "The song starts, and you want to get up and dance, but you feel as big and clumsy as Frankenstein's monster."

Once you have your reader's attention, lead up to your thesis statement. Here is a formula to use as you create your thesis statement.

| Memorable Event | | Effect on Your Life | | Thesis Statement |
|---|---|---|---|---|
| Caught up in a surge of raw emotion from the crowd | **+** | I felt just how strong the pull of "mob mentality" can be. | **=** | Caught up in a surge of raw emotion from the crowd, I felt just how strong the pull of "mob mentality" can be. |

**Memorable Event**      **+** **Effect on Your Life** _____

_____

_____

_____

**= Thesis Statement**

_____

_____

_____

## Middle Paragraphs

In your middle paragraphs, provide support for your thesis statement by
- Telling the story (review your timeline for the most important facts).
- Drawing the reader in with details (mine your sensory chart).
- Explaining the significance of what happened.

## Closing Paragraph

The final paragraph of a personal essay should reflect back on the whole, if possible making a connection that was not visible at the beginning. At the very least, it should restate and reinforce the thesis of the essay. Review the closing paragraph of the readings in this chapter for examples of effective endings.

**Revise** Take a break from your writing. Then come back to it with fresh eyes. If possible, read your personal essay aloud to a friend or family member, and ask if any parts are unclear. Then review your writing with the following checklist. Keep polishing until you can answer every question with a "yes."

**Ideas**

☐ **1.** Do I focus on one main event from my life?

☐ **2.** Did the event I've chosen have an important effect on me?

**Organization**

☐ **3.** Does my opening grab the reader's attention and present a clear thesis?

☐ **4.** Does my middle clearly tell the story (using facts from my timeline)?

☐ **5.** Do I include a variety of details?

☐ **6.** Does my middle make the significance of the event clear?

**Voice**

☐ **7.** Do I tell the story in a way that keeps the reader interested to the end?

**Edit** Prepare a clean copy of your personal essay and use the following checklist to check for errors. Continue until you can answer "yes" to each question.

**Words**

☐ **1.** Do I use correct verb forms (*he saw,* not *he seen*)? (See page 356.)

☐ **2.** Do my subjects and verbs agree (*she speaks,* not *she speak*)? (See pages 282–291.)

☐ **3.** Have I used the right words (*there, their, they're*)?

**Sentences**

☐ **4.** Have I avoided sentence fragments? (See pages 297–302.)

☐ **5.** Have I avoided run-on sentences? (See pages 306–310.)

☐ **6.** Have I avoided improper shifts in sentences? (See pages 314–315.)

**Conventions**

☐ **7.** Have I used commas after long introductory word groups? (See page 396.)

☐ **8.** Have I capitalized first words? (See page 414.)

☐ **9.** Have I capitalized proper nouns and proper adjectives? (See page 414.)

☐ **10.** Have I carefully checked my spelling?

"Aristotle was famous for knowing everything. He taught that the brain exists merely to cool the blood and is not involved in the process of thinking. This is true only of certain persons."

—Will Cuppy

Convit,2010 / Used under license from Shutterstock.com

# 37

# Process Essays

Socrates taught Plato; Plato taught Aristotle; Aristotle taught Alexander the Great; and Alexander conquered the Persian Empire, spreading Greek culture so thoroughly that it affected the Byzantine Empire well into the fifteenth century, nearly two millennia after his death. The fact that we're still familiar with Greek mythology and with cities like Sparta and Athens says something about that effect even today.

Millennia-long though it may be, that spread of thought is a process nevertheless. We can describe it in steps, thereby better understanding the whole.

## Learning Outcomes

**LO1** Understand, read, and analyze process essays.

**LO2** Write your own process essay.

## What do you think?

From your own understanding, how is the human brain involved in the process of thinking?

Answers will vary.

# LO1 Understanding Process Essays

This chapter contains three example process essays, along with questions you can
use as tools to help analyze each reading. At the end of the chapter are writing
guidelines for creating a process essay of your own.

**SQ3R**  When you read, become involved with the text by using the SQ3R approach.

- **Survey:** Prepare by reading "About the Author," skimming the essay, and
  noting any vocabulary words.
- **Question:** Make a list of questions you expect to have answered by the
  essay.
- **Read:** Read the essay, noting any steps in the process that is being
  described.
- **Recite:** Recite any steps in order to make sure you understand and
  remember them.
- **Review:** Scan the essay again, looking for details you might have missed
  or answers to any remaining questions you may have. Answer the
  questions provided to help you analyze the essay.

---

## Essay List:

**"Conversational Ballgames":** Nancy Masterson Sakamoto uses two
very different types of ballgames as analogies to contrast Japanese
and American conversational styles.

---

**"How Our Skins Got Their Color":** Dr. Marvin Harris argues that the
natural skin tone of the human race is brown, then explains how
Europeans developed white skin from that base, and the parallel
development of black skin in sub-Saharan Africa. His essay is
based upon explanation of another process: the human body's use
of sunlight to create vitamin D, and its use of that substance to
absorb calcium.

---

**"Sorry, What's Your Name Again? 6 Steps to Relieve the Most Common
Memory Worry":** In this how-to process, Roger Seip offers a multi-
sensory strategy for remembering the names of new people you
meet.

Don Hammond/Design Pics/Corbis

# Conversational Ballgames
## by Nancy Masterson Sakamoto

**About the Author**

Nancy Masterson Sakamoto is the author of the book *Polite Fiction: Why Japanese and Americans Seem Rude to Each Other*. Born in Los Angeles in 1931, she went on to marry a Japanese man and taught American studies in Japan from 1972 to 1982. She then returned to the U.S. and became a professor at Shitennoji Gakuen University in Honolulu.

Nancy Masterson Sakamoto, "Conversational Ballgames," Polite Fictions, Tokyo: Kinseido, Ltd., 1982.

1    After I was married and had lived in Japan for a while, my Japanese gradually improved to the point where I could take part in simple conversations with my husband, his friends, and family. And I began to notice that often, when I joined in, the others would look startled, and the conversation would come to a

5   halt. After this happened several times, it became clear to me that I was doing something wrong. But for a long time, I didn't know what it was.

Finally, after listening carefully to many Japanese conversations, I discovered what my problem was. Even though I was speaking Japanese, I was handling the conversation in a Western way.

10   Japanese-style conversations develop quite differently from Western-style conversations. And the difference isn't only in the languages. I realized that just as I kept trying to hold Western-style conversations even when I was speaking Japanese, so were my English students trying to hold Japanese-style conversations even when they were speaking English. We were unconsciously playing en-

15   tirely different conversational ballgames.

A Western-style conversation between two people is like a game of tennis. If I introduce a topic, a conversational ball, I expect you to hit it back. If you agree with me, I don't expect you simply to agree and do nothing more. I expect you to add something—a reason for agreeing, another example, or a remark to carry

20   the idea further. But I don't expect you always to agree. I am just as happy if you question me, or challenge me, or completely disagree with me. Whether you agree or disagree, your response will return the ball to me.

And then it is my turn again. I don't serve a new ball from my original starting line. I hit your ball back again from where it has bounced. I carry your idea

25   further, or answer your questions or objections, or challenge or question you. And so the ball goes back and forth.

If there are more than two people in the conversation, then it is like doubles in tennis, or like volleyball. There's no waiting in line. Whoever is nearest and quickest hits the ball, and if you step back, someone else will hit it. No one stops

30   the game to give you a turn. You're responsible for taking your own turn and no one person has the ball for very long.

A Japanese-style conversation, however, is not at all like tennis or volleyball, it's like bowling. You wait for your turn, and you always know your place in line. It depends on such things as whether you are older or younger, a close friend or a relative stranger to the previous speaker, in a senior or junior position, and so on. 35

The first thing is to wait for your turn, patiently and politely. When your moment comes, you step up to the starting line with your bowling ball, and carefully bowl it. Everyone else stands back, making sounds of polite encouragement. Everyone waits until your ball has reached the end of the lane, and watches to see 40 if it knocks down all the pins, or only some of them, or none of them. Then there is a pause, while everyone registers your score.

Then, after everyone is sure that you are done, the next person in line steps up to the same startling line, with a different ball. He doesn't return your ball. There is no back and forth at all. And there is always a suitable pause between 45 turns. There is no rush, no impatience.

No wonder everyone looked startled when I took part in Japanese conversations. I paid no attention to whose turn it was, and kept snatching the ball halfway down the **alley** and throwing it back at the bowler. Of course the conversation fell apart, I was playing the wrong game. 50

This explains why it can be so difficult to get a Western-style discussion going with Japanese students of English. Whenever I serve a volleyball, everyone just stands back and watches it fall. No one hits it back. Everyone waits until I call on someone to take a turn. And when that person speaks, he doesn't hit my ball back. He serves a new ball. Again, everyone just watches it fall. So I call on 55 someone else. This person does not refer to what the previous speaker has said. He also serves a new ball. Everyone begins again from the same starting line, and all the balls run parallel. There is never any back and forth.

Now that you know about the difference in the conversational ballgames, you may think that all your troubles are over. But if you have been trained all 60 your life to play one game, it is no simple matter to switch to another, even if you know the rules. Tennis, after all, is different from bowling.

**Vocabulary**

**alley**
in bowling, a single lane with a foul line at one end, pins at the other, and a gutter along each side

**Process Diagrams**

I. Topic _____
(Chronological Order)

| Step 1 |
| --- |

↓

| Step 2 |
| --- |

↓

| Step 3 |
| --- |

II.

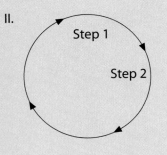

Step 1

Step 2

**Think Critically**  Review the process diagrams to the left. Which do you think best suits an American conversation and which a Japanese? Explain.

Answers will vary.

_____

_____

_____

_____

_____

_____

**About the Author**

Dr. Marvin Harris (1927-2001) was chair of the Anthropology department at Columbia University, then a Graduate Research Professor at the University of Florida. He also served as the Chair of the General Anthropology Division for the American Anthropological Association. During his life he published 16 books and wrote a series of essays he titled *Our Kind*.

Marvin Harris, "How Our Skins Got Their Color," *Our Kind: Who We Are, Where We Came From, and Where We Are Going*, Harper-Collins, 1989.

## How Our Skins Got Their Color
## by Marvin Harris

1      Most human beings are neither very fair nor very dark, but brown. The extremely fair skin of northern Europeans and their descendants, and the very black skins of central Africans and their descendants, are probably special adaptations. Brown-skinned ancestors may have been shared by modern-day blacks
5    and whites as recently as 10,000 years ago.

Human skin owes its color to the presence of particles known as melanin. The primary function of melanin is to protect the upper levels of the skin from being damaged by the sun's ultraviolet rays. This radiation poses a critical problem for our kind because we lack the dense coat of hair that acts as a sunscreen for most
10   mammals. . . . Hairlessness exposes us to two kinds of radiation hazards: ordinary sunburn, with its blisters, rashes, and risk of infection; and skin cancers, including malignant melanoma, one of the deadliest diseases known. Melanin is the body's first line of defense against these afflictions. The more melanin particles, the darker the skin, and the lower the risk of sunburn and all forms of skin can-
15   cer. This explains why the highest rates for skin cancer are found in sun-drenched lands such as Australia, where light-skinned people of European descent spend a good part of their lives outdoors wearing scanty attire. Very dark-skinned people such as heavily **pigmented** Africans of Zaire seldom get skin cancer, but when they do, they get it on depigmented parts of their bodies—palms and lips.

20      If exposure to solar radiation had nothing but harmful effects, natural selection would have favored inky black as the color for all human populations. But the sun's rays do not present an **unmitigated** threat. As it falls on the skin, sunshine converts a fatty substance in the **epidermis** into vitamin D. The blood carries vitamin D from the skin to the intestines (technically making it a hormone rather
25   than a vitamin), where it plays a vital role in the absorption of calcium. In turn, calcium is vital for strong bones. Without it, people fall victim to the crippling diseases **rickets** and **osteomalacia**. In women, calcium deficiencies can result in a deformed birth canal, which makes childbirth lethal for both mother and fetus.

Vitamin D can be obtained from a few foods, primarily the oils and livers
30   of marine fish. But inland populations must rely on the sun's rays and their own

skins for the supply of this crucial substance. The particular color of a human population's skin, therefore, represents in large degree a trade-off between the hazards of too much versus too little solar radiation: acute sunburn and skin cancer on the one hand, and rickets and osteomalacia on the other. It is this trade-off that largely accounts for the **preponderance** of brown people in the world and for the general tendency for skin color to be darkest among equatorial populations and lightest among populations dwelling at higher **latitudes**.

At middle latitudes, the skin follows a strategy of changing colors with the seasons. Around the **Mediterranean** basin, for example, exposure to the summer sun brings high risk of cancer but low risk for rickets; the body produces more melanin and people grow darker (i.e., they get suntans). Winter reduces the risk of sunburn and cancer; the body produces less melanin, and the tan wears off.

The **correlation** between skin color and latitude is not perfect because other factors—such as the availability of foods containing vitamin D and calcium, regional cloud cover during the winter, amount of clothing worn, and cultural preferences—may work for or against the predicted relationship. Arctic-dwelling Eskimo, for example, are not as light-skinned as expected, but their **habitat** and economy afford them a diet that is exceptionally rich in both vitamin D and calcium.

Northern Europeans, obliged to wear heavy garments for protection against the long, cold, cloudy winters, were always at risk for rickets and osteomalacia from too little vitamin D and calcium. This risk increased sometime after 6000 B.C., when pioneer cattle herders who did not exploit marine resources began to appear in northern Europe. The risk would have been especially great for the brown-skinned Mediterranean peoples who migrated northward along with the crops and farm animals. Samples of **Caucasian** skin (infant **penile foreskin** obtained at the time of **circumcision**) exposed to sunlight on cloudless days in Boston (42°N) from November through February produced no vitamin D. In Edmonton (52°N) this period extended from October to March. But further south (34°N) sunlight was effective in producing vitamin D in the middle of the winter. Almost all of Europe lies north of 42°N. Fair-skinned, nontanning individuals who could utilize the weakest and briefest doses of sunlight to synthesize vitamin D were strongly favored by natural selection. During the frigid winters, only a small circle of a child's face could be left to peek out at the sun through the heavy clothing, thereby favoring the survival of individuals with **translucent** patches of pink on their cheeks characteristic of many northern Europeans. (People who could get calcium by drinking cow's milk would also be favored by natural selection. . . .)

If light-skinned individuals on the average had only 2 percent more children survive per generation, the changeover in the skin color could have begun 5,000 years ago and reached present levels well before the beginning of the Christian era. But natural selection need not have acted alone. Cultural selection may also have played a role. It seems likely that whenever people consciously or unconsciously had to decide which infants to nourish and which to neglect, the advantage would go to those with lighter skin, experience having show that such individuals tended to grow up to be taller, stronger, and healthier than their darker siblings. White was beautiful because white was healthy.

To account for the evolution of black skin in equatorial latitudes, one has merely to reverse the combined effects of natural and cultural selection. With the sun directly overhead most of the year, and clothing a hindrance to work and survival, vitamin D was never in short supply (and calcium was easily obtained from vegetables). Rickets and osteomalacia were rare. Skin cancer was the main problem, and what nature started culture amplified. Darker infants were favored by parents because experience showed that they grew up to be freer of disfiguring and lethal **malignancies**. Black was beautiful because black was healthy.

80

**Vocabulary**

**malignant**
malicious, intending damage

**Evaluate**  What processes are explained in this essay?

Possible answers:

• Development of skin color

• Migration of early people into Europe

• Formation of vitamin D and absorption of calcium

**Diagram**  Label the diagram below with steps from one of the processes in the essay. (Add more arrows as needed.)

Answers will vary.

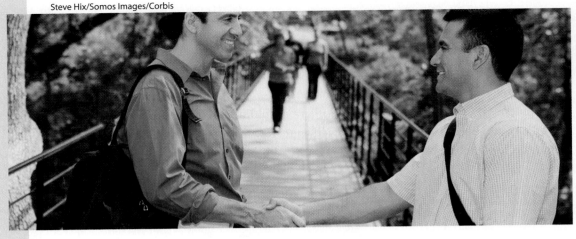

## About the Author

A former stand-up comedian, Roger Seip is now a nationally known motivational speaker for organizations such as Harley Davidson, Northwestern Mutual, and the National Association of Realtors.

Roger Seip, "Sorry, What's Your Name Again? 6 Steps to Relieve the Most Common Memory Worry," Freedom Personal Development Blog, July 27, 2009.

## Sorry, What's Your Name Again? 6 Steps to Relieve the Most Common Memory Worry
### by Roger Seip

If you live in fear of forgetting people's names, sometimes within mere seconds of being introduced to them, you're not alone. Surveys show that 83% of the population worries about their inability to recall people's names. Ironically, while most of us hate having our names forgotten or mispronounced, the majority of us claim we just "aren't good at remembering names" or putting faces together with names when we meet people again. *(1, 5)*

If you have difficulty recalling names, you know that the two most common scenarios are forgetting the name instantaneously upon being introduced to someone new, and failing to recall the name of someone you've met and interacted with in the past and should know but just can't pull up from your memory bank. *(10)*

Forgetting names becomes more than just an embarrassing social **faux pas** in sales. Straining to recall a name can so preoccupy you that you are unable to fully pay attention to your client or prospect. He or she may perceive you not only as unfocused and easily distracted, but also as not very bright if you're unable to devote your full attention to him or her. Even worse, if you forget the name of a client with whom you've worked in the past, he or she may view your memory **lapse** as a betrayal of trust, which can cost you a great deal of money if that client severs the relationship. *(15)*

### Integrating Learning Styles to Improve Name Recall

While common, this frustrating phenomenon of forgetting names can be relatively easy to overcome when you commit to taking steps to improve your memory. The most important key to really effective learning of any kind is understanding that there are three learning styles: visual, **auditory**, and kinesthetic (physically interactive). The more you can apply all three of these styles to a task, the more quickly and solidly you will learn anything. *(20, 25)*

Practice each of the following steps to improve your name recollection in every sales and social situation.

1. When you're first introduced to someone, look closely at his or her face and try to find something unique about it. Whether you find a distinctive quality

## Vocabulary

**faux pas**
blunder (French for "false step")

**lapse**
short break

**auditory**
involving hearing

or not is **irrelevant**; by really looking for a memorable characteristic in a new face, you're incorporating the visual learning style. And a word of advice: if you do find something that really stands out about someone's face, don't say anything! Within minutes of meeting someone new, it's generally a bad idea to exclaim, "Whoa! That's a huge nose!"

2. The next step **utilizes** both auditory and kinesthetic learning styles. When you meet someone, slow down for five seconds, and concentrate on listening to him or her. Focus on the prospect and repeat his or her name back in a conversational manner, such as "Susan. Nice to meet you, Susan." Also make sure to give a good firm handshake, which establishes a physical connection with the prospect.

3. Creating a mental picture of someone's name incorporates the visual sense again. Many people have names that already are pictures: consider Robin, Jay, Matt, or Dawn to name just a few. Some names will require you to play with them a bit to create a picture. Ken, for example, may not bring an immediate image to your mind, but a "can" is very close. Or you might envision a Ken doll. The point is not to create the best, most creative mental image ever, so don't get caught up in your head during this step of the process, thinking, "Oh, that's not a very good picture. What's a better one?" The worst thing you can do when learning is to stress yourself out and overthink the process. If an image doesn't come to you right away, skip it and do it later. You'll undo all of your good efforts if you're staring dumbly at your prospect, insisting, "Hey. Hold still for a minute while I try to turn your name into a picture!"

4. Once you've identified a mental image that you associate with a person's name, the next step is to "glue" that image to the person's face or upper body. This bridges the gap many people experience between being able to recall faces but not the names that belong to those faces. If you met a new prospect named Rosalind, for example, you might have broken her name down into the memorable image of "rose on land." Now you must create a mental picture that will stick with you as long as you need it and pop into your head every time you meet her; this should be something fun, even a little odd, that will bring "rose on land" to mind when you see her face. You might imagine her buried up to her neck in earth, with roses scattered around her, for example. Because you created the image, it will come up next time you see her and enable you to recall her name.

5. At the end of the conversation, **integrate** auditory learning by repeating the prospect's name one more time, but don't ever overuse someone's name in an effort to place it more firmly in your mind. Use the prospect's name only right at the beginning of the conversation, and then again at the end; if you feel like you can do so naturally, you might insert someone's name once or twice in a natural fashion during the course of the conversation, too. But if you've ever had a **stereotypically** pushy salesperson use your name a dozen times in a five minute conversation, you know how annoying, even weird, this can be, so don't overdo it.

**Vocabulary**

**irrelevant**
not applicable

**utilize**
to put to use

**integrate**
to merge into a unified whole

**stereotypically**
in an oversimplified way

6. Writing is a form of kinesthetic learning—you're getting a part of your body involved in the learning process—so if you're really serious about wanting to remember people's names for the long term, keep a name journal or a log of important people you meet, and review it periodically.

**Forget Me Not: It's the Effort That Matters Most**

The most important thing to know about this memory process is that even when it doesn't work, it still works! For example, if you get stuck trying to make a picture out of someone's name, skip it for now. The next day, when you have a chance, give the matter a few minutes of concentrated thought. If you still can't get a picture, stop and take up the matter a week later. Even if you're still unsuccessful at creating a mental image, you've thought about the prospect's name so much, there's now no way you'll ever forget it! So you've actually accomplished what you set to do in the first place.

People can't remember names for one main reason: they're just not paying attention. This process forces you to think. If, for example, you struggle with the step of creating a mental picture, the other steps—looking at the prospect closely, shaking his or her hand confidently and repeating the name a few times—are easy to do, will solidify the name in your memory, and will ultimately convey a positive image of you to clients and prospects. That positive image will certainly make you memorable to prospects, enabling you to close more deals and increase your bottom line.

**Respond** Do you have trouble remembering names? If so, how do you deal with that trouble? If not, how do you react to people who do?

Answers will vary.

Workplace

This essay focuses on a critical skill for success in business and life— remembering people's names.

# L◯2 Writing a Process Essay

**Prewrite** Brainstorm a cluster to identify processes you are interested in explaining. List possible topics in the bubbles below. (Add more bubbles if necessary.) Answers will vary.

**Learning Outcomes**

Write your own process essay.

## Make an Idea Cluster

**Choose one:** Put a star next to the process that you think would make the best subject.

## Do Your Research

Make sure you fully understand the subject you have chosen. Read what experts have to say about the process and take careful notes.

_____

_____

_____

_____

_____

_____

_____

_____

# Outline the Steps

**Prewrite** Make a list of the steps from beginning to end of your process. Use one of the diagrams below as a guide.

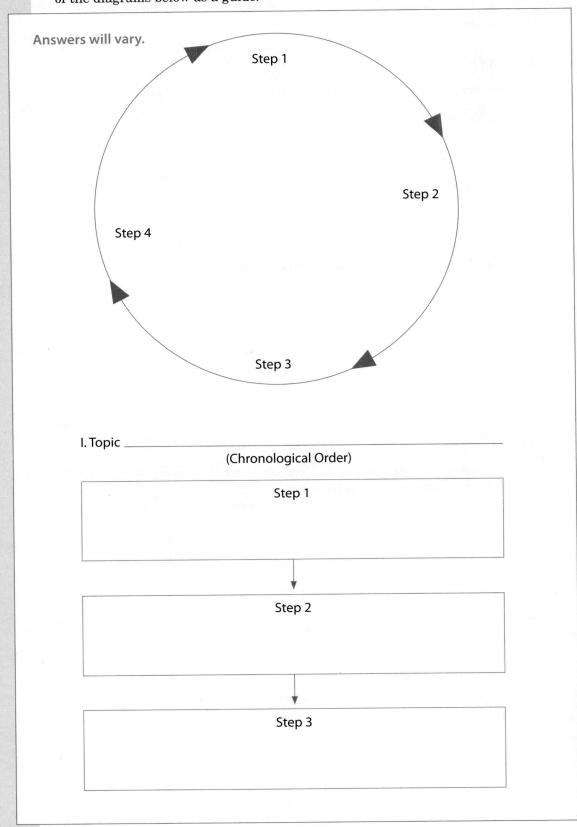

Answers will vary.

Step 1

Step 2

Step 4

Step 3

I. Topic _____

(Chronological Order)

Step 1

Step 2

Step 3

**Draft** Create a strong opening, middle, and closing for your process essay. Use the supports below as you create each part. Answers will vary.

## Opening Paragraph

Capture your reader's attention in the first line of your essay. Think of why your reader should care about this process. Use one of the following strategies:

- **Connect to the reader:** "Saving for the future may seem impossible while you're in school."

- **Ask a question:** "Have you ever wondered how a dolphin, an air-breathing creature, is born at sea?"

- **Begin with action:** "Your chest tightens, throat clenching and unclenching; your tongue undulates, mouth opening and closing; and vibrating puffs of air burst forth—you speak."

Once you have your reader's attention, lead up to your thesis statement. Here is a formula to use as you create your thesis statement.

| **Main Point** | **Importance to Reader** | **Thesis Statement** |
|---|---|---|
| Setting your blog, newsfeed, and social media to automatically synchronize | is actually very easy | Setting your blog, newsfeed, and social media to automatically synchronize is actually very easy. |

**Main Point** ☐ **+ Importance to Reader** _____

_____

_____

**= Thesis Statement**

_____

_____

_____

## Middle Paragraphs

In your middle paragraphs, expand upon your thesis statement by
- Presenting the steps of the process.
- Defining any special terms.
- Explaining how any needed equipment is to be used.
- Identifying any safety issues.

## Closing Paragraph

The final paragraph should help to "set" the process in the reader's mind. You might review the most important details and end by restating your main point, or you might conclude with a reminder of the significance of the process.

**Revise** Take a break from your writing. Then come back to it with fresh eyes. If possible, have a friend or family member read the essay and then perform the process while you watch to see what may not be clear. Then review your writing with the following checklist. Keep polishing until you can answer every question with a "yes."

### Ideas

☐ **1.** Is the process I have chosen interesting to other people?

☐ **2.** Do I include all the needed details about steps, equipment, and safety issues?

### Organization

☐ **3.** Does my opening grab the reader's attention and present a clear thesis?

☐ **4.** Does my middle fully explain the steps of the process?

☐ **5.** Are the steps in clear order of sequence or importance?

☐ **6.** Does my ending remind the reader of the main point and of the significance of the process?

### Voice

☐ **7.** Is the voice both friendly and professional?

**Edit** Prepare a clean copy of your personal essay and use the following checklist to check for errors. Continue until you can answer "yes" to each question.

### Words

☐ **1.** Do I use correct verb forms (*he saw,* not *he seen*)? (See page 356.)

☐ **2.** Do my subjects and verbs agree (*she speaks,* not *she speak*)? (See pages 282–291.)

☐ **3.** Have I used the right words (*there, their, they're*)?

### Sentences

☐ **4.** Have I avoided sentence fragments? (See pages 297–302.)

☐ **5.** Have I avoided run-on sentences? (See pages 306–310.)

☐ **6.** Have I avoided improper shifts in sentences? (See pages 314–315.)

### Conventions

☐ **7.** Have I used commas after long introductory word groups? (See page 396.)

☐ **8.** Have I capitalized first words? (See page 414.)

☐ **9.** Have I capitalized proper nouns and proper adjectives? (See page 414.)

☐ **10.** Have I carefully checked my spelling?

"In theory, there is no difference between theory and practice. In practice there is."

—Yogi Berra

Sue Hammond/Flickr/Getty Images

# 38

# Comparison-Contrast Essays

In Lewis Carroll's *Alice in Wonderland,* the Mad Hatter wonders aloud, "Why is a raven like a writing desk?" A few pages later, we learn that this riddle has no answer. But the riddle does tickle the mind, so much so that Sam Loyd later quipped that a raven was like a writing desk "because Poe wrote on both."

When you note the similarities between two things—a raven and a writing desk, for example—you are comparing them. When you note the differences, you are contrasting them. An essay that compares and contrasts two things creates a strong understanding of both subjects. It also explores surprising connections between things.

## Learning Outcomes

**LO1** Understand, read, and analyze comparison-contrast essays.

**LO2** Write your own comparison-contrast essay.

### What do you think?

In what other ways is a raven like a writing desk? Write as many as you can think of.

Answers will vary.

# LO1 Understanding Comparison-Contrast Essays

One of the best ways to understand a subject is to compare and contrast it with another. This chapter contains four example comparison-contrast pieces, along with questions and graphics for analyzing each reading. You'll also find writing guidelines for creating a comparison-contrast essay of your own.

**SQ3R** When you read, become involved with the text by using the SQ3R approach.

■ **Survey:** Prepare by reading "About the Author," skimming the writing, and noting any vocabulary words.

■ **Question:** Ask yourself what topics are being compared and contrasted and what organizational pattern is used. Here are three common patterns:

| Point-by-Point | Subject-to-Subject | Similarities-Differences |
|---|---|---|
| Beginning | Beginning | Beginning |
| Point 1 — Subject 1 / Subject 2 | Subject 1 | Similarities |
| Point 2 — Subject 1 / Subject 2 | Subject 2 | Differences |
| Point 3 — Subject 1 / Subject 2 | | |
| Ending | Ending | Ending |

■ **Read:** Carefully read the piece, reviewing the vocabulary words as you encounter them, finding answers to your questions, and judging the effectiveness of the author's comparison and contrast.

■ **Recite:** Stop to repeat important points silently or aloud.

■ **Review:** Analyze the writing by filling in the graphic organizer and answering the questions provided.

---

## Essay List:

**"Truth in Advertising: Military Recruitment Ads Versus Reality":** Student writer Hector Antinoro responds to military recruitment ads at movie theaters.

---

**"Chinese Space, American Space":** Yi-Fu Tuan uses American and Chinese homes to reveal a different attitude toward space, or place, and what it has to say about the two societies.

---

**"Religious Faith Versus Spirituality":** Neil Bissoondath uses his mother's death and cremation to distinguish between faith and spirituality.

---

**"Two Views on Social Order: Conflict or Cooperation?":** Llewellyn H. Rockwell, Jr., argues that the left and the right in United States politics are alike in many ways.

Tim Tadder/Ivy /Corbis

**About the Author**

Hector Antinoro is a former National Guard medic who served two terms in Iraq. He is currently finishing a degree as a registered nurse and hopes to specialize in geriatric care. In his spare time, he likes to read poetry by Primo Levi.

## Truth in Advertising:
## Military Recruitment Ads Versus Reality
## by Hector Antinoro

1   Attend pretty much any movie nowadays, and you'll sit through two or three military recruitment ads. Although the details vary—an Air Force command station guiding a satellite out of the path of space junk, a Marine strike force clearing a Middle-Eastern building, a National Guard squad rescuing flood

5   victims—they all bear one thing in common: Drama. These ads make military life seem exciting; in reality, it's generally boring, full of what service people call "hurry up and wait." The ads make military service seem full of glory; actually, it's usually thankless and often downright **demeaning**. (Ask anyone who has ever been assigned **KP** duty.) The ads portray an **idealized** individual heroism, but modern

10  soldiers are the most effective in history because of their teamwork. Finally, the ads use the dramatic word "honor"; in reality, most soldiers will tell you what they learn from service is self-respect. Yes, military service is a noble occupation, something every young person should experience. It's just not as glamorous as the movie-theater ads would have you believe.

**Think Critically** Antinoro uses a point-by-point comparison to contrast recruitment ads and actual military service. His first points are clear opposites, his final ones more subtle. Why do you believe he chose this organization? What effect does it have on your own opinion toward recruitment ads?

Answers will vary.

**Write** Write your own "Truth in Advertising" paragraph, comparing features of an ad campaign to your experience with reality. Answers will vary.

**Vocabulary**

**demeaning**
causing a feeling of low status

**KP**
manual labor in a military mess hall (literally "kitchen police")

**idealized**
an imaginary perfection

**About the Author**

Yi-Fu Tuan was born in China and later moved to the United States. He is now a geography professor in Madison, Wisconsin. In this essay, Tuan compares the ways in which American and Chinese cultures create a different perception of place, and what this implies about the two societies.

Yi-Fu Tuan, "Chinese Space, American Space," Connelly, Get Writing: Sentences and Paragraphs 2e, Wadsworth. 1413033504.

# Chinese Space, American Space
## by Yi-Fu Tuan

Americans have a sense of space, not of place. Go to an American home in exurbia, and almost the first thing you do is drift toward the picture window. How curious that the first compliment you pay your host inside his house is to say how lovely it is outside the house! He is pleased that you should admire his **vistas**. This distant horizon is not merely a line separating earth from the sky; it is a symbol of the future. The American is not rooted in his place, however lovely: his eyes are drawn by the expanding space to a point on the horizon, which is his future.

By contrast, consider the traditional Chinese home. Blank walls enclose it. Step behind the **spirit wall** and you are in a courtyard with perhaps a miniature garden around a corner. Once inside his private compound, you are wrapped in an **ambiance** of calm beauty, an ordered world of buildings, pavement, rock, and decorative vegetation. But you have no distant view: nowhere does the space open out before you. Raw nature in such a home is experienced only as weather, and the only open space is the sky above. The Chinese is rooted in his place. When he has to leave, it is not for the promised land on the terrestrial horizon, but for another world altogether along the vertical, religious axis of his imagination.

The Chinese tie to place is deeply felt. Wanderlust is an alien sentiment. The Taoist classic *Tao Te Ching* captures the ideal of rootedness in place with these words: "Though there may be another country in the neighborhood so close that they are within sight of each other and the crowing of cocks and barking dogs in one place can be heard in the other, yet there is no traffic between them; and throughout their lives the two people have nothing to do with each other." In theory if not in practice, farmers have ranked high in Chinese society. The reason is not only that they are engaged in a "root" industry of producing food but that, unlike **pecuniary** merchants, they are tied to the land and do not abandon their country when it is in danger.

Nostalgia is a recurrent theme in Chinese poetry. An American reader of translated Chinese poems may well be taken aback—even put off—by the

1

5

10

15

20

25

frequency, as well as the sentimentality, of the lament for home. To understand the
30  strength of this sentiment, we need to know that Chinese desire for stability and
rootedness in place is prompted by constant threat of war, exile, and the natural
disasters of flood and drought. Forcible removal makes the Chinese keenly aware
of their loss. By contrast, Americans move, for the most part, voluntarily. Their
nostalgia for hometown is really longing for a childhood to which they can return:
35  in the meantime the future beckons and the future is "out there," in open space.

When we criticize American rootlessness, we tend to forget that it is a result
of ideals we admire, namely social mobility and optimism about the future. When
we admire Chinese rootedness, we forget that the word "place" means both a
location in space and position in society: to be tied to place is also to be bound to
40  one's station in life, with little hope of betterment. Space symbolizes hope; place,
achievement and stability.

**Insight**
Reflect on what sort
of space you are most
comfortable in. Is it an
American space, or one
from another society?

**Analyze**  Complete the point-by-point graphic below to analyze Yi-Fu Tuan's
comparison of Chinese and American sense of space. In the left column, list
details the author provides about Chinese attitudes; in the right column, list
corresponding American attitudes.

**Sense of Space**    Example answers:

| Chinese Attitudes | American Attitudes |
| --- | --- |
| Enclosed | Vistas |
| Calm | Future |
| Order | Social mobility |
| Nostalgia | Optimism |
| Stability | |
| Rootedness | |

**Think Critically**  Tuan describes both benefits and problems with the Chinese
perception of space. What benefits and problems does he describe for the American
perception? How would you summarize the primary message of the essay?

Answers will vary.

_____

_____

_____

_____

_____

_____

**Write**  Write an essay about a place that you know well that has changed
significantly over time—perhaps your home, your neighborhood, a favorite
business, a school you attended, or some other location. Compare the place then
(in the past) to the place now (today). Answers will vary.

## About the Author

Neil Bissoondath is a journalist and author who was born in Trinidad and later immigrated to Canada. In this essay, he explores his own spiritual experience following his mother's death, comparing and contrasting it with religious faith (and glancingly with scientific certainty).

Neil Bissoondath, "Religious Faith Versus Spirituality," Flachmann/Flachmann/MacLennan, Reader's Choice, Fifth Canadian Edition, Pearson Education Canada, 0131979760.

# Religious Faith Versus Spirituality
## by Neil Bissoondath

*Wait till someone you love dies. You'll see. You'll know God exists. You'll want* 1
*Him to.* The prediction, repeated with minimal variation through the years by believers challenged by my nonbelief, was never offered as a promise but as a vague threat, and always with a sense of satisfied superiority, as if the speakers relished the thought that one day I would get my **comeuppance**. 5

They were, without exception, enthusiastic practitioners of their respective faiths—Roman Catholics, Presbyterians, Hindus, Muslims, God-fearing people all. Which was, to me, precisely the problem: Why all this fear?

And then one day, without warning, my mother died. Hers was the first death to touch me to the quick. Her cremation was done in the traditional Hindu 10 manner. Under the direction of a **pundit**, my brother and I performed the ceremony, preparing the body with our bare hands, a contact more intimate than we'd ever had when she was alive.

As I walked away from her flaming **pyre**, I felt myself soaring with a lightness I'd never known before. I was suddenly freed from days of physical and emotional 15 **lassitude**, and felt my first inkling of the healing power of ritual, the solace that ceremony can bring.

Still, despite the pain and the unspeakable sense of loss, the oft-predicted discovery of faith eluded me. I remained, as I do today, a nonbeliever, but I have no doubt that I underwent a deeply spiritual experience. This was when I began to 20 understand that religious faith and spirituality do not necessarily have anything to do with each other—not that they are incompatible but that they are often mutually exclusive.

Western civilization has spent two thousand years blurring the distinction between the two, and as we enter the third millennium we are hardly more at 25 peace with ourselves than people were a thousand years ago. Appreciating the distinction could help soothe our anxieties about the days to come.

Spirituality is the individual's ability to wonder at, and delight in, the

### Vocabulary

**comeuppance**
deserved repayment for a wrong attitude

**pundit**
a Hindu scholar or "wise man"

**pyre**
a pile of wood for cremating a body

**lassitude**
weariness, fatigue, or lethargy

indecipherable, like a baby marveling at the wiggling of its own toes. It is to be
30 at ease with speculation, asking the unanswerable question and accepting that any answer would necessarily be incomplete, even false. It is recognizing that if scientific inquiry has inevitable limits, so too do religious explanations, which base themselves on unquestioning acceptance of the unprovable: neither can ever fully satisfy.

35     A sense of the spiritual comes from staring deep into the formation of a rose or a **hibiscus** and being astonished at the intricate delicacy of its symmetry without needing to see behind its perfection of form the fashioning hand of a deity.

    It comes from watching your child being born and gazing for the first time
40 into those newly opened eyes, from holding that child against your chest and feeling his or her heartbeat melding with yours.

    It comes from gazing up into the sparkling solitude of a clear midnight sky, secure in the knowledge that, no matter how alone you may feel at moments, the message of the stars appears to be that you most **indisputably** are not.

45     At such moments, you need no **dogma** to tell you that the world seen or unseen, near or distant, is a wonderful and mysterious place. Spirituality, then, requires neither science nor religion, both of which hunger after answers and reassurance—while the essence of spirituality lies in the opening up of the individual to dazzlement. Spirituality **entails** no worship.

50     At the very moment of my mother's cremation, her brother, trapped thousands of miles away in England by airline schedules, got out his photographs of her and spread them on his coffee table. He reread her old letters and spent some time meditating on the life that had been lived—his way, at the very moment flames consumed her body, of celebrating the life and saying farewell, his way of engaging with the spiritual.

**Analyze** Complete the T-graph to analyze Bissoondath's comparison of faith and spirituality. In the left column list details about faith; in the right list details about spirituality.   Answers will vary.

| Religious Faith | Spirituality |
|---|---|
| | |
| | |
| | |
| | |

**Think Critically** How does science fit into Bissoondath's essay? Where would you place it in the T-graph above? How does your placement reflect on your own experiences with science and with religion?

  Answers will vary.

_____

_____

_____

**Vocabulary**

**hibiscus**
a type of shrub or tree with large flowers

**indisputably**
without question; unable to be disputed

**dogma**
an official doctrine concerning faith or religion

**entail**
to involve or require

## About the Author

Llewellyn H. Rockwell, Jr., is chairman of the Ludwig von Mises Institute, a think tank devoted to libertarian political and social theory. He served as Congressman Ron Paul's chief of staff from 1978-1982.

Llewellyn H. Rockwell, Jr., "Two Views on Social Order: Conflict or Cooperation?" http://mises.org/daily/2612.

# From "Two Views on Social Order: Conflict or Cooperation?" by Llewellyn H. Rockwell, Jr.

There are two clear and present dangers to liberty in America. One is known as the Left, and the other is known as the Right. They are dangerous because they seek to use government to mold society into a form they seek, rather than the form that liberty achieves if society is left on its own. 1

I'm going to assume that the Left and the Right come to their views sincerely, that their passion for using government is driven by some fear that the absence of government would yield **catastrophe**. So the burden of my talk today will be to identify and explain the common thread that connects the worldview of the Left and the Right, and suggest that they are both wrong about the capacity of society, whether it is defined locally or internationally, to manage itself. . . . 5 10

After the [American] revolution, when government began to regroup and **reconsolidate**, . . . the liberal idea [of pure liberty] began to gain **detractors**. John Adams, whom Jefferson beat in the great presidential election of 1800, never stopped resenting Jefferson's suspicions toward power and opposition to practically everything the federal government wanted to do. It was Jefferson's conviction that liberty yielded social cooperation; it was Adams's view that liberty could only be established and sustained through government authority. These two opposing views persist to this day. 15

Adams went so far as to level a familiar accusation against Jefferson's faith in pure liberty. Adams wrote him in 1813: 20

"You never felt the terrorism of Shays' Rebellion in Massachusetts . . . You certainly never felt the terrorism excited by Genet in 1793, when ten thousand people in the streets of Philadelphia, day by day, threatened to drag Washington out of his house and effect a revolution in the government. . . . I have no doubt you were fast asleep in philosophical tranquility when . . . Market Street was as full of men as could stand by one another, and even before my door when some of my **domestics**, in frenzy, determined to sacrifice their lives in my defence. . . . What think you of terrorism, Mr. Jefferson?" 25

## Vocabulary

**catastrophe**
a terrible disaster

**reconsolidate**
to bring scattered elements back together

**detractor**
someone who insults or argues against

**domestic**
a household servant

. . . What Adams conveniently overlooked is that the rebellion of which he
spoke was actually sparked by taxation and government-backed credit expansion.
There would have been no need for a revolt had government not created the
conditions that led to it. . . . From Shays' Rebellion to 9-11, we see two worldviews
of society at work. One sees the government as a source of liberty and order, and
fears society without the state more than any conceivable alternative. The other
sees government as a source of disorder that uses that disorder to enhance its
power and material resources at the expense of society. . . .

The Left and the Right in this country hold to the first view. The **successors** to
Jefferson hold to the second view, which in Jefferson's time was called the liberal
view, and which today is called the libertarian view. . . .

Let us begin with the Left. They believe society has fundamental flaws and
deep-rooted conflicts that keep it in some sort of structural imbalance. All these
conflicts and **disequilibria** cry out for government fixes, for leftists are certain that
there is no social problem that a good dose of power can't solve.

If the conflicts they want are not there, they make them up. They look at
what appears to be a happy **suburban subdivision** and see pathology. They see an
apparently happy marriage and imagine that it is a mask for abuse. They see a
thriving church and think the people inside are being manipulated by a **cynical**
and corrupt pastor. Their view of the economic system is the same. They see poor
peasants in the Third World drinking a Coke or making Nikes, and they cry foul.
They figure that prices don't reflect reality but instead are set by large players.
There is a power imbalance at the heart of every exchange, domestically and
internationally. The labor contract is a **veneer** that covers exploitation.

To the brooding leftist, it is inconceivable that people can work out their
own problems, that trade can be to people's mutual advantage, that society can be
essentially self-managing, or that attempts to use government power to reshape
and manage people might backfire. Their faith in government knows few limits;
their faith in people is thin or nonexistent. This is why they are a danger to
liberty.

The remarkable fact about the conflict theory of society held by the Left
is that it ends up creating more of the very **pathologies** that they believe have
been there from the beginning. The surest way to drive a wedge between labor
and **capital** is to regulate the labor markets to the point that people cannot make
voluntary trades. Both sides begin to fear each other. It is the same with relations
between races, sexes, the abled and disabled, and any other groups you can name.
It is the same with international relations. A **tariff** or trade sanction is nothing but
war by another means. The best path to creating conflict where none need exist is
to put a government bureaucracy in charge. . . .

The traditional and correct answer to the conflict theory is that there is
essentially nothing government can do to improve the workings of society. During
the Great Depression, for example, most everyone on the Left thought that
government was the only way out. The hard Left favored communist revolution.
The soft Left favored the New Deal. The old liberals pointed out that it was

**successor**
person who takes a position
after someone else

**disequilibria**
lack of balance

**suburban subdivision**
a section of housing outside
of a city

**cynical**
distrustful

**veneer**
a thin covering to hide a
rough inner surface

**pathology**
study of disease, or diseased
condition

**capital**
money and other such
resources

**tariff**
a tax on imported goods,
specifically to raise their price

government itself that brought about the crisis, and that more government intervention could only make matters worse. This was a rational response, but it did not carry the day. 75

After the Second World War, we saw the emergence of a strange creature in American life, something that called itself conservatism. It was opposed to the Left in American life, particularly that branch that was sympathetic to communism. It counseled vague solutions like **prudence** in public affairs. But in a crucial way, it adopted one **tenet** of the leftist worldview: it rejected old liberalism as a vision 80 for how society can work in the absence of government. It adopted a conflict view of society, a different brand rooted in the **assertions** of Hobbes rather than Marx. The idea that conflict was at the very heart of society, absent government, was a key aspect of this view.

This new thing called conservatism adopted some of the **rhetoric** of the Old 85 Right. It defended property and enterprise in economic affairs. But what was critical was the introduction of a notion that society, if left to its own devices, would collapse into chaos. This was particularly true in international affairs. So while the Cold War was originally an invention of the Democrat Harry Truman, it was tailor-made to appeal to conservatives who were looking for an ideological 90 enemy to slay. It is one thing to say that communism is an evil **ideological** system; it is another to say that we cannot rest until every communist is killed and every communist government wiped off the face of the earth.

What happened to the **noninterventionist** views of the Old Right? They were **predicated** on the idea that there could be a leaderless world order, that nations 95 could get along without one overarching authority and source of law. But after the war, that too began to change. A new conviction arose.

Russell Kirk wrote in 1954 that "civilized society requires distinctions of order, wealth, and responsibility; it cannot exist without true leadership . . . society longs for just leadership. . . ." He contrasted this view with what he considered the 100 **erroneous** opinion of Ludwig von Mises, whom he attacks over the course of many pages. Mises, wrote Kirk, had exaggerated faith in the rationality of individuals. Kirk, in contrast, sees that all of history is governed by two great forces: love and hate. Neither are rational impulses. In order to achieve the triumph of love over hate, wrote Kirk, the conservative "looks upon government as a great power for 105 good."

And so conservatives threw themselves behind the force of government to achieve their aims, and no matter how many wicked things government did over the years under conservative control, they always told themselves that it was surely better than the much-feared alternative of an unmanaged society. . . . 110

At the end of the Cold War, many conservatives panicked that there would be no more great causes into which the state could enlist itself. There were about 10 years of books that sought to **demonize** someone, somewhere, in the hope of creating a new enemy. Maybe it would be China. Maybe it would be the culture war. Maybe it should be drugs. From their point of view, 9-11 presented the 115 opportunity they needed, and thus began the newest unwinnable war: the Global War on Terror.

So must government rule every aspect of life until every last terrorist is wiped off the face of the earth? Must we surrender all our liberty and property to 120 this cause, as the regime and its apologists suggest?

This view of society is certainly not sustainable in these times or in the future. Ever more of daily life consists in **seceding** from the state and its **apparatus** of edicts and regulations. In the online world, billions of deals are made every day that require virtually no government law to enforce. The technology that is 125 pushing the world forward is not created by the state but by private enterprise. The places we shop and the communities in which we live are being created by private developers. Most businesses prefer to deal with private courts. We depend on insurance companies, not police, to reduce the risks in life. We secure our homes and workplaces through private firms.

130 What's more, these days we see all around us how liberty generates order and how this order is self-sustaining. We benefit daily, hourly, minute by minute, from an order that is not imposed from without but rather generated from within, by that remarkable capacity we have for pursuing self-interest while benefiting the whole. Here is the great mystery and majesty of social order, expressed so well 135 in the act of economic exchange.

I've spoken about the problem of those who look at society and see nothing but conflict and no prospect for cooperation. It is a view shared by the Left and the Right. Truly there is an actual conflict at the root of history, but it is not the one most people understand or see. It is the great struggle between freedom and 140 **despotism**, between the individual and the state, between the voluntary means and **coercion**. We know where we stand. We stand with the future of freedom.

Gary Hathaway,2010 / Used under license from Shutterstock.com

**Analyze** Complete the following Venn diagram. In the center section, list similarities between the Left and Right. In the outer sections, list details unique to that subject. **Answers will vary.**

Left                    Right

Similarities

**Evaluate** Write a paragraph explaining in what ways you believe the author is correct. Then write one explaining in what ways you believe he is incorrect. Finally, write a concluding paragraph that summarizes your response to the essay.

**Answers will vary.**

_____

_____

_____

_____

_____

_____

_____

_____

**Read Further** Visit the mises.org Web site to read the full essay. Does the additional material there change your understanding of this issue? Explain why or why not. (Use your own paper.) **Answers will vary.**

# LO2 Writing a Comparison-Contrast Essay

**Prewrite** To begin writing, you need a topic. Using an "essentials of life" checklist like the one below, choose a topic that suggests two subjects to compare. For example, "clothing" might suggest comparing the way two friends dress. Similarly, "technology" might suggest comparing the merits of two different cell phones, or even two different cell-phone plans. Use the list as a springboard for your own ideas.    Answers will vary.

## Essentials of Life Checklist

| Clothing | Goals | Community |
|---|---|---|
| Housing | Measurement | Arts |
| Food | Machines | Faith |
| Education | Intelligence | Commerce |
| Family | Agriculture | Heat |
| Friends | Environment | Laws |
| Love | Plant life | Science |
| Senses | Property | Technology |
| Energy | Health | Work |
| Entertainment | Medicine | Hobbies |
| Recreation | Books | Public service |
| Personality | Tools | Natural resources |
| Communication | Exercise | Personal rights |

**WAC**

As this checklist shows, comparing and contrasting are applicable in all subjects and all parts of life.

In each lettered space, write a topic of your choice from the checklist above. Then, below each topic, list two subjects to compare.

**A. Topic**

| Subject 1: | Subject 2: |
|---|---|
| | |

**B. Topic**

| Subject 1: | Subject 2: |
|---|---|
| | |

**C. Topic**

| Subject 1: | Subject 2: |
|---|---|
| | |

**Prewrite** Complete the Venn diagram below. Write your two subjects on the lines provided. In the center section, list similarities between the two subjects. In each outer section, list details that are unique to that subject.

Answers will vary.

Similarities

**Speaking & Listening**

Make sure to share your writing with a classmate. Read your essay aloud to the person, and then discuss the work together. Switch roles and have your partner read her or his writing. Discuss it. Provide positive, helpful feedback.

Choose three or more points to compare and contrast. Then choose a pattern of organization. Use a point-by-point pattern, a subject-to-subject pattern, or a similarities-and-differences pattern.

| Point-by-Point | | Subject-to-Subject | Similarities-Differences |
|---|---|---|---|
| Beginning | | Beginning | Beginning |
| Point 1 | Subject 1 | | Similarities |
| | Subject 2 | Subject 1 | |
| Point 2 | Subject 1 | | |
| | Subject 2 | | Differences |
| Point 3 | Subject 1 | Subject 2 | |
| | Subject 2 | | |
| Ending | | Ending | Ending |

**Draft** Create a strong opening, middle, and closing for your essay. Use the supports below as you create each part. Answers will vary.

## Opening Paragraph

Capture your reader's attention in the first line of your essay. Then lead up to your thesis statement. Here is a formula to use as you create your thesis statement.

- **Make a statement:** The barrio of my youth is vanishing.
- **Ask a question:** Why is it that we can never go home again?
- **Use a quotation:** "I've seen this neighborhood change—twice."

**Two Subjects**

> Print books and e-books

**+**

**Thought or Feeling**

> though different, both have their own conveniences

**=**

**Thesis Statement**

> Although some people think reading print books or e-books is an either/or decision, both are convenient at different times and places.

**Two Subjects**

+ **Thought or Feeling** _____

_____

_____

_____

**= Thesis Statement**

_____

_____

_____

_____

## Middle Paragraphs

In the middle paragraphs, compare the two subjects, using your organizational pattern. Also use transitions to help the reader follow your ideas:

**Transitions That Compare**

| | | | | | |
|---|---|---|---|---|---|
| as | as well | also | both | in the same way | much as |
| much like | one way | like | likewise | similarly | |

**Transitions That Contrast**

| | | | |
|---|---|---|---|
| although | even though | by contrast | but |
| on the one hand | on the other hand | otherwise | though |
| still | while | yet | however |

## Closing Paragraph

In your closing, share a final thought, pointing out a key similarity or difference between the subjects you have compared.

**Revise** Improve your writing. First ask a classmate to read your essay. Then discuss your work, using the following checklist. Continue making improvements until you can answer "yes" to each question.

**Ideas**

☐ **1.** Do I compare and contrast two subjects?

☐ **2.** Do I include a variety of details (facts, quotations, anecdotes)?

**Organization**

☐ **3.** Do I introduce my subjects in the opening?

☐ **4.** Have I used a pattern of organization in the middle part?

☐ **5.** Have I used transitions to connect my sentences?

☐ **6.** Do I share a final thought about the comparison in my ending?

**Voice**

☐ **7.** Do I sound knowledgeable and interested in my subjects?

**Edit** Prepare a clean copy of your essay and use the following checklist to check for errors. When you can answer "yes" to a question, check it off. Continue working until all items are checked.

**Words**

☐ **1.** Do I use correct verb forms (*he saw,* not *he seen*)? (See page 356.)

☐ **2.** Do my subjects and verbs agree (*she speaks,* not *she speak*)? (See pages 282–291.)

☐ **3.** Have I used the right words (*there, their, they're*)?

**Sentences**

☐ **4.** Have I avoided sentence fragments? (See pages 297–302.)

☐ **5.** Have I avoided run-on sentences? (See pages 306–310.)

☐ **6.** Have I avoided improper shifts in sentences? (See pages 314–315.)

**Conventions**

☐ **7.** Have I used commas after long introductory word groups? (See page 396.)

☐ **8.** Have I capitalized first words? (See page 414.)

☐ **9.** Have I capitalized proper nouns and proper adjectives? (See page 414.)

☐ **10.** Have I carefully checked my spelling?

> "The ultimate result of shielding men from the effects of
> folly is to fill the world with fools."
> —Herbert Spencer

James Steidl.,2010 / Used under license from Shutterstock.com

# 39

# Cause-Effect Essays

Set a match to a fuse, and sparks will fly. Let that fuse ignite a stick of dynamite, and the resulting explosion can cause much weightier things to fly—earth, stone, brick, and so on. That simple match becomes the cause of tremendous destruction.

If the explosion was set to bring down a wall of salt in a mine, however, this single destructive act can result in much good—ice melted from winter roads, foods preserved, and meals seasoned, just to name a few benefits.

Match to fuse, fuse to dynamite, explosion to a harvest of salt, salt to roads and foods—each step involves a cause-effect relationship. In this chapter, you will read about several more such relationships and be called upon to evaluate their significance.

## Learning Outcomes

**LO1** Understand, read, and analyze cause-effect essays.

**LO2** Write your own cause-effect essay.

## What do you think?

Study the image and quotation. What does each say to you about cause and effect?

Answers will vary.

# LO1 Understanding Cause-Effect Essays

Within this chapter you will find three example essays using a cause-effect approach. You will also find questions and graphic organizers you can use as tools to help analyze each reading. At the end of the chapter are writing guidelines for creating a cause-effect essay of your own.

**SQ3R** When you read, become involved with the text by using the SQ3R approach.

- **Survey:** Prepare by reading "About the Author," skimming the essay, and noting any vocabulary words.
- **Question:** Ask yourself what cause-and-effect relationships you predict from the essay.
- **Read:** Read the essay, noting the causes leading to or effects resulting from the main topic.
- **Recite:** Recite the main details of the cause-and-effect relationship the author provides.
- **Review:** Answer the questions provided and use the graphic organizers to help you analyze the essay.

## Essay List:

**"Yes, Accidents Happen. But Why?":** Robert Strauss discusses the difficulties in determining the causes behind traffic accidents.

**"Spanglish Spoken Here":** Janice Castro describes the way in which the Spanish language is merging with English in the United States, creating a unique blend of the two.

**"Why Schools Don't Educate":** New York State Teacher of the Year John Taylor Gatto argues that our modern school system fails our society by turning out students who are disconnected from the real world.

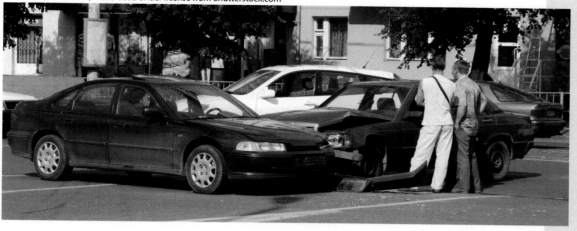

**About the Author**

Robert Strauss is a journalist whose work has appeared in the *New York Times, Los Angeles Times, Washington Post, Sports Illustrated,* and *Fortune,* among other places. He is also a member of the creative-writing faculty at the University of Pennsylvania.

Robert Strauss, "Yes, Accidents Happen. But Why?" New York Times, October 24, 2007.

## Yes, Accidents Happen. But Why?
### by Robert Strauss

1    When Fred Mannering takes his **vintage** MG sports car out for a spin, he always leaves plenty of room between the car in front of him and the MG. He brakes slowly and deliberately. He rarely speeds, and if he were to go fast, it would be only on a superhighway with little traffic.

5    "My other car is newer, with good antilock brakes and air bags, so I don't take nearly as much care," said Dr. Mannering, a Purdue University professor of **civil engineering** who studies the causes and results of traffic accidents. In that way, he may reflect the behavior of the average driver, governed by hard-to-quantify influences.

10    Dr. Mannering's study of accidents in Washington State from 1992 to 1997, a period during which air bags and antilock brakes became prevalent, showed that counter to what would seem logical, there was no major reduction in accidents even with the spread of two seemingly effective safety features.

    "It just shows how hard it is to determine what causes an accident," he
15    said. "The one thing you might conclude—it's called an offset hypothesis—is that people have an acceptance of a level of safety. If they felt safer because of the air bags and brakes, then maybe they drove faster or switched the radio on and off more to, so to speak, **compensate**.

    "What seems like an exact science—determining who or what causes
20    accidents—is actually quite difficult," Dr. Mannering said.

    Insurance companies, carmakers, inventors, safety advocates and clearly drivers themselves all have an interest in learning about what might reduce the number of accidents or at least make them less severe. Yet there is surprisingly little data to help them.

25    "Speeding causes crashes," said Anne McCartt, senior vice president for research at the Insurance Institute for Highway Safety, a nonprofit group financed by auto insurers. "Running through a red light causes crashes. Drinking alcohol certainly causes crashes, but to what extent? That has been difficult to determine."

30    Rob Foss, a senior research scientist at the University of North Carolina

**Vocabulary**

**vintage**
valuable due to its age; classic

**civil engineering**
the design of public works such as roads and bridges

**compensate**
balance out or make up for

Highway Safety Research Center, confirmed the **elusive** nature of pinpointing the causes. "I guess all we can safely say we know with certainty is that virtually all crashes are caused by a series of things coming together all at once," he said. "Driving after you have too much to drink is dangerous, but, strangely, we don't know how much, despite laws that have alcohol limits. Many people take trips after having too much to drink and manage to get home." 35

Part of the problem stems from the limitations of researchers' information. Often they depend on police reports, which can be reliable for some things, like what kind of car is involved or the extent of injuries. But other factors—like distractions— may not exist in police reports. A driver is unlikely, for one, to tell an officer that he was using a cellphone, especially if he thinks it will increase his liability. 40

"Putting in place a good crash investigation and maintaining good data for these kinds of analyses is complicated and thus expensive," said Peter Kissinger, chief executive of the AAA Foundation for Traffic Safety. "It's not the kind of thing which a political leader in a state has the patience to see through. They would rather put some money for roads as opposed to investing in something as unsexy as maintaining a good crash **database**." 45

The Strategic Highway Research Program at the National Academy of Sciences may change that. The program will gather raw data from about 1,000 cars equipped with minicameras, motion-detection sensors and other devices to monitor cars and their drivers. The program expands a pilot study done at Virginia Tech University. 50

The Virginia study came to some **preliminary** conclusions:

- Nearly 80 percent of crashes and 65 percent of near crashes were caused by distractions that made the driver look away for up to three seconds. 55
- Drivers ages 18 to 20 were up to four times more likely to have an **inattention**-related accident than older drivers.
- Driver drowsiness was involved in 20 percent of all crashes.
- All 14 of the rear-end crashes in the study happened when the lead car was stopped. 60

"For the last 30 years, the emphasis has been on injury prevention and modification of vehicles because that seemed to be where the payoff was," said Dr. Kenneth Campbell, chief program officer for safety at the Strategic Highway Research Program, who will direct the five-year study. "That has slowed." He said that traffic fatalities in the United States have remained at about 40,000 a year for the last decade or so. 65

"Now the technology is available to separate out things like alcohol use and different kinds of distractions, and the condition in which people keep a car and all sorts of variables," he said. "It is long in coming, but soon we'll know what really does cause car accidents." 70

**Analyze** This essay includes two separate cause-effect relationships. The first suggests reasons (causes) for crashes (the effect); the second describes difficulties (causes) in drawing firm conclusions (an effect).

Make a list of suspected causes for crashes. Next, make a list of reasons those causes are so difficult to pin down. Number the items in each list by supposed order of importance. Write a journal entry describing your thoughts about the subject.

## Vocabulary

**elusive**
difficult to track

**database**
a computer file that organizes information for easy searching and reference

**preliminary**
initial, prior to a full set

**inattention**
lack of attention, distractedness

472

**About the Author**

Janice Castro is an assistant professor at Northwestern University's journalism school. She served as a reporter, a writer, and an editor at *Time Magazine* for over 20 years and has freelanced for many other publications.

Janice Castro,"Spanglish Spoken Here,"Time, July 11, 1988.

## Spanglish Spoken Here
## by Janice Castro

1    In Manhattan a first-grader greets her visiting grandparents, happily exclaiming, "Come here, sientate!" Her bemused grandfather, who does not speak Spanish, nevertheless knows she is asking him to sit down. A Miami personnel officer understands what a job applicant means when he says, "Quiero un part 
5    time." Nor do drivers miss a beat reading a billboard alongside a Los Angeles street advertising CERVEZA—SIX-PACK!

This free-form blend of Spanish and English, known as Spanglish, is common **linguistic** currency wherever concentrations of Hispanic Americans are found in the U.S. In Los Angeles, where 55 percent of the city's 3 million inhabitants 
10    speak Spanish, Spanglish is as much a part of daily life as sunglasses. Unlike the broken-English efforts of earlier immigrants from Europe, Asia and other regions, Spanglish has become a widely accepted conversational mode used casually—even playfully—by Spanish-speaking immigrants and native-born Americans alike.

Consisting of one part **Hispanicized** English, one part Americanized Spanish 
15    and more than a little fractured **syntax**, Spanglish is a bit like a Robin Williams comedy routine: a crackling line of cross-cultural **patter** straight from the melting pot. Often it enters Anglo homes and families through the children, who pick it up at school or at play with their young Hispanic contemporaries. In other cases, it comes from watching TV; many an **Anglo** child watching Sesame Street has 
20    learned *uno dos tres* almost as quickly as one two three.

Spanglish takes a variety of forms, from the Southern California Anglos who bid farewell with the utterly silly "hasta la bye-bye" to the Cuban-American drivers in Miami who *parquean* their *carros*. Some Spanglish sentences are mostly Spanish, with a quick detour for an English word or two. A **Latino** friend 
25    may cut short a conversation by glancing at his watch and excusing himself with the explanation that he must "ir al supermarket."

Many of the English words transplanted in this way are simply handier than their Spanish counterparts. No matter how distasteful the subject, for example, it is still easier to say "income tax" than *impuesto sobre la renta*. At the same time, 
30    many Spanish-speaking immigrants have adopted such terms as VCR, microwave

### Vocabulary

**linguistic**
concerning languages

**Hispanic**
a person of Latin American (see page 474) descent living in the USA

**syntax**
the ordering of words into phrases and sentences.

**patter**
rapid speech

**Anglo**
a Caucasian living in the USA

**Latino**
See "Hispanic," above.

## Insight

Do you speak a hybrid language? Which languages are combined? Where do you use this hybrid?

and dishwasher for what they view as largely American phenomena. Still other English words convey a cultural context that is not **implicit** in the Spanish. A friend who invites you to *lonche* most likely has in mind the brisk American custom of "doing lunch" rather than the **languorous** afternoon break traditionally implied by *almuerzo*. 35

Mainstream Americans exposed to similar **hybrids** of German, Chinese or Hindi might be mystified. But even Anglos who speak little or no Spanish are somewhat familiar with Spanglish. Living among them, for one thing, are 19 million Hispanics. In addition, more American high school and university students sign up for Spanish than for any other foreign language. 40

Only in the past ten years, though, has Spanglish begun to turn into a national slang. Its popularity has grown with the explosive increases in U.S. immigration from **Latin American** countries. English has increasingly collided with Spanish in retail stores, offices and classrooms, in pop music and on street corners. Anglos whose ancestors picked up such Spanish words as *rancho, bronco,* 45 *tornado* and *incommunicado*, for instance, now freely use such Spanish words as *gracias, bueno, amigo* and *por favor*.

Among Latinos, Spanglish conversations often flow easily from Spanish into several sentences of English and back again. "It is done unconsciously," explains Carmen Silva-Corvalan, a Chilean-born associate professor of linguistics at the 50 University of Southern California, who speaks Spanglish with relatives and neighbors. "I couldn't even tell you minutes later if I said something in Spanish or in English."

Spanglish is a sort of code for Latinos: the speakers know Spanish, but their hybrid language reflects the American culture in which they live. Many lean to 55 shorter, clipped phrases in place of the longer, more graceful expressions their parents used. Says Leonel de la Cuesta, an assistant professor of modern languages at Florida International University in Miami: "In the U.S., time is money, and that is showing up in Spanglish as an economy of language." Conversational examples: *taipiar* (type) and *winshi-wiper* (windshield wiper) replace *escribir a maquina* 60 and *limpiaparabrisas*.

Major advertisers, eager to tap the estimated $134 billion in spending power wielded by Spanish-speaking Americans, have ventured into Spanglish to promote their products. In some cases, attempts to sprinkle Spanish through commercials have produced embarrassing **gaffes**. A Braniff airlines ad that sought 65 to tell Spanish-speaking audiences they could settle back *en* (in) luxuriant *cuero* (leather) seats, for example, inadvertently said they could fly without clothes (*encuero*).

A fractured translation of the Miller Lite slogan told readers the beer was "Filling, and less delicious." Similar **blunders** are often made by Anglos trying to 70 impress Spanish-speaking pals. But if Latinos are amused by mangled Spanglish, they also recognize these goofs as a sort of friendly acceptance. As they might put it, *no problema*.

## Vocabulary

**implicit**
clearly conveyed, though not directly expressed

**languorous**
slow and relaxed

**hybrid**
a mixture from two or more backgrounds

**Latin America**
all of the Americas south of the USA

**gaffe**
an ignorant or careless mistake in language

**blunder**
a foolish or clumsy error

**Analyze** Which of these cause/effect diagrams best illustrates the essay? Why?

Cause ↘
Cause → Effect
Cause ↗

Cause ↗ Effect
Cause → Effect
↘ Effect

Answers will vary.

**Explain** What is the main effect or main cause in the essay?

The main effect is the hybridization of Spanish and English.

**Analyze** How do the details of the essay proceed from that cause or lead to that effect?

Specific examples are given to explain where and why Spanglish occurs. Examples of where include Manhattan, Los Angeles, Miami, and other areas of Hispanic population. Examples of why include children's exposure to both languages, the "economy of language" of "income tax" versus *impuesto sobre la renta*," Hispanic adoption of American culture, and advertising adopting Spanish terms.

**Reflect** How does Spanglish, or the melding of other languages, affect your own life? In what ways is Spanglish unique from other meldings or similar to them?

Answers will vary.

## About the Author

New York State Teacher of the Year, and three-time NYC Teacher of the Year, John Taylor Gatto held a variety of jobs— including Army medic, scriptwriter, and audio publisher—before beginning to teach. He is now a public speaker on the topic of education.

John Taylor Gatto, "Why Schools Don't Educate," Acceptance speech for New York City Teacher of the Year Award, January 31, 1990.

## Why Schools Don't Educate
## by John Taylor Gatto

I accept this award on behalf of all the fine teachers I've known over the years who've struggled to make their transactions with children honorable ones: men and women who are never **complacent**, always questioning, always wrestling to define and redefine endlessly what the word education should mean. A "Teacher of the Year" is not the best teacher around—those people are too quiet to be easily uncovered—but a standard-bearer, symbolic of these private people who spend their lives gladly in the service of children. This is their award as well as mine.

We live in a time of great social crisis. Our children rank at the bottom of nineteen industrial nations in reading, writing, and arithmetic. The world's narcotic economy is based upon our own consumption of this commodity. If we didn't buy so many powdered dreams, the business would collapse—and schools are an important sales outlet. Our teenage-suicide rate is the highest in the world—and suicidal kids are rich kids for the most part, not poor. In Manhattan, 70 percent of all new marriages last less than five years.

Our school crisis is a reflection of this greater social crisis. We seem to have lost our identity. Children and old people are penned up and locked away from the business of the world to an **unprecedented** degree; nobody talks to them anymore. Without children and old people mixing in daily life, a community has no future and no past, only a continuous present. In fact, the term "community" hardly applies to the way we interact with each other. We live in networks, not communities, and everyone I know is lonely because of that. In some strange way, school is a major actor in this tragedy, just as it is a major actor in the widening gulfs among social classes. Using school as a sorting mechanism, we appear to be on the way to creating a **caste system**, complete with untouchables who wander through subway trains begging and sleep on the streets.

I've noticed a fascinating phenomenon in my twenty-nine years of teaching— that schools and schooling are increasingly **irrelevant** to the great **enterprises** of

1

5

10

15

20

25

the planet. No one believes anymore that scientists are trained in science classes, or politicians in civics classes, or poets in English classes. The truth is that schools
30 don't really teach anything except how to obey orders. This is a great mystery to me, because thousands of humane, caring people work in schools as teachers and aides and administrators, but the abstract logic of the institution overwhelms their individual contributions. Although teachers do care and do work very, very hard, the institution is psychopathic; it has no conscience. It rings a bell, and the
35 young man in the middle of writing a poem must close his notebook and move to a different cell, where he learns that humans and monkeys derive from a common ancestor.

Our form of compulsory schooling is an invention of the state of Massachusetts, from around 1850. It was resisted—sometimes with guns—by an estimated 80
40 percent of the Massachusetts population, with the last outpost, in Barnstable on Cape Cod, not surrendering its children until the 1880s, when the area was seized by the militia and the children marched to school under guard.

Now, here is a curious idea to ponder: Senator Ted Kennedy's office released a paper not too long ago claiming that prior to compulsory education the state
45 literacy rate was 98 percent, and after it the figure never again climbed above 91 percent, where it stands in 1990. I hope that interests you.

Here is another curiosity to think about: The home-schooling movement has quietly grown to a size where 1.5 million young people are being educated entirely by their own parents. Last month the education press reported the amazing news
50 that children schooled at home seem to be five, or even ten years ahead of their formally trained peers in their ability to think.

I don't think we'll get rid of schools any time soon, certainly not in my lifetime, but if we're going to change what's rapidly becoming a disaster of ignorance, we need to realize that the institution "schools" very well, but it does not "educate";
55 that's inherent in the design of the thing. It's not the fault of bad teachers or too little money spent. It's just impossible for education and schooling to be the same thing.

Schools were designed by Horace Mann and Barnas Sears and W. R. Harper of the University of Chicago and Edward Thorndike of Columbia Teachers College
60 and others to be instruments for the scientific management of a mass population. Schools are intended to produce, through the application of formulas, formulaic human beings whose behavior can be predicted and controlled.

To a very great extent, schools succeed in doing this. But our society is disintegrating, and in such a society, the only successful people are self-reliant,
65 confident, and individualistic—because the community life that protects the dependent and weak is dead. The products of schooling are, as I've said, irrelevant. Well-schooled people are irrelevant. They can sell film and razor blades, push paper and talk on telephones, or sit mindlessly before a flickering computer terminal, but as human beings they are useless—useless to others and useless
70 to themselves.

## Vocabulary

**humane**
compassionate, sympathetic

**institution**
an established organization, system, or practice

**psychopathic**
mentally ill

**compulsory**
mandatory, enforced

The daily misery around us is, I think, in large measure caused by the fact that—as social critic Paul Goodman put it thirty years ago—we force children to grow up **absurd**. Any reform in schooling has to deal with school's absurdities.

It is absurd and anti-life to be part of a system that compels you to sit in confinement with only people of exactly the same age and social class. The system effectively cuts you off from the immense diversity of life and the **synergy** of variety. It cuts you off from your own past and future, sealing you in a continuous present, much the same way television does.

It is absurd and anti-life to be part of a system that compels you to listen to a stranger reading poetry when you want to learn to construct buildings, or to sit with a stranger discussing the construction of buildings when you want to read poetry.

It is absurd and anti-life to move from cell to cell at the sound of a gong for every day of your youth, in an institution that allows you no privacy and even follows you into the **sanctuary** of your home, demanding that you do its "homework."

"How will they learn to read?" you say, and my answer is: "Remember the lessons of Massachusetts." When children are given whole lives instead of age-graded ones in cell blocks, they learn to read, write, and do arithmetic with ease, if those things make sense in the life that unfolds around them.

But keep in mind that in the United States almost nobody who reads, writes, or does arithmetic gets much respect. We are a land of talkers; we pay talkers the most and admire talkers the most, and so our children talk constantly, following the public models of television and schoolteachers. It is very difficult to teach "the basics" anymore, because they really aren't basic to the society we've made.

Two institutions at present control our children's lives: television and schooling, in that order. Both reduce the real world of wisdom, **fortitude**, **temperance**, and justice to a never-ending, nonstop abstraction. In centuries past, the time of a child or adolescent would be occupied in real work, real charity, real adventure, and the real search for mentors who might teach what he or she really wanted to learn. A great deal of time was spent in community pursuits, practicing affection, meeting and studying every level of the community, learning how to make a home, and dozens of other tasks necessary to becoming a whole man or woman.

But here is the **calculus** of time the children I teach must deal with:

Out of the 168 hours in each week, my children sleep 56. That leaves them 112 hours a week out of which to **fashion** a self.

My children watch 55 hours of television a week according to recent reports. That leaves them 57 hours a week in which to grow up.

My children attend school 30 hours a week, use about 6 hours getting ready, going and coming home, and spend an average of 7 hours a week in homework—a total of 45 hours. During that time, they are under constant **surveillance**, have no private time or private space, and are disciplined if they try to assert individuality in the use of time or space. That leaves 12 hours a week out of which to create

## Vocabulary

**absurd**
ridiculously meaningless

**synergy**
convergence of mutually beneficial actions

**sanctuary**
a place of safety and protection

**fortitude**
strength of will

**temperance**
self-control

**calculus**
method of calculation

**fashion**
as a verb, to craft or create

**surveillance**
close watch

a unique consciousness. Of course, my kids eat, and that takes some time—not
115  much, because they've lost the tradition of family dining, but if we allot 3 hours
a week to evening meals, we arrive at a net amount of private time for each child
of 9 hours.

It's not enough. It's not enough, is it? The richer the kid, or course, the less
television he watches but the rich kid's time is just as narrowly **proscribed** by
120  a somewhat broader catalog of commercial entertainments and his inevitable
assignment to a series of private lessons in areas seldom of his actual choice.

And these things are oddly enough just a more cosmetic way to create
dependent human beings, unable to fill their own hours, unable to **initiate** lines
of meaning to give substance and pleasure to their existence. It's a national
125  disease, this dependency and aimlessness, and I think schooling and television
and lessons—the entire **Chautauqua** idea—has a lot to do with it.

Think of the things that are killing us as a nation—narcotic drugs, brainless
competition, recreational sex, the pornography of violence, gambling, alcohol, and
the worst pornography of all—lives devoted to buying things, accumulation as
130  a philosophy—all of them are addictions of dependent personalities, and that is
what our brand of schooling must inevitably produce.

I want to tell you what the effect is on children of taking all their time from
them—time they need to grow up—and forcing them to spend it on abstractions.
You need to hear this, because no reform that doesn't attack these specific
135  **pathologies** will be anything more than a **façade**.

1. The children I teach are **indifferent** to the adult world. This defies the
   experience of thousands of years. A close study of what big people were up
   to was always the most exciting occupation of youth, but nobody wants to
   grow up these days and who can blame them? Toys are us.
140
2. The children I teach have almost no curiosity, and what little they do
   have is **transitory**; they cannot concentrate for very long, even on things
   they choose to do. Can you see a connection between the bells ringing
   again and again to change classes and this phenomenon of **evanescent**
   attention?
145
3. The children I teach have a poor sense of the future, of how tomorrow is
   **inextricably** linked to today. They live in a continuous present; the exact
   moment they are in is the boundary of their consciousness.

4. The children I teach are ahistorical; they have no sense of how the past
   has **predestined** their own present, limiting their choices, shaping their
150  values and lives.

5. The children I teach are cruel to each other; they lack compassion for
   misfortune, they laugh at weakness, and they have contempt for people
   whose need for help shows too plainly.

6. The children I teach are uneasy with intimacy or **candor**. They cannot
155  deal with genuine intimacy because of a lifelong habit of preserving a
   secret self inside an outer personality made up of artificial bits and pieces

## Vocabulary

**proscribed**
prohibited

**initiate**
begin, launch

**Chautauqua**
a traveling lecture series to
entertain and educate

**pathology**
illness

**façade**
a false front on a building

**indifferent**
uncaring

**transitory**
short-lived

**evanescent**
vanishing like vapor

**inextricable**
unable to be separated

**predestined**
predetermined by destiny

**candor**
openness in communicating
personal feelings

of behavior borrowed from television or acquired to manipulate teachers. Because they are not who they represent themselves to be, the disguise wears thin in the presence of intimacy, so intimate relationships have to be avoided.                                                                                                                    160

7. The children I teach are materialistic, following the lead of schoolteachers who materialistically "grade" everything—and television mentors who offer everything in the world for sale.

8. The children I teach are dependent, passive, and timid in the presence of new challenges. This timidity is frequently masked by surface **bravado**,   165 or by anger or aggressiveness, but underneath is a vacuum without fortitude.

I could name a few other conditions that school reform will have to tackle if our national decline is to be arrested, but by now you will have grasped my thesis, whether you agree with it or not. Either schools, television, or both have   170 caused these pathologies. It's a simple matter of arithmetic: between schooling and television, all the time children have is eaten up. That's what has destroyed the American family; it is no longer a factor in the education of its own children.

What can be done?

First, we need a ferocious national debate that doesn't quit, day after day,   175 year after year, the kind of continuous emphasis that journalism finds boring. We need to scream and argue about this school thing until it is fixed or broken beyond repair—one or the other. If we can fix it, fine; if we cannot, then the success of home schooling shows a different road that has great promise. Pouring the money back into family education might kill two birds with one stone, repairing families   180 as it repairs children.

Genuine reform is possible, but it shouldn't cost anything. We need to rethink the fundamental **premises** of schooling and decide what it is we want all children to learn, and why. For 140 years this nation has tried to impose objectives from a lofty command center made up of "experts," a central **elite** of social engineers.   185 It hasn't worked. It won't work. It is a gross betrayal of the democratic promise that once made this nation a noble experiment. The Russian attempt to control Eastern Europe has exploded before our eyes. Our own attempt to impose the same sort of central **orthodoxy**, using the schools as an instrument, is also coming apart at the seams, albeit more slowly and painfully. It doesn't work because its   190 fundamental premises are mechanical, antihuman, and hostile to family life. Lives can be controlled by machine education, but they will always fight back with weapons of social pathology—drugs, violence, self-destruction, indifference, and the symptoms I see in the children I teach.

It's high time we looked backward to regain an educational philosophy that   195 works. One I like particularly well has been a favorite of the ruling classes of Europe for thousands of years. I think it works just as well for poor children as for rich ones. I use as much of it as I can manage in my own teaching—as much, that is, as I can get away with, given the present institution of compulsory schooling.

**480**

<sup>200</sup> At the core of this elite system of education is the belief that self-knowledge is the only basis of true knowledge. Everywhere in this system, at every age, you will find arrangements that place the child alone in an unguided setting with a problem to solve. Sometimes the problem is fraught with great risks, such as the problem of getting a horse to gallop or making it jump. But that, of course,
<sup>205</sup> is a problem successfully solved by thousands of elite children before the age of ten. Can you imagine anyone who has mastered such a challenge ever lacking confidence in his or her ability to do anything? Sometimes the problem is that of mastering solitude, as Thoreau did at Walden Pond, or Einstein did in the Swiss **customshouse**.

<sup>210</sup> One of my former students, Roland Legiardi-Laura, though both his parents were dead and he had no inheritance, rode a bicycle across the U.S. alone when he was hardly out of boyhood. Is it any wonder that in manhood he made a film about Nicaragua, although he had no money and no prior experience with filmmaking, and that it was an international award winner—even though his regular work
<sup>215</sup> was as a carpenter?

Right now we are taking from our children the time they need to develop self-knowledge. That has to stop. We have to invent school experiences that give a lot of that time back. We need to trust children from a very early age with independent study, perhaps arranged in school, but which takes place away from
<sup>220</sup> the institutional setting. We need to invent a **curriculum** where each kid has a chance to develop uniqueness and self-reliance.

A short time ago, I paid seventy dollars and sent a twelve-year-old girl with her non-English-speaking mother on a bus down the New Jersey coast. She took the police chief of Sea Bright to lunch and apologized for polluting his beach with
<sup>225</sup> a discarded Gatorade bottle. In exchange for this public apology, I had arranged for the girl to have a one-day **apprenticeship** in small-town police procedures. A few days later, two more of my twelve-year-old kids traveled alone from Harlem to West Thirty-first Street, where they began apprenticeships with a newspaper editor. Next week, three of my kids will find themselves in the middle of the Jersey
<sup>230</sup> swamps at six in the morning studying the mind of a trucking-company president as he dispatches eighteen-wheelers to Dallas, Chicago, and Los Angeles.

Are these "special" children in a "special" program? No, they're just nice kids from central Harlem, bright and alert, but so badly schooled when they came to me that most of them couldn't add or subtract with any **fluency**. And not a single
<sup>235</sup> one knew the population of New York City, or how far it is from New York to California.

Does that worry me? Of course. But I am confident that as they gain self-knowledge, they'll also become self-teachers—and only self-teaching has any lasting value.

<sup>240</sup> We've got to give kids independent time right away, because that is the key to self-knowledge, and we must reinvolve them with the real world as fast as possible so that the independent time can be spent on something other than

**Vocabulary**

**customshouse**
building where vessels are cleared after paying a tax

**curriculum**
set of educational courses

**apprenticeship**
learning by working with an expert

**fluency**
graceful use of a skill

mere abstractions. This is an emergency. It requires drastic action to correct. Our children are dying like flies in our schools. Good schooling or bad schooling, it's all the same: irrelevant. <sup>245</sup>

What else does a restructured school system need? It needs to stop being a parasite on the working community. I think we need to make community service a required part of schooling. It is the quickest way to give young children real responsibility.

For five years I ran a **guerrilla** school program where I had every kid, rich and <sup>250</sup> poor, smart and **dipsy**, give 320 hours a year of hard community service. Dozens of those kids came back to me years later and told me that this one experience had changed their lives, had taught them to see in new ways, to rethink goals and values. It happened when they were thirteen, in my Lab School program— made possible only because my rich school district was in chaos. When "stability" <sup>255</sup> returned, the lab closed. It was too successful, at too small a cost, to be allowed to continue; we made the expensive, elite programs look bad.

There is no shortage of real problems in this city. Kids can be asked to help solve them in exchange for the respect and attention of the adult world. Good for kids, good for the rest of us. <sup>260</sup>

Independent study, community service, adventures in experience, large doses of privacy and solitude, a thousand different apprenticeships—these are all powerful, cheap, and effective ways to start a real reform of schooling. But no large-scale reform is ever going to repair our damaged children and our damaged society until we force the idea of "school" open—to include family as the main <sup>265</sup> engine of education. The Swedes realized this in 1976, when they effectively abandoned state adoption of unwanted children and instead spent national time and treasure on reinforcing the family so that children born to Swedes were wanted. They reduced the number of unwanted Swedish children from six thousand in 1976 to fifteen in 1986. So it can be done. The Swedes just got tired <sup>270</sup> of paying for the social wreckage caused by children not being raised by their natural parents, so they did something about it. We can, too.

Family is the main engine of education. If we use schooling to break children away from parents—and make no mistake, that has been the central function of schools since John Cotton announced it as the purpose of the Bay Colony schools <sup>275</sup> in 1650 and Horace Mann announced it as the purpose of Massachusetts schools in 1850—we're going to continue to have the horror show we have right now.

The curriculum of family is at the heart of any good life. We've gotten away from that curriculum—it's time to return to it. The way to sanity in education is for our schools to take the lead in releasing the stranglehold of institutions on <sup>280</sup> family life, to promote during school time **confluences** of parent and child that will strengthen family bonds. That was my real purpose in sending the girl and her mother down the Jersey coast to meet the police chief.

I have many ideas on how to make a family curriculum, and my guess is that a lot of you will have many ideas, too, once you begin to think about it. Our <sup>285</sup>

**Vocabulary**

**guerrilla**
someone who battles by irregular means, against a superior force

**dipsy**
variant of "dippy," meaning foolish

**confluence**
where two or more things flow together

greatest problem in getting the kind of **grass-roots** thinking going that could reform schooling is that we have large, **vested interests** profiting from schooling just exactly as it is, despite **rhetoric** to the contrary.

290 We have to demand that new voices and new ideas get a hearing, my ideas and yours. We've all had a bellyful of authorized voices on television and in the press. A decade-long, free-for-all debate is called for now, not more "expert" opinions. Experts in education have never been right; their "solutions" are expensive, self-serving, and always involve further **centralization**. Enough.

Time for a return to democracy, individuality, and family.

295 I've said my piece. Thank you.

**Analyze** In your opinion, which of these cause/effect diagrams best illustrates the essay? Defend your choice. What is the main effect or main cause in the essay, and what does it result from or lead to?

> The second diagram: Gatto argues that "our form of compulsory schooling is an invention of the state of Massachusetts," and that statistics show a 98 percent literacy rate for that state before its institution, with a maximum 91 percent literacy rate after. From this cause he explains many educational and societal ills.

**Reflect** Obviously, not everyone agrees with Mr. Gatto. What do you believe about the future of education in the United States?

> Answers will vary.

**Vocabulary**

**grass roots**
the basic level of a society rather than its power structures

**vested interest**
someone with a personal stake or gaining a special benefit

**rhetoric**
art of speaking effectively, a term often used to describe misleading arguments

**centralization**
yielding control to a small group

# LO2 Writing a Cause-Effect Essay

**Prewrite** Start by thinking of a cause-and-effect relationship that interests you. Are you concerned about child obesity? Does the effect of an increasingly global economy fascinate you? Make a list of possible topics. Answers will vary.

## Make a List

_____     _____
_____     _____
_____     _____
_____     _____
_____     _____
_____     _____

**Choose one:** Put a star next to a topic that seems doable in the amount of time you have.

## Research and Organize

Find out all you can about the topic you have chosen. Then fill in one of the diagrams below with details to include in your essay. Add more boxes if you need them.

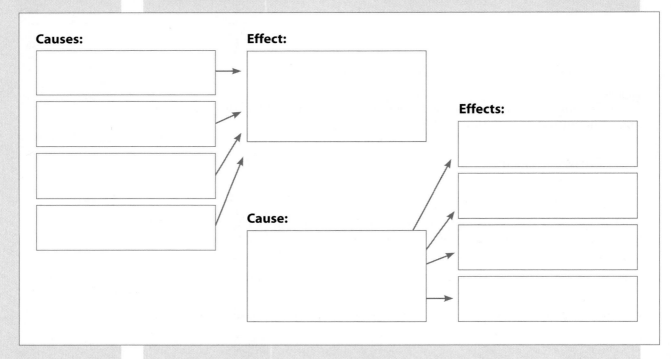

**Draft** Create a strong opening, middle, and closing for your cause-and-effect essay. Answers will vary.

## Opening Paragraph

The opening of your cause-and-effect essay should grab your reader's attention and clearly introduce the topic. It must present your claim that *this* cause results in *these* effects, or *these* causes yield *this* effect. You can use one of the following strategies to start:

- **Ask a question:** "Why is audio and video reporting banned from public courtrooms?"
- **Begin with action:** "Just one year ago, 12-year-old Sana was taken from her home, handed a machete, and sent to fight against soldiers in her government's army."
- **Connect to the reader:** "Picture a street full of people, some real and some imaginary, but because of a psychosis, you are unable to tell which is which."

Once you have your reader's attention, lead up to your thesis statement. Here is a formula to use as you create your thesis statement.

| Main Point | | Causes or Effects | | Thesis Statement |
|---|---|---|---|---|
| The Niger delta has suffered 50 years of oil contamination. | **+** | sabotage, theft, corporate mismanagement | **=** | Africa's Niger delta has suffered 50 years of oil contamination, from a combination of sabotage, theft, and corporate mismanagement. |

**Main Point** + **Importance to Reader** _____

[blank box] _____

_____

_____

**= Thesis Statement**

_____

_____

_____

## Middle Paragraphs

In your middle paragraphs, defend your thesis statement by fully explaining each cause or effect of that main point. In general, you should devote at least a paragraph to each cause or effect. Arrange them from most important to least important or vice versa.

## Closing Paragraph

The final paragraph should summarize the cause-and-effect relationship to help cement it in the reader's mind. You may also use this paragraph to make recommendations for changes to the situation, or to call the reader to act in some way.

**Revise** Take a break from your writing. Then come back to it with fresh eyes. If possible, have a friend or family member read the essay and make suggestions. Then review your writing with the following checklist. Keep polishing until you can answer every question with a "yes."

**Ideas**

☐ **1.** Is the cause-and-effect relationship clear?

☐ **2.** Do I cover all the important causes or effects of the main topic?

**Organization**

☐ **3.** Does my opening grab the reader's attention and present a clear thesis?

☐ **4.** Does my middle fully explain all the causes or effects?

☐ **5.** Are the causes or effects covered in the most effective order?

☐ **6.** Does my ending summarize the cause-and-effect relationship and leave the reader with something more to think about?

**Voice**

☐ **7.** Is the voice both friendly and professional?

**Edit** Prepare a clean copy of your personal essay and use the following checklist to check for errors. Continue until you can answer "yes" to each question.

**Words**

☐ **1.** Do I use correct verb forms (*he saw,* not *he seen*)? (See page 356.)

☐ **2.** Do my subjects and verbs agree (*she speaks,* not *she speak*)? (See pages 282–291.)

☐ **3.** Have I used the right words (*there, their, they're*)?

**Sentences**

☐ **4.** Have I avoided sentence fragments? (See pages 297–302.)

☐ **5.** Have I avoided run-on sentences? (See pages 306–310.)

☐ **6.** Have I avoided improper shifts in sentences? (See pages 314–315.)

**Conventions**

☐ **7.** Have I used commas after long introductory word groups? (See page 396.)

☐ **8.** Have I capitalized first words? (See page 414.)

☐ **9.** Have I capitalized proper nouns and proper adjectives? (See page 414.)

☐ **10.** Have I carefully checked my spelling?

—David Hume

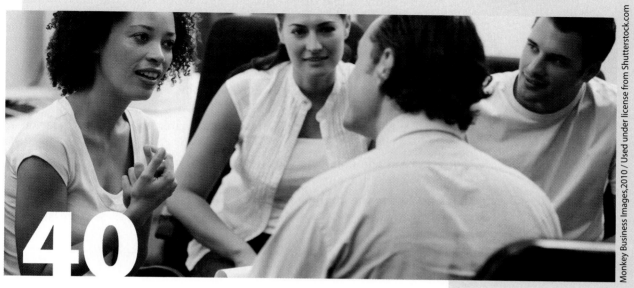

Monkey Business Images, 2010 / Used under license from Shutterstock.com

# 40

# Argument Essays

You may think of the word "argue" as meaning heated conversation, with shouts flying. Actually, the word is more related to discussion, reasoning, and debate, as when lawyers argue a case in court. Obviously, a judge wouldn't allow them to bellow at each other, and a jury wouldn't be convinced if they did. Instead, lawyers lay out their evidence and reasoning, seeking to convince. In the same way, the essay writers in this chapter each present an argument, hoping to convince you. Notice the different ways in which they make their case.

## Learning Outcomes

**LO1** Understand, read, and analyze argument essays.

**LO2** Write your own argument essay.

## What do you think?

What experience have you had with presenting an argument? How effective have your efforts been?

Answers will vary.

Understand, read, and
analyze argument essays.

Argumentation is very
important for all classes.
Knowing how to state a
position, support it, and
defend it will serve you
well throughout college
and life beyond.

# LO1 Understanding Argument Essays

Within this chapter you will find three example argument essays. Each is followed by questions to help analyze the reading. At the end of the chapter are writing guidelines for creating an argument essay of your own.

**SQ3R** When you read, become involved with the text by using the SQ3R approach.

- **Survey:** Prepare by reading "About the Author," skimming the essay, and noting any vocabulary words.
- **Question:** Ask yourself to predict what the writer hopes to convince you of.
- **Read:** Read the essay, noting the value of supporting arguments and concessions the author makes.
- **Recite:** Recite the main points of the argument.
- **Review:** Answer the questions provided to help you analyze the essay.

## Essay List:

**"Why I Changed My Mind on the Death Penalty":** Lance Morrow argues that while state executions are part of a social contract to maintain civilization, our own culture has become so chaotic that executions no longer serve that purpose.

**"A Modest Proposal: Guys Shouldn't Drive Till 25":** In the tradition of Jonathan Swift, Joyce Gallagher points out that great tragedy could be avoided, and many public benefits gained, by refusing a driver's license to the most accident-prone sector of our society: young males aged 15-25.

**"Choosing Virginity":** Lorraine Ali and Julie Scelfo interview a handful of young people who have committed themselves to abstaining from sex until after marriage.

Christian Schmidt/Cusp/Corbis

**About the Author**

Lance Morrow has been a professor of journalism at Boston University and a journalist and essayist for *Time* magazine. He is also the author of several nonfiction books.

Lance Morrow, "Why I Changed My Mind on the Death Penalty," Time, May 3, 2000.

## Why I Changed My Mind on the Death Penalty
## by Lance Morrow

1      Christina Marie Riggs, a nurse in Arkansas and a single mother, killed her two children—Justin, 5, and Shelby Alexis, 2—by giving them injections of **potassium chloride** and then smothering them with a pillow. She wrote a suicide note, and apparently tried to kill herself with an overdose of 28 antidepressant
5    tablets. She survived.

       Or she did until last night, when the state of Arkansas put Riggs to death by lethal injection at the state prison in Varner. She was the first woman to be executed in Arkansas since 1845.

       The state of Arkansas played the part of Jack Kevorkian in a case of assisted
10   suicide. Christina Riggs said she wanted to die. She had dropped all legal appeals. She wanted to be with her children in heaven. Just before Riggs died, she said, "I love you, my babies." Some people said she had killed them because she was severely depressed. The prosecutor, on the other hand, called her "a self-centered, selfish, **premeditated** killer who did the unspeakable act of taking her own
15   children's lives."

       So where do we stand on capital punishment now? (And, incidentally, isn't it grand that we seem to be overcoming, at the speed of light, our reluctance to execute women? Bless you, Gloria Steinem.)

       Review the state of play:

20   **Deterrence** is an unreliable argument for the death penalty, I think, because deterrence is unprovable.

       The fear of executing the wrong man (a more popular line of **demurral** these days) is an unreliable argument against all capital punishment. What if there are many witnesses to a murder? What if it's Hitler? Is capital punishment OK
25   in cases of unmistakable guilt? George W. Bush says that he reviews each case to make sure he is absolutely certain a person did it before he allows a Texas execution to go ahead.

       I have argued in the past that the death penalty was justified, in certain brutal cases, on the basis of the social contract. That is: Some hideous crimes
30   demand the ultimate punishment in order to satisfy the essentially civilizing deal

**Vocabulary**

**potassium chloride**
an odorless salt used in some state executions

**premeditated**
planned ahead of time

**deterrence**
a preventative

**demurral**
hesitation or objection

that we make with one another as citizens. We forgo individual revenge, **deferring** to the law, but depend upon a certainty that the law will give us a justice that must include appropriate harshness. I favored the Texas folk wisdom: "He needs killing." If the law fails in that task, I said, and people see that evil is **fecklessly** tolerated, then the social contract disintegrates. Society needs a measure of **homeopathic** revenge. 35

But I have changed my mind about capital punishment.

I think the American atmosphere, the American imagination (news, movies, books, music, fact, fiction, entertainment, culture, life in the streets, **zeitgeist**) is now so filled with murder and violence (gang wars, random shootings not just in housing projects but in offices and malls and schools) that violence of any kind—including solemn execution—has become merely a part of our cultural routine and joins, in our minds, the passing parade of stupidity/**psychosis**/chaos/ entertainment that Americans seem to like, or have come to deserve. In Freudian terms, the once forceful (and patriarchal) American **Superego** (arguably including the authority of law, of the presidency, of the military, etc.) has collapsed into a great dismal swamp of **Id**. 40 45

And in the Swamp, I have come to think, capital punishment has lost whatever cautionary social force it had—its exemplary meaning, its power to proclaim, as it once arguably did, that some deeds are, in our fine and virtuous company, intolerable. 50

I think those arguing in favor of capital punishment now are indulging in a form of **nostalgia**. Capital punishment no longer works as a morality play. Each execution (divorced from its moral meaning, including its capacity to shock and to warn the young) simply becomes part of the great messy **pageant**, the vast and **voracious** stupidity, the Jerry Springer show of American life. 55

Maybe most of our moral opinions are formed by emotions and **aesthetic** reactions. My opinion is this: Capital punishment has lost its moral meaning. Having lost its moral meaning, it has become as immoral as any other expression of violence. And therefore we should stop doing it.

**Analyze** | What is Morrow's main argument?

Capital punishment has become just another spectacle, has lost its

meaning, and should be done away with.

What are his supporting points?

Answers will vary.

Do you agree or disagree? Why?

Answers will vary.

### Vocabulary

**defer**
delegate to someone else

**fecklessly**
weakly, irresponsibly

**homeopathic**
a medical treatment to create immunity by small, repeated exposure

**zeitgeist**
the spirit of a cultural time period

**psychosis**
insanity involving a break with reality

**Superego**
sense of moral responsibility, conscience

**Id**
instinctual drives

**nostalgia**
longing for the past

**pageant**
a spectacle or an exhibition

**voracious**
endlessly hungry

**aesthetic**
artistic sense of beauty

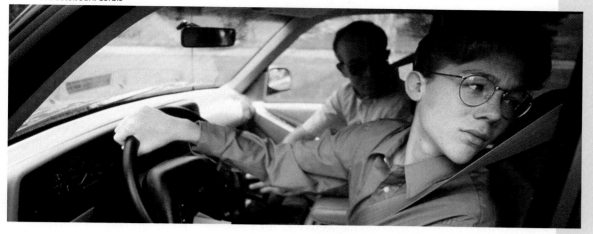

**About the Author**

Joyce Gallagher is a freelance writer. In this essay, she suggests a radical solution for a problem commonly ignored.

Joyce Gallagher, "A Modest Proposal: Guys Shouldn't Drive Till 25," Brandon/Brandon, Sentences, Paragraphs, and Beyond: With Integrated Readings 6e, Wadsworth, 2011. 0495802131.

# A Modest Proposal: Guys Shouldn't Drive Till 25
## By Joyce Gallagher

1    In the year 2001, 57,480 people were killed in motor vehicle accidents.* That figure is within a few hundred of being the same number as those killed in the Vietnam War. We took drastic measures back in the early 1970s and ended that war in a way shocking to some: we left. The time has come for another drastic

5    scheme. We need to recognize the main causes of this highway carnage and take action. According to the U.S. Department of Transportation, 25.1 percent of the roadway fatalities involve an age group constituting only 14.5 percent of the driving public. That group is in the age range from 15 to 25. Within that group, one half are males. They are three times more likely to be involved in roadway

10   fatalities, meaning that about 7 percent of males are responsible for more than 16 percent of roadway fatalities. This proposal may be a hard sell for politicians, but it is time for us to step forward boldly and raise the legal driving age for males nationally to 25.

     Some may protest that it is unfair to punish the good young male drivers for

15   the sins of their irresponsible peers. But we're already discriminating by group. Surely we all agree that drivers of a certain age should not be allowed to drive. That age varies from state to state, but it is around 15. We have concluded that those younger than 15 are too immature. We don't say that those under 15 should be treated individually, not even on the basis of gender. Instead, we exclude

20   the offending group. With my proposal, we would simply move the legal age of male drivers to 25, lumping those of similar age and sex together for the good of society.

     For you who would like to point out that some oldsters are also menaces on the roadways, I would say that those over 88 are equal only to those between

25   15 and 25 for being involved in fatal crashes. Moreover, the crashes by super-seniors are likely to be caused by physical and mental impairments, which can be detected by periodic tests and remedied by pulled licenses, whereas the young, often irresponsible and impatient, are more likely to be guided by thrill-seeking impulses, tantrums, and other byproducts of testosterone, all of which are

30   hopelessly glandular.

*All statistics in this article are from the U.S. Bureau of Transportation Statistics: www.bts.gov.

**Vocabulary**

**carnage**
bloody slaughter

**constitute**
form or compose

**impairment**
something that damages or reduces an ability

**testosterone**
a hormone responsible for male characteristics

**glandular**
produced by glands

Although one **salient** reason—that this group of young males is responsible for the deaths of so many fellow citizens—is enough support for the proposed law, there are many side benefits for society.

- While the male 15-25 age group is waiting to drive motor vehicles, they would have time to improve their cultural lives and lay groundwork for better 35 driving skills and improved mental and physical health.

- Many youngsters would customarily ride with statistically superior female or elder drivers and could learn from the relatively good examples they witness.

- Being no more dependent on driving almost everywhere, the male 40 youngsters would walk more or ride bikes or skateboards, providing them wholesome exercise so often neglected in our **paunchy**, weight-challenged society.

- As a group they would also use more public transportation, relieving traffic congestion on our roadways and reducing congestion in the air we breathe.

- Support for public transportation projects would soar, and cars might 45 cease to be near the center of our lives.

- Car payment money now **impoverishing** so many young males might go toward savings, education, home improvement, self-improvement, and family activities.

- Gratitude from young male drivers for the rides provided by female spouses 50 and other loved ones could promote affectionate and appreciative relationships and diminish road rage.

The only exceptions to this new national law would be for the military and for public security and emergency agencies. Within the armed services, male **personnel** under 25 would be allowed to drive on foreign soil or on military property 55 at any time. Male drivers working for police, fire, rescue, and ambulance services would drive only when on duty and their permits would be terminated for any serious traffic **infraction**. No doubt, some male youngsters, obsessed with driving motor vehicles, would join our public service **sectors**, making our national security and **infrastructural** services stronger so we could all sleep more peacefully. 60

Probably some males would protest this law and would try to **circumvent** it with devious strategies. Such resistance could be easily combated. For example, those who attempt to cross-dress or dye their hair gray for the purpose of obtaining a driver's license could be charged with a felony.

Several people who have read my modest proposal have suggested that 65 young men are victims of their own bodies and could plead a "testosterone **dementia** defense." Therefore, they should be allowed to take injections of **estrogen** to neutralize the male hormones raging like tiny bulls within their systems. However, even these critics would surely concede that there could be a feminizing reaction to estrogen, one both psychological and physiological. Because 70 of those possible side effects, wives of young men might find estrogen therapy unacceptable. A youthful bride might willingly bear the burden of transporting her husband to work and back, whereas she would almost certainly **recoil** at the thought of his wearing her bra.

Some might argue that improved drivers' education programs in our school 75

## Vocabulary

**salient**
notably significant, rising above

**paunchy**
fat

**impoverishing**
making poor

**personnel**
the people employed in an organization

**infraction**
violation

**sector**
a subdivision of a society

**infrastructural**
dealing with the framework of an organization, the resources of a society

**circumvent**
find a way around

**dementia**
a type of insanity

**estrogen**
a hormone responsible for female characteristics

**recoil**
shrink back, flinch away in disgust

systems, better public transportation, the production of vehicles that are no more powerful and threatening than they need be, a reduced speed limit, counseling and restrictions for repeat offenders, and a stricter enforcement of existing laws represent a wiser approach to our national problem. However, because those ideas have failed to **resonate**, and young males have continued to put the pedal to the metal in a flood of blood, it is time for a simple statement that will fit on your bumper sticker:

80

**Vocabulary**

**resonate**
to echo within or spread throughout

> **Guys Shouldn't Drive Till 25**

Joe Bator/Surf/Corbis

**React** How does this essay make you feel? If you are male, how do you think a female would react to the essay? If you are female, how do you think a male would react?

Answers will vary.

_____

_____

_____

_____

**Analyze** What is Gallagher truly suggesting?

We should better implement current programs like driver education, public

transportation, reasonable vehicles, reduced speed limits, treatment of

repeat offenders, and enforcement of existing laws.

_____

**Think Critically** Is Gallagher's approach effective? Why or why not? What suggestions might you have for a different approach?

Answers will vary.

_____

_____

_____

_____

Jacques M. Chenet/Documentary/Corbis

## About the Author

Lorraine Ali is a contributing editor for *Newsweek* and a reporter for various other publications. Julie Scelfo is a *New York Times* reporter.

Lorraine Ali and Julie Scelfo, "Choosing Virginity," Newsweek, December 9, 2002.

# Choosing Virginity
## by Lorraine Ali and Julie Scelfo

**A New Attitude: Fewer teenagers are having sex. As parents and** 1
**politicians debate the merits of abstinence programs, here's what the**
**kids have to say.**

There's a sexual revolution going on in America, and believe it or not, it has
nothing to do with Christina Aguilera's bare-it-all video "Dirty." The uprising is 5
taking place in the real world, not on "The Real World." Visit any American high
school and you'll likely find a growing number of students who watch **scabrous**
TV shows like "Shipmates," listen to Eminem—and have decided to remain
**chaste** until marriage. Rejecting the get-down-make-love **ethos** of their parents'
generation, this wave of young adults represents a new counterculture, one clearly 10
at odds with the mainstream media and their routine use of sex to boost ratings
and peddle product.

According to a recent study from the Centers for Disease Control, the number
of high-school students who say they've never had sexual intercourse rose by
almost 10 percent between 1991 and 2001. Parents, public-health officials and 15
sexually **beleaguered** teens themselves may be relieved by this "let's not" trend.
But the new **abstinence** movement, largely fostered by cultural conservatives and
**evangelical** Christians, has also become hotly controversial. . . .

The debate concerns public policy, but the real issue is personal choice. At the
center of it all are the young people themselves, whose voices are often drowned 20
out by the political **cacophony**. Some of them opened up and talked candidly to
*Newsweek* about their reasons for abstaining from sex until marriage. It's clear
that religion plays a critical role in this extraordinarily private decision. But
there are other factors as well: caring parents, a sense of their own unreadiness,
the desire to gain some **semblance** of control over their own destinies. Here are 25
their stories.

### The Wellesley Girl

Alice Kunce says she's a **feminist**, but not the "army-boot-wearing, shaved-
head, I-hate-all-men kind." The curly-haired 18-year-old Wellesley College
sophomore—she skipped a grade in elementary school—looks and talks like what 30
she is: one of the many bright, outspoken students at the liberal Massachusetts
women's college. She's also a virgin. "One of the empowering things about the
feminist movement," she says, "is that we're able to assert ourselves, to say no to
sex and not feel pressured about it. And I think guys are kind of getting it. Like,
'Oh, not everyone's doing it.'" 35

But judging by just about every TV program or movie targeted at teens, everyone is doing it. Alice grew up with these images, but as a small-town girl in Jefferson City, Mo., most teen shows felt alien and alienating. "You're either a prudish person who can't handle talking about sex or you're out every Saturday night getting some," she says. "But if you're not sexually active and you're willing to discuss the subject, you can't be called a prude. How do they market to that?" The friend from back home she's been dating since August asked not to be identified in this story, but Alice doesn't mind talking candidly about what they do—or don't do. "Which is acceptable? Oral, vaginal or anal sex?" she asks. "For me, they're all sex. In high school, you could have oral sex and still call yourself a virgin. Now I'm like, 'Well, what makes one less **intimate** than the other?'"

Alice, a regular churchgoer who also teaches Sunday school, says religion is not the reason she's chosen abstinence. She fears **STDs** and pregnancy, of course, but above all, she says, she's not mature enough emotionally to handle the deep intimacy sex can bring. Though most people in her college, or even back in her Bible-belt high school, haven't made the same choice, Alice says she has never felt **ostracized**. If anything, she feels a need to speak up for those being **coerced** by aggressive abstinence groups. "Religious pressure was and is a lot greater than peer pressure," says Alice, who has never taken part in an abstinence program. "I don't think there are as many teens saying 'Oh come on, everybody's having sex' as there are church leaders saying 'No, it's bad, don't do it. It'll ruin your life.' The choices many religious groups leave you with are either no sex at all or uneducated sex. What happened to educating young people about how they can protect themselves?"

## The Dream Team

Karl Nicoletti wasted no time when it came to having "the talk" with his son, Chris. It happened five years ago, when Chris was in sixth grade. Nicoletti was driving him home from school and the subject of girls came up. "I know many parents who are wishy-washy when talking to their kids about sex. I just said, 'No, you're not going to have sex. Keep your pecker in your pants until you graduate from high school.'"

Today, the 16-year-old from Longmont, Colo., vows he'll remain abstinent until marriage. So does his girlfriend, 17-year-old Amanda Wing, whose parents set similarly strict rules for her and her two older brothers. "It's amazing, but they did listen," says her mother, Lynn Wing. Amanda has been dating Chris for only two months, but they've known each other for eight years. On a Tuesday-night dinner date at Portabello's (just across from the Twin Peaks Mall), Amanda asks, "You gonna get the chicken parmesan again?" Chris nods. "Yep. You know me well." They seem like a long-married couple—except that they listen to the Dave Matthews Band, have a 10:30 weeknight **curfew** and never go beyond kissing and hugging. (The guidelines set by Chris's dad: no touching anywhere that a soccer uniform covers.)

"Society is so run by sex," says Chris, who looks like Madison Avenue's **conception** of an All-American boy in his **Abercrombie** sweat shirt and faded baggy jeans. "Just look at everything—TV, movies. The culture today makes it seem OK to have sex whenever, however or with whoever you want. I just disagree with that." Amanda, who looks **tomboy** comfy in baggy brown **cords**, a white T shirt, and chunky-soled shoes, feels the same way. "Sex should be a special thing that doesn't need to be public," she says. "But if you're abstinent, it's like you're the one set aside from society because you're not 'doing it.'"

The peer pressure in this town of 71,000 people in the shadow of the Rocky Mountains is **substantially** less than in cosmopolitan Denver, 45 minutes away. ("It

## Vocabulary

**intimate**
very closely associated, as in something privately shared

**STDs**
Sexually Transmitted Diseases

**ostracized**
excluded from a group, shunned

**coerced**
compelled by forcefulness or threat

**curfew**
requirement to return home

**conception**
in this case, an idea

**Abercrombie**
short for "Abercrombie & Fitch," a clothing store specializing in outdoor fashions

**tomboy**
a girl who behaves in traditionally boyish ways

**cords**
short for "corduroy" pants, made of a ribbed cotton fabric

**substantial**
real, true, not imaginary

figures you had to come all the way out here to find a virgin," one local said.) Chris joined a Christian abstinence group called Teen Advisors this year. "We watched their slide show in eighth grade and it just has pictures of all these STDs," he says. "It's one of the grossest things you've ever seen. I didn't want to touch a girl, like, forever." He now goes out once a month and talks to middle schoolers about abstinence. Amanda saw the same presentation. "It's horrible," she says. "If that doesn't scare kids out of sex, nothing will." Could these gruesome images put them off sex for life? Chris and Amanda say no. They're sure that whoever they marry will be disease-free.

To most abstaining teens, marriage is the golden light at the end of the **perilous** tunnel of dating—despite what their parents' experience may have been. Though Amanda's mother and father have had a long and stable union, Karl Nicoletti separated from Chris's mother when Chris was in fifth grade. His **fiancée** moved in with Chris and Karl two years ago; Chris's mother now has a year-and-a-half-old son out of **wedlock**. Chris and Amanda talk about marriage in the abstract, but they want to go to college first, and they're looking at schools on opposite sides of the country. "I think we could stay together," Chris says. Amanda agrees. "Like we have complete trust in each other," she says. "It's just not hard for us." Whether the bond between them is strong enough to withstand a long-distance relationship is yet to be seen. For now, Chris and Amanda mostly look ahead to their next weekly ritual: the Tuesday pancake lunch.

### The Survivor

Remaining a virgin until marriage is neither an easy nor a common choice in Latoya Huggins's part of Paterson, N.J. At least three of her friends became single mothers while they were still in high school, one by an older man who now wants nothing to do with the child. "It's hard for her to finish school," Latoya says, "because she has to take the baby to get shots and stuff."

Latoya lives in a chaotic world: so far this year, more than a dozen people have been murdered in her neighborhood. It's a life that makes her sexuality seem like one of the few things she can actually control. "I don't even want a boyfriend until after college," says Latoya, who's studying to be a beautician at a technical high school. "Basically I want a lot out of life. My career choices are going to need a lot of time and effort."

Latoya, 18, could pass for a street-smart 28. She started thinking seriously about abstinence five years ago, when a national outreach program called Free Teens began teaching classes at her church. The classes reinforced what she already knew from growing up in Paterson—that discipline is the key to getting through your teen years alive. Earlier this year she dated a 21-year-old **appliance** salesman from her neighborhood, until Latoya heard that he was hoping she'd have sex with him. "We decided that we should just be friends," she explains, "before he cheated on me or we split up in a worse way."

So most days Latoya comes home from school alone. While she waits for her parents to return from work, she watches the Disney Channel or chills in her basement bedroom, which she's decorated with construction-paper cutouts of the names of her favorite pop stars, such as Nelly and Aaliyah. She feels safe there, she says, because "too many bad things are happening" outside. But bad things happen inside, too: last year she opened the door to a neighbor who forced his way inside and attempted to rape her. "He started trying to take my clothes off. I was screaming and yelling to the top of my lungs and nobody heard." Luckily, the phone rang. Latoya told the intruder it was her father, and that if she didn't answer he would come home right away. The man fled. Latoya tries not to think about what happened, although she feels "like dying" when she sees her attacker

90

95

100

105

110

115

120

125

130

135

**Vocabulary**

**perilous**
dangerous

**fiancée**
French term for a woman engaged to be married; *fiancé,* a man engaged to be married.

**wedlock**
marriage

**appliance**
any of a variety of household machines

<sup>140</sup> on the street. (Her parents decided not to press charges so she wouldn't have to **testify** in court.) Her goal is to graduate and get a job; she wants to stay focused and independent. "Boys make you feel like you're special and you're the only one they care about," she says. "A lot of girls feel like they need that. But my mother loves me and my father loves me, so there's no gap to fill."

<sup>145</sup>
## The Beauty Queen

Even though she lives 700 miles from the nearest ocean, Daniela Aranda was recently voted Miss Hawaiian Tropic El Paso, Texas, and her parents couldn't be prouder. They've displayed a picture of their bikini-clad daughter **smack-dab** in the middle of the living room. "People always say to me 'You don't look like a <sup>150</sup> virgin'," says Daniela, 20, who wears super sparkly eye shadow, heavy lip liner and a low-cut black shirt. "But what does a virgin look like? Someone who wears white and likes to look at flowers?"

Daniela models at Harley-Davidson fashion shows, is a cheerleader for a local soccer team called the Patriots and hangs out with friends who work at <sup>155</sup> Hooters. She's also an evangelical Christian who made a vow at 13 to remain a virgin, and she's kept that promise. "It can be done," she says. "I'm living proof." Daniela has never joined an abstinence program; her decision came from strong family values and deep spiritual convictions.

Daniela's arid East El Paso neighborhood, just a mile or so from the Mexican <sup>160</sup> border, was built atop desert dunes, and the sand seems to be reclaiming its own by swallowing up back patios and sidewalks. The city, predominantly Hispanic, is home to the Fort Bliss Army base, breathtaking **mesa** views—and some of the highest teen-pregnancy rates in the nation. "There's a lot of girls that just want to get pregnant so they can get married and get out of here," Daniela says.

<sup>165</sup> But she seems content to stay in El Paso. She studies business at El Paso Community College, dates a UTEP football player named Mike and works as a sales associate at the A'gaci Too clothing store in the Cielo Vista Mall. She also tones at the gym and reads—especially books by the Christian author Joshua Harris. In *Boy Meets Girl,* she's marked such passages as "Lust is never satisfied" <sup>170</sup> with a pink highlighter. She's also saved an article on A. C. Green, the former NBA player who's become a spokesman for abstinence. "My boyfriend's coach gave it to him because the other guys sometimes say, 'Are you gay? What's wrong with you?' It's proof that if a famous man like Green can do it, so can he."

Daniela has been dating Mike for more than a year. He's had sex before, but <sup>175</sup> has agreed to remain abstinent with her. "He's what you call a born-again virgin," she says. "Or a secondary abstinent, or something like that. We just don't put ourselves in compromising situations. If we're together late at night, it's with my whole family."

Daniela knows about temptation: every time she walks out onstage in a <sup>180</sup> bathing suit, men take notice. But she doesn't see a contradiction in her double life as virgin and beauty queen; rather, it's a personal challenge. "I did Hawaiian Tropic because I wanted to see if I could get into a bikini in front of all these people," she says. "I wasn't thinking, 'Oh, I'm going to win.' But I did, and I got a free trip to Houston's state finals. I met the owner of Hawaiian Tropic. It's like, <sup>185</sup> wow, this is as good as it gets."

## The Ring Bearer

Lenee Young is trying to write a paper for her Spanish class at Atlanta's Spelman College, but as usual she and her roommates can't help getting onto the subject of guys. "I love Ludacris," Lenee gushes. "I love everything about him. <sup>190</sup> Morris Chestnut, too. He has a really pretty smile. Just gorgeous." But Lenee, 19,

### Insight

What views of sexuality are typical in your culture? How do these views match up with those of U. S. society at large?

### Vocabulary

**testify**
make sworn statements

**smack-dab**
exactly

**mesa**
Spanish word for "table"; a rock formation with steep sides and a flat top

has never had a boyfriend, and has never even been kissed. "A lot of the guys in high school had already had sex," she says. "I knew that would come up, so I'd end all my relationships at the very beginning." Lenee decided back then to remain a virgin until marriage, and even now she feels little temptation to do what many of her peers are doing behind closed **dormitory** doors. "I feel that part of me hasn't been triggered yet," she says. "Sex is one of those things you can't miss until you have it." 195

Last summer she went with a friend from her hometown of Pittsburgh to a Silver Ring Thing. These popular free events **meld** music videos, **pyrotechnics**, and live teen comedy sketches with **dire** warnings about STDs. Attendees can buy a silver ring—and a Bible—for $12. Then, at the conclusion of the program, as techno music blares, they recite a pledge of abstinence and don their rings. "My friend, who's also a virgin, said I needed to go so I could get a ring," Lenee says. "It was fun, like the music and everything. And afterwards they had a dance and a bonfire." 200 205

The idea of abstinence was not new to Lenee. In high school she participated in a program sponsored by the University of Pittsburgh Medical Center called Postponing Sexual Involvement. Her mother had discussed it with her—once—the week before she left for college. Two of her closest friends are also virgins; the trio jokingly call themselves The Good Girls Club. But student life can sometimes be a shock to her **sensibilities**. "Another friend of mine and this guy were talking about how they didn't use a **condom**. He said, 'I like it raw.' I was like, 'Oh, my goodness.'" 210

And then there was the recent party that began with truth-or-dare questions. The first one: have you ever kissed a boy? Young was the only woman who said no, and everybody in the room was stunned. "Are you serious? We gotta find you a boyfriend!" But Lenee wasn't embarrassed. "I don't feel like I've missed out," she says. "I just feel like my time will come." Until then, she sports that shiny silver ring. 215

**The Renewed Virgin** 220

Lucian Schulte had always planned to wait until he was married to have sex, but that was before a warm night a couple of years ago when the green-eyed, lanky six-footer found himself with an unexpected opportunity. "She was all for it," says Lucian, now 18. "It was like, 'Hey, let's give this a try.'" The big event was over in a hurry and lacked any sense of intimacy. "In movies, if people have sex, it's always romantic," he says. "Physically, it did feel good, but emotionally, it felt really awkward. It was not what I expected it to be." 225

While the fictional teens of *American Pie* would have been clumsily overjoyed, Lucian, raised Roman Catholic, was plagued by guilt. "I was worried that I'd given myself to someone and our relationship was now a lot more serious than it was before," he says. "It was like, 'Now, what is she going to expect from me?'" Lucian worried, too, about disease and pregnancy. He promised himself never again. 230

Lucian, now an engineering major at the University of Alberta in Canada, is a "renewed virgin." His parents are strong proponents of chastity, and he attended school-sponsored abstinence classes. But the messages didn't hit home until he'd actually had sex. "It's a pretty special thing, and it's also pretty serious," he says. "Abstinence has to do with 'Hey, are you going to respect this person?'" He has dated since his high-school affair, and is now hoping a particular cute coed from Edmonton will go out with him. "But I'll try to restrict myself to kissing," he says. "Not because I think everything else is bad. But the more you participate with someone, the harder it's going to be to stop." 235 240

**Vocabulary**

**dormitory**
in college, a residence hall

**meld**
mix into a whole

**pyrotechnics**
fireworks

**dire**
involving disaster

**sensibilities**
emotional sensitivity

**condom**
a sheath covering the penis during sexual intercourse, to prevent pregnancy and transmission of disease

It's not easy to practice such restraint, especially when those around him do
not. Lucian lives in a single room, decorated with ski-lift tickets and a "Scooby-
Doo" poster, in an all-male dorm, but he says most students "get hitched up, sleep
245 around, and never see each other again." Meanwhile he does his best to push his
own sexual urges from his mind. "I try to forget about it, but I have to say it sucks.
Homework is a good thing to do, and going out for a run usually works." He also
goes to Sunday mass. Lucian figures he can hold out until he's married, which he
hopes will be by the time he's 30. "I'm looking forward to an intimate experience
250 with my wife, who I'll truly love and want to spend the rest of my life with," says
Lucian. "It's kind of corny, but it's for real."

### Teens & Sexuality

Raised in the age of AIDS and better educated about sex and abstinence,
more teens are saying "no." Condom use is up and teen pregnancy is down. A look
255 at the trends:

**Safer Sex:** Today, 25% more students say they used a condom during their
last sexual encounter than those surveyed a decade ago.

**Sex Ed:** 89% have been educated about **AIDS**.

**Race:** Black students are 40% more likely to have had sex than whites.

**Vocabulary**

**AIDS**
acquired immunodeficiency
syndrome, a sexually
transmitted disease

**Reflect** How would you summarize the authors' own opinions about teen
abstinence? Answers will vary.

_____

_____

_____

Do the authors ever actually state those opinions? What words seem to express
them? List specific examples.

_____

_____

_____

Summarize the argument of one young person who was interviewed for this essay.
Are any counterarguments offered? How does this affect the overall message?

_____

_____

_____

_____

_____

_____

# LO2 Writing an Argument Essay

**Prewrite** To select a topic for an argument essay, start by making a cluster of
subjects you have opinions about. **Answers will vary.**

## Make a Cluster

Add more bubbles and lines as needed. Continue clustering until an idea
excites you. Put a star next to that idea.

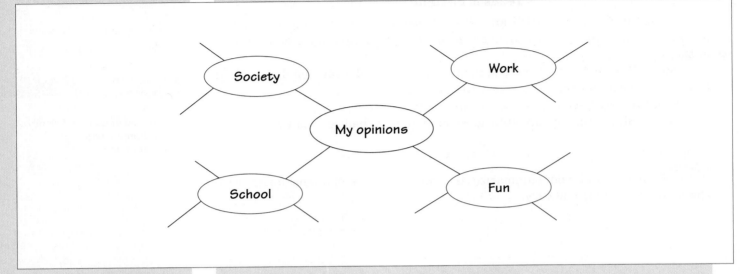

## Freewrite

Prepare to write your argument essay by freewriting. Write until you run
out of ideas for supporting your position. Then freewrite every argument
you can imagine against your position.

**Draft** Create a strong opening, middle, and closing for your argument essay.
Answers will vary.

## Opening Paragraph

The opening paragraphs of an argument essay should catch your reader's attention, provide any needed background to introduce the topic, and then make that introduction. You can use one of the following rhetorical strategies to start:

- **Make a logical claim:** "Judging films by their special effects is like judging people by their looks."

- **Present yourself as an authority:** "Having grown up with country-western music, I can attest to its essentially moral nature."

- **Appeal to the reader's emotion:** "Lowering a student's grades for poor class attendance is double punishment, intended to cause failure, not encourage success."

Once you have your reader's attention, lead up to your thesis statement. Here is a formula to use as you create your thesis statement.

**Your Topic**

nuclear weapons

**+**

**Your Feeling About It**

are a necessary deterrent to other nuclear weapons

**=**

**Thesis Statement**

In a world where nuclear weapons are possible, owning nuclear weapons is a necessity.

**Your Topic**

**+ Your Feeling About It** _____

_____

_____

_____

**= Thesis Statement**

_____

_____

_____

## Middle Paragraphs

In your middle paragraphs, defend your thesis statement by providing supporting reasons. Follow the rhetorical approach of your opening paragraphs, making a logical argument, speaking as an authority, or appealing to your audience's feelings about the subject. To strengthen your position, also address opposing views and make any needed concessions.

## Closing Paragraph

Your final paragraph should make a firm conclusion based on the support presented in your middle paragraphs. You may also use this paragraph to call for action from the reader or to point out related subjects for further discussion.

**Revise** Take a break from your writing for a while. Then come back to it with fresh eyes or have a friend or family member read the essay and make suggestions. When you are confident of the contents, review your writing with the following checklist. Keep polishing until you can answer every question with a "yes."

**Ideas**

☐ **1.** Is my position clear clear?

☐ **2.** Do I include the most persuasive reasons for taking this position?

**Organization**

☐ **3.** Does my opening grab the reader's attention?

☐ **4.** Does my middle convincingly present support, address counterarguments, and make necessary concessions?

☐ **5.** Does my ending make an effective conclusion?

☐ **6.** Does my ending make a call to action?

**Voice**

☐ **7.** Does the voice convey an effective rhetorical position: arguing logic, establishing my authority, or appealing to the reader's concerns?

**Edit** Prepare a clean copy of your personal essay and use the following checklist to check for errors. Continue until you can answer "yes" to each question.

**Words**

☐ **1.** Do I use correct verb forms (*he saw,* not *he seen*)? (See page 356.)

☐ **2.** Do my subjects and verbs agree (*she speaks,* not *she speak*)? (See pages 282–291.)

☐ **3.** Have I used the right words (*there, their, they're*)?

**Sentences**

☐ **4.** Have I avoided sentence fragments? (See pages 297–302.)

☐ **5.** Have I avoided run-on sentences? (See pages 306–310.)

☐ **6.** Have I avoided improper shifts in sentences? (See pages 314–315.)

**Conventions**

☐ **7.** Have I used commas after long introductory word groups? (See page 396.)

☐ **8.** Have I capitalized first words? (See page 414.)

☐ **9.** Have I capitalized proper nouns and proper adjectives? (See page 414.)

☐ **10.** Have I carefully checked my spelling?

# Index

Valentin Agapov/2010. Used under license from Shutterstock.com

3dfoto/2010. Used under license from Shutterstock.com

Maximmal/2010. Used under license from Shutterstock.com

James Steidl 2010/used under license from www.shutterstock.com

# Reading-Writing Connection

To succeed in college, students must approach writing and reading not as assignments to complete, but rather as opportunities to learn and to think. In this way, writing and reading are means to an end, rather than ends unto themselves. Students also must appreciate the unique relationship between the two tasks. Writing aids reading; reading provides ideas for writing.

## Writing to Learn (page 2-3)

Writing to learn is ungraded writing, carried out to help students understand concepts introduced in lectures, discussions, lab work, and readings. Essentially, writing to learn consists of having students write freely about the subjects and concepts they are studying. In these writings, students can explore topics under discussion, argue for or against particular points of view, reflect on their work on specific projects, and so on. Writing as a learning strategy is part of the larger writing-across-the-curriculum movement.

## Writing to Share Learning (page 4)

The focus of *WRITE 1* and *WRITE 2* is writing to share learning—the paragraphs, essays, and reports students turn in for evaluation. Both texts cover the writing process, writing paragraphs, writing essays, the conventions of the language, and so on. While writing to learn helps students explore and form their thoughts, writing to share learning helps them clarify and fine-tune them. In this way, both types of writing stimulate thinking and learning.

## Reading to Learn (pages 8-13)

Reading to learn is an approach that leads to more productive academic reading. It includes, among other things, previewing the text, reading the text, making annotations, engaging in exploratory writing during the reading, and summarizing the text after the reading. Employing such strategies helps students take control of their college-level reading.

## Reading Graphics (pages 14-15)

In college-level texts, significant portions of information is communicated via charts, tables, and diagrams. As a result, students need to understand how to read a graphic: scanning it, studying the specific parts, considering and questioning the image, and reflecting on its effectiveness. This skill is often overlooked in developmental and introductory courses.

Figure 36.2 Complex Web Site Map

## Understanding Assignments (pages 18-19)

Students, too often, approach their writing and reading assignments without the proper forethought, and as a result, they don't carry out their work in the appropriate way. So students must be made aware that understanding the dynamics of each assignment is critical: Are they expected to inform or to persuade in a writing assignment? Who is the intended audience in the material they are reading? *WRITE 1* and *WRITE 2* introduce students to the STRAP strategy, which helps them identify the dynamics of both writing and reading assignments. (*See the back of this card.*)

Students use the STRAP strategy to analyze their writing and reading assignments. The strategy consists of answering questions about these five features: *subject, type, role, audience,* and *purpose.* Once they answer the questions, they'll be ready to get to work. This chart shows how the strategy works:

| For Writing Assignments | | For Reading Assignments |
|---|---|---|
| What specific topic should I write about? | **Subject** | What specific topic does the reading address? |
| What form of writing *(essay, article)* will I use? | **Type** | What form *(essay, text chapter, article)* does the reading take? |
| What position *(student, citizen, employee)* should I assume? | **Role** | What position *(student, responder, concerned individual)* does the writer assume? |
| Who is the intended reader? | **Audience** | Who is the intended reader? |
| What is the goal *(to inform, to persuade)* of the writing? | **Purpose** | What is the goal of the material? |

## Using the Traits (pages 20-21)

Students sometimes struggle to understand why a text works or does not work. Without this understanding, they have a hard time developing their own writing, discussing the writing of their peers, and/or analyzing reading material. *WRITE 1* and *WRITE 2* use the traits of writing as a guide to effective prose. A working knowledge of the traits helps students become more thoughtfully involved in their writing and reading. (Traits side notes appear throughout the text.)

- **Ideas** The main points and supporting details in writing and  reading material
- **Organization** The overall structure of the material
- **Voice** The personality of the writing—how the writer speaks to the reader
- **Word Choice** The writer's use of words and phrases
- **Sentence Fluency** The flow of the sentences
- **Conventions** The correctness or accuracy of the language
- **Design** The appearance of the writing

## Using Graphic Organizers (pages 22-23)

Struggling students find visuals such as graphic organizers helpful when they are writing and learning. Graphic organizers work well for collecting details during the prewriting stage; they also work well when students are gleaning key concepts and ideas from essays and articles they are assigned to read.

# Further Readings

To learn more about writing to learn and the traits of writing, refer to the following publications.

Collins, James L. *Strategies for Struggling Writers.* Guilford Press, 1998.

Mayher John S., Nancy Lester, and Gordon M. Pradl. *Learning to Write / Writing to Learn.* Heinemann, 1983.

Spandel, Vickie. *Creating Writers Through 6-Trait Writing.* Allyn & Bacon, 2008.

# Writing Process

Educators Donald M. Murray and Donald H. Graves led a group of others in shifting the focus of writing from product to process. They explored the "moves" that different writers made at different stages as they developed a piece of writing. Though the steps in the process have had various names throughout time, the terms used in *WRITE 1* and *WRITE 2* are prewriting, writing, revising, editing, and publishing.

## Prewriting

This phase begins when the writer first starts to think about an idea. Prewriting may begin with a formal writing assignment (as is often the case in academic writing), or it may begin with inspiration, or even a niggling idea that won't let go. During prewriting, the writer focuses on ideas and organization and does the following:

- **Analyzes the rhetorical situation**—the writer's role, the subject of the writing, the purpose, the medium or form, the audience, and the context. In terms of academic writing, this task involves understanding the assignment.

- **Selects a topic** by brainstorming possible ideas and narrowing them down to a specific topic that fits all parts of the rhetorical situation.

- **Gathers information about the topic** through personal reflection, questioning, and research. At this stage, graphic organizers, lists, and notes help writers generate or discover ideas and keep track of them.

- **Finds a focus,** deciding which specific thought or feeling about the topic that the writer wants to explore. Finding a focus involves sizing the project, making sure it is not too large or too small to be covered in the form required.

- **Organizes details** by creating a quick list or a more formal topic or sentence outline. The organizational structure is often dictated by the writer's purpose (to inform, persuade, entertain, reflect) and by the form of the writing.

## Writing

This phase involves creating a first draft—pouring words onto a page or into a computer. The writing phase is informed and guided by the prewriting work, but the writer should feel free to innovate and experiment. At this phase, the writer should focus on ideas, organization, and voice while creating a three-part structure:

- **Opening:** The opening should catch the reader's attention and identify the writer's subject and focus. In a paragraph, the opening is the topic sentence. In an essay, the opening is the first paragraph or so, providing background and introducing the topic.

- **Middle:** The middle should support the opening. In a paragraph, the middle consists of sentences of different levels, presenting main points and supporting details. In an essay, the middle consists of paragraphs, each of which focuses on a main point and develops it.

- **Closing:** The closing should bring the writing to an effective end, perhaps by revisiting the opening, by summing up the main points, or by providing an important final thought. In a paragraph, the closing is a final sentence, and in an essay, it is a paragraph.

## Revising

Revising involves making large-scale changes to writing, improving it in the most important ways. A peer review at this stage can help the writer discover what is working and what could work better in a specific piece of writing. During revising, the writer (and peer reviewers) should focus on the "Big Three" traits: ideas, organization, and voice. There are four basic revising moves:

- **Adding**—providing answers to some of the 5 W's and H, or adding engaging, surprising, or varied details to bolster a claim
- **Cutting**—removing ideas that are off topic, redundant, obvious, or otherwise unhelpful in conveying the writer's message
- **Rearranging**—putting it in a more effective order or creating a smoother flow of thought, often using transition words and phrases
- **Rewriting**—experimenting to find the best way to express each idea, and reworking parts that did not convey the message in the first draft

## Editing

Editing involves making small-scale changes to improve style and correctness. During editing, the writer should focus on the "Little Three" traits:

- **Words**—using specific nouns, active verbs, and modifiers that clarify, and avoiding wordiness, deadwood, and clichés
- **Sentences**—varying sentence beginnings, lengths, and style
- **Conventions**—correcting punctuation, capitalization, usage, spelling, and grammar

| Correction Marks | |
| --- | --- |
| ⌐ | delete |
| d̲ | capitalize |
| ⌀ | lowercase |
| ∧ | insert |
| ⌃ | add comma |
| ? ∧ | add question mark |
| word ∧ | add word |
| ⊙ | add period |
| ◯ | spelling |
| ∿ | switch |

## Publishing

Publishing is simply the act of sharing writing, whether in an official publication or simply by reading it aloud to classmates or family members. Publishing is the step in which writing becomes true communication, the ideas in the writer's mind entering the minds of a real audience.

# A Recursive Process

Writing rarely moves straight forward through this process. Instead, writers in one stage may go back to a previous stage, or jump ahead to a later one. The needs of the rhetorical situation dictate the order of steps.

Process Chart
Prewrite — Write — Revise — Edit — Publish

# Further Readings

For further readings into the writing process, see the following publications.

Graves, Donald H. *Writing: Teachers & Children at Work.* Heinemann, 2003.
Murray, Donald M. *Learning by Teaching.* Boyton/Cook Heinemann, 1982.
VanderMey, Randall et al. *COMP: Write.* Wadsworth Cengage Learning, 2010.

# History of the Traits of Writing

The writing traits date back to the 1960s, when researcher Paul Diederich gathered a group of 50 professionals to determine what elements make up strong writing. In reviewing numerous student papers, the group uncovered a common pattern of characteristics, or traits, that made some papers more effective than others. Years later a group of teachers in Beaverton, Oregon, and Missoula, Montana, replicated Diederich's work and settled on a similar set of traits. Since then, the traits—ideas, organization, voice, word choice, sentence fluency, correctness—have become a cornerstone of writing instruction in schools throughout the world. *WRITE 1* and *WRITE 2* describe the six traits in detail, as well as adding a seventh trait—appropriate design.

## The Traits of Writing

### Strong Ideas

Good writing starts with an interesting idea. A writer should include plenty of effective ideas and details in his or her writing. And all of the information needs to hold the reader's interest.

### Logical Organization

Effective writing has a clear overall structure—with a beginning, a middle, and an ending. Each paragraph should have a topic sentence, and transitions should link the ideas.

### Fitting Voice

In the best writing, the writer's voice comes through. Voice is a writer's unique way of saying things. It shows that he or she cares about the writing. Furthermore, voice should fit the form. A personal essay should convey a different voice than a formal expository essay.

### Well-Chosen Words

In strong writing, nouns and verbs are specific and clear, and modifiers add important information. The word choice should also fit the purpose and audience.

### Smooth Sentences

The sentences in good writing should read smoothly from one to the next. Sentence variety gives the writing flow and energy, while each sentence carries the meaning of the essay or article.

### Correct Copy

Strong writing is easy to read because it follows the conventions or rules of the language.

### Appropriate Design

The design should follow the guidelines established by the instructor.

## Connecting the Process and the Traits

The writing process makes writing easy by breaking the job into five recursive steps. The traits identify the key elements to consider at each step. Together the process and the traits help writers assess and improve their writing. The first three traits—ideas, organization, and voice—deal with big issues and thus dominate the early stages of the writing process (prewriting and writing). Meanwhile, words, sentences, conventions, and design become important later in the process (revising, editing, and publishing). See how the process and traits connect in the chart below.

| Process | Traits |
|---|---|
| **Prewriting** | **Ideas:** selecting a topic, collecting details about it, forming a thesis<br>**Organization:** arranging the details<br>**Voice:** establishing your stance (objective, personal) |
| **Writing** | **Ideas:** connecting your thoughts and information<br>**Organization:** following your planning<br>**Voice:** sounding serious, sincere, interested, . . . |
| **Revising** | **Ideas:** reviewing for clarity and completeness<br>**Organization:** reviewing for structure/arrangement of ideas<br>**Voice:** reviewing for appropriate tone |
| **Editing** | **Word choice:** checking for specific nouns, verbs, and modifiers<br>**Sentences:** checking for smoothness and variety<br>**Conventions:** checking for correctness |
| **Publishing** | **Design:** evaluating the format |

## Traits Across the Spectrum

The writing traits work well with all writing forms and disciplines. Each discipline has its own specific ideas and organizational structures that writers should follow. And any form of writing benefits from strong words, smooth sentences, correctness, and effective design.

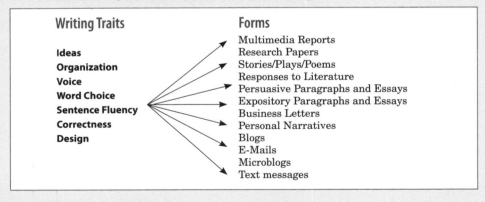

**Writing Traits**

Ideas
Organization
Voice
Word Choice
Sentence Fluency
Correctness
Design

**Forms**

Multimedia Reports
Research Papers
Stories/Plays/Poems
Responses to Literature
Persuasive Paragraphs and Essays
Expository Paragraphs and Essays
Business Letters
Personal Narratives
Blogs
E-Mails
Microblogs
Text messages

## Further Readings

For further readings into the traits of writing, see the following publications.

Diederich, Paul B. *Measuring Growth in English.* National Council of Teachers of English, 1974.
VanderMey, Randall et al. *COMP: Write.* Wadsworth Cengage Learning, 2010.

# Paragraph Patterns

Before writers can throw themselves into the drafting stage, they must first find a focus and consider the various patterns of organization. In college-level writing, students will need to introduce their focus in the form of a thesis statement (or in a topic sentence if they are writing a paragraph). A strong thesis statement states a particular feeling, feature, or part of a specific topic.

## Forming a Thesis Statement

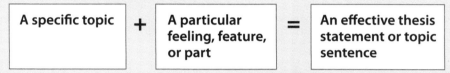

| A specific topic | **+** | A particular feeling, feature, or part | **=** | An effective thesis statement or topic sentence |

Once students establish a thesis, they should identify an appropriate pattern of organization to organize the information that supports it. As a result, students will begin drafting with a sense of purpose, focus, and organization.

## Patterns of Organization

- Use **chronological order** (time) when you are sharing a personal experience, telling how something happened, or explaining how to do something.
- Use **spatial order** (location) for descriptions, arranging information from left to right, top to bottom, from the edge to the center, and so on.
- Use **order of importance** when you are taking a stand or arguing for or against something. Either arrange your reasons from most important to least important or the other way around.
- Use **deductive organization** if you want to follow your thesis statement with basic information—supporting reasons, examples, and facts.
- Use **inductive organization** when you want to present specific details first and conclude with your thesis statement.
- Use **compare-contrast organization** when you want to show how one topic is different from and similar to another one.

## Choosing a Pattern of Organization

How do students decide on an appropriate pattern of organization? Here are two strategies they can use:

1. **Study the thesis statement or topic sentence.** It will indicate how to organize the ideas.

2. **Review the information or research gathered during prewriting.** Decide which ideas support the thesis and arrange them according to the appropriate method of organization.

# Forming a Meaningful Whole

A meaningful whole in writing means the writer connects all of his or her thoughts and feelings about a specific topic into a complete draft—one with clear beginning, middle, and ending parts. Forming a meaningful whole for a paragraph means including a topic sentence, body sentences, and a closing sentence. For an essay, it means including an opening part (including a thesis statement), a number of supporting paragraphs, and a closing paragraph.

**Paragraph Structure**

**Topic Sentence**
A **topic sentence** names the topic.

**Detail Sentences**
**Detail sentences** support the topic.

**Closing Sentence**
A **closing sentence** wraps up the paragraph.

**Essay Structure**

**Opening Paragraph**
The **opening paragraph** draws the reader into the essay and provides information that leads to a thesis statement. The thesis statement tells what the essay is about.

**Middle Paragraphs**
The **middle paragraphs** support the thesis statement. Each middle paragraph needs a topic sentence, a variety of detail sentences, and a closing sentence.

**Closing Paragraph**
The **closing paragraph** finishes the essay by revisiting the thesis statement, emphasizing an important detail, providing the reader with an interesting final thought, and/or looking toward the future.

# Levels of Detail

College writing requires students use a certain level of depth in their writing. When they make a point, they should fully explain it with specific examples and details before they move to the next point. The process of making important points and supporting them with details is at the core of most writing. To write with depth, students should include different levels of detail. Here are three basic levels:

- **Level 1:** A **controlling sentence** (usually a topic sentence) names a topic or makes a main point.
- **Level 2:** A **clarifying sentence** explains a level 1 sentence.
- **Level 3:** A **completing sentence** adds details to complete the point.

Exceptional writers may add a fourth level of detail, elaborating on the point with anecdotes, examples, quotations, and so on.

# Teaching Complete Sentences

Students learn less from worksheets about identifying and correcting sentences than from writing and correcting their own sentences. As a result, many of the activities in this book prompt students to write their own simple, compound, and complex sentences, to create their own prepositional and participial phrases, and so on. Real writing is key.

## Subjects and Verbs

At base, every sentence is the connection between a subject and verb. The instruction in the "Sentence Basics" chapter thus focuses on subjects and verbs, and then on special types of subjects and special types of verbs. The other words in the sentence either complete these words (as is the case with direct and indirect objects and object complements) or modify them.

## Adjectives and Adverbs

Adjectives, of course, modify nouns and words that function as nouns. Adverbs modify verbs, adjectives, and other adverbs or words that function as such. These definitions might seem a bit esoteric to students, so instead of focusing on definitions, focus on function. Adjectives and adverbs answer basic questions.

| **Adjective Questions** | **Adverb Questions** |
|---|---|
| *Which?* | *How?* |
| *What kind of?* | *When?* |
| *How many?/How much?* | *Where?* |
| | *Why?* |
| | *To what degree?* |
| | *How often?/How long?* |

Impress on students that words that answer these questions are functioning as adjectives or adverbs. These questions become important not so much for identifying words and phrases in writing, but for helping students expand their sentences and create deeper, more thought writing.

## Simple, Compound, and Complex Sentences

A simple sentence is a subject and a verb that express a complete thought. A compound sentence is a pair of simple sentences joined with a comma and a coordinating conjunction *(and, but, or, nor, for, so, yet.)* The conjunction coordinates the sentences by showing they are of equal importance. A complex sentence is a pair of simple sentences joined with a subordinating conjunction. The conjunction subordinates one sentence to another by making one sentence into a dependent clause.

The chapter "Simple, Compound, and Complex Sentences" goes into detail about these sentence structures, giving students practice forming each type. Students should then apply their learning in the writing they are doing elsewhere.

**Subordinating Conjunctions**

| | |
|---|---|
| after | so that |
| although | that |
| as | though |
| as if | till |
| as long as | unless |
| because | until |
| before | when |
| even though | whenever |
| if | where |
| in order that | whereas |
| provided that | while |
| since | |

## Avoiding Sentence Fragments

A sentence must have a subject and verb and must express a complete thought. To check sentences, have students find the subject (single underline) and the verb (double underline) and then determine if the words express a complete thought. A fragment is missing one or more of these features, but it can be fixed by supplying what is missing.

**Fragment Missing a Subject**
Works all summer. ————————→

**Sentence With a Subject**
**Roger** works all summer.

**Fragment Missing a Verb**
His construction company. ————————→

**Sentence With a Verb**
His construction company **thrives**.

**Fragment Missing a Subject and Verb**
With three projects. ————————→

**Sentence With a Subject and Verb**
**They are busy** with three projects.

**Fragment Missing a Complete Thought**
When they work. ————————→

**Sentence With a Complete Thought**
When they work, **the company thrives**.

*Note:* When a subject and verb are present but a complete thought is not, usually the words are a dependent clause. A dependent clause begins either with a subordinating conjunction (*after, because, though, etc.*) or with a relative pronoun (*who, which, that*).

## Avoiding Run-On Sentences and Comma Splices

Just as fragments can result from splitting up a complex sentence, run-ons and comma splices can result from incorrectly creating a compound sentence. A run-on is a pair of sentences joined without a comma and coordinating conjunction. A comma splice occurs when only a comma is used to join sentences. Either error can be corrected by supplying **both** a comma and a coordinating conjunction (or by joining the sentences with a semicolon).

**Run-On (Missing Both)**
Roger works hard he is tired. ————————→

**Compound Sentence Joined Correctly**
Roger works hard, **and** he is tired.

**Comma Splice (Missing Conjunction)**
Roger works hard, he is tired. ————————→

**Compound Sentence Joined Correctly**
Roger works hard, **and** he is tired.

*Note:* Fragments, run-ons, and comma splices in student writing may be signs that students are experimenting with sentences, trying to combine them in compound and complex forms. Treat these errors, then, as signs of growth. Help students recognize and correct them, but do so in the context of authentic writing.

# Teaching Sentence Variety

Variety is more than just the spice of life. The reason the Food and Drug Administration recommends a varied diet is not for sake of spice, but because our bodies need different types of nutrients from different sources. Sentence variety is similar. Yes, varied sentences spice up writing and read more smoothly, but the deeper reason for variety is that different types, kinds, and structures of sentences convey different kinds of thoughts. Sentence variety makes for deeper and more "nutrient-rich" thinking.

## Simple, Compound, and Complex

Simple, compound, and complex sentences are covered in their own chapter, which focuses on creating these structures rather than identifying them. Students need to understand that these three structures work well for different kinds of thinking:

- **Simple sentences** provide ideas in a straightforward way.
- **Compound sentences** connect simple sentences equally. Different coordinating conjunctions create different connections.

  additions: *and*          contrasts: *but, yet*

  options: *or, nor*        causes: *for, so*
- **Complex sentences** connect simple sentences in a more nuanced way, making one depend on the other. Note the relationships created by the subordinating conjunctions in complex sentences.

  time: *after, as, as long as, before, since, until, when, whenever, while*

  contrasts: *although, as if, even though, though, unless, until, whereas, while*

  causes: *as, as long as, because, if, in order that, since, so that, when, whenever*

## Medium, Long, and Short

Just as different sentence structures create special relationships between ideas, different sentence lengths are suited to different sizes of ideas. Students should not vary the length of sentences randomly. Instead, they should use different lengths for different purposes in their writing.

- **Medium sentences** (10-20 words) work well to express most ideas.

  When I read the advertisement online, I wrote my résumé and cover letter and sent them in.
- **Long sentences** (over 20 words) work well to express complex ideas.

  After waiting anxiously to hear from the employer, I received a call requesting an interview, went in to meet the department manager, toured the facility, and completed a test.
- **Short sentences** (under 10 words) work well to make a point.

  I got the job!

## Varied Beginnings

On the surface, the reason to vary the beginnings of sentences is to keep them from sounding repetitive and predictable. At a deeper level, varying beginnings provides the chance to insert a transition word, phrase, or clause that helps make clear the connection between a sentence and what has come before.

- Transition word:  However, I won't start work until July.
- Transition phrase:  With all the arrangements, I won't start work until July.
- Transition clause:  Though I am eager to begin, I won't start work until July.

## Varying the Kinds of Sentences

Throughout *WRITE 1* and *WRITE 2,* students are prompted to create statements, questions, commands, and conditional sentences. These kinds of sentences are taught in context—for example, using command verbs when teaching the reader how to perform a process. Additional instruction in the kinds of sentences appear in the online bonus chapters "End Punctuation" and "Sentence Analysis." The key point is for students to understand the uses of the different kinds of sentences in their writing:

- **Statements** provide information about the subject. Use them most often.

  I was one of 25 applicants for the job.

- **Questions** ask for information about the subject. Use them to engage the reader.

  What made me stand out from the other applicants?

- **Exclamations** express strong emotion. Use them sparingly in academic writing.

  I had the best attitude!

- **Commands** tell the reader what to do. (They have an implied subject—*you.*) Use them to call the reader to act.

  Show a positive attitude when you interview.

- **Conditional** sentences show that one situation depends on another.

  If you have a good attitude and résumé, then the interviewer will notice.

*Note:* Each of these kinds of sentences represents a different kind of thinking. Using a variety of sentence kinds in writing stimulates deeper and broader thought.

## Modifying Phrases and Clauses

The "Sentence Basics" chapter deals with creating sentence style by adding modifying phrases and clauses. Instead of focusing on the daunting names of such word groups—participial phrases, infinitive phrases, subordinate clauses—the exercises focus on the function of these groups. Do they answer an adjective question or an adverb question?

| **Adjective Questions** | **Adverb Questions** |
|---|---|
| *Which?* | *How?* |
| *What kind of?* | *When?* |
| *How many?/How much?* | *Where?* |
| | *Why?* |
| | *To what degree?* |
| | *How often?/How long?* |

If you ask one of these questions, students will likely respond verbally with a modifying phrase or clause that you could identify but they could not. Identification is not as important as use. Help students see that if the words answer an adjective or adverb question, those words can be used like an adjective or adverb.

# Combining Sentences

Sentence combining is a proven strategy for improving sentence style, especially among struggling writers, who often produce short, choppy, repetitive sentences. *WRITE 1* and *WRITE 2* focus on three main approaches to combining sentences. The first two approaches, coordination and subordination, help writers make new connections between ideas. The third approach, moving and deleting, helps writers remove accidental repetition and create sentences with greater meaning.

## Coordination

The word "coordinate" means "make equal" or "place in the same rank." A coordinating conjunction places two ideas on an equal footing. Coordinating conjunctions can connect words, phrases, or clauses in an equal way.

| Coordinating Conjunctions | | | | | | |
|---|---|---|---|---|---|---|
| and | but | or | nor | for | so | yet |

When a coordinating conjunction is used to create a compound sentence, a comma should precede the conjunction.

| | |
|---|---|
| **Choppy sentences:** | The book is late. I need to turn it in. |
| **Combined sentences:** | The book is late, **so** I need to turn it in. |

If the sentences are joined without a conjunction and comma, a run-on sentence results. If the sentences are joined with the comma but without the conjunction, a comma-splice results. Compound sentences require both the comma and the conjunction (or just a semicolon).

## Subordination

The word "subordinate" means "make unequal" or "place in a lower rank." A subordinating conjunction makes one idea depend upon another idea. The subordinating conjunction appears before the clause that is less important, making it dependent.

| | |
|---|---|
| **Choppy sentences:** | The book is due. The library is closed. |
| **Combined sentences:** | **Though** the book is due, the library is closed. |
| **Combined sentences:** | The book is due **though** the library is closed. |

If the dependent clause comes first, it should be followed by a comma.

| Subordinating Conjunctions | |
|---|---|
| after | so that |
| although | that |
| as | though |
| as if | till |
| as long as | unless |
| because | until |
| before | when |
| even though | whenever |
| if | where |
| in order that | whereas |
| provided that | while |
| since | |

## Moving and Deleting

When sentences repeat content, the best way to combine them is to delete the repetition and merge the rest. The "Sentence Style" chapter includes instruction and exercises for combining by moving and deleting. Again, students should select the combining strategy that improves their thinking rather than one that just improves the flow of words.

| | |
|---|---|
| **Repetitive sentences:** | I plan to be a nurse. I want to work in a hospital. |
| **Combined sentences:** | I plan to be a nurse **in a hospital**. |

# Expanding Sentences

Often struggling writers create sentences that provide little information. A writer who has eked out four say-nothing sentences does not need to combine them into two say-nothing sentences. Instead, the writer should expand the sentences. The best way to get writers to expand sentences is to have them answer the 5 W's and H about a sentence and add some of their answers to the original. This approach taps into spoken English, which is much more fluent for most struggling writers than written English is. For that reason, expanding works well as a partner or group activity.

| | |
|---|---|
| **Say-nothing sentence:** | She works there. |
| Who works there? | my friend Stacy |
| What does she do? | She's a pediatrics nurse. |
| Where does she work? | at Lakeside Memorial Hospital |
| When does she work? | She works nights. |
| Why does she work? | to support her son |
| How does she work? | cheerfully |
| **Expanded sentence:** | My friend Stacy cheerfully works nights as a pediatrics nurse at Lakeside Memorial Hospital. |

# Modeling Sentences

Sentence modeling is similar to copying a masterpiece, stroke for stroke. The focus required to replace each word in a sentence makes students think about how the original sentence was built. Modeling explores word choice, syntax, and semantics. Students can construct participial phrases, absolute phrases, and appositives without being frightened by the difficult names of these structures. When students build appositives and understand their use, they may well ask, "What is this thing called?" That's the point at which the word *appositive* is meaningful to the student.

| | |
|---|---|
| **Original Sentence:** | Storms are sensual feasts—the cold wet touch of rain, the smell of damp soil, the percussive crack of thunder, the brilliant flashes of lightning. |
| | —Eli King |
| **Modeled Sentence:** | Morning on the lake was a languid treat—the soft wet slap of oars, the coils of rising mist, the watery murmur of waves, the dark, welling depths. |

The "Sentence Style" chapter includes a number of sentences from literary figures, and these are valuable to model. However, students may find it even more valuable to model sentences from their areas of study. An engineer builds a sentence in a different way than an accountant or a nurse or a social worker. Encourage students to submit "great sentences" they find outside the classroom, perhaps from their area of study. You might even give them an extra credit point for each sentence they bring in. At the start of class, then, you can write such a sentence on the board, discuss what makes it great, and have everyone in class model the sentence.

## Noun

The distinction between common and proper nouns is mainly an issue for ensuring correct capitalization. However, forming the plurals of nouns can be challenging, especially given the special rules for nouns ending in *s, ch, f,* and *y,* as well as irregular plurals such as *children.* It's important to directly teach these issues to those who have trouble with them, but the only way students will internalize these rules is to use them consistently in authentic writing.

The "Noun" chapter also provides instruction about count and noncount nouns as well as articles and noun markers. Native speakers of Standard English often use these parts of speech correctly without even being aware of their existence, while those who speak English as a second language may be aware of them but may struggle with them. Provide direct instruction and practice as needed.

## Pronoun

Pronouns may be just stand-ins for nouns, but these little words carry a lot of information. Personal pronouns must match their antecedents in person, number, and gender and have the correct case for their role in the sentence. Here is a chart of these forms of personal pronouns.

| Person | Singular | | | Plural | | |
|---|---|---|---|---|---|---|
| | Nom. | Obj. | Poss. | Nom. | Obj. | Poss. |
| First (speaking) | I | me | my/mine | we | us | our/ours |
| Second (spoken to) | you | you | your/yours | you | you | your/yours |
| Third (spoken about) masculine | he | him | his | they | them | their/theirs |
| feminine | she | her | her/hers | they | them | their/theirs |
| neuter | it | it | its | they | them | their/theirs |

With indefinite pronouns, agreement errors are common. The material in the "Pronoun" chapter provides direct instruction on these issues, but mastery will come in authentic writing.

## Verb

Verbs come in three basic classes—action, linking, and helping verbs. Understanding the uses of each class will help students form better sentences. Verbs also reflect number, voice, and tense, as shown in the chart below.

| | Active Voice | | Passive Voice | |
|---|---|---|---|---|
| | Singular | Plural | Singular | Plural |
| **Present Tense** | I see<br>you see<br>he/she/it sees | we see<br>you see<br>they see | I am seen<br>you are seen<br>he/she/it is seen | we are seen<br>you are seen<br>they are seen |
| **Past Tense** | I saw<br>you saw<br>he saw | we saw<br>you saw<br>they saw | I was seen<br>you were seen<br>it was seen | we were seen<br>you were seen<br>they were seen |
| **Future Tense** | I will see<br>you will see<br>he will see | we will see<br>you will see<br>they will see | I will be seen<br>you will be seen<br>it will be seen | we will be seen<br>you will be seen<br>they will be seen |
| **Present Perfect Tense** | I have seen<br>you have seen<br>he has seen | we have seen<br>you have seen<br>they have seen | I have been seen<br>you have been seen<br>it has been seen | we have been seen<br>you have been seen<br>they have been seen |
| **Past Perfect Tense** | I had seen<br>you had seen<br>he had seen | we had seen<br>you had seen<br>they had seen | I had been seen<br>you had been seen<br>it had been seen | we had been seen<br>you had been seen<br>they had been seen |
| **Future Perfect Tense** | I will have seen<br>you will have seen<br>he will have seen | we will have seen<br>you will have seen<br>they will have seen | I will have been seen<br>you will have been seen<br>it will have been seen | we will have been seen<br>you will have been seen<br>they will have been seen |

## Adjective and Adverb

Adjectives modify nouns, and adverbs modify verbs, adjectives, and other adverbs. Once students understand adjectives and adverbs, they will better understand word groups that function like adjectives and adverbs. Instead of loading writers down with the names of phrases and clauses, teach them the adjective and adverb questions. If a word, phrase, or clause answers one of these questions, it is probably functioning as an adjective or adverb.

| **Adjective Questions** | **Adverb Questions** |
| --- | --- |
| *Which?* | *How?* |
| *What kind of?* | *When?* |
| *How many?/How much?* | *Where?* |
| | *Why?* |
| | *To what degree?* |
| | *How often?/How long?* |

The chapter "Adjective and Adverb" includes an activity on teaching the order of adjectives. This is, once again, a feature of language that native English speakers use without thought, but that may need to be directly taught to ESL students.

## Conjunction

Conjunctions show the relationships between ideas. Here are the three types of conjunctions and the relationships they show:

- **Coordinating conjunctions** connect ideas in an equal way, showing the following:
  **Additions:** *and*
  **Contrasts:** *but, yet*
  **Options:** *or, nor*
  **Causes:** *for, so*
- **Correlative conjunctions** stress the equality of two ideas, showing the following:
  **Inclusion:** *both / and, not only / but also*
  **Exclusion:** *neither / nor*
  **Options:** *whether / or*
- **Subordinating conjunctions** make one idea depend on another, showing the following:
  **Time:** *after, as, as long as, before, since, until, when, whenever, while*
  **Contrasts:** *although, as if, even though, though, unless, until, whereas, while*
  **Causes:** *as, as long as, because, if, in order that, since, so that, that, when, whenever*

## Preposition

Prepositions create special relationships between nouns and other words in the sentences. The preposition and its object (a noun or pronoun) form a prepositional phrase, which functions as an adjective or adverb. As such, the prepositional phrase can answer the adjective or adverb questions listed above.

The chapter "Conjunction and Preposition" features four small prepositions that are used very frequently in English—*by, at, on,* and *in.* Native speakers of English use these words correctly without knowing the rules for them, but often ESL writers will need to learn the rules through direct instruction and then apply them to their writing.